FOR
TODAY

STUDY BIBLE AND COMMENTARY
ROMANS EDITION

LIFE FOR TODAY
Study Bible and Commentary
Romans Edition

ISBN 1-881541-13-4

Printed in the United States of America

LIFE

FOR

TODAY

STUDY BIBLE AND COMMENTARY
ROMANS EDITION

Andrew Wommack

For more information on the monthly *Life For Today* program and other areas of ministry write to:

Europe: Andrew Wommack Ministries of Europe
P.O. Box 35
Coventry, CV1 2DN
ENGLAND

All Others: Andrew Wommack Ministries, Inc.
P.O. Box 3333
Colorado Springs, CO 80934
U.S.A.

CONTENTS

Preface.....i

List of Heading Divisions in the Book of Romans.....ii

Books of the Old and New Testaments.....iii

Miscellaneous Abbreviations.....iii

Introduction to the Book of Romans.....iv

Features of Your Life For Today Study Bible.....vi

How to Use Your Life For Today Study Bible.....vii

Life For Today Study Bible and Commentary.....655

Supplemental Study Aids and Charts

Conversion Chart.....S1
To use in conjunction with the Andrew Wommack Ministries Life For Today partnership program

Footnote Index.....F1
All the footnotes in this Study Bible indexed and cross referenced by subject matter

PREFACE

This study Bible and commentary is the product of a call the Lord has placed on my life to be a teacher to the body of Christ. Along with that call is a God-given desire to help bring His body *"to the unity of the faith, and of the knowledge of the Son of God, unto a perfect man, unto the measure of the fulness of Christ..."* (Eph. 4:13).

God's Word, the Holy Bible, is given for that exact purpose (2 Tim. 3:16-17 and 2 Pet. 1:3-4) and this study Bible and commentary is meant to be a tool to help bring that to pass in your life.

This volume, the *Romans Edition,* is the third of the *Life For Today* series. The first went into print in 1991 (with a revision in 1992) under the title of the *Gospels Edition,* and the second went into print in 1994 titled *The Acts of the Apostles Edition*. This adaptation of our monthly *Life For Today* study pages is an ongoing process, and my goal is to eventually have all of the New Testament represented by a *Life For Today* bound volume.

This study Bible and commentary represents over twenty-six years of diligently seeking revelation of the scriptures. I have put eight years of work into the *Gospels Edition* alone, averaging over one hour on each verse. My staff has also spent countless hours helping with the references, some footnotes, and all the logistics of producing this work.

This work combines the best of many different resources so that the reader will have access to Hebrew and Greek word meanings, other commentaries, Bible dictionaries, and my own teaching on scripture in one volume.

"And now, brethren, I commend you to God, and to the word of His grace, which is able to build you up and to give you an inheritance among all them which are sanctified" (Acts 20:32).

Andrew Wommack

LIST OF HEADING DIVISIONS IN THE BOOK OF ROMANS		
	Reference	Beg. Pg. #
Paul's Calling and Desire to Come to the Romans	1:1-15	655
The Gospel of Christ and the Righteousness it Reveals	1:16-17	658
God's Wrath Revealed Against the Unrighteousness of Men	1:18-20	659
Results of Turning From God's Revelation	1:21-32	660
God's Judgment of Self-Righteous & Religious People	2:1-16	662
The Jews Have the Law But Don't Keep It	2:17-27	665
The True Jew	2:28-29	667
Does the Jew Have Advantage?	3:1-8	668
The Purpose of the Law: The Universal Guilt of Man	3:9-20	669
Righteousness Needed and Provided by God	3:21-31	672
Justification by Faith Illustrated From the O. T.	4:1-8	674
Justification is Apart From Circumcision or Religious Ordinances	4:9-12	676
Justification is by Faith Apart From Law	4:13-25	678
The Benefits of Justification by Faith	5:1-11	681
Sin and Death Came by Adam	5:12-14	684
The Results of Being "In Adam" or "In Christ" Contrasted	5:15-21	686
Deliverance From Sin by Union with Christ	6:1-10	688
Dead to Sin, Alive to God	6:11-19	690
Servants of Sin Now Servants of God	6:20-23	693
Man Under Law and His Deliverance Through Christ	7:1-6	694
Sin Taking Occasion by the Law	7:7-14	696
The Effects of Trying to Live by Law or Self-Effort	7:15-23	698
Giving Up and Accepting God's Provision for Deliverance	7:24-25	699
Walking After the Spirit, Not After the Flesh	8:1-17	700
The Hope of Total Salvation	8:18-25	705
The Spirit's Help in Weakness	8:25-28	707
God is for Us	8:29-39	708
Paul's Personal Feelings for Lost Israel	9:1-5	710
Election According to Grace	9:6-29	711
Righteousness of Law vs. Righteousness of Faith	9:30-33	717
Righteousness of Law says "Do," Righteousness of Faith says "Done"	10:1-13	719
The Gospel Heard but Rejected	10:14-21	722
A Remnant According to Grace	11:1-6	724
Israel's Fall and Blinding	11:7-12	725
The Saving of the Nations Through Israel's Fall	11:13-22	726
Israel Restored; God's Mercy Shown to All	11:23-32	727
A Praise to God For His Wisdom	11:33-36	729
Presenting Our Bodies and Renewing Our Minds	12:1-3	729
The Exercising of God's Grace Gifts	12:4-8	732
The Practical Living of Christ's Life	12:9-21	734
Submission to Governing Authority	13:1-7	738
Love—The Fulfilling of the Law	13:8-10	740
Cast Off the Works of Darkness and Put on Christ	13:11-14	742
Christian Liberty and Questionable Things	14:1-23	743
Bearing Other's Weaknesses and Not Pleasing Ourselves	15:1-7	748
Christ, the Savior of Jew and Gentile	15:8-13	749
Ministering Christ to the Nations	15:14-21	750
Paul's Desire is to Visit Rome	15:22-33	751
Paul Sends Greetings	16:1-16	753
Warning Concerning Divisions and Offenses	16:17-20	756
Final Greeting and Benediction	16:21-27	758

THE NAMES AND ORDER

OF THE

BOOKS OF THE OLD AND NEW TESTAMENTS

with abbreviations of their names, and the number of chapters in each

The Old Testament

Genesis	Gen.	50	2 Chronicles	2 Chr.	36	Daniel	Dan.	12
Exodus	Ex.	40	Ezra		10	Hosea	Hos.	14
Leviticus	Lev.	27	Nehemiah	Neh.	13	Joel		3
Numbers	Num.	36	Esther	Est.	10	Amos		9
Deuteronomy	Dt.	34	Job		42	Obadiah	Obad.	1
Joshua	Josh.	24	Psalms	Ps.	150	Jonah	Jon.	4
Judges	Jud.	21	Proverbs	Prov.	31	Micah	Mic.	7
Ruth		4	Ecclesiastes	Eccl.	12	Nahum	Nah.	3
1 Samuel	1 Sam.	31	Song of Solomon	Song	8	Habakkuk	Hab.	3
2 Samuel	2 Sam.	24	Isaiah	Isa.	66	Zephaniah	Zeph.	3
1 Kings	1 Ki.	22	Jeremiah	Jer.	52	Haggai	Hag.	2
2 Kings	2 Ki.	25	Lamentations	Lam.	5	Zechariah	Zech.	14
1 Chronicles	1 Chr.	29	Ezekiel	Ezek.	48	Malachai	Mal.	4

The New Testament

Matthew	Mt.	28	Ephesians	Eph.	6	Hebrews	Heb.	13
Mark	Mk.	16	Philippians	Phil.	4	James	Jas.	5
Luke	Lk.	24	Colossians	Col.	4	1 Peter	1 Pet	5
John	Jn.	21	1 Thessalonians	1 Th.	5	2 Peter	2 Pet.	3
The Acts	Acts	28	2 Thessalonians	2 Th.	3	1 John	1 Jn.	5
Romans	Rom.	16	1 Timothy	1 Tim.	6	2 John	2 Jn.	1
1 Corinthians	1 Cor.	16	2 Timothy	2 Tim.	4	3 John	3 Jn.	1
2 Corinthians	2 Cor.	13	Titus	Ti.	3	Jude		1
Galatians	Gal.	6	Philemon	Phile.	1	The Revelation	Rev.	22

MISCELLANEOUS ABBREVIATIONS

ABUV = The New Testament, American Bible Union Version
Amp = Amplified New Testament
ASV = American Standard Version
CEV = Contemporary English Version
KJV = King James Version
KSB = Heb.-Gk. Key Study Bible (Spiros Zodhiates)
LB = The Living Bible
NASB = New American Standard Bible: New Testament
NEB = New English Bible: New Testament
NIV = New International Version
NKJV = New King James Version
TCNT = Twentieth Century New Testament
Alf = New Testament (Henry Alford)
Bas = New Testament-Basic English
Bauer = Greek-English Lexicon (Walter Bauer)
Beck = New Testament in the Language of Today (William F. Beck)
Ber = Berkley Version of the New Testament
Berry = Greek-English Lexicon (George Ricker Berry)
Con. = Epistles of Paul (W.J.Conybeare)
GGNT = Galatians in the Greek N.T. (Kenneth S. Wuest)
Gspd = New Testament: An American Translation (Edgar J. Goodspeed)
HZNT = An Die Römer Handbuch Zun Neuen Testament (Ernst Käsemann)
Knox = New Testament in the Translation of Monsignor Ronald Knox
Lam = New Testament According to the Eastern Texts (George M. Lamsa)
LNT = Manual Greek Lexicon of N.T. (G. Abbott-Smith)
Mof = New Testament: A New Translation (James F. Moffatt)
Mon = Centenary Translation: The New Testament in Modern English (Helen Barret Montgomery)
Nor = New Testament: A New Translation (Olaf M. Norlie)
Phi = New Testament in Modern English (J.B. Phillips)
Rienecker = Linguistic Key to the Greek N.T. (Fritz Rienecker and Cleon Rogers
Rieu = Book of Acts (C.H. Rieu)
Rieu = The Four Gospels (E.V. Rieu)
Rhm = Emphasized New Testament: A New Translation (J.B. Rotherham)
RWP = Word Pictures in the New Testament (A. T. Robertson)
SH = A Critical and Exegetical Commentary on the Epistle to the Romans (William Sanday and Arthur C. Headlam)
Strong = Strong's Exhaustive Concordance (James Strong)
Tay = Living Letters: (Kenneth N. Taylor)
TDNT = Theological Dictionary of the New Testament (Gerhard Kittel and Gerhard Friedrich)
Thayer = Thayer's Greek-English Lexicon
TSK = Treasury of Scriptural Knowledge
Unger = Unger's Bible Dictionary
Vincent = A Critical and Exegetical Commentary on the Epistles to the Philippians and to Philemon The International Critical Commentary
W. E. Vine = An Expository Dictionary of Biblical Words (W.E. Vine)
Wey = The New Testament in Modern Speech (Richard Francis Weymouth)
William = The Acts of the Apostles: Black New Testament Commentary (C. S. C. Williams)
WMNT = Word Meanings in the New Testament (Ralph Earle)
Wms = The New Testament: A Translation in the Language of the People (Charles B. Williams)
Wuest = Romans in the Greek New Testament (Erdman's)
WWS = Wuest's Word Studies of the Greek N.T.
Zon = Zondervan Pictorial Encyclopedia

INTRODUCTION TO THE BOOK OF ROMANS

The book of Romans is the longest and the clearest exposé by the apostle Paul on the gospel. This book contains the doctrinal foundation for the Christian faith and it is for this reason that it was arranged first in order among the epistles of the New Testament. The truths presented here must be understood before proceeding to other doctrinal matters.

In this letter, Paul deals with a larger number of doctrinal issues than in any other of his epistles. His treatment of the doctrine of salvation by grace through faith is so masterfully done that its divine inspiration cannot be questioned. The depth in which Paul treats these great subjects shows that this knowledge was truly given to him by the direct revelation of God (Gal. 1:12).

An understanding of the truths in Romans 3 transformed Martin Luther's personal life and ignited the fires of the reformation that shook the world. Indeed, an understanding of the truths expressed in this book are essential not only to the salvation of every individual, but also to the maturing and success of every Christian.

AUTHORSHIP

Paul is undoubtedly the author of the letter to the Romans. The first verse of this epistle clearly states so (Rom. 1:1). There is no dissenting opinion of this among the early writings of the church. The writer also sends greetings to Priscilla and Aquila (see note 2 at Acts 18:2, p. 604), his helpers, and also to Timotheus, his workfellow (Rom. 16:21). The book of Acts confirms these were close workers with Paul.

THE RECIPIENTS OF THE BOOK OF ROMANS

Paul addressed this letter to all the Christians that were in Rome (Rom. 1:7). There is no scriptural account of any apostolic mission to take the gospel to Rome, so it may therefore be supposed that these Christians were converts from the day of Pentecost when the Holy Spirit was given (Acts 2:10), and the personal witness of believers as they traversed the empire.

These saints in Rome were a diverse group. There were Gentiles who had come from pagan worship to trust in Jesus as their Savior, and there were devout Jews who had believed in Jesus as the Jewish Messiah. This gave rise to many problems among the believers, which were aggravated no doubt, by the fact that no apostle had been to Rome to settle disputes and provide doctrinal teaching and guidance.

The Jewish Christians were adamant that the Gentiles had to convert to Judaism through the rite of circumcision. They lacked proper teaching in the revelation of grace that was given to Paul. Therefore, Paul felt an obligation, as the apostle to the gentiles (Rom. 11:13), to instruct them in these matters and hence, this letter.

DATE AND PLACE OF WRITING

This letter to the Romans was probably written during Paul's third missionary trip around A.D. 57-58 when Paul was in Corinth or that vicinity (Acts 20:2-3).

The date can be deduced from some of Paul's statements in Rom. 15:25-28 about how he was headed to Jerusalem to take the offering of the saints in Macedonia (see note 1 at Acts 16:9, p. 593) and Achaia (see note 11 at Acts 18:12, p. 605) to the poor saints in Judaea (see note 1 at Jn. 4:3, p. 100). This places the writing of this book towards the end of Paul's third missionary trip (see note 2 at Acts 18:23, p. 607) as he headed for Jerusalem.

Phebe, a servant of the church in Cenchrea (see note 1 at Acts 18:18, p. 606), was the one who carried this epistle to the church in Rome (Acts 16:1; subscript Acts 16:27). So, it can be supposed that Paul was in Phebe's home town of Cenchrea or Corinth (see note 1 at Acts 18:1, p. 604) when he wrote this letter.

CONTENT

The book of Romans contains the most detailed explanation of salvation by grace through faith in the scriptures. The book can be outlined as follows:

I. Introduction 1:1-15
II. Presentation of Gospel 1:16-8:39
 A. All men guilty 1:18-3:20
  1. Gentiles guilty 1:18-32
  2. Jews guilty 2:1-3:9
  3. Conclusion-all guilty 3:9-31
 B. O.T. examples of justification by faith 4:1-25
 C. Justification imputed just as sin was imputed 5:1-21
 D. Dead to sin 6:1-13
 E. Not under law 6:14-7:13
 F. Reason for law-our carnality 7:14-25
 G. Triumph of grace 8:1-39
III. Justification for inclusion of Gentiles 9:1-11:36
IV. Exhortations to holy living 12:1-13:14
V. Instructions on how to live the Gospel in
 front of a weak brother 14:1-15:21
VI. Mentioning of future travels 15:22-33
VII. Salutations 16:1-27

ABOUT THE AUTHOR

Some facts about Paul's persecution of the church, his conversion, and the intervening time until the beginning of his ministry has been dealt with in note 4 at Acts 7:58, page 543; note 1 at Acts 9:1, page 551; note 1 at Acts 9:26, page 556. Information about Paul's life after the close of the book of Acts is included in note 1 at Acts 28:30, page 653. Many notes about Paul's exploits, character and hardships are found throughout the book of Acts.

FEATURES OF THE LIFE FOR TODAY STUDY BIBLE AND COMMENTARY

(3)

DOES THE JEW HAVE AN ADVANTAGE?

(1)
a Gk.-"perissos"- superiority; pre-eminence
Dict.- a factor favorable or conducive to success; benefit or profit; gain; a relatively favorable position; the condition of being ahead
b Gk.-"ioudaios"- Jewish as respects birth; race; religion
see note 10 at Jn. 8:33, p. 232
(9)
c Dict.- benefit; advantageous gain or return
d Gk.-"peritome"- circumcision: the rite, condition, or people (Strong)
The extinction of the passions and the removal of spiritual impurity (Thayer)
From Gk.-"peri-temno"- to cut around
(2)
see note 4 at Jn. 7:22, p. 224
see note 1 at Acts 11:2, p. 565
see note 2 at Acts 15:1, p. 585
see note 3 at Acts 16:3, p. 591
Dt. 10:16
30:6
Jer. 4:4
9:26
Rom. 4:10
4:11-12
Col. 2:11-12
(4)
e great in every way (TCNT)
much in every way (NIV)
f Gk.-"proton"- firstly in importance
g Gk.-"pisteuo"- to be intrusted with a thing

CHAPTER 3

(10)

WHAT advantage[a] then[1] hath the Jew?[b] or
what profit[c] *is there* of circumcision?[d]
2 *Much every way:[e] chiefly,[f] because[2]
that unto them were committed[g] the oracles[3]
of God.
3 For what if some did not believe?[h]
shall their unbelief[i] make the faith[j] of God[4]
without effect?[5]
4 *God forbid:[6] yea, let[7] God be true,[k]
but every man a liar;[l] as it is written,[8] That
thou mightest be justified[m] in thy sayings,[n]
and mightest overcome[o] when thou art
judged.[p]

(8)
h Rom. 10:16
Heb. 4:2
i see note 3 at Mt. 17:20, p. 211
see note 2 at Lk. 8:51, p. 159
see note 2 at Mk. 6:5, p. 163
see notes 2-3 at Mk. 8:23, p. 200
see note 2 at Mt. 17:20, p. 210
see note 2 at Jn. 20:25, p. 498
see note 4 at Acts 9:38, p. 558
see note 14 at Acts 12:16, p. 572
j shall their want of faith make of none effect the faithfulness of God (ASV)-
Num. 23:19
1 Sam. 15:29
2 Tim. 2:13
Ti. 1:2
k Jn. 14:6
3:33
2 Cor. 1:18
Ti. 1:2
Heb. 6:18
l Gk.-"pseustes"- a falsifier; from Gk.-"pseudo-mai"- to utter an untruth or at-tempt to deceive by falsehood-
Rom. 3:10-12
1 Jn. 2:4, 22
4:20
(6)
m i.e. show or regard as just or innocent; be righteous
n Gk.-"logos"- something said including the thought
o Gk.-"nikao"- to subdue; conquer; prevail; get the victory
p Gk.-"krino"- call in question; judge

(7)

PARALLEL SCRIPTURE FOR ROMANS 3:2

MARK 7:13

13 Making the word of God of none effect through your tradition, which ye have delivered: and many such like things do ye.

(5)

O.T. SCRIPTURE CITED IN ROMANS 3:4

PSALM 51:4

4 Against thee, thee only, have I sinned, and done this *evil in thy sight: that thou mightest be justified when thou speakest,* and *be clear when thou judgest.*

(11)

Footnotes for Romans 3:1-8

1 (Rom. 3:1) Paul had just proven that the Jews were just as guilty as the pagans who they disdained (see note 1 at Rom. 2:1, p. 662). This led to the question, "What advantage is there in being a Jew then?" Paul gives the most important answer to that question in verse two (see note 2 at verse 2, below) and then addresses the issue more in Romans 9:4-5.

2 (Rom. 3:2) The main advantage (see ref. f at this verse) that the Jews had over others was that God had committed His Word unto them. They not only had the intuitive knowledge of God (see note 2 at Rom. 1:18, p. 659) but they had a written record of God's instructions which should have served as an added restraint from departing from God. They, however, had missed the true intent of God's law and therefore were not taking advantage of the benefits God's Word afforded them.

3 (Rom. 3:2) The Greek word for "oracles" is "logion" which means, "an utterance of God." Therefore, this is speaking of the Word of God that was committed to the Jews. In the Old Testament, the word "oracle" was also used to designate the innermost part of the temple since the ark of the covenant was kept there (1 Ki. 6:5; 6:16,19-23,31; 7:49; 8:6,8; 2 Chr. 3:16; 4:20; 5:7,9; Ps. 28:2).

The word "oracles" is used four times in the New Testament (Acts 7:38; Rom. 3:2; Heb. 5:12; 1 Pet. 4:11). In each of these instances, the word is clearly referring to the Word of God.

4 (Rom. 3:3) Paul is using the phrase "the faith of God" in this verse interchangeably with the word "oracle" in verse two. He is saying that the unbelief of the Jews did not make the Word of God or the promises of God without effect. Therefore, the Word of God is the faith of God. No wonder faith comes by hearing God's Word; God's Word contains His faith.

5 (Rom. 3:3) Paul is asking the question, "If some of the Jews did not believe God's Word, does that make God's Word of no effect?" The answer to this question is a resounding no in verse four. However, Mark 7:13 says we make the word of God of none effect through our tradition. What's the harmony between these two verses?

An individual can make God's Word of no effect in his personal life. Hebrews 4:2 says God's Word will not profit us unless we mix it with faith. So the Word will not profit anyone who doesn't believe it, but God's Word itself doesn't lose any power. That is what Paul is stating here. The unbelief of the Jewish nation as a whole did not void the promises of God concerning salvation through a Savior. The promises of salvation were of no effect to the individuals who rejected Jesus, but to anyone who will put his faith in Jesus as Messiah, the Word of God still has its power to save.

6 (Rom. 3:4) This is the first of ten times that Paul uses this expression in the book of Romans (here; Rom. 3:6,31; 6:2,15; 7:7,13; 9:14; 11:1,11). He also uses this expression three other times in his other epistles (1 Cor. 6:15; Gal. 2:17; 6:14).

The Greek words that are used are "me ginomai" meaning "let it not be! far be it! God forbid!" and express emphatic denial of the false conclusion that someone might draw from his teaching.

7 (Rom. 3:4) This phrase "let God be true, but every man a liar" is given in response to the question of verse 3 (see note 5 at Rom. 3:3, above). Paul is stating that God and His promises are always true even if men don't believe Him. However, there can be other applications of this truth which will benefit us greatly.

When anyone or anything contradicts a promise to us in God's Word we need to reckon God to be true and that person or thing a lie. We need to believe that what God's Word says about our prosperity is true (2 Cor. 8:9; 3 Jn. 2) instead of what our checkbook says. We need to believe that we [were] healed by His stripes (Isa. 53:5; Mt. 8:17; 1 Pet. 2:24) instead of believing what the x-rays show. In every aspect of our lives, we need to believe God's Word above what we see or hear.

8 (Rom. 3:4) This is a quotation from David out of Psalm 51:4 when he was repenting of his sin with Bathsheba and the murder of her husband. David was admitting his sinfulness and proclaiming God's complete justification in judging his sin in whatever way He saw fit. David's sin had not made God unholy, it made him unholy. In David's sinfulness, he now saw the holiness of God clearer than ever.

This is what Paul is drawing from this Old Testament passage. He was saying that in a similar manner, God retained His holiness even when His people were unholy. It was the Jews who suffered from not believing God's Word, not God.

1. Greek Words Defined–
Greek words and renderings to aid in understanding the English Translation.

2. Other Commentary Footnotes–
References to other footnotes and references in Gospels or Acts LFT Bible.

3. Headings–
Short headings summarizing the content of the passage.

4. Translation Clarification–
Other translations used for broader explanations.

5. O.T. Scriptures Cited–
O.T. scriptures partially or fully quoted in the N.T. Indicated by asterisks at beginning of verse.

6. Passage Explanations–
For better understanding of terminology.

7. Parallel Scriptures–
A parallel passage that in some way relates to, or further clarifies passage. Indicated by asterisks at beginning of verse.

8. Related Scripture References–
For in–depth topical studies.

9. Dictionary Definitions–
To aid in understanding the meaning of words.

10. Reference Letters/Footnote Numbers–
Indicate various material relating to the passage. See Number 10 on p. vii for specific information.

11. Commentary Footnotes–
Comprehensive footnotes to aid and enrich study.

For a listing of additional study aids, please see the Table of Contents.

HOW TO USE YOUR LIFE FOR TODAY STUDY BIBLE

1. GREEK WORDS DEFINED-Definitions of Greek words are given to add clarity to the passage. You can also compare these Greek definitions with other verses to see if the same Greek word was translated by multiple English words or vice-versa. For instance, the Greek word "dikaioo" has been translated several ways in English (see ref. m, Rom. 3:4, p. 668; see ref. c, Rom. 4:2, p. 674)

2. OTHER COMMENTARY FOOTNOTES-Many topics are too broad to be covered fully in one footnote. Therefore, a comparison of related footnotes is very beneficial. Once a topic has been successfully dealt with, there will not be another note, but rather a reference back to previous notes.

3. HEADINGS-*The Romans Edition* has been divided into 51 different headings. These are arranged in the order of the scriptures themselves.

4. TRANSLATION CLARIFICATION-Similar to the definitions of Greek words, these are other translations used to provide additional understanding.

5. O.T. SCRIPTURES CITED-This is a great convenience which allows the reader to see every Old Testament scripture that was quoted in the text, printed right in front of him. There are many advantages to be gained by diligently comparing the New Testament quotes with the exact wording of the Old Testament scripture (see note 8 at Rom. 3:4, p. 668).

6. PASSAGE EXPLANATIONS-These marginal entries put many hard to understand or outdated expressions used in the KJV into modern terminology.

7. PARALLEL SCRIPTURES-These are Related Scripture references (#7, p. vi), which have been selected from the reference columns and printed nearby for your convenience and enrichment as you study.

8. RELATED SCRIPTURE REFERENCES-The greatest commentary on scripture is the scripture itself. Therefore, these related scriptures are listed to guide you to other scriptures that correspond to the one you are studying.

9. DICTIONARY DEFINITIONS-Many times a dictionary definition will add understanding to a word that is even better than the Greek definition. This is especially helpful with many of the archaic English words which were a very good translation, but have lost their meaning in modern English.

10. REFERENCE LETTERS/FOOTNOTE NUMBERS-These small alphabetical letters within the scripture verses allow you to quickly identify scripture references, Greek definitions, dictionary definitions, scripture clarifications and translations, as well as other related footnotes and material that would relate to the passage. The small numbers in the text indicate a footnote written in reference to the word, phrase, or scripture verse in which the number appears.

11. COMMENTARY FOOTNOTES-There are over 2300 *Life For Today* footnotes (in the Gospels Edition, the Acts of the Apostles Edition, and the Romans Edition combined) written from a Spirit-filled perspective. These are equivalent to having a comprehensive Bible dictionary, encyclopedia, and commentary all wrapped up into one. Many difficult passages and seeming contradictions are dealt with and clarified. The "How To" of applying the biblical truth is also emphasized.

ROMANS

PAUL'S CALLING AND DESIRE TO COME TO THE ROMANS

a see Intro. to Romans, p. iv
see note 4 at Acts 7:58, p. 543
see note 1 at Acts 9:1, p. 551
see note 1 at Acts 9:26, p. 556
see note 1 at Acts 28:30, p. 653
b see note 1 at Lk. 9:46, p. 215
c see note 5 at Jn. 1:41, p. 40
see note 2 at Mt. 16:16, p. 202
see note 3 at Acts 4:26, p. 526
d see note 2 at Lk. 6:13, p. 109
see note 3 at Acts 14:4, p. 581
Rom. 1:5
11:13
e Acts 13:2-4
Gal. 1:15
f see note 5 at Acts 20:24, p. 618
see note 7 at Mt. 24:14, p. 396
Rom. 1:9,16-17
15:16, 29
16:25
g Acts 26:6
Ti. 1:2
h see note 1 at Acts 11:27, p. 569
Acts 10:43
Rom. 3:21
i 1 Cor. 15:3-4
j see note 5 at Mk. 1:1, p. 30
Jn. 3:16
Rom. 1:9
Acts 8:37
9:20
Rom. 8:3, 29-32
1 Cor. 1:9
1 Jn. 1:3
4:9-10, 15
5:13
k see note 3 at Lk. 1:43, p. 12

CHAPTER 1

PAUL,[a] a servant[1b] of Jesus Christ,[c] called
to be an apostle,[2d] separated[e] unto the gospel[f]
of God,
2 (Which he had promised[g] afore[3] by his
prophets[h] in the holy scriptures,)[i]
3 Concerning his Son[j] Jesus Christ[c] our
Lord,[k] which was made of the seed of
David[l] according to the flesh;[m]
4 And declared[n] *to be* the Son[j] of God
with power,[o] according to the spirit of
holiness,[p] by the resurrection[q] from the
dead:[4]
5 By whom we have received grace[5r]
and apostleship,[d] for obedience[6] to the faith[s]
among all nations,[t] for his name:[u]

l see note 5 at Jn. 1:41, p. 40
see note 2 at Lk. 18:39, p. 343
m i.e. according to His human nature
n Gk.-"horizo"- to mark out; to appoint; decree; specify
o i.e. in a striking, triumphant, and miraculous manner (Amp)
p Rom. 8:11
q see note 1 at Acts 1:3, p. 509
see note 1 at Mt. 22:23, p. 378
see note 3 at Lk. 24:39, p. 496
r see note 5 at Acts 20:24, p. 618
Jn. 1:16
1 Cor. 15:10
Gal. 1:15-16
2:9
Eph. 3:2-9
s i.e. to the obedience that comes from faith (NIV)-
Rom. 16:26
Acts 6:7
2 Cor. 10:4-6
Heb. 5:9
t see note 2 at Lk. 2:32, p. 22
see note 1 at Acts 10:1, p. 559
see note 4 at Acts 10:11, p. 561
see note 1 at Acts 10:35, p. 563
see note 1 at Acts 11:22, p. 568
see note 2 at Acts 10:28, p. 562
u Acts 15:14

Footnotes for Romans 1:1-5

1 (Rom. 1:1) Out of the six Greek words for "servant" used in the New Testament, Paul used one of the most slavish terms possible. The word used in this passage is "doulos" and comes from the root word "deo" which means "bind." So, Paul is literally speaking of himself as being a bondman or slave of Jesus Christ — a slave by free choice; yet owned and purchased by Jesus Christ (1 Cor. 6:19-20).

The idea of being a love-slave by choice comes from Old Testament passages such as Exodus 21:2-6 and Deuteronomy 15:12-17. If an Israelite bought a Hebrew slave, he had to set him free in the seventh year. However, if the slave loved his master and said, *"I will not go away from thee,"* then a hole was to be bored through the lobe of his ear pronouncing him a bond-slave forever.

By the use of this word, Paul is declaring Jesus as his absolute Master, yet indicating the idea of his expression of love and free choice to the one whom he serves.

2 (Rom. 1:1) Notice that Paul spoke of his servitude to Christ before he mentioned his apostleship. This reveals Paul's priorities and humility, which were key factors in his success.

3 (Rom. 1:2) The concept of the gospel (see note 5 at Acts 20:24, p. 618) was not new. Galatians 3:8 says that the Lord preached the gospel unto Abraham. Also, Moses gave the conditions of the gospel in Deuteronomy 30:11-14, which Paul quoted in Romans 10:6-7 as he explained faith as the only condition to receiving God's grace. Jesus Himself said that the law of Moses, the prophets, and the psalms were full of prophecies concerning Him (Lk. 24:44).

The gospel was woven throughout the Old Testament scriptures. Indeed, the job of the Old Testament law was to "shut us up" or constrain us towards the gospel (Gal. 3:23). In this sense, there is no conflict between the Old Testament law and the New Testament grace. The Old Testament ministry of law was only temporary (Gal. 3:19) until the gospel could be put into effect by the sacrifice of Jesus.

The conflict between law and grace comes when people try to mix the two. As Jesus described in His parables about the new wine in the old wine skin and the new patch on the old garment (see note 1 at Lk. 5:36, 38, p. 93), the two covenants are not compatible.

The Old Testament law paved the way for the gospel and pointed men towards the gospel. If the law is used to point out man's need and bring him to his knees through hopelessness of self-salvation, then the gospel is used to provide salvation and relationship, there is no conflict. Conflict arises only when individuals refuse to use faith in God's grace as the only means of salvation and insist that some degree of adherence to law is required for justification (see note 2 at Lk. 9:55, p. 245; see note 1 at Lk. 16:16, p. 301).

4 (Rom. 1:4) The resurrection of Jesus from the dead is the greatest witness of all to the validity of Jesus' claims (see note 1 at Acts 1:3, p. 509).

5 (Rom. 1:5) This is the first of twenty-four times the term "grace" is used in Paul's epistle to the Romans. The Greek word for grace is "charis" and is translated many different ways throughout the New Testament. It is translated: favor, thanks, gracious, thankworthy, thank, thanked, pleasure, liberality, and acceptable. The most common way it is translated is by the word "grace" which is used 129 times in the New Testament.

According to Thayer's Greek-English Lexicon, "the word 'charis' (grace) contains the idea of kindness which bestows upon one what he has not deserved. The New Testament writers used 'charis' pre-eminently of that kindness by which God bestows favors even upon the ill-deserving."

Another form of the Greek word "charis" (grace) is "charisma" and is translated "gift." Vines Expository Dictionary defines "charisma" as "a gift of grace, a gift involving grace on the part of God as the donor." In other words, "charisma" is a specific form or manifestation of the grace of God. It is used to describe as a free gift: righteousness (Rom. 5:16-17); spiritual gifts (1 Cor. 12:28-31; Rom. 12:6-8); eternal life (Rom. 6:23); the five ministry gifts (Eph. 4:11); celibacy (1 Cor. 7:7); healings (1 Cor. 12:9, 28, 30); and miraculous intervention (2 Cor. 1:11).

6 (Rom. 1:5) The Greek word used here for obedience is "hupakoe" and means "attentive hearkening; that is by implication, compliance or submission."

Many times in the New Testament faith and obedience are linked together (Acts 6:7; Rom. 16:26; Jas. 2:14-22; 1 Pet. 1:21). This is because the origin and historical development of the words "believe" and "obey" are closely related. What you believe is what you will do.

If you really believed that the building you were in was on fire, you would do something. Different people might do different things but it is inconceivable that anyone who really believed the building was on fire would do nothing. The New Testament calls this a *"work of faith"* (1 Th. 1:2-3; 2 Th. 1:11) which is an action corresponding to and induced by what a person believes. This differs from a work of the law in that works of the law require no faith and are works of one's own resources without any reference, reliance, or trust in God (Gal. 2:16; 3:12; 5:4; Rom. 3:28; 4:15-16; 9:30-32).

ROMANS

PAUL'S CALLING AND DESIRE TO COME TO THE ROMANS (cont'd)

CHAPTER 1

6 *Among whom are ye also the called[7a]
of Jesus Christ:
7 To all that be in Rome,[b] beloved[8c] of
God, called[a] *to be* saints:[d] Grace[e] to you and
peace[f] from God our Father,[g] and the Lord
Jesus Christ.
8 *First, I thank[h] my God[i] through Jesus
Christ for you all, that your faith[9] is spoken
of throughout the whole world.[j]

PARALLEL SCRIPTURES FOR ROMANS 1:6

ROMANS 8:28-30

28 And we know that all things work together for good to them that love God, to them who are the called according to his *purpose.*

29 For whom he did foreknow, he also did predestinate to be *conformed to the image of his Son, that he might be the firstborn among many brethren.*

30 Moreover whom he did predestinate, them he also called: and whom he called, them he also justified: and whom he justified, them he also glorified.

PARALLEL SCRIPTURE FOR ROMANS 1:8

1 THESSALONIANS 1:8

8 For from you sounded out the word of the Lord not only in Macedonia and Achaia, but also in every place your faith to God-ward is spread abroad; so that we need not to speak any thing.

a Gk.-"kletos"- invited; i.e. appointed; a saint- Rom. 8:28-30; 9:24; 1 Cor. 1:9; Gal. 1:6; 1 Th. 2:12; 2 Th. 2:14; 2 Tim. 1:9; Heb. 3:1; 1 Pet. 2:9, 21; 2 Pet. 1:10; Rev. 17:14
b Acts 2:10; 23:11; 28:14, 16
c Gk.-"agapetos"- esteemed; dear; favorite. Dict.- held in great affection; to love thoroughly- Rom. 9:25; Col. 3:12; 1 Tim. 6:2
d see note 5 at Acts 9:13, p. 555
e Gk.-"charis"- a common greeting employed by Paul, Peter, and John- 1 Cor. 1:3; 2 Cor. 1:2; Gal. 1:3; Eph. 1:2; Phil. 1:2; Col. 1:2; 1 Th. 1:1; 2 Th. 1:2; 1 Tim. 1:2; 2 Tim. 1:2; Ti. 1:4; Phile. 3; 1 Pet. 1:2; 2 Pet. 1:2; 2 Jn. 3; Rev. 1:4-5
f see note 37 at Jn. 14:27, p. 434; see notes 38-39 at Jn. 14:27, p. 434; see note 91 at Jn. 16:33, p. 442; see note 2 at Lk. 24:38, p. 496
g see note 29 at Mt. 6:9, p. 79
h see note 4 at Lk. 17:18, p. 314
i see note 1 at Jn. 1:1, p. 2
j see note 2 at Lk. 15:4, p. 292; see note 4 at Acts 19:10, p. 609; see note 109 at Jn. 17:21, p. 446; see note 5 at Mt. 28:19, p. 504

Footnotes for Romans 1:6-8

7 (Rom. 1:6) This verse states that we are *"the called of Jesus Christ."* The next verse states to what Jesus has called us. He called us to be saints (see note 5 at Acts 9:13, p. 555). God's grace has extended the call (or invitation) to every person to become a saint through salvation (Ti. 2:11), but not everyone chooses to respond positively to this call. If an individual rejects God's call, then God chooses to reject that person (Lk. 12:9; 1 Jn. 2:23). Therefore the statement of Matthew 22:14, *"For many are called, but few* are *chosen."*

8 (Rom. 1:7) It is one of the greatest truths of the Bible, and also one of the hardest to comprehend, that we are the objects of God's love. God didn't just pity us or feel some sense of moral obligation to save us; He saved us because of His infinite love for us (Jn. 3:16). An experiential understanding of God's love is the key to being filled with all the fullness of God (Eph. 3:19).

9 (Rom. 1:8) This is quite a statement! It is to be understood that this is speaking of the known Roman world, but this is still an astounding fact. These believers who had never had an apostolic visit and, as far as we know, had very little teaching, had such a strong faith in the Lord that stories of that faith had spread throughout the world. This is quite a contrast with many churches today that haven't even impacted their neighborhoods with the gospel of Christ.

ROMANS

PAUL'S CALLING AND DESIRE TO COME TO THE ROMANS (cont'd)

CHAPTER 1

9 *For God is my witness,[k] whom I serve with my spirit[l] in the gospel[m] of his Son, that without ceasing I make mention of you always in my prayers;
10 Making request,[n] if by any means now at length I might have a prosperous journey by the will of God[o] to come unto you.
11 For I long to see you,[p] that I may impart[10] unto you some spiritual gift,[q] to the end ye may be established;[r]
12 *That is, that I may be comforted together with you by the mutual faith both of you and me.[s]
13 Now I would not have you ignorant, brethren, that oftentimes I purposed to come unto you, (but was let[11] hitherto,) that I might have some fruit[t] among you also, even as among other Gentiles.[u]
14 I am debtor[12v] both to the Greeks, and to the Barbarians;[13] both to the wise, and to the unwise.[w]
15 So, as much as in me is,[x] I am ready to preach[y] the gospel[m] to you that are at Rome[b] also.[14]

PARALLEL SCRIPTURES FOR ROMANS 1:9

JOHN 4:23-24

23 But the hour cometh, and now is, when the true worshippers shall worship the Father in spirit and in truth: for the Father seeketh such to worship him.
24 God is a Spirit: and they that worship him must worship him *in spirit and in truth.*

PARALLEL SCRIPTURES FOR ROMANS 1:12

EPHESIANS 4:4-6

4 There is *one body, and one Spirit, even as ye are called in one hope of your calling;*
5 One Lord, one faith, one baptism,
6 One God and Father of all, who is *above all, and through all, and in you all.*

k Dict.- one who furnishes evidence- 2 Cor. 1:23; 11:31; Gal. 1:20; Phil. 1:8; 1 Th. 2:5
l i.e. with my spiritual self, or all my heart (Ber, Phi)
m Gk.-"euaggelion"- a good message; good news; see note 5 at Acts 20:24, p. 618; see note 7 at Mt. 24:14, p. 396
n Rom. 15:30-32; 1 Th. 3:10-11; Phile. 22
o Acts 18:21; 21:14; 1 Cor. 4:19; Jas. 4:15
p Rom. 15:23, 32; 2 Cor. 9:14; Phil. 1:8; 2:26; 4:1
q Rom. 15:29; Acts 8:15-17; 19:6; 1 Cor. 12:1-11; Gal. 3:5; Eph. 4:8-12; see note 3 at Jn. 4:39, p. 58; see note 3 at Jn. 1:48, p. 42; see note 13 at Mk. 16:17, p. 507
r Gk.-"sterizo"- to make stable; to strengthen; make firm- Rom. 16:25; Acts 16:5; 2 Cor. 1:21; 1 Th. 3:2; 2 Th. 2:17; 3:3; 1 Pet. 5:10; 2 Pet. 1:12
s I mean that we may be mutually strengthened by your faith and mine (Ber)
t Jn. 15:16; Col. 1:6; Phil. 4:17
u see note 2 at Lk. 2:32, p. 22; see note 1 at Acts 10:44, p. 564; see note 45 at Mt. 6:32, p. 83
v Gk.-"opheiletes"- an ower; i.e. person indebted- Rom. 13:8; 1 Cor. 9:16-23
w i.e. to the cultured and uncultured; to the educated and uneducated (Amp, LB)
x and so, for my part (TCNT)
y see note 2 at Acts 8:5, p. 545; see note 3 at Acts 8:6, p. 545; see note 2 at Acts 20:7, p. 615; see note 2 at Acts 14:4, p. 581; Acts 10:42; 16:10; 17:3; 1 Cor. 1:23; 2 Cor. 2:12; 4:5

Footnotes for Romans 1:9-15

10 (Rom. 1:11) Two things are very significant in Paul's statement here. First, we see that spiritual gifts can be imparted or passed from one person to another. This is the whole purpose of the presbytery laying hands on an individual during ordination, as Paul reminds Timothy (1 Tim. 4:14).

Secondly, spiritual gifts help establish or strengthen an individual. This is in stark contrast to what some critics of the gifts of the Holy Spirit claim. As Paul said in 1 Corinthians 14:3-4, the gifts of the Spirit operating in the church produce edification, exhortation, and comfort; in private use they edify the individual.

11 (Rom. 1:13) The word "let" that was used here is an old English word which means "hindered." It is still used in that sense in the sports of tennis and table tennis.

Paul was saying that he had purposed many times to travel to Rome, but he had been hindered up to this point. In Romans 15:22 Paul clearly states what his hindrance was: that others, closer to where he was, had not heard the gospel yet. In other words, he was hindered from bringing the gospel to Rome because there were so many other places that needed him just as much. However, in Romans 15:23, Paul says that he had presented the gospel to every region in those parts (probably the area of Corinth—see Date and Place of Writing in the Introduction to the Book of Romans, p. iv), and he was now ready to begin his journey to Rome.

12 (Rom. 1:14) Paul was making this statement in a spiritual sense. He was expressing his sense of obligation to share the gospel of Jesus Christ with all men. This was one of the attitudes of Paul that motivated him to travel to the ends of the known world and constantly lay his life on the line for the sake of Christ. Likewise, those who seek to be used of God today need to recognize that their duty to share Christ with a dying world is not optional.

13 (Rom. 1:14) In Paul's day the term "barbarian" was not an offensive term. It was simply used to distinguish anyone who did not speak the Greek language, or later to identify anyone who was not of the Hellenic race.

14 (Rom. 1:15) Paul has now dispensed with the preliminaries and is beginning to present his defense of the gospel, which was his primary purpose of writing.

ROMANS

THE GOSPEL OF CHRIST AND THE RIGHTEOUSNESS IT REVEALS

a Dict.- reluctant through fear of shame
Dict.- "shame"- a painful emotion caused by a strong sense of guilt, embarrassment, unworthiness, or disgrace-
Ps. 119:46
Mk. 8:38
2 Tim. 1:8, 12, 16
1 Pet. 4:16
b Gk.-"euaggelion"- a good message; good news
see note 7 at Mt. 24:14, p. 396
see note 5 at Acts 20:24, p. 618
Rom. 15:19, 29
Lk. 2:10-11
1 Cor. 9:12, 18
2 Cor. 2:12
4:4
Gal. 1:7
1 Tim. 1:11

CHAPTER 1

16 For I am not ashamed[a] of the gospel[b]
of Christ:[c] for it is the power[1d] of God[e] unto[f]
salvation[g] to every one[h] that believeth;[2i] to
the Jew[j] first, and also to the Greek.[k]
17 For therein is the righteousness[l] of
God[e] revealed[m] from faith[3n] to faith: as it is
written,[o] The just[p] shall live[4] by faith.[n]

c see note 5 at Jn. 1:41, p. 40
see note 2 at Mt. 16:16, p. 202
see note 3 at Acts 4:26, p. 526
d Gk.-"dunamis"- force; miraculous power; ability; might; strength; mighty work
see note 5 at Acts 1:8, p. 509
e Jer. 5:14
1 Cor. 1:18-24
2:4
1 Th. 1:5
Heb. 4:12
Jer. 23:29
see note 1 at Jn. 1:1, p. 2
f Gk.-"eis"- a preposition that often signifies result; i.e. the gospel is the power of God resulting in salvation

continued on center column

References continued from column 4

g Gk.-"soteria"- rescue; safety; deliverance; health; saving; salvation; a derivative of "sozo"
see note 7 at Acts 2:21, p. 515
see note 93 at Jn. 17:2, p. 444
see note 2 at Mt. 8:17, p. 68
h Rom. 1:5
Jn. 3:15-16
Acts 2:39
Rom. 3:29
10:13
Rev. 3:20
i Gk.-"pisteuo"- to have faith in, upon, or with respect to, a person or thing; to entrust, esp. one's spiritual well-being to Christ; commit; to trust
see note 1 at Acts 10:44, p. 564
see note 2 at Acts 15:1, p. 585
see note 3 at Acts 16:31, p. 597
see note 6 at Mt. 24:13, p. 396
j see note 10 at Jn. 8:33, p. 232
k Rom. 3:29-30
4:9-12
9:24
10:12
Acts 18:5-6
20:21
26:20
l Gk.-"dikaiosune"- the state acceptable to God which becomes a sinner's possession through that faith by which he embraces the grace of God offered him in the expiatory death of Jesus Christ; justification (Thayer)
m Dict.- to make known what has heretofore been kept secret
n Gk.-"pistis"- reliance upon Christ; belief; believe
see note 1 at Acts 10:44, p. 564
see note 3 at Acts 16:31, p. 597
see note 6 at Mt. 24:13, p. 396
o Hab. 2:4
Gal. 3:11
Heb. 10:38
p Gk.-"dikaios"- righteous; a state of being right, or right conduct

Footnotes for Romans 1:16-17

1 (Rom. 1:16) The gospel is the power of God that releases the effects of salvation in our lives (see ref. f, this verse). Salvation is much more than just being born again. This refers to every benefit to which the believer is entitled through Jesus (see ref. g, this verse). Therefore, if we are not experiencing the abundance that Jesus provided for us—in any area of our lives—then we are having a problem understanding and/or believing the gospel.

The term "gospel" has become so familiar to Christians that the true meaning and understanding has been lost. As discussed in note 5 at Acts 20:24, page 618 and note 7 at Matthew 24:14, page 396, the truths of the gospel are not commonly preached or understood in many churches. **This is the reason that so many Christians are not walking in all the benefits of their salvation.** They don't have the power of the gospel working in them.

If a person needs healing, it's in the gospel. If deliverance is needed, it's in the gospel. Prosperity, answered prayer, joy, peace, love; they are all found through understanding and believing the gospel.

2 (Rom. 1:16) Most English words that end with the suffix "eth" in the Bible, carry the idea of an act or process which continues. So, the man that "believeth" is a man who has believed and is continuing to believe.

In the Greek language the word that was translated "believeth" here, is a present participle which expresses the idea of a continuous and repeated action. Therefore, the faith that results in salvation cannot be abandoned and still produce its results (Heb. 6:4-6; 10:29; Col. 1:21-23). It may appear to be abandoned, as in the case of Peter when he denied the Lord (Lk. 22:57-62), but Jesus had prayed that his "faith fail not" (see note 2 at Lk. 22:32, p. 429).

The scriptures present true Bible faith as an ongoing experience, not a one-time action.

3 (Rom. 1:17) The expression *"from faith to faith"* describes the means whereby righteousness is given and retained. God's righteousness cannot be earned; it can only be acquired through faith. As proof that righteousness received by faith is not a new idea or concept, Paul quotes Habakkuk 2:4, *"The just shall live by faith"* (also quoted in Gal. 3:11 and Heb. 10:38).

4 (Rom. 1:17) The just shall **live** by faith. They don't just visit faith every once and awhile, or vacation there once a year, they **live** in and by faith.

ROMANS

GOD'S WRATH REVEALED AGAINST THE UNRIGHTEOUSNESS OF MEN

a Gk.-"orge"- that in God which stands opposed to man's disobedience; obduracy, and sin, and manifests itself in punishing the same (Thayer) see note 4 at Jn. 3:36, p. 52 see note 4 at Acts 12:23, p. 573 Ps. 2:12 78:49 90:11 Rom. 2:5 Jn. 3:36 Eph. 5:6 Col. 3:6 Rev. 6:16-17 19:15
b see note 1 at Jn. 1:1, p. 2
c Gk.-"apokalupto"- to take off the cover; disclose

CHAPTER 1

18 For the wrath[1a] of God[b] is revealed[c]
from heaven[d] against all[2] ungodliness[e] and
unrighteousness[f] of men, who hold the
truth in unrighteousness;[g]

19 Because that which may be known of
God is manifest in them;[h] for God[b] hath
shewed *it* unto them.
20 For the invisible things of him[i] from
the creation of the world[j] are clearly seen,
being understood by the things that are
made,[k] *even* his eternal power[l] and
Godhead;[3m] so that they are without excuse:[n]

d Gk.-"ouranos"- heaven as the abode of God see note 2 at Mk. 12:25, p. 380
e Gk.-"asebeia"- want of reverence towards God; impiety; wickedness- Ps. 1:1 Ti. 2:12 2 Pet. 2:5-6 3:7 Jude 4, 15, 18
f Gk.-"adikia"- injustice; wrongfulness of character; life or act; iniquity; unjust- Rom. 1:29 2:8-9 Dt. 25:16 Isa. 55:7 1 Cor. 6:9 2 Th. 2:12 2 Pet. 2:13-15 1 Jn. 1:9

continued on center column

References continued from column 4

g who suppress the truth by their unrighteousness; i.e. who curtail or prohibit the truth, that keep the truth from being revealed- Rom. 1:19, 28, 32 2:3, 15-23 2 Th. 2:10
h lies plain before their eyes; made plain in their inner consciousness (NEB, Amp)
i i.e. God- Heb. 11:27
j ever since the world was made (Con)
k have been clearly perceptible and understandable through the things He has made (Nor)
l Gk.-"dunamis"- miraculous power; might; strength; mighty work
m Gk.-"theiotes"- divinity; divine nature
n Dict.- a plea or explanation offered to elicit pardon; the reason or ground for excusing Syn.– forgive- Ps. 19:1-4 Rom. 2:1

Footnotes for Romans 1:18-20

1 (Rom. 1:18) Paul's purpose in writing verses 18-20 is to explain why the gospel is the power of God unto salvation (v. 16). The problem was that then, just as now, most people felt the way to get people to come to God was to condemn them and scare them out of Hell. People doubted that Paul's good news of the love of God would be enough to cause repentance.

Therefore, Paul begins to prove that every person already has an instinctive knowledge of God's wrath against their sin. We don't need to prove God's wrath. God has already done that. What people need to know is the good news that God placed His wrath for our sins upon His own Son so that we could be completely forgiven. This good news will draw men to God more than the bad news will ever drive men to God.

2 (Rom. 1:18) In Romans 1:18-20, Paul is declaring that God has revealed Himself to all mankind. Old Testament scriptures proclaim that God has revealed Himself to everyone through nature (Ps. 19:1-3), but Paul is stating here that there is an intuitive revelation of God within every man.

There are five words used in these three verses to describe the extent to which God has revealed Himself to mankind that are worth special note. Any one of these five words used by itself would have made a strong argument for Paul's case. However, the combination of these words in just two sentences emphasizes the certainty of Paul's claims.

The use of the word "all" in verse 18 shows the extent to which God has revealed Himself. God has placed a witness within every man against **all** ungodliness and unrighteousness.

In verse 19, the Greek word that was translated "manifest" is the same word that was also translated "shewed" in this same verse. The word is "phaneroo" and it means "to render apparent; manifestly declare; make manifest; shew." This word makes it very clear that this instinctive or intuitive knowledge is not so subtle that it can be overlooked. God gives every individual the right to choose, but there can be no doubt that every person has, at one time, clearly seen and understood (v. 20) the basic truths of God's existence.

In verse 20, Paul says this inner witness of God causes the individual to "clearly see" the invisible things of God and even "understand" the Godhead. The Greek word that was translated "clearly see" is the word "kathorao" and means "to behold fully; i.e. distinctly apprehend." This leaves no doubt that every person who has ever walked the earth has had a clear revelation of God. The use of the word "understand" emphatically states that God not only gave them knowledge but the understanding to use that knowledge.

Therefore, no one will be able to stand before God on judgment day and say "God is not fair." He has given every person who has ever lived, regardless of how remote or isolated they may have been, the opportunity to know Him. They are without excuse.

Someone might say, "If all this is true, then why can't you observe more of this intuitive knowledge of God in the lives of those who have not heard the gospel?" Paul gives the answer to this in verses 21-23 (see note 1 at v. 21, p. 660).

3 (Rom. 1:20) The dictionary definition of the word "Godhead" is, "God, or the essential and divine nature of God." Therefore, Paul is stating that God has given every person an intuitive revelation of His divine nature. What a statement! And what a responsibility when men will have to stand before God and answer for the perversions they have perpetrated in the name of God. In their hearts, they knew better.

ROMANS

RESULTS OF TURNING FROM GOD'S REVELATION

CHAPTER 1

21 Because that, when they knew[a] God,[1] they glorified[b] *him* not as God, neither were thankful; but became vain[c] in their imaginations,[d] and their foolish[e] heart[f] was darkened.[g]

22 Professing[h] themselves to be wise,[i] they became fools,[j]

23 And changed the glory[k] of the uncorruptible God[l] into an image[m] made like to corruptible[n] man, and to birds, and fourfooted beasts,[o] and creeping things.[p]

24 Wherefore God also gave[2] them up[q] to uncleanness[r] through the lusts[s] of their own hearts,[f] to dishonour[t] their own bodies between themselves:[u]

25 Who changed[v] the truth of God into a lie, and worshipped[w] and served the creature[x] more than the Creator, who is blessed[y] for ever. Amen.

26 For this cause God gave them up unto vile affections:[z] for even their women[3] did change the natural[aa] use into that which is against nature:[bb]

a Gk.-"ginosko"- to know; understand; perceive; have knowledge of
see note 2 at Rom. 1:18, p. 659
Rom. 1:19, 28
Jn. 1:9
3:19

b Gk.-"doxazo"- to praise; extol; magnify; hold in honor-
Ps. 50:23
86:9
Lk. 17:15-18
Rev. 14:7

c Gk.-"mataioo"- to render or become foolish, wicked, or idolatrous
Dict.- empty; lacking substance; to no use or purpose; foolish-
2 Ki. 17:15
Isa. 44:9
Jer. 2:5
10:3-8, 14-15
16:19
Eph. 4:17-18
1 Pet. 1:18

d i.e. reasonings, thoughts, and thinking-
Gen. 6:5
8:21
Eph. 4:17-18

e without discernment or understanding

f see note 3 at Mt. 12:34, p. 131

g to shut out the light-
Mt. 6:23
Jn.1:4-5

h Latin-"pro"- forth; in public; "fateri"- to acknowledge; confess
Def.- to declare publicly

i Dict.- having wisdom or discernment for what is true

j Dict.- one who shows himself, by words or actions, to be deficient in judgment, sense, or understanding; a stupid or thoughtless person-
1 Cor. 1:19-21
3:18-19

k exalted honor, majestic beauty, and splendor-
Ps. 106:20

l see note 1 at Jn. 1:1, p. 2

m Dt. 4:15-18
5:8
Ps. 115:4-8
135:15-18
Isa. 40:18-20
Ezek. 8:9-12
Acts 17:29
1 Cor. 12:2
1 Pet. 4:3
Rev. 9:20

n immoral; perverted; depraved; impure; contaminated; unclean; mortal; perishable-
1 Cor. 15:50, & 53-54

o i.e. animals

p i.e. reptiles

q Ps. 81:11-12
Hos. 4:17-18
Mt. 15:14
Acts 7:42
2 Th. 2:10-12

r Gk.-"akatharsia"- impurity; morally defiled

s Gk.-"epithumia"- a longing or desire; esp. for what is forbidden

continued on center column

References continued from column 4

t translated in the N.T. to despise; dishonour; entreat shamefully, and suffer shame-
1 Cor. 6:13,18
1 Th. 4:4
2 Tim. 2:20-22

u Rom. 1:27
Lev. 18:22

v Rom. 1:23

w see note 1 at Mt. 8:2, p. 86

x reverenced and worshiped the things made instead of the maker (Con)
Gk.-"ktisis"- creation; i.e. thing created-
Rom. 1:23
Mt. 6:24
10:37
2 Tim. 3:4
1 Jn. 2:15-16

y Gk.-"eulogetos"- adorable; to praise and celebrate with praises-
2 Cor. 1:3
11:31
Eph. 1:3
1 Tim. 1:11
6:15
1 Pet. 1:3

z Gk.-"pathos"- passion (esp. concupiscence); (inordinate) affection; lust-
Gen. 19:5
Lev. 18:22-28
Dt. 23:17-18
Jud. 19:22
1 Cor. 6:9
Eph. 4:19
1 Tim. 1:10
Jude 7

aa Gk.-"phusikos"- physical; i.e. instinctive

bb Gk.-"phusis"- the nature of things; the force, laws, order, of nature; as opposed to what is monstrous; abnormal; perverse; that which is contrary to nature's laws; against nature (Thayer)

Footnotes for Romans 1:21-25

1 (Rom. 1:21) As Paul explained in Romans 1:18-20 (see note 2 at Rom. 1:18, p. 659), every person who has ever lived has had God reveal Himself to them, but this verse is explaining that revelation is not always received. Each individual has the freedom of choice.

In verses 21-23, Paul describes different characteristics of those who reject God's revelation. These could also be descriptive of progressive steps that one takes away from the true revelation of God.

The first step in rejecting God is not to glorify Him as the supreme, all knowing, unquestionable God. This is what happened with Adam and Eve in the Garden of Eden. They questioned God's intent behind His command (Gen. 3:1-6). They ceased to magnify and honor (see ref. b at this verse) God as they once did. Submission to God as supreme is always humbling and therefore "self" rebels. This is very prevalent today.

Secondly, they were not thankful. This is always a sign that self is exalting itself above God. A selfless person can be content with very little. A self-centered person cannot be satisfied. Thankfulness is a sign of humility and cultivating a life of thankfulness will help keep "self" in its proper place.

After these first two steps have been taken, then the individual's mind is free to begin imagining foolish, wicked, and idolatrous thoughts (see ref. c at this verse). This leads to a hardened heart (*"foolish heart was darkened"*– see note 10 at Mk. 6:52, p. 179) and being reprobate (see note 6 at v. 28, p. 661).

2 (Rom. 1:24) This phrase *"God gave them up"* is used twice in this passage (here and in verse 26) and the phrase *"God gave them over"* is used once (v. 28). These phrases are drawing on the fact that there is a God-given intuitive knowledge inside of every person that would prevent him from committing such depraved acts (see note 2 at Rom. 1:18, p. 659). However, because of our free choice, God will not continue to force that restraint upon us against our will. If a person persists in his rebellion against this conviction of God, He will give that person up to his own heart's lust.

Therefore, a person who is committing some of the terrible acts spoken of here (idolatry, homosexuality, etc.) and says that he has no conviction about it is either lying (Rom. 1:18-20) or he has been given over to a reprobate mind (see note 6 at v. 28, p. 661) by God.

Footnote 3 for Romans 1:26 on p. 661

ROMANS

RESULTS OF TURNING FROM GOD'S REVELATION (continued)

cc Gk.-"aschemosune"- an indecency; that which is immodest; shameful
dd Dict.- to award compensation to; pay; make a return for
ee suffering in their own bodies and personalities the inevitable consequences and penalty of their wrongdoing (Amp)- Rom. 1:23-24
ff necessary (as binding); used only here and at Lk. 15:32
gg Dict.- to keep or hold in one's possession; to keep in mind; remember

CHAPTER 1

27 And likewise also the men, leaving
the natural[aa] use of the woman, burned in
their lust one toward another; men with
men working that which is unseemly,[cc] and
receiving in themselves that recompence[dd]
of their error[ee] which was meet.[4ff]
28 And even as they did not like[5] to
retain[gg] God in *their* knowledge,[hh] God gave
them over to a reprobate[6ii] mind, to do those
things which are not convenient;[jj]

hh Prov. 1:7, 22, 29 5:12-13 Rom. 8:7-8 1 Cor. 15:34
ii Gk.-"adokimos"- undiscerning; not distinguishing; void of judgment; in this text it may be understood as an abominable mind; a mind to be abhorred by God and man (KSB)- Jer. 6:30 2 Cor. 13:5-7 2 Tim. 3:8 Ti. 1:16
jj not fitting; not proper; inappropriate- Eph. 5:4 Phile. 8

Footnote for Romans 1:26 from p. 660; Footnotes for Romans 1:27-28

3 (Rom. 1:26) Verses 26 and 27 are speaking of lesbianism and homosexuality. If any one could doubt the clear statements of the Old Testament scriptures that this is an abomination to God (Lev. 18:22; 20:13; Dt.23:17-18), then these scriptures should forever settle the question.

4 (Rom. 1:27) This is speaking of the emotional and physical consequences of homosexuality. Paul here says these consequences are "meet." The word that Paul used (Gk.-"dei") is found in 100 verses, but it is only translated "meet" one other time in the New Testament (Lk. 15:32). All other times the translation clearly denotes something that is necessary (behoved; must; need; needful; ought; oughtest; should).

This implies that these consequences (such as disease) are prescribed payment for such acts. Add to this the use of the word "recompense" (meaning "payment or compensation for an act") in this same verse and it clearly looks as if physical and emotional scars are God's judgement upon this sin.

These natural consequences of sin are not necessarily God's direct punishment on the individuals who commit these acts. Anyone who participates in homosexuality, which is expressly forbidden by God, is bringing punishment on themselves. It's like the law of gravity. Many people are killed when they violate this God-given law but it is not accurate to say God killed them. They killed themselves. There was no malice on God's part.

Likewise, God established natural laws governing sexual behavior. Marriage was given while man was still in a perfect state (Gen. 2) and it is very possible that God never imagined man perverting such a beautiful gift (Jer. 7:31). When someone violates God's sexual order, they are destroying themselves just as surely as someone who tries to breathe under water or walk off a cliff.

This verse is saying that the devastation that many homosexuals experience in their bodies is an appropriate payment for someone who has willfully perverted the perfect gift of marriage that God gave to us before the Fall. But this does not mean that God hates all homosexuals and is personally punishing them. If that were so, some of the diseases we see would not be selective. All homosexuals would contract these diseases.

No, these maladies occur naturally when God's perfect order is perverted. God hates homosexuality, but loves the individuals who are homosexuals. If homosexuals will turn to God and put faith in Jesus as their Savior, they can be saved just the same as anyone else.

5 (Rom. 1:28) The reason they did not like to retain God in their knowledge is because the knowledge of God would have convicted them and restrained them from committing such acts. This is the same motivation behind the actions of those who oppose Christianity so strongly today. People want to sin without anyone convicting them.

6 (Rom. 1:28) The Greek word translated "reprobate" is "adokimos" and it means "undiscerning; not distinguishing; void of judgment." In this text it may be understood as "an abominable mind, a mind to be abhorred by God and man" (KSB).

This is describing the state of a person who has "passed the point of no return" with God. As the context explains, God has revealed Himself to every person who has ever walked the earth. But there comes a point where God's Spirit will not strive with man any longer (Gen. 6:3). When that happens, the individual is hopelessly damned because no one can come to the Father except the Spirit draws him (see note 8 at Jn. 6:44, p. 184; see note 6 at Acts 24:25 p. 635).

Therefore a reprobate person is a person whom God has abandoned and there is no hope of salvation for them. Paul applied this term to Christians who had renounced their faith in Christ (2 Cor. 13:5-7; 2 Tim. 3:8; Ti. 1:16; see note 5 at Acts 5:5, p. 528).

Some people may fear that they are reprobate because of some sin or blasphemy (see note 1 at Mt. 12:31, p. 128) that they have uttered. However, as these verses describe, a reprobate person is past feeling remorse or conviction. If anyone is repentant over some terrible action, then that itself is proof that the Spirit of God is still drawing him and he is not reprobate. A reprobate person wouldn't care.

ROMANS

RESULTS OF TURNING FROM GOD'S REVELATION (continued)

CHAPTER 1

29 Being filled with all unrighteousness,[7]
fornication, wickedness, covetousness,[a]
maliciousness;[b] full of envy,[c] murder,
debate,[d] deceit,[e] malignity;[f] whisperers,[g]
30 Backbiters,[h] haters of God,[i]
despiteful,[j] proud, boasters,[k] inventors of
evil things,[l] disobedient to parents,[m]
31 Without understanding,[n] covenant-
breakers,[o] without natural affection,[8]
implacable,[p] unmerciful:
32 Who knowing[9] the judgment of
God,[q] that they which commit such things
are worthy of death,[r] not only do the same,
but have pleasure[s] in them that do them.

a i.e. greed- Ps. 10:3 Col. 3:5
b Dict.- the desire to harm others, or to see others suffer; ill will; spite
c i.e. jealousy
d to quarrel or argue
e deception and trickery
f Dict.- intense ill will or hatred; great malice
g i.e. gossips- Prov. 16:28 26:20 2 Cor. 12:20
h Dict.- to slander the character or reputation of (an absent person)- Prov. 25:23
i Prov. 8:36 Jn. 7:7 15:23-24
j Dict.- an act of defiance; insult; offense
k Ps. 52:1 94:4 97:7 Jas. 3:5 4:16 Jude 16

l Ps. 99:8 106:39 Eccl. 7:29
m Dt. 21:18-21 Prov. 30:17 Mt. 10:21 15:4 2 Tim. 3:2
n Rom. 1:20-21 3:11 Prov. 18:2 Jer. 4:22 Mt. 15:16
o 2 Tim. 3:3
p Dict.- incapable of appeasement
q i.e. they are fully aware of God's righteous decree (Amp)- Rom. 1:18, 21 2:1-5, 21-23
r Rom. 6:23 2 Sam. 12:5-7 Prov. 14:12 Jas 1:15
s Gk.-"suneudokeo"- assent to; feel gratified with; be pleased- Ps. 50:18 Hos. 7:3 Mk. 14:10-11

Footnotes for Romans 1:29-32

7 (Rom. 1:29) It is very interesting to see some of the things included in this list of abominations that many people would not consider sin, or certainly not a "bad" sin like others on the list. For instance, the word "debate" means "to quarrel or argue." Some people think that is perfectly okay, but Paul lists it right along with murder and sexual sins.

The word "whisperers" means "gossips." A "backbiter" is a person who slanders the character or reputation of another when they are not present. Pride is listed among these sins that are an abomination to God, as well as being disobedient to parents. A "covenant-breaker" is a person who can not be trusted to keep his word.

The truth is, there are no little sins or acceptable sins. All unrighteousness is sin (1 Jn. 5:17) and should be rejected.

8 (Rom. 1:31) Although this phrase "without natural affection" has been interpreted by many to mean homosexual acts, the Greek word suggests something different. The Greek word that is used is "astorgos" which literally means "hard-hearted towards kindred." This describes someone who is unloving and without the natural tenderness that a mother would express towards a child. Therefore, Paul is describing a hardhearted person who is void of love and tenderness.

9 (Rom. 1:32) When God turns an individual over (see note 2 at Rom. 1:24, p. 660) to a reprobate mind (see note 5 at Rom. 1:28, p. 661), they do not lose their knowledge of what's right and wrong; they just lose God's conviction about it. They still know they are wrong but they don't care.

GOD'S JUDGMENT OF SELF-RIGHTEOUS & RELIGIOUS PEOPLE

CHAPTER 2

THEREFORE[1] thou art inexcusable,[2a] O
man, whosoever thou art that judgest:[3] for
wherein thou judgest another, thou
condemnest[b] thyself; for thou that judgest
doest the same things.[c]

a Gk.-"anapologetos"- indefensible; without excuse

b Gk.-"katakrino"- to give judgment against; to judge worthy of punishment
c Rom. 2:3, 21-23

Footnotes for Romans 2:1

1 (Rom. 2:1) In the preceding chapter, Paul had conclusively proved that the Gentiles were guilty before God. They had no excuse for their vile actions (Rom. 1:20). This, no doubt, pleased the Jews. That's exactly what they believed and what they had been arguing. They maintained that unless these Gentiles converted to Judaism and observed the law of Moses (specifically the law of circumcision), they could not be saved.

However, after Paul had taken full advantage of the Jews' prejudice, he turns his arguments to the Jews, showing them that they are just as guilty or even more guilty than the Gentiles. He ends this chapter with statements about the Gentiles' faith being superior to the Jews' circumcision and concludes a true Jew is born of faith, not of the flesh (Rom. 2:28-29).

Thus the second chapter proves the Jews, or religious persons are just as guilty before God as the heathen. Then in the third chapter Paul draws this all together by proclaiming that since everyone—Jew and Gentile—is in "the same boat," then all can be saved by one method of salvation, through faith.

2 (Rom. 2:1) From a human perspective, some people have obtained a level of holiness that gives them the right to judge others. However, when viewed from God's standpoint, we are all sinners and one sinner has no justification for condemning a fellow sinner (see note 46 at Mt. 7:1, p. 83). We may not be doing the exact same transgressions, but we are guilty of being lawbreakers (Jas. 2:10) and are, therefore, disqualified from being the judge.

Also, whenever one condemns another, he is showing that he has a knowledge of right and wrong and therefore can no longer claim ignorance for his own offenses. As verse two explains, we are better off to leave the judging to God.

3 (Rom. 2:1, 3) The Greek word that is rendered "judgest" three times in this verse and once in verse three is the word "krino." It is speaking of a harsh, condemning type of judging that was warned against in Matthew 7:1. There is a Greek word "anakrino" which signifies discernment which is encouraged in scripture (see note 46 at Mt. 7:1, p. 83).

ROMANS

GOD'S JUDGMENT OF SELF-RIGHTEOUS & RELIGIOUS PEOPLE (cont'd)

CHAPTER 2

2 But we are sure that the judgment[d] of
God is according to truth[e] against them
which commit such things.
3 And thinkest thou this, O man, that
judgest[3] them which do such things, and
doest the same,[4] that thou shalt escape[f] the
judgment[d] of God?
4 Or despisest[g] thou the riches[h] of his
goodness[i] and forbearance[j] and longsuffering;[k] not knowing that the goodness[l]
of God leadeth thee to repentance?[5m]
5 But after thy hardness[n] and impenitent[o]
heart[p] treasurest[q] up unto thyself[6] wrath[r]
against the day of wrath[r] and revelation[s] of
the righteous judgment[t] of God;
6 *Who will render to every man
according to his deeds:[7u]

PARALLEL SCRIPTURE FOR
ROMANS 2:6

JOB 34:11

11 For the work of a man shall he render unto him, and cause every man to find according to his *ways.*

Footnotes for Romans 2:2-6

4 (Rom. 2:3) These pious Jews could have argued with Paul that they were not committing the same sins that these heathens were, but in reality they were. They may not have worshiped idols, but they were covetous, which Colossians 3:5 reveals is idolatry. They may not have committed adultery, but they had lusted in their hearts, which Jesus said was equal to adultery (Mt. 5:28). They may not have murdered anyone, but they had hated, which was the same root sin (Mt. 5:21-22).

When viewed in this way, judgment for others disappears and mercy comes to light.

5 (Rom. 2:4) This is a radical statement that the Jews of Paul's day and the religious legalists of our day reject. They refuse to accept that the goodness of God is sufficient motivation for people to turn from sin. They insist that fear of punishment is a superior motivator.

It is true that fear is a more familiar motivator to most people. Even a lost man or carnal Christian can identify with fear and respond to it. But as 1 John 4:18 states, *"fear hath torment."* Those who respond to God through fear will also be tormented with thoughts of doubt and condemnation as to whether they have done enough. Fear will move some towards God but it is inferior to love. There is nothing that fear can do that love can't do better and without the side effect of torment.

Those who were motivated to seek God because of fear if they didn't, will cease to be motivated when things are going good. They become the ones who only pray when they are in trouble. Those who come to God because of His goodness will see God as the source of their success and continue to serve God in the good and the bad times.

The world, and especially religion, has used negative reasons to motivate people. The gospel uses the positive reason of God's great love to draw men unto God. We need to renew our minds to line up with God's thinking.

6 (Rom. 2:5) The apostle James said, *"For he shall have judgment without mercy, that hath shewed no mercy; and mercy rejoiceth against judgment"* (Jas. 2:13). Those who show mercy will be shown mercy. But those who are hardhearted and unmerciful will reap the same when they stand before the judgment seat of God.

7 (Rom. 2:6) Verses 6-16 are speaking of the final judgment of God at the end of this world. The Lord will judge us and render a due reward according to every man's work. Although this is true, some have taken these scriptures to mean the opposite of what Paul is saying in context here.

From the context, we see that Paul is preaching that Jews and Gentiles alike have all sinned and come short of the glory of God (Rom. 3:23). Therefore, no one can be saved by his actions (Rom. 3:20). The only way to be saved is through faith in Jesus and what He did for us (Rom. 3:24-28). Therefore, these verses cannot be contradicting everything else that Paul is saying by proclaiming that acceptance by God is based on performance.

No, the action that will be rewarded with eternal life is the action of faith (Jn. 3:16). Faith alone saves, but saving faith is never alone. True faith has actions (Jas. 2:17-20). The Greek word that is translated "do not obey" in verse 8 means "to disbelieve (willfully and perversely): not believe; unbelieving." So it is faith that is the issue even though actions are being spoken of.

Therefore, to those whose faith is causing them to patiently continue in well doing (v. 7), they will receive eternal life. But to those whose rejection of God's mercy causes them to disobey (disbelieve) the truth, they will receive indignation and wrath; tribulation and anguish (vv. 8-9).

d Gk.-"krima"- a decision; a sentence- Rom. 2:5; 9:14; Gen. 18:25; Ps. 9:4, 7-8; 11:5-7; 96:13; 98:9; Acts 17:31

e Gk.-"aletheia"- in accordance with fact; justly; without partiality

f Prov. 11:21; 16:5; Mt. 23:33; Heb. 2:3; 12:25

g Dict.- to regard with contempt or disdain; to look down on

h Rom. 11:33; Ps. 86:15; 104:24; Eph. 1:18; 2:4, 7; 3:8,16; Phil. 4:19; Col. 1:27

i Gk.-"chrestotes"- kindness; gentleness- Ps. 117:2; 119:76; Isa. 54:10; Jon. 4:2; Eph. 2:7; Ti. 3:4

j Dict.- tolerance and restraint in the face of provocation; patience- Rom. 3:25; 9:22

k Dict.- patiently enduring wrongs or difficulties; patient endurance- Gal. 5:22; Ex. 34:6; Num. 14:18; 1 Tim. 1:16; 1 Pet. 3:20; 2 Pet. 3:9,15

l i.e. kindness see ref. i, this heading

m see note 1 at Mt. 3:2, p. 30; see note 3 at Lk. 15:18, p. 294; see note 2 at Mt. 27:3, p. 469; see note 8 at Acts 6:11, p. 535

n see note 10 at Mk. 6:52, p. 179; see note 3 at Mt. 13:15, p. 136; see note 1 at Mt. 16:8, p. 198; see note 3 at Mk. 8:17, p. 199; Ex. 8:15; 1 Sam. 6:6; 2 Chr. 26:16; Ps. 95:8; Prov. 29:1; Ezek. 3:7; Dan. 5:20; Zech. 7:11-12; Heb. 3:13, 15; 4:7

o Dict.- not penitent; unrepentant

p see note 3 at Mt. 12:34, p. 131

q Gk.-"thesaurizo"- to amass; lay up; reserve; same word as at Jas. 5:3

r Gk.-"orge"- punishment; anger, indignation; vengeance see note 4 at Jn. 3:36, p. 52; see note 4 at Acts 12:23, p. 573; Job 21:30; Prov. 11:4; 2 Pet. 2:9; 3:7; Rev. 6:17

s Gk.-"apokalupsis"- disclosure; manifestation

t Gk.-"dikaiokrisia"- a just sentence

u Ps. 62:12; Mt. 16:27; 1 Cor. 3:8; Rev. 2:23; 20:12; 22:12

ROMANS

GOD'S JUDGMENT OF SELF-RIGHTEOUS & RELIGIOUS PEOPLE (cont'd)

CHAPTER 2

7 *To them who by patient[a] continuance[b] in well[c] doing seek for glory[d] and honour[e] and immortality,[f] eternal life:[g]

8 But unto them that are contentious,[h] and do not obey[i] the truth,[j] but obey unrighteousness,[k] indignation[l] and wrath,[m]

9 Tribulation[n] and anguish,[o] upon every soul of man that doeth evil, of the Jew first, and also of the Gentile;[p]

10 *But glory, honour,[e] and peace,[q] to every man that worketh good,[r] to the Jew[s] first, and also to the Gentile:[t]

11 For there is no respect of persons[u] with God.

12 For as many as have sinned without law[v] shall also perish[w] without law: and as many as have sinned in the law shall be judged[x] by the law;

13 (For not the hearers of the law *are* just[y] before God, but the doers[z] of the law shall be justified.[aa]

PARALLEL SCRIPTURE FOR ROMANS 2:7

HEBREWS 6:12, 15

12 That ye be not slothful, but followers of them who through faith and patience inherit the promises.

15 And so, after he had patiently endured, he obtained the promise.

2 TIMOTHY 4:7-8

7 I have fought a good fight, I have finished my *course, I have kept the faith:*

8 Henceforth there is laid up for me a crown of righteousness, which the Lord, the righteous judge, shall give me at that day: and not to me only, but unto all them also that love his appearing.

PARALLEL SCRIPTURE FOR ROMANS 2:10

ISAIAH 48:18, 22

18 O that thou hadst hearkened to my commandments! then had thy peace been as a river, and thy righteousness as the waves of the sea:

22 There is *no peace, saith the LORD, unto the wicked.*

a cheerful or hopeful endurance; constancy- Jas. 1:4 Rom. 8:25 Ps. 27:14 37:34 Lam. 3:25-26 Mt. 24:12-13 Lk. 8:15 Gal. 6:9 Heb. 6:12,15 10:35-36 Jas. 5:7-8

b Dict.- an uninterrupted succession; unbroken course

c Gk.-"agathos"- "good" in any sense

d Gk.-"doxa"- dignity; honor; praise; worship- 2 Th. 2:14 Rom. 8:18 Jn. 5:44 2 Cor. 4:16-18 Col. 1:27 1 Pet. 1:7-8 4:13-14

e Gk.-"time"- esteem; esp. of the highest degree; dignity; honor; appearing in the rewards of the future life (Thayer)

f Gk.-"aphtharsia"- incorruptibility; unending existence; deathlessness Dict.- one not subject to death; imperishable- 1 Cor. 15:53-54 2 Tim. 1:10

g see note 3 at Jn. 3:36, p. 52 see note 94 at Jn. 17:3, p. 444 Rom. 6:23 1 Jn. 2:25

h Gk.-"eritheia"- self-seeking; a partisan and factious spirit- Prov. 13:10 1 Cor. 11:16 Ti. 3:9 Jas. 3:16

i Gk.-"apeitheo"- to disbelieve (willfully and perversely); not believe; unbelieving

j Jn. 14:6 17:17

k Gk.-"adikia"- wrongfulness of character, life, or act; iniquity; unjust- 2 Th. 2:10-12

l Gk.-"thumos"- fierceness; wrath; anger; passion- Heb. 10:27, 31 Ps. 90:11 Nah. 1:6 Rev. 14:10

m Gk.-"orge"- anger; indignation; vengeance

n Gk.-"thlipsis"- pressure; affliction; anguish; burdened; persecution; trouble- 2 Th. 1:6

o Gk.-"steno-choria"- narrowness of room; i.e. calamity; distress Dict.- an agonizing physical or mental pain; torment; torture

p see ref. t, this heading- Rom. 1:10, 16 3:29-30 4:9-12 9:24 10:12 15:8-9 Acts 13:46 18:5-6 20:21 26:20

q Gk.-"eirene"- quietness; rest; set at one again Dict.- the absence of hostilities; harmonious relations; inner contentment; free from strife- Isa 26:3 Rom. 5:1 8:6 14:17 15:13 Ps. 29:11 37:37 Isa. 32:17 48:18, 22 Lk. 1:79 Jn. 14:27 16:33 Gal. 5:22 Phil. 4:7

r Isa. 32:17 Acts 10:35 Jas. 3:18

continued on center column

References continued from column 4

s see note 10 at Jn. 8:33, p. 232

t see note 45 at Mt. 6:32, p. 83 see note 1 at Jn. 12:23, p. 359 see note 3 at Lk. 7:9, p. 117 see note 2 at Lk. 2:32, p. 22 see ref. p, this heading

u Gk.-"prosopolepsia"-partiality; i.e. favoritism; from the Gk.-"prosopoleptes"- an accepter of a face (individual); i.e. spec. one exhibiting partiality- Dt. 10:17 16:19 2 Chr. 19:7 Job 34:19 Prov. 24:23-24 Mt. 22:16 Lk. 20:21 Acts 10:34 Gal. 2:6 Eph. 6:9 Col. 3:25

v Gk.-"anomos"- not subject to the Jewish law

w Gk.-"apollumi"- to incur the loss of the true or eternal life; to be delivered up to eternal misery (Thayer)

x Gk.-"krino"- same as at Rom. 2:1, p. 662 see note 3 at Rom. 2:1, p. 662 Rom. 3:19-20 4:15 7:7-11 Gal 3:10 Jas. 2:10

y Gk.-"dikaios"- equitable (in character or act); by implication: innocent; holy

z Gk.-"poietes"- a performer- Rom. 2:25 Dt. 5:1 30:12-14 Ezek. 20:11

aa see note 13 at Acts 13:39, p. 579 see note 21 at Jn. 8:56, p. 234 see note 22 at Jn. 8:57, p. 234 see note 5 at Jn. 11:52, p. 312 see note 2 at Acts 15:1, p. 585 see note 1 at Mt. 26:2, p. 410 Rom. 4:2-5 Ps. 143:2 Lk. 18:14 Acts 13:39 Gal. 3:11-12

ROMANS

GOD'S JUDGMENT OF SELF-RIGHTEOUS & RELIGIOUS PEOPLE (cont'd)

bb Gk.-"ergon"- the course of action demanded by the law
cc see note 3 at Mt. 12:34, p. 131 see note 10 at Mk. 7:21, p. 191
dd see note 9 at Rom. 2:15, this page
ee Gk.-"summartureo"- to testify jointly; i.e. corroborate by evidence; testify unto

CHAPTER 2

14 For when the Gentiles, which have not the law, do by nature[8] the things contained in the law, these, having not the law, are a law unto themselves:

15 Which shew the work[bb] of the law written in their hearts,[cc] their conscience[9dd] also bearing witness,[ee] and *their* thoughts the mean while accusing[ff] or else excusing[gg] one another;)

16 In the day when God[hh] shall judge the secrets[ii] of men by Jesus Christ[jj] according[10] to my gospel.[kk]

ff Dict.- to charge with a shortcoming or error; to bring charges against
gg Dict.- to make allowance for (a shortcoming); overlook; condone
hh see note 1 at Jn. 1:1, p. 2
ii Gk.-"kruptos"- concealed; private; hidden; inward
jj see note 5 at Jn. 1:41, p. 40 see note 3 at Acts 4:26, p. 526
kk see note 7 at Mt. 24:14, p. 396 see note 5 at Acts 20:24, p. 618

Footnotes for Romans 2:14-16

8 (Rom. 2:14) This is speaking of the intuitive knowledge of God described in chapter 1 (see note 2 at Rom. 1:18, p. 659).

9 (Rom. 2:15) Our conscience is the part of us that bears witness as to what is right and wrong. This happens through our thoughts either accusing or excusing us. Our conscience is a part of our soul (see note 2 at Mt. 22:37, p. 383), which can be deduced from the fact that even a Christian's conscience can be defiled (1 Cor. 8:7), evil (Heb. 10:22), and weak (1 Cor. 8:7,10), which the born-again spirit cannot be (see note 3 at Mt. 26:41, p. 448).

A good conscience is essential to faith. Without a good conscience, our faith is made shipwrecked (1 Tim. 1:19). A good conscience produces confidence (1 Jn. 3:21; Heb. 10:35). An evil conscience condemns us (1 Jn. 3:20).

It is possible that God created man without a conscience and that the conscience was acquired through the tree of the knowledge of good and evil. The name of that tree is descriptive of the function of the conscience.

The conscience is referred to by name 31 times in 29 verses in the New Testament (Jn. 8:9; Acts 23:1; 24:16; Rom. 2:15; 9:1; 13:5; 1 Cor. 8:7,10,12; 10:25, 27-29; 2 Cor. 1:12; 4:2; 1 Tim. 1:5,19; 3:9; 4:2; 2 Tim. 1:3; Ti. 1:15; Heb. 9:9,14; 10:2, 22; 13:18; 1 Pet. 2:19; 3:16, 21).

10 (Rom. 2:16) This is quite a statement of authenticity for the gospel which Paul preached. God didn't get His understanding of the gospel from Paul, but Paul received his revelation of the gospel from God. He was so sure of this that he could make statements like this, and that of Galatians 1:8-12.

THE JEWS HAVE THE LAW BUT DON'T KEEP IT

a see note 10 at Jn. 8:33, p. 232 Rom. 2:28-29 9:4-7 Mt. 3:9 Jn. 8:33 2 Cor. 11:22 Gal. 2:15 Phil. 3:3-7 Rev. 2:9 3:9
b Gk.-"epanapauomai"- to lean upon; trust to
c see note 2 at Mt. 19:17, p. 329 Rom. 9:4, 32 Lk. 10:26-28 Jn. 5:45 7:19 9:28-29
d Gk.-"kauchaomai"- to glory in God; i.e. the knowledge of God; intimacy with Him; his favors- Jn. 8:41
e Phil. 1:10 1 Th. 5:21

CHAPTER 2

17 Behold, thou art called[1] a Jew,[a] and
restest[b] in the law,[c] and makest thy boast[d] of
God,
18 And knowest *his* will, and approvest[e]
the things that are more excellent,[f] being
instructed[g] out of the law;
19 And art confident[h] that thou thyself
art a guide[i] of the blind,[j] a light[k] of them
which are in darkness,
20 An instructor[l] of the foolish,[m] a
teacher[n] of babes,[o] which hast the form[p] of
knowledge and of the truth in the law.

f Gk.-"diaphero"- to test, prove, the things that differ; i.e. to distinguish between good and evil; lawful and unlawful (Thayer)
g Rom. 15:4 Ps. 19:8 119:98-100, & 104-105, 130 Prov. 6:23 2 Tim. 3:15-17
h Dict.- having assurance or certainty- 1 Cor. 8:1-2 Prov. 26:12 Isa. 5:21
i Gk.-"hodegos"- a conductor; leader; teacher
j Gk.-"tuphlos"- opaque (as if smoky); i.e. (by analogy) blind (physical or mental)
k Gk.-"phos"- used of one in whom continued on center column

References continued from column 4

wisdom and spiritual purity shine forth, and who imparts the same to others (Thayer)- Isa. 49:6 Mt. 4:16 5:14 Lk. 1:79 Acts 26:18 Phil. 2:15
l Gk.-"paideutes"- a trainer; i.e. teacher or discipliner; to educate
m Gk.-"aphron"- mindless; i.e. stupid; ignorant; unwise
n see note 3 at Mt. 5:2, p. 73 see note 5 at Mt. 28:19, p. 504
o Gk.-"nepios"- not speaking; i.e. an infant (minor); a simple-minded person; immature; childish- Mt. 11:25 1 Cor. 3:1 Heb. 5:13 1 Pet. 2:2
p Gk.-"morphosis"- formation; i.e. appearance; semblance- Rom. 6:17 2 Tim. 1:13 3:5

Footnotes for Romans 2:17-20

1 (Rom. 2:17) It is true that the Jews had been given the Word of God, which gave them a superior knowledge of God. However, since they had not kept the law, their superior knowledge had just made them more accountable than other people (see note 5 at Lk. 12:48, p. 272).

ROMANS

THE JEWS HAVE THE LAW BUT DON'T KEEP IT (continued)

CHAPTER 2

21 Thou therefore which teachest
another, teachest thou not thyself?[a] thou
that preachest a man should not steal, dost[2]
thou steal?[b]
22 Thou that sayest a man should not
commit adultery,[c] dost thou commit
adultery?[c] thou that abhorrest[d] idols,[e] dost
thou commit sacrilege?[f]
23 Thou that makest thy boast[g] of the
law, through breaking the law dishonourest[h]
thou God?
24 For the name of God is blasphemed[i]
among the Gentiles[j] through you, as it is
written.[k]
25 For circumcision[l] verily[m] profiteth,[n]
if thou keep the law:[3] but if thou be a
breaker[o] of the law, thy circumcision[l] is
made uncircumcision.
26 Therefore if the uncircumcision keep[p]
the righteousness of the law,[4] shall not his
uncircumcision be counted[q] for
circumcision?[l]
27 And shall not uncircumcision which
is by nature,[r] if it fulfil[s] the law, judge[t] thee,
who by the letter[u] and circumcision[l] dost
transgress[o] the law?

a Ps. 50:16-21 Mt. 23:3 Lk. 11:46 Gal. 6:13
b Isa. 56:11 Ezek. 22:12-13,27 Mic. 3:11 Mt. 21:13 23:14
c see note 6 at Mt. 19:9, p. 324 Jer. 7:9-10 9:2 Ezek. 22:11 Jas. 4:4
d Gk.-"bdelusso"- to stink; to be disgusted; i.e. detest; abhor
e Gk.-"eidolon"- an image; i.e. for worship; a heathen god; a false god
f Gk.-"hierosuleo"- to be a temple robber; from Gk.-"hierosulos"- a temple-despoiler; robber of churches- Mk. 11:17
g Dict.- to bring about with excessive pride; to take pride in, or be enhanced by, the possession of

h Dict.- something that causes loss of honor, respect, or reputation; disgrace; shame
i Gk.-"blasphemeo"- defame; rail on; revile; speak evil; to speak reproachfully Dict.- to speak of God or something sacred in an irreverent or impious manner; to revile; execrate- Isa. 52:5 Ezek. 36:20-23 1 Tim. 6:1 Ti. 2:5
j see note 45 at Mt. 6:32, p. 83 see note 1 at Acts 10:1, p. 559 see note 1 at Acts 11:22, p. 568 see note 3 at Acts 14:27, p. 584
k 2 Sam. 12:14

continued on center column

References continued from column 4

l Gk.-"peritome"- circumsion (the rite, the act, the condition, or the people). From Gk.-"peritemno"- to cut around- Rom. 2:28-29 4:11-12 Gal. 5:3-6 6:15 Eph. 2:11-12
m i.e. indeed profiteth
n Gk.-"opheleo"- to be useful; i.e. to benefit
o Gk.-"parabates"- a violator; transgressor
p Gk.-"phulasso"- obey; take care not to violate; to observe
q Gk.-"logizomai"- a thing is reckoned as, or to be something; i.e. as availing for, or equivalent to, something; as having the like force and weight (Thayer)
r Gk.-"phusis"- natural production, native disposition, constitution, or usage
s Rom. 8:4 13:10 Gal. 5:14
t Gk.-"krino"- condemn; damn- Mt. 12:41-42
u Gk.-"gramma"- that which has been written; the written law of Moses

Footnotes for Romans 2:21-27

2 (Rom. 2:21) The Jews took pride in their keeping of the law, but there wasn't any Jew who could boast that he had kept the law perfectly (see note 4 at Mk. 10:20, p. 329). *"All have sinned and come short of the glory of God"* (Rom. 3:23). Paul highlights three areas in which they boasted of their own holiness, but he reveals that they were actually sinners in these very things.

They boasted that they didn't steal, but Paul reveals that they did steal. Jesus also rebuked the Pharisees for stealing. This is not the typical type of theft, but what we would call "white collar crime" (see ref. b, this page).

Paul says that they were adulterers, even though they prided themselves on not committing adultery. They were guilty of spiritual adultery if nothing else (Jas. 4:4) and Jesus had revealed that adultery was also a sin of the heart, even if there was no action (Mt. 5:28).

They also thought they were not idolatrous, but Paul convicts them on this count also. He uses the word "sacrilege" which refers to them being temple robbers, thereby making direct reference to their covetousness which is idolatry (Col. 3:5).

Therefore, even though they had a form of godliness, they were sinners just like the Gentiles, and their hypocrisy gave the Gentiles a reason to blaspheme God. This leads Paul to proclaim that the Jews' claim to some kind of special covenant with God is made void through their breaking of the law. In the third chapter of Romans, he goes on to draw the conclusion that everyone, Jew and Gentile, is in the same condition of sin and needs the same salvation through Christ.

3 (Rom. 2:25) If a Jew could keep the law perfectly, then the Jewish covenant that was sealed with the sign of circumcision would give him an advantage over others. But that has never, and can never happen. No one can keep the law, and the law was not given to provide a way to God (see note 2 at Mt. 19:17, p. 329). Therefore, because no Jew has ever kept the law perfectly, they are the same as uncircumcised in the sight of God.

4 (Rom. 2:26) Notice that Paul did not say that the uncircumcision kept the law. Instead he mentions them keeping the "righteousness" of the law (v. 26) and "fulfilling" the law (v. 27)— there is a difference. A person can fulfill the righteousness of the law through faith in Jesus, but no one, Jew or Gentile, can keep the law.

ROMANS

THE TRUE JEW

CHAPTER 2

28 *For he is not a Jew,[a] which is one
outwardly;[b] neither *is that* circumcision,[1c]
which is outward[b] in the flesh:[d]
29 *But he[2] *is* a Jew, which is one
inwardly;[e] and circumcision *is that* of the
heart,[3f] in the spirit,[g] *and* not in the letter;[4]
whose praise[h] *is* not of men, but of God.[i]

PARALLEL SCRIPTURE FOR ROMANS 2:28

REVELATION 2:9

9 I know thy works, and tribulation, and poverty, (but thou art rich) and I know *the blasphemy of them which say they are Jews, and are not, but* are *the synagogue of Satan.*

PARALLEL SCRIPTURES FOR ROMANS 2:29

2 CORINTHIANS 3:6

6 Who also hath made us able ministers of the new testament; not of the letter, but of the spirit: for the letter killeth, but the spirit giveth life.

ROMANS 7:6

6 But now we are delivered from the law, that being dead wherein we were held; that we should serve in newness of spirit, and not in the oldness of the letter.

a Gk.-"ioudaios"-Jewish as respects birth, race, and religion
see note 10 at Jn. 8:33, p. 232
Rom. 9:4-7
Ps. 135:4
Isa. 48:1-2
Mt. 3:9
Jn. 8:33, 44
Gal. 2:15
6:15
Phil. 3:3-7
Rev. 2:9
3:9

b Gk.-"phaneros"-externally; openly; outwardly manifest; i.e. to be plainly recognized or known (Thayer)

c Gk.-"peritome"-circumcision; the rite, condition, or people (Strong)
The extinction of the passions and the removal of spiritual impurity (Thayer)
From Gk.-"peritemno"- to cut around
see note 4 at Jn. 7:22, p. 224
see note 1 at Acts 11:2, p. 565
see note 2 at Acts 15:1, p. 585
Dt. 10:16
30:6
Jer. 4:4
9:26
Rom. 4:10-12
Col. 2:11-12

d nor is outward bodily circumcision real circumcision (TCNT)

e Dict.- on or in the inside; within-
1 Sam. 16:7
Mt. 23:25-28
Lk. 11:39
17:21

f see note 1 at Mt. 16:8, p. 198
see note 3 at Mt. 12:34, p. 131
see note 10 at Mk. 7:21, p. 191
see note 3 at Mt. 13:15, p. 136
see note 3 at Mk. 8:17, p. 199
see note 10 at Mk. 6:52, p. 179
see note 6 at Mk. 11:23, p. 367
see notes 2-3 at Jn. 14:1, p. 431

g see note 3 at Mt. 26:41, p. 448
see note 6 at Mk. 11:23, p. 367
Jn. 3:5-8
Phil. 3:3

h Gk.-"epainos"-laudation; a commendation bestowed by one-
Jn. 5:44
12:43
1 Cor. 4:5
2 Cor. 10:18

i Gk.-"theos"-the supreme divinity
see note 1 at Jn. 1:1, p. 2

Footnote for Romans 2:28-29

1 (Rom. 2:28) As with so many commandments of the Old Testament, circumcision was an outward sign of a greater inward reality. Paul uses this term "sign" in referring to the circumcision of Abraham in Romans 4:11. The Jews of the first century had ignored the circumcision of the heart and had focused all their attention on the flesh (1 Sam. 16:7). Paul is clarifying that it is the condition of the heart that makes someone a child of God, not the flesh.

2 (Rom. 2:29) This is a remarkable statement. Paul is saying that those who have been born again through faith in Jesus have been circumcised in their heart (Col. 2:11-12) and are the true Jews. They aren't Jews in nationality or religion, but they are the true people of God. Paul deals with this in more detail in Romans 9 and clearly makes a case that Gentiles who are united with Christ in the new birth are now God's people. Paul makes the same point in Galatians 3, saying that anyone who is saved through faith in Jesus is now Abraham's seed and heirs according to the promise (Gal. 3:16, 22, 26-29). This leaves no doubt that the church is now God's chosen people on earth.

This does not mean that God has forsaken the Jews. Paul once again deals with that issue in Romans 9. There are still prophesies which apply to the physical nation of Israel which will be fulfilled. However, the New Testament church composed of Jews and Gentiles, is now God's kingdom on earth.

3 (Rom. 2:29) Paul's statement here definitely places the spirit in the heart of man. This has led some to believe that the heart and spirit are the same, but 1 Peter 3:4 refers to the spirit of man as the hidden man of the heart, implying that the spirit comprises only a part of the heart. The heart of man is actually made up of two parts, the soul and the spirit. This is the reason the scripture speaks of having two minds in our hearts (Jas. 4:8) and why we must believe with all our heart (Acts 8:37), not just a part (see note 3 at Mt. 12:34, p. 131).

4 (Rom. 2:29) The Greek word that is used here for "letter" is "gramma" and literally means, "a writing; i.e. a letter, epistle, book, etc." Paul is saying that circumcision is spiritual rather than natural. True circumcision is a born-again nature and not a mark in the flesh.

ROMANS

DOES THE JEW HAVE ADVANTAGE?

CHAPTER 3

WHAT advantage[a] then[1] hath the Jew?[b] or
what profit[c] *is there* of circumcision?[d]
2 *Much every way:[e] chiefly,[f] because[2]
that unto them were committed[g] the oracles[3]
of God.

3 For what if some did not believe?[h]
shall their unbelief[i] make the faith[j] of God[4]
without effect?[5]
4 *God forbid:[6] yea, let[7] God be true,[k]
but every man a liar;[l] as it is written,[8] That
thou mightest be justified[m] in thy sayings,[n]
and mightest overcome[o] when thou art
judged.[p]

PARALLEL SCRIPTURE FOR ROMANS 3:2

MARK 7:13

13 Making the word of God of none effect through your tradition, which ye have delivered: and many such like things do ye.

O.T. SCRIPTURE CITED IN ROMANS 3:4

PSALM 51:4

4 Against thee, thee only, have I sinned, and done this *evil in thy sight: that thou mightest be justified when thou speakest,* and *be clear when thou judgest.*

Footnotes for Romans 3:1-4

1 (Rom. 3:1) Paul had just proven that the Jews were just as guilty as the pagans whom they disdained (see note 1 at Rom. 2:1, p. 662). This led to the question, "What advantage is there in being a Jew then?" Paul gives the most important answer to that question in verse two (see note 2 at v. 2, below) and then addresses the issue more in Romans 9:4-5.

2 (Rom. 3:2) The main advantage (see ref. f, this verse) that the Jews had over others was that God had committed His Word unto them. They not only had the intuitive knowledge of God (see note 2 at Rom. 1:18, p. 659), but they had a written record of God's instructions which should have served as an added restraint from departing from God. They, however, had missed the true intent of God's law, and therefore were not taking advantage of the benefits God's Word afforded them.

3 (Rom. 3:2) The Greek word for "oracles" is "logion" which means, "an utterance of God." Therefore, this is speaking of the Word of God that was committed to the Jews. In the Old Testament, the word "oracle" was also used to designate the innermost part of the temple, since the ark of the covenant was kept there (1 Ki. 6:5, 16, 19-23, 31; 7:49; 8:6, 8; 2 Chr. 3:16; 4:20; 5:7, 9; Ps. 28:2).

The word "oracles" is used four times in the New Testament (Acts 7:38; Rom. 3:2; Heb. 5:12; 1 Pet. 4:11). In each of these instances, the word is clearly referring to the Word of God.

4 (Rom. 3:3) Paul is using the phrase "the faith of God" in this verse interchangeably with the word "oracle" in verse two. He is saying that the unbelief of the Jews did not make the Word of God or the promises of God without effect. Therefore, the Word of God is the faith of God. No wonder faith comes by hearing God's Word; God's Word contains His faith.

5 (Rom. 3:3) Paul is asking the question, "If some of the Jews did not believe God's Word, does that make God's Word of no effect?" The answer to this question is a resounding "no" in verse four. However, Mark 7:13 says we make the Word of God of none effect through our tradition. What's the harmony between these two verses?

An individual can make God's Word of no effect in his personal life. Hebrews 4:2 says God's Word will not profit us unless we mix it with faith. So the Word will not profit anyone who doesn't believe it, but God's Word itself doesn't lose any power. That is what Paul is stating here. The unbelief of the Jewish nation as a whole did not void the promises of God concerning salvation through a savior. The promises of salvation were of no effect to the individuals who rejected Jesus, but to anyone who will put his faith in Jesus as Messiah, the Word of God still has its power to save.

6 (Rom. 3:4) This is the first of ten times that Paul uses this expression in the book of Romans (here; Rom. 3:6, 31; 6:2,15; 7:7,13; 9:14; 11:1,11). He also uses this expression three other times in his other epistles (1 Cor. 6:15; Gal. 2:17; 6:14).

The Greek words that are used are "me ginomai" meaning "let it not be! far be it! God forbid!" and express emphatic denial of the false conclusion that someone might draw from his teaching.

7 (Rom. 3:4) This phrase *"let God be true, but every man a liar"* is given in response to the question of verse 3 (see note 5 at Rom. 3:3, above). Paul is stating that God and His promises are always true even if men don't believe Him. However, there can be other applications of this truth which will benefit us greatly.

When anyone or anything contradicts a promise made to us in God's Word, we need to reckon God to be true and that person or thing to be lying. We need to believe that what God's Word says about our prosperity is true (2 Cor. 8:9; 3 Jn. 2), instead of what our checkbook says. We need to believe that we [were] healed by His stripes (Isa. 53:5; Mt. 8:17; 1 Pet. 2:24), instead of believing what the x-rays show. In every aspect of our lives, we need to believe God's Word above what we see or hear.

8 (Rom. 3:4) This is a quotation from David out of Psalm 51:4 when he was repenting of his sin with Bathsheba and the murder of her husband. David was admitting his sinfulness and proclaiming God's complete justification in judging his sin in whatever way He saw fit. David's sin had not made God unholy, it made him unholy. In David's sinfulness, he now saw the holiness of God more clearly than ever.

This is what Paul is drawing from this Old Testament passage. He was saying that in a similar manner, God retained His holiness even when His people were unholy. It was the Jews who suffered from not believing God's Word, not God.

a Gk.-"perissos"- superiority; pre-eminence Dict.- a factor favorable or conducive to success; benefit or profit; gain; a relatively favorable position; the condition of being ahead

b Gk.-"ioudaios"- Jewish as respects birth; race; religion see note 10 at Jn. 8:33, p. 232

c Dict.- benefit; advantageous gain or return

d Gk.-"peritome"- circumcision: the rite, condition, or people (Strong) The extinction of the passions and the removal of spiritual impurity (Thayer) From Gk.-"peritemno"- to cut around see note 4 at Jn. 7:22, p. 224 see note 1 at Acts 11:2, p. 565 see note 2 at Acts 15:1, p. 585 see note 3 at Acts 16:3, p. 591 Dt. 10:16 30:6 Jer. 4:4 9:26 Rom. 4:10-12 Col. 2:11-12

e great in every way (TCNT) much in every way (NIV)

f Gk.-"proton"- firstly in importance

g Gk.-"pisteuo"- to be intrusted with a thing

h Rom. 10:16 Heb. 4:2

i see note 3 at Mt. 17:20, p. 211 see note 2 at Lk. 8:51, p. 159 see note 2 at Mk. 6:5, p. 163 see notes 2-3 at Mk. 8:23, p. 200 see note 2 at Mt. 17:20, p. 210 see note 2 at Jn. 20:25, p. 498 see note 4 at Acts 9:38, p. 558 see note 14 at Acts 12:16, p. 572

j shall their want of faith make of none effect the faithfulness of God (ASV)- Num. 23:19 1 Sam. 15:29 2 Tim. 2:13 Ti. 1:2

k Jn. 14:6 3:33 2 Cor. 1:18 Ti. 1:2 Heb. 6:18

l Gk.-"pseustes"- a falsifier; from Gk.-"pseudomai"- to utter an untruth or attempt to deceive by falsehood- Rom. 3:10-12 1 Jn. 2:4, 22 4:20

m Gk.-"dikaioo"- to render; i.e. show or regard as just or innocent; be righteous

n Gk.-"logos"- something said including the thought

o Gk.-"nikao"- to subdue; conquer; prevail; get the victory

p Gk.-"krino"- call in question; judge

ROMANS

DOES THE JEW HAVE ADVANTAGE? (continued)

CHAPTER 3

5 But[9] if our unrighteousness[a] commend[b]
the righteousness of God, what shall we
say? *Is* God unrighteous who taketh vengeance?[c] (I speak as a man)[10]
6 God forbid: for then how[11] shall God
judge[d] the world?[e]
7 For if the truth of God hath more
abounded[f] through my lie unto his glory;[g]
why yet am I also judged[d] as a sinner?
8 And not *rather,* (as we be slanderously[h]
reported, and as some affirm[i] that we say,)[12]
Let us do evil, that good may come? whose
damnation[j] is just.[k]

a Gk.-"adikia"- wrongfulness of character, life, or act; unjust; iniquity
b Gk.-"sunistao"- to show; prove; establish; exhibit
c Gk.-"orge"- punishment; anger; indignation; wrath- Heb. 10:29-31 12:29 Rom. 12:19 Ps. 58:10-11 94:1-2 Nah. 1:2 2 Th. 1:6-9
d Gk.-"krino"- to distinguish; i.e. decide judicially; to try; condemn; punish; avenge; sentence- Ps. 9:8 50:6 96:13 98:9 Acts 17:31
e Gk.-"kosmos"- the world including its inhabitants
f Gk.-"perisseuo"- to superabound; be the better; excel; increase
g but, you say, if a falsehood of mine has brought great honor to God by bringing out his truthfulness (Gspd) see note 9 at Rom. 3:5, this page
h Gk.-"blasphemeo"- to speak impiously; blaspheme; defame; rail on; revile; speak evil- Mt. 5:11 1 Pet. 3:16-17
i Dict.- to declare positively or firmly; maintain to be true
j Gk.-"krima"- condemnation; judgment
k Gk.-"endikos"- in the right; i.e. equitable; just Dict.- consistent with moral right

Footnotes for Romans 3:5-8

9 (Rom. 3:5) Paul had just explained that the Jews' faithlessness did not make God unfaithful to His Word (see note 5 at Rom. 3:3, p. 668). Therefore, when you consider how unfaithful we have been to God, it makes God's mercy and faithfulness appear even greater. So this brings up new questions, "If my unrighteousness reveals God's righteousness, or causes it to be seen in an even greater way, then am I actually helping God? Would it be right for God to judge me for something like that?" Of course, Paul's answer to that is another "God forbid."

It is true that man would never have seen the love and goodness of God as clearly if we had not sinned, but that does not mean our sin was a good thing. This is one piece of information that the Lord never wanted us to know by experience. No one will be able to tell God on judgment day that his sin just helped God reveal how great His mercy was. The Lord will be totally just in bringing His judgment on all those who refuse His offer of mercy given through Jesus, His Son.

10 (Rom. 3:5) Paul is saying that the logic he had just been using was not from God but was carnal. He was not saying this as God's spokesman but was expressing a thought that opponents of the gospel held, so he could expose the error in it. Therefore, he gave a disclaimer in parenthesis that this was not God's wisdom, but man's.

11 (Rom. 3:6) Paul is saying that if this were true (v. 5), God couldn't judge the world, and it is a well-established fact in scripture that God will judge the world (see ref. d, this verse). Therefore, this argument has to be rejected.

12 (Rom. 3:8) Paul preached the grace of God as no one else recorded in scripture (see note 2 at Acts 15:1, p. 585). This led many people to slander him and his teaching by accusing him of encouraging people to sin. This was totally untrue. The grace of God teaches us to deny ungodliness and worldly lust (Ti. 2:11-12). Here, Paul shows his total rejection of those allegations by saying that the damnation of those people is just. He also "raises the stakes" for anyone who wants to criticize those who proclaim the grace of God. According to Paul, they will be damned.

THE PURPOSE OF THE LAW: THE UNIVERSAL GUILT OF MAN

CHAPTER 3

9 What then? are we[a] better[b] *than they?*[1c]
No, in no wise: for we have before proved
both Jews[d] and Gentiles,[e] that they are all
under sin;[f]
10 *As it is written, There is none
righteous,[g] no, not one:

PARALLEL SCRIPTURE FOR
ROMANS 3:10-12

PSALM 14:1-3

THE FOOL hath said in his heart, There
is *no God. They are corrupt, they have*
done abominable works, there is *none*
that doeth good.
2 *The LORD looked down from*
heaven upon the children of men, to see
if there were any that did understand,
and *seek God.*
3 *They are all gone aside, they are* all
together become filthy: there is *none*
that doeth good, no, not one.

a i.e. Jews
b Gk.-"proechomai"- to hold oneself before others; be better; superior- Rom. 3:22-23 Isa. 65:5 Lk. 7:39 18:9-14
c i.e. the Gentiles
d see note 10 at Jn. 8:33, p. 232 Rom. 9:4-7 Mt. 3:9 Jn. 8:33-44 Rev. 2:9 3:9
e see note 45 at Mt. 6:32, p. 83 see note 3 at Lk. 7:9, p. 117 see note 1 at Jn. 12:23, p. 359 see note 1 at Acts 10:1, p. 559 see note 3 at Acts 14:27, p. 584
f Gal. 3:22
g Gk.-"dikaios"- equitable in character or act; innocent; holy; just; right- Rom. 3:23 Jer. 17:9 Mt. 15:19 Mk. 7:21-22 10:18 Gal. 5:19-21 Eph. 2:1-3 1 Jn. 1:8-10

Footnotes for Romans 3:9-10

1 (Rom. 3:9) In Romans 1:18-32, Paul proved that the Gentiles were guilty before God for their actions because of an intuitive knowledge of God (see note 2 at Rom. 1:18, p. 659). In Romans 2, Paul proved that the Jews were even worse off than the Gentiles because they had been given the Word of God and yet had not kept it (see note 1 at Rom. 2:1, 662).

Now, in chapter three, he brings all this together and concludes that every one (Jew or Gentile, religious or pagan, moral or immoral) is guilty before God. Paul cites many Old Testament scriptures to verify this claim (see Parallel and O.T. Scriptures for vv. 10-18, above and on p. 670) and to show that this is not some new doctrine. Faith in the sacrificial death of a savior was God's plan of redemption all along.

Paul's arguments in Romans 3:9-18 provide the reason for salvation by grace through faith (Eph. 2:8) and refute the doctrines of every other religion.

Man is so destitute that he cannot save himself; he has to have a savior. Therefore, every other religion is wrong because it doesn't provide a savior. To some degree or another, the other religions of the world teach that the burden of salvation is upon our own shoulders.

In contrast, Christianity has a Savior, and not just some man. God Himself provided salvation for mankind. Within the ranks of those who claim Christianity, this is also the pivotal issue. Any deviation from trust in Jesus and His imputed righteousness to reliance on our own holiness for right standing with God is error.

Therefore, the truth expressed in these verses is critical to understanding God's plan of salvation. Since man could never "make up" for his sins, God did what man could not do. He paid the price Himself. No other method of payment is acceptable.

ROMANS

THE PURPOSE OF THE LAW: THE UNIVERSAL GUILT OF MAN (cont'd)

CHAPTER 3

11 *There is none that understandeth,[a]
there is none that seeketh[b] after God.
12 *They are all gone out of the way,[c]
they are together become unprofitable;[d]
there is none that doeth good,[e] no, not one.[f]
13 *Their throat *is* an open sepulchre;[g]
with their tongues[h] they have used deceit;[i]
the poison of asps[j] *is* under their lips:
14 *Whose mouth[k] *is* full of cursing[l] and
bitterness:[m]
15 *Their feet *are* swift to shed blood:[n]
16 *Destruction[o] and misery[p] *are* in their
ways:[q]
17 *And the way[r] of peace[s] have they
not known:[t]
18 *There is no fear of God before their
eyes.[u]

PARALLEL SCRIPTURES FOR ROMANS 3:10-12

PSALM 53:1-3

THE FOOL *hath said in his heart,* There is *no God. Corrupt are they, and have done abominable iniquity:* there is *none that doeth good.*

2 *God looked down from heaven upon the children of men, to see if there were* any *that did understand, that did seek God.*

3 *Every one of them is gone back: they are altogether become filthy;* there is *none that doeth good, no, not one.*

PARALLEL SCRIPTURE FOR ROMANS 3:14-18

ISAIAH 64:6

6 *But we are all as an unclean* thing, *and all our righteousnesses* are *as filthy rags; and we all do fade as a leaf; and our iniquities, like the wind, have taken us away.*

PARALLEL SCRIPTURE FOR ROMANS 3:18

PSALM 36:1

THE *transgression of the wicked saith within my heart,* that there is *no fear of God before his eyes.*

O.T. SCRIPTURES CITED IN ROMANS 3:13

PSALM 5:9

9 *For* there is *no faithfulness in their mouth; their inward part* is *very wickedness; their throat* is *an open sepulchre; they flatter with their tongue.*

PSALM 140:3

3 *They have sharpened their tongues like a serpent; adders' poison* is *under their lips. Selah.*

PSALM 10:7

7 *His mouth is full of cursing and deceit and fraud: under his tongue* is *mischief and vanity.*

PARALLEL SCRIPTURES FOR ROMANS 3:15-17

ISAIAH 59:7-8

7 *Their feet run to evil, and they make haste to shed innocent blood: their thoughts* are *thoughts of iniquity; wasting and destruction* are *in their paths.*

8 *The way of peace they know not; and* there is *no judgment in their goings: they have made them crooked paths: whosoever goeth therein shall not know peace.*

a Gk.-"suniemi"- the man of understanding; i.e. a good and upright man (as having knowledge of those things which pertain to salvation) [Thayer]- Rom. 1:22, 28 Ps. 14:2-4 53:2, 4 Prov. 1:7 Jer. 4:22 Mt. 13:13, 14, 19 1 Jn. 2:20, 27 5:20

b Gk.-"ekzeteo"- to search out; i.e. investigate; crave; seek after carefully and diligently- Isa. 9:13 31:1 55:6 Rom. 8:7

c all have swerved from the right path (Mon)- Ex. 32:8 Ps. 14:3 Isa. 53:6 59:8 1 Pet. 2:25

d Gk.-"achreioo"- to render useless; i.e. spoil- Mt. 25:30 Phile. 11

e Gk.-"chrestotes"- excellence in character or demeanor; gentleness; kindness

f Ps. 53:1 Eccl. 7:20 Isa. 64:6

g Gk.-"taphos"- a grave; tomb; i.e. filthy like the stench from an open grave (Tay)- Ps. 5:9 Jer. 5:16 Mt. 23:27-28

h Gk.-"glossa"- the tongue; by impl. a language- Rom. 3:4 Ps. 5:9 12:3-4 36:3 52:2 57:4 Isa. 59:3 Jer. 9:3-5 Mt. 12:34-35 Jas. 3:5-8

i Dict.- misrepresentation; deception; trick; wile; falseness; to victimize persons for the most part by underhand means

j Gk.-"aspis"- used of a serpent- Ps. 140:3

k Gk.-"stoma"- by impl. language and its relations

l Dict.- to invoke evil, calamity, or injury upon; to damn; to swear at; abuse profanely- Ps. 10:7 59:12 109:17-18 Jas. 3:10

m Dict.- exhibiting or proceding from strong animosity

n They are quick to kill (Tay)- Prov. 1:16 6:18 Isa. 59:7

o Gk.-"suntrimma"- concussion or utter fracture; i.e. complete ruin

p Gk.-"talaiporia"- wretchedness; i.e. calamity

q i.e. their paths

r Gk.-"hodos"- a road; journey; highway

s Gk.-"eirene"- prosperity; quietness; rest; set at one again- Isa. 57:21 59:8 Mt. 7:14 Lk. 1:79 Rom. 5:1

t Gk.-"ginosko"- be aware of; perceive; understand

u Gen. 20:11 Ps. 36:1 Prov. 8:13 16:6 23:17 Lk. 23:40 Rev. 19:5

ROMANS

THE PURPOSE OF THE LAW: THE UNIVERSAL GUILT OF MAN (cont'd)

v Rom. 3:2 2:12-18 6:14 1 Cor. 9:20-21 Gal. 3:19 3:23-25 4:5, 21 5:18 1 Tim. 1:9
w Rom. 1:20 2:1 Ps. 107:42 Ezek. 16:63 Mt. 22:12-13
x Gk.-"hupodikos"- under sentence; i.e. condemned- Rom. 3:23 2:1-2
y Dict.- for that reason
z Gk.-"ergon"- to work; toil as an effort; labour; doing
aa Gk.-"sarx"- a human being

CHAPTER 3

19 Now[2] we know that what things
soever the law saith, it saith to them who
are under[3] the law:[v] that every mouth may
be stopped,[w] and all the world may become
guilty[x] before God.[4]
20 *Therefore[y] by the deeds[z] of the law
there shall no flesh[aa] be justified[bb] in his
sight[cc] for by the law *is* the knowledge[dd] of
sin.[ee]

PARALLEL SCRIPTURE FOR ROMANS 3:20

PSALM 143:2

2 *And enter not into judgment with
thy servant: for in thy sight shall no man
living be justified.*

bb Gk.-"dikaioo"- to render; i.e. show or regard as just or innocent; be righteous see note 13 at Acts 13:39, p. 579 see note 21 at Jn. 8:56, p. 234 see note 22 at Jn. 8:57, p. 234 see note 1 at Lk. 10:28, p. 253 see note 3 at Lk. 10:29, p. 253 see note 2 at Acts 15:1, p. 585 see note 1 at Mt. 26:2, p. 410
cc Ps. 130:3
dd Gk.-"epignosis"- recognition; i.e. full discernment; acknowledgment
ee Gk.-"hamartia"- offence; from Gk.-"hamartano"- to miss the mark; to err; offend; trespass see note 17 at Mt. 5:28, p. 75 see note 11 at Jn. 8:34, p. 232 see note 17 at Jn. 8:44, p. 234

Footnotes for Romans 3:19-20

2 (Rom. 3:19) Paul had conclusively proven that both Jews and Gentiles were sinners (see note 1 at Rom. 3:9, p. 669) and therefore incapable of saving themselves through their own works of righteousness. They both needed a savior. He now begins to reveal that the means of that salvation is through faith in Jesus the Messiah, and not through our moral goodness.

3 (Rom. 3:19) This very clear statement by Paul comes as a complete shock to most Christians. Christianity as a whole has embraced the Old Testament law and most Christians have never thought that the law was not intended for them. However, Paul is saying that the law was given to the Jews. The purpose of that law was to produce guilt (see note 4 at this verse, below), therefore, anyone who is denying his guilt before God can profit from its condemning effect (2 Cor. 3:9; 1 Tim. 1:9). But a Christian who embraces the Old Testament law (not everything that is in the Old Testament is law) as God's gift to them has misunderstood its purpose.

That is not to say that a Christian should reject the Old Testament as God's holy Word, God forbid. It certainly is God's Word and is, therefore, profitable for doctrine, reproof, etc. (2 Tim. 3:16). However, it needs to be interpreted in light of the new covenant. Jesus not only set us free from the curse of the law (Gal. 3:13), He also set us free from the law itself (Rom. 4:16; 6:14-15; 7:4-6; 8:2; 2 Cor. 3:7; Gal. 2:19; 3:24-25; 4:21; 5:18; Eph. 2:14-15; Col. 2:14; 1 Tim. 1:9; Heb. 7:18-19; 8:7-13; 10:8-9). A desire to live under the commands of the Old Testament law is a return to bondage and a misunderstanding of our new covenant in Jesus (note 2 at Lk. 9:55, p. 245; see note 1 at Lk. 16:16, p. 301; see note 6 at Lk. 19:8, p. 344).

4 (Rom. 3:19) Paul begins to make a series of radical statements here. Radical because the Jews of his day, just like many church people of our day, thought that the law of God was given so that we could earn our salvation through keeping it. That wasn't its purpose. The law was not given for the purpose of producing justification (Rom. 3:20, 28; 4:13; Gal. 2:16; 3:11; 5:4; Ti. 3:5).

The law was given to kill (2 Cor. 3:7) and condemn (2 Cor. 3:9). The law strengthened sin (1 Cor. 15:56) and made sin come alive (Rom. 7:9). The law gave sin an occasion against us to deceive us and work all manner of lust in us (Rom. 7:8, 11). In short, the law strengthened our enemy, sin, not us.

Why would God give us something that strengthened our enemy? Because sin had already beat us and we didn't know it. Mankind was deceived into thinking that although we weren't perfect, surely our sins weren't that bad. We really are pretty good people and the outcome would be "okay." The only thing that is wrong with that thinking is that God doesn't grade on a curve. It doesn't matter if you are better than someone else. All have sinned and come short of the glory of God (v. 23) and the wages for sin (any sin) is death (Rom. 6:23).

James 2:10 says, *"For whosoever shall keep the whole law, and yet offend in one* ***point****, he is guilty of all."* If a person commits **any** sin he is guilty of them all. It's similar to breaking a window. It doesn't matter how big a hole you make in the window. If it's broken, the whole window has to be replaced. If we break even the slightest command, we are guilty of breaking them all.

So God had to break the deception that people had fallen into, of thinking they were surely good enough to be accepted by God. The way He did this was to give the law. It made sin and its lust come alive in us. To those who would receive it, it became obvious that if this holy perfection of the law was what God demanded, no one could be saved by his own goodness.

That was the point that God wanted to make and that is the point that Paul is making here. No one can be saved by keeping the law because all have sinned and come short of the law's perfection (v. 23).

Therefore, the law stripped us of every excuse and made us guilty before God. The law gave us a knowledge of just how sinful we were and removed any deception of us ever being saved because we were such "nice guys" in comparison to others. As Paul said in Galatians 3:23, *"But before faith came, we were kept under the law, shut up unto the faith which should afterwards be revealed."* The law took away every hope of salvation except faith in a savior. That was the purpose of the law.

ROMANS

RIGHTEOUSNESS NEEDED AND PROVIDED BY GOD

CHAPTER 3

21 But now the righteousness[a] of God without[1b] the law[c] is manifested,[d] being witnessed[e] by the law[f] and the prophets;[g]

22 Even the righteousness of God[2] *which is* by faith[h] of[3] Jesus Christ[i] unto all[j] and upon all[j] them that believe:[k] for there is no difference:[4]

23 For[5] all[l] have sinned,[m] and come short[n] of the glory[6o] of God;

a Gk.-"dikaiosune"- equity of character or act; justification- Dan. 9:24 Rom. 1:17 5:19, 21 10:3-4 Gen. 15:6 Isa. 45:24-25 54:17 Jer. 23:5-6 33:16 1 Cor. 1:30 2 Cor. 5:21 Phil. 3:9

b Gk.-"choris"- at a space; i.e. separately or apart from the law

c i.e. the principle of the law; doing, earning, and achieving certain standards in order to be accepted by God

d Gk.-"phaneroo"- to render apparent; appear; shew self

e Gk.-"martureo"- to be a witness; i.e. testify; give evidence; bear record; give testimony

f see note 1 at Mt. 26:24, p. 420 Dt. 18:15-19 Lk. 24:44 Jn. 1:45 3:14 5:46-47 Acts 26:22

g see note 1 at Mt. 26:24, p. 420 see note 3 at Acts 13:15, p. 577 Rom. 1:2 16:26 Acts 3:21-25 10:43 28:23 Gal. 3:8 1 Pet. 1:10

h Gk.-"pistis"- persuasion; i.e. credence; moral conviction; reliance upon Christ for salvation; belief; believe see note 2 at Lk. 1:6, p. 6 see note 21 at Jn. 8:56, p. 234 see note 22 at Jn. 8:57, p. 234 see note 3 at Lk. 10:29, p. 253 see note 5 at Jn. 11:52, p. 312 see note 2 at Acts 15:1, p. 585 Rom. 4:3-13, & 20-22 5:1 Phil. 3:9

i see note 2 at Mt. 16:16, p. 202 see note 5 at Jn. 1:41, p. 40

j Rom. 4:11 10:12

k Gk.-"pisteuo"- to have faith (in, upon, or with respect to, a person); i.e. to entrust one's spiritual well-being to Christ; commit to trust; put trust in

l Gk.-"pas"- the whole; anyone; everyone

m Gk.-"hamartano"- to miss the mark; to err; offend; sin; trespass- Rom. 3:9, 19 2:1 11:32 Eccl. 7:20 Gal. 3:22 1 Jn. 1:8-10

n Heb. 4:1

o Rom. 5:2 1 Th. 2:12 2 Th. 2:14 1 Pet. 4:13 5:1, 10

Footnotes for Romans 3:21-23

1 (Rom. 3:21) This is another one of Paul's radical statements (see note 4 at Rom. 3:19, p. 671) that was diametrically opposed to the Jewish thinking of his day. Mercy and grace were present in the Old Testament but it was typified in the OldTestament sacrifices which were incorporated in the law. Therefore, the Jews had come to think that the only way God would grant any forgiveness was through fulfilling the law as much as possible and then offering the appropriate sacrifice prescribed in the law for any sins. For Paul to say that a person could be righteous apart from the law (see ref. b, this verse) was unthinkable.

Paul didn't end there though, he went on to say that this method of receiving right standing with God was promised under the Old Testament law and prophets. This meant that Paul was not putting forth a new doctrine, but expounding the true doctrine which the Old Testament law and prophets had advocated all along. This left no doubt that the Jews' trust in the Old Testament law for justification was never God's intent. They had misunderstood and misapplied the law in this area.

Likewise today, many religious people misunderstand the true intent of the Old Testament law (see notes 3-4 at Rom. 3:19, p. 671).

2 (Rom. 3:22) Paul makes an even clearer presentation of this truth in Romans 9:30-10:9. The Jews were seeking to produce their own righteousness that was according to their holy actions that conformed to the law. Paul is speaking of a different type of righteousness—not a human righteousness that was flawed, but the perfect righteousness of God Himself.

Through faith in Jesus, we can receive the very righteousness of God as a gift (2 Cor. 5:21). God's righteousness is infinitely better in quality and quantity that man's puny righteousness (Isa. 64:6). No one can ever be justified in the sight of God based on his own righteousness which comes through acts of holiness. One must have God's righteousness which only comes through faith in the Lord Jesus Christ as Savior. Paul said in Philippians 3:9, *"And be found in him, not having mine own righteousness, which is of the law, but that which is through the faith of Christ, the righteousness which is of God by faith." This is "the righteousness of God"* which Paul is referring to here.

3 (Rom. 3:22) Notice that Paul did not say that this righteousness of God came by faith **in** Jesus Christ. No, it comes by the faith **of** Jesus Christ. There is a big difference.

Our faith does not produce our righteousness. Jesus obtained righteousness (the perfect righteousness of God) through His faith and offers it to everyone who will believe on Him as Lord. Therefore, our faith (which is also a gift from God—Eph. 2:8) just receives what Jesus has already obtained for us through His faith. Jesus obtained our justification and righteousness through His faith (Gal. 2:16).

4 (Rom. 3:22) The only difference between Jew and Gentile, or the moral and immoral, is in the sight of men. From God's point of view there is no difference. All have sinned and come short of the glory of God (Rom. 3:23; Jas. 2:10).

5 (Rom. 3:23) As explained in note 1 at Romans 3:9, page 669, this is one of the pivotal doctrines of scripture. Jesus only came to save sinners (1 Tim. 1:15). Unless an individual acknowledges that he is a sinner, he cannot be saved. Romans 4:5 says that God justifies the ungodly. Therefore, until a person admits he is ungodly, he cannot be saved.

A person has to be stripped of all other means of salvation (Jn. 14:6) before they can receive Jesus as their Savior. That was the purpose of the Old Testament law (see note 4 at Rom. 3:19, p. 671) and that is the argument that Paul has given in Romans 1:21-23. Therefore, the truth of universal guilt before God that is expressed in this verse is true in all its applications.

However, in context, this verse is just a stepping stone to an even greater truth that is expressed in verses 24-26. Because the whole world is guilty before God, He has provided one way of salvation for everyone. In the same way that everyone is guilty, so everyone has already been justified freely by God's grace.

That does not mean everyone is saved. Everyone has had the sacrificial offering of Jesus made for his sins by grace (1 Tim. 4:10; 1 Jn. 2:2) but grace alone doesn't save. We have to put faith in what God has provided for us by grace (Eph. 2:8). Therefore, although the price has been paid for the sins of the whole world, only those who receive it by faith will benefit from the salvation that Jesus offers.

6 (Rom. 3:23) The Greek word that was translated "glory" here is "doxa," and according to W.E. Vine, it means "the manifested perfection of His character, especially His righteousness of which all men fall short." A simple way of saying this is that all men fall short of Jesus. Jesus is the glory of the Father (Jn. 1:14; 2 Cor. 4:6; Heb. 1:3; Rev. 21:23).

A common mistake that people make is comparing themselves with other people (2 Cor. 10:12). Nearly everyone has heard, "if the hypocrites down there at church make it, then I'll make it." The only thing wrong with that thinking is that the hypocrites down there at church aren't God's "measuring stick." Everyone is going to be compared to Jesus, the glory of God, and therefore, everyone will come up short. We all need a savior.

ROMANS

RIGHTEOUSNESS NEEDED AND PROVIDED BY GOD (continued)

CHAPTER 3

24 Being justified[p] freely[7q] by his grace[r]
through[8s] the redemption[t] that is in Christ[i]
Jesus:
25 Whom God hath set forth *to be* a
propitiation[u] through[s] faith[h] in his blood,[v]
to declare[w] his righteousness for the
remission[x] of sins that are past,[9y] through
the forbearance[z] of God;
26 To declare, *I say,* at this time his[10]
righteousness:[w] that he might be just,[aa] and
the justifier of him which believeth in
Jesus.[bb]
27 Where *is* boasting[cc] then?[11] It is
excluded. By what law? of works?[dd] Nay:
but by the law[12] of faith.[h]
28 Therefore we conclude[ee] that a man
is justified[p] by faith[h] without[ff] the deeds[dd] of
the law.
29 *Is he* the God of the Jews[gg] only? *is
he* not also of the Gentiles?[hh] Yes, of the
Gentiles also:[ii]

References continued from column 4

aa Gk.-"dikaios"- equitable (in character or act); innocent; holy; righteous-
Dt. 32:4
Isa. 45:21
Zech. 9:9
Rev. 15:3
bb Rom. 3:30
4:5
8:33
Gal. 3:8-14
see ref. p, this heading
see ref. h, p. 672
cc Dict.- to brag about one's own accomplishments; to speak with pride-
Rom. 4:2
1 Cor. 1:29-31
4:7
Eph. 2:8-10
dd Gk.-"ergon"- to work; toil; by impl. an act
see note 3 at Acts 9:36, p. 558
see note 1 at Rom. 3:21, p. 672
Rom. 9:11, 32
11:6
Gal. 2:16
ee Dict.- to reach a decision; to form a final judgment
ff see ref. b, p. 672
Rom. 3:20-22
8:3
Acts 13:38-39
Gal. 2:16
3:11-14, 24
Phil. 3:9
gg see note 10 at Jn. 8:33, p. 232
hh see note 45 at Mt. 6:32, p. 83
see note 1 at Acts 10:1, p. 559
see note 3 at Acts 14:27, p. 584
ii Rom. 1:16
9:24-26
15:9-13
Ps. 72:17
Jer. 16:19
Hos. 1:10
Zech. 2:11
Mal. 1:11
Mk. 16:15
Lk. 24:46-47
Acts 9:15
22:21
26:17
Gal. 3:28-29
Col. 3:11

Footnotes for Romans 3:24-29

7 (Rom. 3:24) Justification is not something to be earned, but a gift to be received. Seeking to earn salvation is the only sin that will prevent a person from being saved because you can not submit yourself to the righteousness of God which comes as a gift through faith as long as you are seeking to establish your own righteousness (Rom. 10:3).

8 (Rom. 3:24) Grace is God's ability given to us on an unearned, undeserved basis. However, this grace comes through the redemption that Jesus provided. Therefore, there can be no grace in our lives apart from faith in Jesus. Romans 5:2 says, *"By whom also we have access by faith into this grace wherein we stand, and rejoice in hope of the glory of God."*

9 (Rom. 3:25) This verse is speaking of the sins that were committed under the old covenant, before the sacrifice of Jesus was made. Those sins were also paid for by the blood of Jesus. The Old Testament sacrifices were only types and shadows of the true sin offering that Jesus made. It was impossible for the blood of bulls and of goats to ever take away sins (Heb. 10:4).

The Lord dealt with sins under the Old Testament through His forbearance. In a similar way that a person gives a check or credit card in exchange for the real currency desired, so the Lord gave the Old Testament sacrifices. However, just as these substitutes would be unacceptable if there was no reality to back them up, so the Old Testament sacrifices only served as a token of the real sacrifice of Jesus that would pay for sin (Heb. 9:13-14).

10 (Rom. 3:26) Paul restates this amazing fact that it is the righteousness of Jesus that has been given us (see note 2 at Rom. 3:22, p. 672). We don't just have enough righteousness to let us slip into heaven. We have been given Jesus' righteousness. First Corinthians 1:30 says, *"But of him are ye in Christ Jesus, who of God is made unto us wisdom, and righteousness, and sanctification, and redemption."* Jesus is my righteousness! Second Corinthians 5:21 says, *"For he hath made him* to be *sin for us, who knew no sin; that we might be made the righteousness of God in him."*

11 (Rom. 3:27) Boasting, bragging, or pride about our holiness or spiritual accomplishments are sure signs that we don't understand justification by grace through faith as Paul was teaching it here. If we acknowledge that we are no better than anyone else regardless of our conduct, and that the only way we obtained peace with God was through putting faith in what Jesus did for us, then there is no room for boasting about our achievements. It was the accomplishments of Jesus that saved us.

Pride is the root of all divisions in the church today (see note 11 at Acts 20:30, p. 619). Therefore, the prevalence of division in the church is a painful testimony to the lack of this foundational truth of justification by grace through faith.

12 (Rom. 3:27) Notice that Paul refers to the **law** of faith. Faith is governed by law, just as gravity or electricity is. If we would view faith as a law, rather than something that sometimes works and other times doesn't, we would begin to get very different results.

The law of electricity has been here on earth since creation. Man has observed it in such things as lightening and static electricity, but it was not until someone believed that there were laws that governed the activity of electricity that progress began to be made in putting it to use. Likewise, none deny the existence of faith, but it is only when an individual begins to understand that there are laws that govern faith and then begins to learn what those laws are that faith begins to work for him.

p Gk.-"dikaioo"- to render (show or regard as) just or innocent
see note 13 at Acts 13:39, p. 579
see note 5 at Jn. 11:52, p. 312
see note 2 at Lk. 1:6, p. 6
see note 21 at Jn. 8:56, p. 234
see note 22 at Jn. 8:57, p. 234
see note 3 at Lk. 10:29, p. 253
see note 2 at Acts 15:1, p. 585
Isa. 53:11
Mt. 20:28
Rom. 5:9, 16-19
1 Cor. 6:11
Ti. 3:5-7
q Gk.-"dorean"- gratuitously, without a cause, as a gift
r Gk.-"charis"- graciousness of manner or act; favour; gift-
Rom. 4:4-5, 16
Eph. 1:7
2:8-9
Ti. 3:7
s Gk.-"dia"- denoting the channel of an act
t Gk.-"apolutrosis"- ransom in full; i.e. riddance; deliverance; salvation
see note 7 at Mk. 10:45, p. 340
see note 1 at Mt. 26:2, p. 410
Rom. 5:9
Isa. 53:11
Mt. 20:28
Eph. 1:6-7
Col. 1:14
1 Tim. 2:6
Ti. 2:14
Heb. 9:12
1 Pet. 1:18-20
Rev. 5:9

u Gk.-"hilasterion"- an atoning victim; mercy seat (Strong)
Christ, through His expiatory death, is the personal means by whom God shows the mercy of His justifying grace to the sinner who believes (Vine)
Dict.- to conciliate an offended power; appease; especially, a conciliatory offering to a god. In ancient Jewish ceremony, the mercy seat-
1 Jn. 2:2
4:10
v Rom. 5:9
Jn. 6:53-58
Col. 1:20-23
Heb. 10:18-20
w Dict.- to reveal or manifest-
Rom. 3:26
Ps. 22:31
40:10
50:6
97:6
x Gk.-"aphesis"- deliverance; freedom; liberty; release from bondage; forgiveness; pardon of sins, letting them go as if they had not been committed; remission of penalty
see note 5 at Acts 10:43, p. 564
Mt. 26:28
Lk. 1:77
3:3
24:47
Acts 2:38
10:43
Heb. 9:22
10:18
y Gk.-"proginomai"- to be already; i.e. have previously transpired
z Gk.-"anoche"- self-restraint; i.e. tolerance
Dict.- tolerance and restraint in the face of provocation; patience
continued on center column

ROMANS

RIGHTEOUSNESS NEEDED AND PROVIDED BY GOD (continued)

a i.e. the Jews
b i.e. the Gentiles
c Gk.-"katargeo"- to be (render) entirely idle (useless) see note 5 at Rom. 3:3, p. 668 see note 8 at Mk. 7:13, p. 191 Mt. 5:17 15:6

CHAPTER 3

30 Seeing *it is* one God, which shall
justify the circumcision[a] by[13] faith, and
uncircumcision[b] through faith.
31 Do we then make void[c] the law[14]
through faith? God forbid:[d] yea, we
establish[e] the law.

d see note 6 at Rom. 3:4, p. 668 Lk. 20:16
e Dict.- to settle securely in a position; to cause to be recognized or accepted; to prove the truth of- Rom. 8:4

Footnotes for Romans 3:30-31

13 (Rom. 3:30) There is no reason to believe that Paul is making any distinction between the way the Jews and the Gentiles are justified by his use of the words "by" and "through." The same end (justification) is achieved and faith is the way for both Jew and Gentile to receive it.

14 (Rom. 3:31) Paul had just systematically taken away the Jews' trust in the law for the purpose of justification. This led to the question, "Is the law then useless?" Paul emphatically answers, *"God forbid."*

The real purpose of the law was established (see ref. e, this verse) by the gospel (see note 5 at Acts 20:24, p. 618). The problem with the Jews was that they were using the law for something that God never intended. The law was useless to produce justification. God didn't give the law so that we could keep it and thereby earn justification. The law was given to reveal to us that we could never live up to such a holy standard and thereby drive us to God to call out for mercy (Gal. 3:22-24).

The true purpose of the law is still functional today (see note 4 at Rom. 3:19, p. 671). As 1 Timothy 1:8-10 says, *"But we know that the law is good, if a man use it lawfully; Knowing this, that the law is not made for a righteous man. . . ."* The law is God's way of revealing to man his need. It is powerless to make provision for that need. It's the gospel that provides the power to produce salvation (see note 1 at Rom. 1:16, p. 658).

In chapter four, Paul goes on to use two great men of the Old Testament (Abram and David) as examples of how justification came through faith, not through the law.

JUSTIFICATION BY FAITH ILLUSTRATED FROM THE O. T.

a meaning "father of a multitude"
b i.e. forefather see note 10 at Jn. 8:33, p. 232 see note 14 at Jn. 8:37, p. 232 Isa. 51:2 Mt. 3:9 Lk. 3:8 16:24-25, 29-31 Jn. 8:33, 37-41, & 53, 56 Acts 13:26 2 Cor. 11:22
c Gk.-"dikaioo"- to render (i.e. show or regard as) just or innocent. Trans.- free; justify; be righteous see note 13 at Acts 13:39, p. 579 continued on column 4

CHAPTER 4

WHAT shall we say then that Abraham[a]
our father,[b] as pertaining to the flesh, hath
found?[1]
2 For if Abraham[a] were justified[c] by
works,[d] he hath *whereof* to glory;[e] but not
before God.[2f]

continued from column 1 see note 5 at Jn. 11:52, p. 312 see note 21 at Jn. 8:56, p. 234 see note 22 at Jn. 8:57, p. 234 see note 1 at Lk. 10:28, p. 253 see note 3 at Lk. 10:29, p. 253 see note 2 at Acts 15:1, p. 585 Rom. 5:16-19 1 Cor. 6:11
d Ti. 3:5-7 Gk.-"ergon"- from "ergo"- to work (toil) (as an effort or occupation); by impl. an act; Trans.- deed, doing, labour, work continued on center column

References continued from column 4

see note 3 at Acts 9:36, p. 558 see note 2 at Lk. 11:42, p. 264 Rom. 3:20-28 9:11, 32 11:6 Gal. 2:16 Phil. 3:9
e Dict.- to brag about one's own accomplishments; to speak with pride; boast- Gen. 12:12, 13, 18, & 20 20:9-13 Josh. 24:2 1 Cor. 1:29
f Gal. 3:22

Footnotes for Romans 4:1-2

1 (Rom. 4:1) The question is, "What good then were Abraham's works?" Paul answers this indirectly. Paul states what Abraham's works *were not* good for. They were not good enough to grant him justification in the sight of God. That came by faith (see ref. c, v. 2). He shows that Abraham's works or efforts didn't earn him anything from God. Abraham was justified by faith for over thirteen years (see note 3 at Rom. 4:10, p. 677) before he performed the act of circumcision that the Jews were insisting was necessary for right standing with God (vv. 10-11).

2 (Rom. 4:2) Our own good works will only allow us to boast if we're comparing ourselves with other people (2 Cor. 10:12). However, in the sight of God, not one of us has anything to brag about. We have all come short of the glory of God (see notes 5-6 at Rom. 3:23, p. 672).

ROMANS

JUSTIFICATION BY FAITH ILLUSTRATED FROM THE O.T. (cont'd)

CHAPTER 4

3 *For what saith[g] the scripture?[3] Abraham[4a] believed[5] God,[h] and it was counted[6] unto him for righteousness.[i]

4 Now to him that worketh[j] is the reward[k] not reckoned[l] of grace,[m] but of debt.[7n]

5 But to him that worketh[j] not, but believeth[o] on him that justifieth[c] the ungodly,[8p] his faith[q] is counted[l] for righteousness.[9i]

O.T. SCRIPTURE CITED FOR ROMANS 4:3

GENESIS 15:6

6 And he believed in the LORD; and he counted it to him for righteousness.

g Rom. 9:17, 10:11, 11:2, Mk. 12:10, Jas. 4:5, 2 Pet. 1:20-21
h Gal. 3:6-8, Jas. 2:23
i Gk.-"dikaiosune"- equity (of character or act); justification see ref. d, this heading Rom. 4:5, 9, 4:11, 22-25, Ps. 106:31
j Gk.-"ergazomai"- to toil (as a task, occupation, etc.) see ref. d, this heading
k Gk.-"misthos"- pay for service good or bad. Trans.- hire; reward; wages
l Gk.-"logizomai"- see note 6 at Rom. 4:3, p. 675
m Gk.-"charis"- see note 5 at Rom. 1:5, p. 655, Rom. 4:5, 16, 11:6, Eph. 1:7, 2:8-9, Ti. 3:7
n Gk.-"opheilema"- something owed; i.e. a due- Rom. 11:6
o Rom. 4:24-25, 3:22, 26-30, 5:1-2, 10:10, Jn. 5:24, Acts 13:38-39, Gal. 2:16, 3:8-14, Phil. 3:9
p Rom. 1:17-18, 5:6-8, 1 Cor. 6:9-11, 1 Tim. 1:13-15, Ti. 3:3-7
q Gk.-"pistis"- persuasion; i.e. credence; moral conviction (of religious truth, or the truthfulness of God or a religious teacher) esp. reliance upon Christ for salvation see ref. c, this heading

Footnotes for Romans 4:3-5

3 (Rom. 4:3) Paul is showing an inspired revelation of the Old Testament scriptures. All devout Jews knew the story of Abraham, but they had missed this simple truth that Paul brings out. In Genesis 15:6, the scriptures clearly say that Abraham believed God and God counted Abraham's faith for righteousness. It can't get any clearer than that. Later in this same chapter, Paul refers to the interval of time (over thirteen years—see note 3 at Rom. 4:10, p. 677) between when the scriptures state Abraham was counted righteous and the time when he was circumcised as further proof that Abraham's righteousness was given to him *before* he performed the righteous acts of the law (see note 3 at v. 10, p. 677).

4 (Rom. 4:3) Paul had just made a series of radical statements (see note 4 at Rom. 3:19, p. 671; see note 1 at Rom. 3:21, p. 672) which were hard for these Jews to swallow. He is now going back to Old Testament scripture and the founder of the Jewish nation to prove his assertions. He skillfully uses the very scriptures they had misunderstood to verify his gospel of grace. He also quotes David to draw on two of the most revered men of the Old Testament as examples of salvation by grace through faith.

5 (Rom. 4:3) Hebrews 11:6 says, *"But without faith* it is *impossible to please* him.*"* It was Abraham's faith that pleased God. The Lord promised Abraham that his seed would be as numerous as the stars in the sky and the sand on the seashore and Abraham believed God. That pleased God so much that He counted Abraham righteous right then, even though Abraham had not yet fulfilled the rite of circumcision and he was not living such a holy life.

According to Leviticus 18:9, it was an abomination (Lev. 18:26) for a man to marry a half sister. Sarah, Abraham's wife, was his half sister (Gen. 20:12). Therefore, Abraham's marriage to Sarah was not what pleased God. Abraham had already lied about Sarah being his wife so that he could save his own neck. He was willing to let a man commit adultery with his wife with no objections from him. Immediately after this instance where the Lord counted Abraham's faith for righteousness (Gen. 15:6), Abraham tried to accomplish God's will in the flesh with Hagar (Gen. 16) and then repeated this terrible sin with Sarah again (Gen. 20).

Anyone who really looked at the life of Abraham and the favor that he found with God would have to conclude that it was Abraham's faith that pleased God. It's the same with any of us. The only thing that we can do to please God is put faith in Jesus as our Savior.

6 (Rom. 4:3) The Greek word that was translated "counted" in this verse is the word "logizomai" which means "to take an inventory, i.e. estimate." It is an accounting term that means "to enter in the account book" (Rienecker's—A Linguistic Key to the Greek New Testament). This same word is used 11 times in this chapter. It was translated "counted" twice (vv. 3 and 5), "impute" once (v. 8), "imputed" four times (vv. 11, 22, 23, 24), "imputeth" once (v. 6), and "reckoned" three times (vv. 4, 9, 10). By comparing the different ways this same Greek word was translated into English, it becomes very easy to discern an accurate meaning for it.

7 (Rom. 4:4) Paul is saying that if an individual could be saved by works, then God would be providing that salvation as a payment to that person, and, of course, that doesn't make sense. God is not under obligation or debt to save anyone. Trust in our own works voids grace and likewise trust in God's grace makes faith in our own efforts useless. This is repeated by Paul again in Romans 11:6; *"And if by grace, then* is it *no more of works: otherwise grace is no more grace. But if* it be *of works, then is it no more grace: otherwise work is no more work."*

8 (Rom. 4:5) What a statement!! Paul had been countering the false doctrine that acting righteous could make a person righteous. Now he drops the bomb that God justifies the ungodly! We might add from the context that this is the only kind of person that He justifies. That's because He doesn't have any other kind of people to justify. We've all sinned and come short of the glory of God (see notes 5-6 at Rom. 3:23, p. 672). This verse should forever dispel any delusions that anyone might have of trying to earn God's favor by his or her performance.

9 (Rom. 4:5) Faith in the atonement of Jesus grants us righteousness. Our actions don't grant us righteousness. However, true faith will produce actions (Jas. 2:17) and these actions, or lack thereof, can be used by others to determine where we stand with the Lord (1 Jn. 3:7-10). Although our actions are an indication of our inner faith, they can be misinterpreted and therefore any judgments made based on actions need to be for the purpose of discernment only and not condemnation (see note 46 at Mt. 7:1, p. 83).

ROMANS

JUSTIFICATION BY FAITH ILLUSTRATED FROM THE O.T. (cont'd)

a Gk.-"kathaper"- according as; just as (Thayer)
b Ps. 1:1-3
112:1
Mt. 5:3-12
Gal. 3:8-9, 14
c see note 1 at Jn. 1:1, p. 2
d see note 6 at Rom. 4:3, p. 675
Rom. 4:11, 24
e Rom. 1:16-17
3:22
5:18-19
Isa. 45:24-25
54:17
Jer. 33:16
1 Cor. 1:30
2 Cor. 5:21
Phil. 3:9
2 Pet. 1:1
f Gk.-"choris"- at a space; i.e. separately or apart from
Trans.- beside; by itself; without
g see note 3 at Acts 9:36, p. 558
Rom. 3:20, 27
Eph. 2:8-10
2 Tim. 1:9
h Gk.-"makarios"- supremely blest; fortunate; well off
Trans.- blessed; happy

CHAPTER 4

6 Even[a] as David[10] also describeth the blessedness[b] of the man, unto whom God[c]
imputeth[d] righteousness[e] without[f] works,[g]
7 *Saying, Blessed[h] *are* they whose iniquities are forgiven,[i] and whose sins[j] are covered.[k]
8 *Blessed[h] is the man to whom the Lord[l] will not[11] impute[m] sin.[j]

O.T. SCRIPTURE CITED FOR ROMANS 4:7-8

PSALM 32:1-2

BLESSED is he whose *transgression* is *forgiven,* whose *sin* is *covered.*
2 Blessed is *the man unto whom the LORD imputeth not iniquity, and in whose spirit* there is *no guile.*

Footnotes for Romans 4:6-8

10 (Rom. 4:6) King David (see note 8 at Acts 13:22, p. 578) was living under the old covenant of law (see note 3 at Rom. 3:19, p. 671). However, this scripture that Paul quotes from Psalm 32, as well as the things David wrote in Psalm 51 when repenting for his sins against Uriah and Bathsheba, show that he had a tremendous revelation of the salvation by grace through faith that was coming with the Messiah.

11 (Rom. 4:8) The Greek word that is translated "will not" in this verse is what is called an emphatic negative and it means "not ever." This is the strongest language possible stating that those who receive forgiveness will not ever have their sins held against them. He didn't just say "did not" or "does not" but "will not" implying that even future tense sins have been dealt with, through the sacrificial offering of Jesus, once for all (Heb. 10:10, 14).

Most Christians have the concept that the sins that they committed before they professed faith in Christ were forgiven at salvation, but any sins that are committed after that time are not forgiven until they are repented of and forgiveness is asked. That is not the case.

All our sins, past, present, and future were forgiven us through the one offering of Jesus. If God can't forgive future tense sins, then none of us can be saved because Jesus only died once, nearly 2,000 years ago, before we had committed any sins. **All** our sins have been forgiven.

Why then, 1 John 1:9? *"If we confess our sins, he is faithful and just to forgive us **our** sins, and to cleanse us from all unrighteousness."* This is not speaking of the eternal salvation of our spirit but rather the salvation of our souls (Jas. 1:21; 1 Pet. 1:9). It's our spirits that get born again at salvation, and sin will never be imputed to our born-again spirits. They have been sanctified and perfected forever (Heb. 10:10, 14; 12:23) and cannot sin (1 Jn. 3:9).

However, we are still in the process of saving our souls (Jas. 1:21; 1 Pet. 1:9). When we sin the devil has a legal right to bring his forms of death into our soulish area (Rom. 6:16). How do we get the devil out once he has gotten in? We confess it and God brings that forgiveness that is already a reality in our born-again spirit out into the soulish realm and the devil has no right to stay.

If we had to confess every sin committed after our born-again experience in order to maintain our salvation, no one would ever make it. What if we forgot to confess some sin? That puts the burden of salvation back on us.

We must remember that *"God **is** a Spirit"* (Jn. 4:24) and we must worship Him through our new born-again spirit. Therefore, we truly are blessed because God will not hold any sin against our spirit. Our spirit is clean and pure (Eph. 4:24; Heb. 12:23; 1 Jn. 4:17) and will not change due to our performance.

i Gk.-"aphiemi"- to send from one's self; to send away; to bid go away or depart; yield up; to let go; let alone; let be; to leave, not to discuss; give up a debt, by not demanding it; to give up a thing to one (Thayer)-
Ps. 85:2
130:3-4
Isa. 40:1-2
Jer. 33:8-9
Mic. 7:18-20
Mt. 9:2
Lk. 7:47-50
j Gk.-"hamartia"- offence; sin (-ful)
Gk.-"hamartano"- to miss the mark; i.e. to err, esp. (morally) to sin
k Gk.-"epikalupto"- to conceal
l see note 3 at Lk. 1:43, p. 12
m Dict.- to ascribe a crime or fault to; to attribute to; reckon; to consider; take in account
see note 6 at Rom. 4:3, p. 675

JUSTIFICATION IS APART FROM CIRCUMCISION OR RELIGIOUS ORDINANCES

a Gk.-"makarismos"- beautification; i.e. attribution of good fortune-
Ps. 1:1-3
112:1
Mt. 5:3-12
Gal. 3:8-9, 14
b see note 1 at Acts 11:2, p. 565
see note 2 at Acts 15:1, p. 585
see note 3 at Acts 16:3, p. 591

CHAPTER 4

9 *Cometh this blessedness[a] then[1] upon the circumcision[b] *only,* or upon the uncircumcision[c] also?[d] for we say that faith[e] was reckoned[f] to Abraham for righteousness.

References continued from column 4
Isa. 49:6
Lk. 2:32
Gal. 3:14, 26-28
Eph. 2:11-13
3:8
Col. 3:11
e see notes 21-22 at Jn. 8:56-57, p. 234
see note 2 at Acts 15:1, p. 585
see note 3 at Lk. 10:29, p. 253
f Gk.-"logizomai"- see note 6 at Rom. 4:3, p. 675

Footnotes for Romans 4:9

1 (Rom. 4:9) Paul had previously shown in this chapter that Abraham's faith was what granted him right standing with God (see notes 3 and 5 at Rom. 4:3, p. 675) and he used a quote from David to verify salvation by grace through faith (see note 10 at Rom, 4:6, above). He now returns to the story of Abraham and uses the very religious act which the legalists were demanding compliance with (i.e. circumcision) to further certify that salvation is by grace through faith.

c i.e. Gentiles
see note 2 at Lk. 2:32, p. 22
see note 45 at Mt. 6:32, p. 83
see note 3 at Lk. 7:9, p. 117
see note 3 at Acts 14:27, p. 584
see note 4 at Acts 21:21, p. 623
d Rom. 3:29-30
9:23-24
10:12-13
15:8-19
continued on center column

ROMANS

JUSTIFICATION IS APART FROM CIRCUMCISION OR RELIGIOUS ORDINANCES (continued)

CHAPTER 4

10 *How was it then reckoned?[f] when[2]
he[3] was in circumcision,[g] or in
uncircumcision?[c] Not in circumcision,[g] but
in uncircumcision.[c]
11 *And he received the sign[h] of
circumcision,[g] a seal[4i] of the righteousness[j]
of the faith[e] which *he had yet* being
uncircumcised: that he might be the father[k]
of all them that believe, though they be not
circumcised;[c] that righteousness[j] might be
imputed[f] unto them also:
12 *And the father[k] of circumcision[g] to
them[l] who are not of the circumcision[g]
only, but who also walk[m] in the steps[n] of
that faith[e] of our father[k] Abraham, which *he*
had[5] being *yet* uncircumcised.

PARALLEL SCRIPTURES FOR ROMANS 4:9-12

COLOSSIANS 3:11

11 Where there is neither Greek nor Jew, circumcision nor uncircumcision, Barbarian, Scythian, bond nor *free: but Christ is all, and in all.*

GALATIANS 5:6

6 For in Jesus Christ neither circumcision availeth any thing, nor uncircumcision; but faith which worketh by love.

GALATIANS 6:15

15 For in Christ Jesus neither circumcision availeth any thing, nor uncircumcision, but a new creature.

Footnotes for Romans 4:10-12

2 (Rom. 4:10) The time between when God counted Abraham's faith for righteousness and when Abraham was circumcised was over thirteen years. This can be deduced in the following way. The instance where God counted Abraham righteous took place in Genesis 15:6, which was before the birth of Ishmael (Gen. 16:15). Abraham circumcised Ishmael the same day (Gen. 17:26) that he was circumcised, which Genesis 17:25 says took place when Ishmael was thirteen years old. Therefore, the circumcision of Abraham was at least thirteen years and nine months after his justification by faith in Genesis 15:6.

3 (Rom. 4:10) This truth is so simple and obvious that it is amazing that the legalistic Jews had missed it. Paul explains that God said Abraham was righteous (Gen. 15:6) over thirteen years (see note 2 at this verse, above) before he performed the rite of circumcision (see note 2 at Acts 15:1, p. 585). Now if circumcision was necessary for justification with God, as some Jews were advocating, then Abraham could not have been righteous until after the performing of this act. But God Himself said Abraham was righteous. Therefore, the rite of circumcision (or any other act of obedience) cannot be a prerequisite for justification.

In our day, religious people no longer contend that circumcision is essential for salvation, Paul conclusively disproved that. However, many people are still making the same mistake. They have just substituted some other act of holiness for circumcision. They may have changed cars, but they are headed down the same road to the same destination.

For instance, entire denominations are built around the doctrine that water baptism is essential for salvation. There is no disputing that water baptism is a command of Jesus (Mt. 28:19-20) just as circumcision was a command under the Old Testament (Gen. 17:9-14). However, the same logic that Paul uses here to disprove circumcision as a prerequisite to justification can be used to prove that water baptism is not required before a person can be saved (Ex.—Cornelius; see note 9 at Mk. 16:16, p. 505; see note 1 at Acts 10:44, p. 564; see note 4 at Jn. 3:5, p. 48).

Any condition that must be met for salvation, except faith in what Jesus did for us, is error (Rom. 3:28). This is what Paul called "another gospel" or more accurately a perversion of the gospel (Gal. 1:6-7).

4 (Rom. 4:11) The rite of circumcision was a confirmation (see ref. h and ref. i, this verse) of the righteousness that Abraham had already attained by faith. It was meant to be a constant reminder to him of the covenant between God and himself. It was never intended to be something that Abraham would boast about or use to **show** others his holiness. This was private!

No doubt one of the reasons the Lord chose this act as a sign of the covenant instead of some other act was to prevent the very thing that the Jews were doing. How were you to tell if someone else was circumcised? That's not the kind of thing that is public knowledge. It's between God and that individual. God gave the sign of circumcision because it is a very private act, therefore, He never intended us to use circumcision to judge the righteousness of anyone.

5 (Rom. 4:12) Note that Abraham had faith before he had the action of circumcision. Many people have mistakenly thought that actions produce faith, but that's not so (see note 2 at Lk. 11:42, p. 264; see note 21 at Mt. 23:26, p. 391). Faith produces actions (see note 55 at Mt. 7:21, p. 85; see note 26 at Mt. 25:40, p. 409). Acting right doesn't make a person right, you have to be born again (see note 2 at Jn. 3:3, p. 48).

g Gk.-"peritome"- circumcision (the rite, the condition, or the people) see ref b, this heading 1 Cor. 7:18-19 Gal. 5:6 6:15

h Gk.-"semeion"- an indication Dict.- something that suggests the presence or existence of a fact, condition, or quality not immediately evident; an indication- Ex. 31:13, 17 2 Cor. 1:22

i Gk.-"sphragis"- a signet; by impl. the stamp impressed (as a mark of privacy or genuineness); Dict.- something that serves to authenticate, confirm, or attest- Eph. 1:13 4:30

j Rom. 4:13 3:22 9:30 10:6 Gal. 5:5 Phil. 3:9 Heb. 11:7 2 Pet. 1:1

k Gk.-"pater"- the founder of a race or tribe; forefather; the author of a family or society of persons animated by the same spirit as himself; one who has infused his own spirit into others (Thayer)- Rom. 3:16-18 Gal. 3:7, 29

l Rom. 9:6-7 Mt. 3:9 Gal. 4:22-31

m Gk.-"stoicheo"- from Gk.-"steicho"- to march in (military) rank (to range in regular line; keep step); i.e. (fig.) to conform to virtue and piety Trans.- walk (orderly)

n Gk.-"ichnos"- from Gk.-"ikneomai"- to arrive; a track; Trans.- step

ROMANS

JUSTIFICATION IS BY FAITH APART FROM LAW

CHAPTER 4

13 For the promise,[a] that he should be the heir[b] of the world,[1c] *was* not to Abraham,[d] or to his seed,[e] through the law, but through the righteousness[f] of faith.[g]

14 For if they which are of the law *be* heirs,[b] faith is made void,[2h] and the promise[a] made of none effect:[i]

15 Because the law worketh[3j] wrath:[k] for where no law is, *there is* no transgression.[l]

16 Therefore *it is* of faith,[m] that *it might be* by grace;[n] to the end[o] the promise might be sure[p] to all[4] the seed; not to that only which is of the law, but to that also which is of the faith of Abraham; who is the father[5q] of us all,

a Gen. 12:3
15:4-5
17:4-5
22:15-18
Heb. 6:13-19
b Gk.-"klerono-mos"- a sharer by lot; i.e. an inheritor; by impl. a possessor
Dict.- to come into possession of; possess
c Gk.-"kosmos"- orderly arrangement; i.e. decoration; by impl. the world (in a wide or narrow sense, including its inhabitants); being "heir of the world" is probably referring to all people and all nations of the earth
d Gk.-"Abraam"- the Hebrew patriarch
Heb.-"Abraham"- father of a multitude-
Gen. 17:5
e Gk.-"sperma"- something sown; i.e. seed (including the male sperm; by impl. offspring; spec. a remnant)
see note 10 at Jn. 8:33, p. 232
f Gk.-"dikaiosune"- equity (of character or act); justification;
Trans.- righteousness

g Gk.-"pistis"- persuasion; i.e. credence; mor. conviction (of religious truth, or the truthfulness of God or a religious teacher); esp. reliance upon Christ for salvation
see note 2 at Lk. 1:6, p. 6
see notes 21-22 at Jn. 8:56-57, p. 234
see note 3 at Lk. 10:29, p. 253
Rom. 3:22
9:30
10:6
Gal. 5:5
Phil. 3:9
h Gk.-"kenoo"- to make empty; i.e. to abase; neutralize; falsify-
Rom. 3:31
4:16
Gal. 2:21
3:18-24
5:4
Phil. 3:9
Heb. 7:19
i Gk.-"katargeo"- to be (render) entirely idle (useless)
j Gk.-"katergazomai"- to work fully; i.e. accomplish
k Gk.-"orge"- desire; i.e. violent passion; by impl. punishment-
Dt. 27:26
continued on center column

References continued from column 4

Dt. 29:20-28
2 Ki. 22:13
Rom. 3:19-20
5:13, 20
7:7-11
Jn. 3:36
1 Cor. 15:56
2 Cor. 3:7-9
Gal. 3:10, 19
1 Jn. 3:4
see note 4 at Jn. 3:36, p. 52
see note 4 at Acts 12:23, p. 573
l Gk.-"parabasis"- violation-
Rom. 5:13
m Rom. 3:24-26
5:1
Gal. 3:7-12, 22
see ref. g, this page
n see note 5 at Rom. 1:5, p. 655
see note 5 at Acts 20:24, p. 618
Eph. 2:5, 8
Ti. 3:7
o Dict.- a result; outcome
p Gk.-"bebaios"- stable; Trans. firm; of force; stedfast; sure
q Rom. 4:1, 11-12
4:17-18
Gal. 3:7

Footnotes for Romans 4:13-16

1 (Rom. 4:13) There is no Old Testament scripture that states in these words that Abraham would be heir of the world. The closest scriptures would be when the Lord told Abram that all the families of the earth would be blessed through him (Gen. 12:3) and that he had made Abraham the father of many nations (Gen. 17:4-5).

The Jews had interpreted God's promises to Abraham as being to his physical descendants only. However, this wording of the Old Testament promises to Abraham by the apostle Paul removed any doubt about the Jews being the only ones to be blessed through God's covenant with Abraham. Abraham's true seed is anyone of any nation or language who places faith in Christ as his Savior.

2 (Rom. 4:14) We are either justified by faith in our works without faith in Christ, or we are justified by faith in Christ without faith in our works, but not a combination of the two (Rom. 11:6). Trusting in our own goodness as the reason that God would grant us salvation neutralizes faith and renders God's promise to Abraham useless.

There are Christians who have put their faith in Christ for their eternal salvation, but then fall back into the deception that God is going to bless them and use them based on their performance. This is what happened to the Galatians. Paul told them that Christ had become of no benefit to them if they were trusting in what they did to be justified with God (Gal. 5:4). Likewise today, many Christians do not experience the full effect of their salvation because they are making faith void by trusting in their own goodness.

3 (Rom. 4:15) The law of God released the wrath of God (see note 4 at Jn. 3:36, p. 52). Without the law there was no wrath because without the law there was no transgression. First John 3:4 says, *"Whosoever committeth sin transgresseth also the law: for sin is the transgression of the law."* Therefore, before the law of God was given, men's sins were not being held against them (see note 2 at Rom. 5:13, p. 685).

This is why Abraham was not killed for marrying his half sister (see note 5 at Rom. 4:3, p. 675) and Jacob for marrying his wife's sister (Lev. 18:18). God had not given the law concerning these things yet and, therefore, there was no willful transgression on these men's part. So, when the law of God was introduced, sin revived and we died (see notes 3-4 at Rom. 7:9, pp. 696-697). The law produced death by releasing God's wrath against our sins (see note 4 at Rom. 3:19, p. 671).

Anyone who seeks to keep the law of God for the purpose of being justified in God's sight, will also release the wrath of God in their life. Praise God for Jesus who brought us out from under the law and put us under grace (Rom. 6:14).

4 (Rom. 4:16) Paul makes it very clear here that the seed of Abraham included more than his physical descendants. Jesus taught on this (see note 10 at Jn. 8:33, p. 232; see note 14 at Jn. 8:37, p. 232; see note 16 at Jn. 8:41, p. 232) and Paul mentions this a number of times (Rom. 2:28-29; 4:11-12, 16; ch. 9; Gal. 3).

5 (Rom. 4:16) Since God made salvation available on the basis of faith in what He did, then everyone can be saved. If He would have made our holiness the basis of salvation, then no one could have been saved, *"for all have sinned and come short of the glory of God"* (see note 6 at Rom. 3:23, p. 672).

ROMANS

JUSTIFICATION IS BY FAITH APART FROM LAW (continued)

r Gk.-"ethnos"- a race; i.e. a tribe; spec. a foreign (non-Jewish) one; usually by impl. pagan see note 14 at Jn. 8:37, p. 232
s i.e. in the presence of
t Gk.-"pisteuo"- to have faith (in, upon, or with respect to, a person or thing); to entrust; esp. one's spiritual well being to Christ; Trans. commit (to trust); put in trust with; believe see note 1 at Jn. 20:25, p. 498 see note 4 at Jn. 20:29, p. 498 see note 2 at Mt. 28:17, p. 504 see note 2 at Acts 5:19, p. 530
u see note 1 at Jn. 1:1, p. 2

CHAPTER 4

17 *(As it is written, I have made thee
a father[q] of many nations,)[r] before[s] him
whom he believed,[t] *even* God,[u] who
quickeneth[v] the dead[w] and calleth[x] those
things which be not as though they were.[6]
18 *Who against hope[y] believed[7t] in
hope,[y] that he might become the father[q] of
many nations,[r] according to that which was
spoken, So shall thy seed be.[8]

PARALLEL SCRIPTURES FOR ROMANS 4:17

GENESIS 17:4-5

4 As for me, behold, my covenant is with thee, and thou shalt be a father of many nations.

5 Neither shall thy name any more be called Abram, but thy name shall be Abraham; for a father of many nations have I made thee.

PARALLEL SCRIPTURE FOR ROMANS 4:18

GENESIS 15:5

5 And he brought him forth abroad, and said, Look now toward heaven, and tell the stars, if thou be able to number them: and he said unto him, So shall thy seed be.

v Gk.-"zoopoieo"- to revitalize; Trans. make alive; give life; quicken- Jn. 5:21, 25 6:63 Rom. 8:11 1 Cor. 15:45 Eph. 2:1-5 1 Tim. 6:13
w Gk.-"nekros"- (from -"nekus"- (a corpse) dead (lit. or fig.)
x Dict.- to cry out in a loud tone; announce; proclaim
y Gk.-"elpis"- (from -"elpo"- to anticipate, usually with pleasure) expectation or confidence- Rom. 8:24 5:5 Prov. 13:12

Footnotes for Romans 4:17-18

6 (Rom. 4:17) The phrase, *"and calleth those things which be not as though they were"* is referring to the instance Paul had just cited when God changed Abram's name to Abraham (Gen. 17:5). The name Abram meant "high father." The name Abraham meant "father of a multitude." The Lord changed Abram's name to Abraham one year before the birth of Isaac, thus confessing that Abraham was the father of a multitude before it happened in the physical.

This illustrates God's faith. God says things are so before there is physical proof that they are so. The same thing was done at creation (Gen. 1). God spoke everything into existence and then it was so. He spoke light into existence and then four days later created a source for that light to come from (Gen. 1:3 with 14-19).

God has given us the power to create with faith-filled words (Prov. 18:20-21; see note 4 at Mk. 11:14, p. 363; see note 4 at Mk. 11:23, p. 367). If we are going to operate in God's kind of faith, we have to learn to call those things which are not as though they were.

7 (Rom. 4:18) There was no hope in the natural for Abraham or his wife Sarah. They were both as good as dead when it came to having children at their age. Therefore, they rejected the natural and believed God with a supernatural hope. There is a natural hope which everyone has and there is a supernatural hope that is imparted by God (1 Cor. 13:13). To receive miracles, we have to reject the limitations of natural hope and press on to obtain God's supernatural hope through faith.

8 (Rom. 4:18) Abraham's faith was based on God's Word. Every word of God is powerful and contains the faith of God to bring that word to pass (see note 4 at Mt. 14:29, p. 178). If we will only consider God's Word, then we will only believe (Rom. 8:6; see note 9 at Rom. 4:19, p. 680).

ROMANS

JUSTIFICATION IS BY FAITH APART FROM LAW (continued)

CHAPTER 4

19 And being not weak[a] in faith,[9] he
considered[b] not his own body now dead,[c]
when he was about an hundred years old,
neither yet the deadness[d] of Sarah's[e] womb:
20 He staggered[f] not at the promise of
God through unbelief;[10g] but was strong[11h]
in faith,[i] giving[12] glory[j] to God;
21 And being fully[13] persuaded[k] that,
what he had promised,[l] he was able[14m] also
to perform.[n]
22 And therefore[o] it was imputed[p] to
him for righteousness.
23 Now it was not written for his sake
alone,[q] that it was imputed[p] to him;[15]
24 But for us also, to whom it shall be
imputed,[p] if we believe on him that raised[r]
up Jesus our Lord[s] from the dead;
25 Who was delivered[t] for our offences,
and was raised[r] again for our justification.[u]

References continued from column 4

Rom. 5:6-8
8:3, 32
Isa. 53:5-6, 10-12
2 Cor. 5:21
Gal. 1:4
Eph. 5:2
Ti. 2:14
Heb. 9:28

u Gk.-"dikaiosis"- acquittal; from - "dikaioo"- to render just or innocent
see note 13 at Acts 13:39, p. 579
Rom. 3:22
9:30
10:6
Gal. 5:5
Phil. 3:9
Heb. 10:14

Footnotes for Romans 4:19-25

9 (Rom. 4:19) This verse is telling us how Abraham kept from being weak in faith. The key is what he focused his attention on.

Some translations and many commentators turn this verse around to say the opposite of what the KJV says. For instance, the NIV says, *"without weakening in his faith, he faced the fact that his body was as good as dead,"* etc. However, that type of reasoning is missing one of the great scriptural keys to strong faith.

The word consider is defined as "1. to deliberate upon; examine; study; 4. To take into account; make allowance for; 5. To have regard for; pay attention to." (New American Heritage Dict.) The Greek word that was used is "katanoeo" which simply means "to observe fully."

Therefore, we can see that Abraham **did not** deliberate upon, examine, or study the age of himself and Sarah and the impact that would have on the promise God had given him. He **did not** take those things into account or make any allowance for them. That was not what he paid attention to.

That is amazing, and that is exactly the reason many of us would not be able to receive the same miracle. We consider every negative thing that looks contrary to God's promises and then try to overcome the fear and unbelief that comes through those thoughts with our faith (see note 3 at Mt. 17:20, p. 211). That's not the way Abraham was strong in faith.

Abram was 75 years old when the Lord first promised him that he would have a child and that all the nations of the earth would be blessed through him (Gen. 12:1-4). He was 99 years old in this instance which Paul is citing (Gen. 17:1) and Sarah was 90 years old (Gen. 17:17). Yet, he didn't even take into account the impossibility of what God had promised him.

It is true that Abraham was strong in faith (v. 20) but the thing that made him strong in faith is the fact that he kept his mind stayed on God's promise and equally important is that he kept his mind off anything which would have been contrary to God's promise. Many people desire the same strong faith that Abraham had, but very few desire to control their thinking the way Abraham did.

Faith is a direct result of what we think on. If you think on God's Word, faith comes (Rom. 8:6; 10:17). If you think on other things, unbelief and fear come (Rom. 8:6; see notes in ref. b, this verse). If you want the faith of Abraham working in you, then think the way he thought and never consider anything except God's Word and you will be strong in faith.

10 (Rom. 4:20) From the context of this statement, we can see that the unbelief that Abraham refused to consider was the unbelief that would have come through thinking on the natural facts (see note 9 at v. 19). Many people don't perceive facts as generating unbelief. **We have been led to believe that we have to consider all the facts to make a proper decision, but that's not so with God's Word.**

When we have clear direction from God's Word, we shouldn't consider anything else. Considering "facts" contrary to God's promises will make us stagger in our faith.

11 (Rom. 4:20) Jesus had equated praise with strength (see note 3 at Mt. 21:14, p. 364). Here we see that this is one thing that made Abraham strong in faith. Praise keeps our minds stayed on God and what He is doing. You cannot praise God and keep your mind on the problem. You will fall into complaining every time. This is why praise makes us strong in faith (see note 9 at v. 19, above).

12 (Rom. 4:20) A person who believes the promises of God brings glory to God. Conversely, a person who disbelieves the promises of God dishonors God.

13 (Rom. 4:21) Notice that Abraham wasn't just persuaded. He was **fully** persuaded. Many people have been persuaded that the promises of God are true but they stop short of meditating on God's Word until they become fully persuaded. Strong faith belongs to those who continue in God's Word until all doubt is removed.

14 (Rom. 4:21) This is so obvious that it should go without saying, but the truth is, we really do doubt that God can perform His promises to us. How could this be? The answer lies in the way God made our hearts.

Whatever we focus our attention on is what our heart will believe and whatever we neglect is what our heart will disbelieve (see note 10 at Mk. 6:52, p. 179). If we allow ourselves to meditate on our problems and all the reasons why it looks impossible for God to move in our situations then we will believe that our problems are bigger than God. However, when we keep our minds stayed on the promises of God, nothing is too difficult for God (Jer. 32:17,27).

15 (Rom. 4:23) In verses 23-24, Paul applies all these truths he has discussed about Abraham to us. God is no respecter of persons (Rom. 2:11). If He justified Abraham by faith, He will do the same for us.

a Gk.-"astheneo"- to be feeble (in any sense); Trans. be diseased; impotent folk; sick; weak
see note 3 at Lk. 17:5, p. 305
see note 3 at Mt. 17:20, p. 211
see note 1 at Lk. 8:45, p. 157
see note 8 at Mk. 11:24, p. 367
see note 1 at Jn. 20:25, p. 498
see note 4 at Jn. 20:29, p. 498

b Mt. 6:22-23
2 Cor. 3:18
Heb. 3:1
12:2-3
see note 39 at Mt. 6:22, p. 81
see notes 40-41 at Mt. 6:23, p. 81

c Gk.-"nekroo"- worn out; deprived of power; destroy the strength of; to make dead (Thayer)

d Gk.-"nekrosis"- decease; fig. impotency

e Heb.-"sarah"- lady; princess; queen

f Gk.-"diakrino"- to be divided in one's own mind; to waiver (RWP)

g Gk.-"apistia"- faithlessness; i.e. disbelief; unfaithfulness (disobedience)
see note 3 at Mt. 17:20, p. 211
see note 2 at Mk. 6:5, p. 163
see note 2 at Jn. 20:25, p. 498
see note 2 at Lk. 8:51, p. 159
see notes 2-3 at Mk. 8:23, p. 200
see note 2 at Mt. 17:20, p. 210
see note 14 at Acts 12:16, p. 572

h Gk.-"endunamoo"- to empower
Trans. enable; strength; be strong-
Dan. 11:32
Hag. 2:4
1 Cor. 16:13
continued on column 4

continued from column 1
2 Cor. 12:10
Eph. 6:10
2 Tim. 2:1
see note 3 at Lk. 17:5, p. 305

i see ref. g at Rom. 4:13, p. 678
see note 9 at Rom. 4:19, this page

j Gk.-"doxa"- glory in a wide application; Trans. dignity; glory; honor; praise; worship
see note 4 at Mt. 4:9, p. 38
see note 6 at Mk. 14:4, p. 351
see note 3 at Mt. 21:16, p. 364
see note 4 at Acts 16:25, p. 596
see note 5 at Acts 16:26, p. 596

k Heb. 11:13
Rom 8:38
2 Tim. 1:12

l Heb. 6:13-19

m Gk.-"dunatos"- powerful or capable-
Gen. 18:14
Jer. 32:17, 27
Mt. 19:26
Lk. 1:37, 45

n Dict.- to begin and carry through to completion; do; to fulfill a promise

o Gk.-"dio"- through which thing; i.e. consequently; Trans. for which cause; therefore; wherefore

p see note 6 at Rom. 4:3, p. 675

q Rom. 15:4
1 Cor. 9:10
10:6, 11
2 Tim. 3:16-17

r see note 3 at Mk. 16:6, p. 484
see note 1 at Acts 1:3, p. 509

s see note 3 at Lk. 1:43, p. 12

t Gk.-"paradidomi"- to surrender; i.e. yield up; intrust; transmit-
continued on center column

ROMANS

THE BENEFITS OF JUSTIFICATION BY FAITH

CHAPTER 5

THEREFORE[1] being justified[a] by faith,[b] we have peace[2c] with God through[d] our Lord[e] Jesus[f] Christ:[g]

2 By whom[h] also we have access[3] by faith[i] into this grace[j] wherein we stand,[k] and rejoice[4] in hope[5l] of the glory[m] of God.[6]

PARALLEL SCRIPTURE FOR ROMANS 5:1

ISAIAH 32:17

17 And the work of righteousness shall be peace; and the effect of righteousness quietness and assurance for ever.

a Gk.-"dikaioo"- to render (i.e. show or regard as) just or innocent; Trans. justify- 37 times justifier- once free- once be righteous- once see note 2 at Lk. 9:55, p. 245 see note 1 at Lk. 16:16, p. 301 see note 5 at Jn. 11:52, p. 312 see note 4 at Rom. 3:19, p. 671 see note 1 at Rom. 3:21, p. 672 Rom 5:9, 18

b Rom. 1:17 3:22, 26-28, 30 4:5, 24-25 9:30 10:10 Jn. 3:16-18 5:24 Acts 13:38-39 Gal. 2:16 3:11-14 Phil. 3:9

c Gk.-"eirene"- (from a primary (prim.) verb - "eiro"- to join;) peace (lit. or fig.); by impl. prosperity Trans. peace- 88 times quietness- once rest- once at one again- once see notes 38-39 at Jn. 14:27, p. 434 see notes 90-91 at Jn. 16:33, p. 442 see note 2 at Lk. 24:38, p. 496 Rom. 10:15 14:17 Ps. 85:8-10 Isa. 55:12 Lk. 10:5-6 Jn. 14:27 16:33 Acts 10:36 Eph. 2:14-17 Col. 1:20 3:15

d Gk.-"dia"- a prim. preposition (prep.) denoting the channel of an act- Rom. 6:23 Jn. 20:31 Eph. 2:7

e Gk.-"kurios"- (from -"kuros"- supremacy) supreme in authority; i.e. controller; by impl. Mr. (as a respectful title); Trans. lord- 56 times Lord- 663 times master- 12 times Master- 2 times sir- 13 times owner- once see note 3 at Lk. 1:43, p. 12

f see note 2 at Acts 8:5, p. 545

g see note 5 at Jn. 1:41, p. 40 see note 2 at Mt. 16:16, p. 202

h Jn. 14:6 Eph. 2:18 3:12

i Gk.-"pistis"- persuasion; i.e. credence; moral conviction (of religious truth, of a truthfulness of God or a religious teacher); esp. reliance upon Christ for salvation; constancy in such profession; by extension the system of religious (Gospel) truth itself Trans. faith- 239 times assurance-1 time belief- 1 time fidelity- 1 time them that believe-1 time

continued on center column

References continued from column 4

He which believeth- once (Young) see note 2 at Mt. 21:22, p. 367 see note 3 at Jn. 14:1, p. 431 see note 1 at Jn. 20:25, p. 498 see note 4 at Jn. 20:29, p. 498

j see note 5 at Rom. 1:5, p. 655

k Dict.- to remain unchanged; to be consistent 1 Cor. 15:1 Eph. 6:13-14

l Gk.-"elpis"- (from -"elpo"- to anticipate, usually with pleasure) expectation or confidence Trans. hope- 53 times faith- once see note 6 at Rom. 3:23, p. 672 Rom. 8:24 12:12 15:4, 13 Heb. 11:1

m see note 6 at Rom. 3:23, p. 672 Rom. 2:7 3:23 8:17-18 Ex. 33:18-20 2 Cor. 3:18 4:17 Col. 1:27 Rev. 21:23

Footnotes for Romans 5:1-2

1 (Rom. 5:1) The word "therefore" means, "for that reason; consequently; hence." Paul had just proven through the life of Abraham that justification came by faith. He then made the statement that these truths about Abraham were not written in scripture for his sake alone, but so that we could also be justified by faith (Rom. 4:23-24). So, having established justification by faith, he now moves on to some of the benefits of being justified by faith instead of works.

2 (Rom. 5:1) The first benefit of being justified by faith instead of works that Paul mentions is peace (see ref. c, this verse). **Peace can only come when we relate to God on the basis of faith in what He did for us instead of what we do for Him.** A person who is thinking that he must perform up to some standard to be accepted with God will have no peace. That puts the burden of salvation on our shoulders and we can't bear that load.

We were incapable of living holy enough to please God before we were saved and we are incapable of living holy enough to please God now that we are saved (Heb. 11:6). We got saved by faith and we have to continue to walk with God by faith (Col. 2:6). Not understanding this has caused many Christians who love God to not enjoy the peace that was provided them through faith in Jesus. This is the gospel of peace (Lk. 2:14; Rom. 10:15; Eph. 6:15).

3 (Rom. 5:2) The Greek word that was translated "access" here is the word "prosagoge" and literally means "admission." It was only used three times in the New Testament and it was translated "access" each time (here; Eph. 2:18; 3:12). Faith is our admission or ticket into the grace of God. No one is allowed in without a ticket. Our own good works won't grant us admission. God's grace can only be accessed by faith.

4 (Rom. 5:2) The Greek word that is translated "rejoice" here is the same word that is translated "glory" in the next verse and "joy" in verse 11. That Greek word is "kauchaomai" meaning "to vaunt (in a good or bad sense)." It is derived from an obsolete root word -"aucheo"- meaning "to boast." Paul was rejoicing because of the grace that had been given him and the hope of being glorified with Jesus.

Anybody could rejoice because of those good things, but Paul went on to say that he had the same rejoicing even in the midst of tribulation. Not many people rejoice during the hard times. But Paul could make this boast because he was totally convinced of the faithfulness and unconditional grace of God. Those who can't rejoice during tribulation are not convinced.

5 (Rom. 5:2) Rejoicing and hope are very closely related. We cannot rejoice in trying times if we have no hope. Therefore, hope is very important in the Christian life (see note 12 at Rom. 5:4, p. 683).

6 (Rom. 5:2) The hope that Paul is rejoicing in here is probably what he called the blessed hope in Titus 2:13. In that instance, Paul was clearly referring to the second coming of Jesus. Therefore, what Paul is probably speaking of here is the return of Jesus and becoming like Him (1 Jn. 3:1-2).

ROMANS

THE BENEFITS OF JUSTIFICATION BY FAITH (continued)

a i.e. be full of joy; exult and triumph (Amp) see note 4 at Rom. 5:2, p. 681

CHAPTER 5

3 And not only *so,*[7] but we glory[a] in tribulations[b] also:[8] knowing that tribulation[b] worketh[9] patience;[10]

b Gk.-"thlipsis"- pressures; hardships; sufferings (SH, TDNT) Trans. tribulation-21 times affliction- 17 times trouble- 3 times anguish- once persecution- once to be afflicted- once Rom. 8:35-37 Mt. 5:10-12 Lk. 6:22-23 Acts 5:41 2 Cor. 4:17 11:23-30 12:9-10 Eph. 3:13 Phil. 1:29 2:17-18 Jas. 1:2-3, 12 1 Pet. 3:14

Footnotes for Romans 5:3

7 (Rom. 5:3) Paul had just expressed the joy that he had concerning the second coming of Jesus and the glory that would be revealed in us (Rom. 8:18; see note 6 at v. 2, p. 681). Anybody can rejoice about heaven. But now Paul begins to say that he has that same rejoicing in the midst of tribulations. This is something that very few people can say and Paul is presenting this as a direct result of justification by faith.

When we are believing that God loves us because of our faith in Him and not our performance for Him, then we rejoice; not only in the good times and pleasant things, like thoughts of heaven, but also in the hard times. Our faith remains steadfast. However, those who are trusting in their own efforts will be devastated in times of trouble because they will know they are getting what they deserve and they will feel that they have to clean up their act before they can expect any help. Their attention will be on self instead of Jesus, the author and finisher of their faith (Heb. 12:2).

Paul continues this same thought on through verse 10. In verses 6-8, he illustrates how great the love of God for us was in that He died for us when we were ungodly. Then he draws a conclusion by way of comparison. If God loved us when we were His enemies, then how much more does He love us now that we are His sons. That's the reason he could rejoice even in tribulation. If God could work in his life while he was a sinner to bring him to justification, then how much more, now that he is reconciled to God, will God work whatever comes against him for his good!

8 (Rom. 5:3) People have taken these scriptures to say that God is the one who brings tribulations to accomplish these positive results in our lives. That is not what these scriptures say.

Tribulations exist, not because God creates them, but because there is a battle between the kingdom of God and the kingdom of the devil. And when we operate in faith, God can grant us such victory that we are actually better off because of the battle (see note 9 at this verse, below).

It's just like when an army goes to war. If they win, there are spoils to be gained. But if those soldiers embraced their enemy because of the spoil they were expecting to receive, they would be killed instead of blessed. First, you have to fight and win the war and then, and only then, will the spoils be available. The enemy doesn't come to be a blessing, but a blessing can be obtained from the enemy if we are victorious.

Likewise, tribulations and adversities are not blessings from God (see note 2 at Jn. 9:2, p. 237). They are attacks from the enemy intended to steal away the Word of God out of our lives (see note 5 at Mk. 4:16, p. 137). No man should say that the temptation came from God, for God is not the one who tempts any man (Jas. 1:13). However, there are spoils to be gained when we fight and win over our problems.

If problems were what perfected us, then most Christians would have been perfected long ago and those who experience the greatest problems would be the greatest Christians, but that's not the way it is. God's Word is given to make us perfect, and thoroughly furnished unto every good work (2 Tim. 3:17). God's Word does not need to be supplemented with problems to accomplish its work.

This is a pivotal point. Those who believe God has ordained the problems in their life to work some redemptive virtue will submit to those problems and therefore to Satan, the author of those problems (see note 3 at Lk. 13:16, p. 276). They have to or else, in their way of thinking, they would be rebelling at God. Yet James 4:7 tells us to submit ourselves to God and resist the devil. If Satan can reverse our thinking on this issue and get us to submit to the problems he brings into our lives, he's got us (Rom. 6:16).

Paul is simply rejoicing that even in tribulation, he had the opportunity to use, and therefore strengthen, his patience that had already been given him as a fruit of the Spirit (Gal. 5:22-23) and through the Word of God (Rom. 15:4). And as he believed that, as he stood in patience, he would gain experience that would cause him to hope even more the next time the devil attacked.

Likewise, we can rejoice in tribulation, knowing that regardless of what the devil does we will win and reap the spoils of victory.

9 (Rom. 5:3) The word "worketh" was translated from the Greek word "katergazomai" meaning "to work fully; i.e. accomplish; by implication to finish; fashion." Paul was not saying that tribulations produced patience. Patience comes from the scriptures (Rom. 15:4). But tribulations cause us to use what God has already given us through His Word and we therefore become stronger as a result (see note 8 at this verse, above).

10 (Rom. 5:3) According to the dictionary, patience is "the capacity of calm endurance." The Greek word used for patience here is "hupomone" meaning "cheerful (or hopeful) endurance; constancy." Patience is not a passive word as many people use it, but it is an active word.

Patience is actually faith; faith that is sustained over a long period of time. Patience comes from the scriptures (Rom. 15:4) just as faith does (Rom. 10:17). Patience is a fruit of the Spirit just like faith (Gal. 5:22-23). It was by faith that Moses endured (the definition of patience—Heb. 11:27). It was through faith and patience that Abraham received the promises (Heb. 6:12-15). Not just faith, but a faith that was constant over a twenty-five year period of time.

Therefore, patience is not just passively waiting on God to do something, but it is actively believing for the manifestation of God's promise against all odds, regardless of how long it takes. That kind of faith will make you perfect and complete, not wanting for any good thing (Jas. 1:4).

Patience is a by-product of hope. Romans 8:25 says, *"But if we hope for that we see not,* then *do we with patience wait for*it." When a person has hope firmly established in them, then no obstacle or length of time can keep them from enduring. That's why the scriptures produce patience, because they give us hope (Rom. 15:4).

Therefore, patience, hope, and faith are all intertwined. You can't have one without the others. A person who says he is patiently waiting on God and yet has lost his hope is deceived. Likewise, a person who isn't believing God is not operating in patience. First comes hope from a promise of God's Word. Then faith begins to give substance and evidence to those things that were hoped for (Heb. 11:1) and if time is involved before the manifestation comes, then patience does its work (Jas. 1:4).

ROMANS

THE BENEFITS OF JUSTIFICATION BY FAITH (continued)

CHAPTER 5

4 And patience, experience;[11c] and
experience,[c] hope:[12]
5 And hope[d] maketh not ashamed;[e]
because the love[f] of God is shed[g] abroad in
our hearts[h] by the Holy Ghost[i] which is
given unto us.
6 For when we were yet without[13]
strength,[j] in due time[k] Christ[l] died for the
ungodly.[m]
7 For scarcely[n] for a righteous[o] man will
one die:[14] yet peradventure[p] for a good[q]
man some would even dare to die.[r]
8 But God commendeth[s] his love toward[t]
us, in that, while we were yet sinners,[u]
Christ died for us.[15]

c the temper of the veteran as opposed to that of the raw recruit (SH)
d see ref. l at Rom. 5:2, p. 681
Ps. 71:14
Jer. 17:7-8
Phil. 1:20
2 Th. 2:16
Heb. 6:18-19
e Gk.-"kataischuno"- to shame down; i.e. disgrace or (by impl.) put to the blush; also trans. confound; dishonor
f see note 3 at Jn. 13:35, p. 425
see note 4 at Lk. 11:11, p. 256
see note 1 at Mt. 22:36, p. 382
see note 2 at Jn. 13:34, p. 425
see note 54 at Jn. 15:9, p. 436
see note 56 at Jn. 15:10, p. 436
see note 59 at Jn. 15:12, p. 436
see note 111 at Jn. 17:23, p. 446
see note 1 at Lk. 23:34, p. 475
g Gk.-"ekcheo"- (from-"cheo"- to pour) to pour forth; fig. to bestow; trans. gush (pour) out; run greedily (out); shed (abroad; forth); spill
h see note 3 at Mt. 12:34, p. 131
see note 10 at Mk. 7:21, p. 191
see note 6 at Mk. 11:23, p. 367
see notes 2-3 at Jn. 14:1, p. 431
i see note 1 at Jn. 7:15, p. 224
see note 2 at Lk. 22:24, p. 426
see notes 25-26 at Jn. 14:16, p. 432
see notes 27-29 at Jn. 14:17, p. 432
see note 30 at Jn. 14:18, p. 434
see note 31 at Jn. 14:19, p. 434
continued on column 4

continued from column 1
see note 36 at Jn. 14:26, p. 434
see note 75 at Jn. 16:7, p. 440
see note 84 at Jn. 16:14, p. 440
j Gk.-"asthenes"- weak; infirm; feeble (unable to achieve anything great; destitute of power among men; sluggish in doing right) (Thayer)
k i.e. at the right time (NASV)- Gal. 4:4
l see note 2 at Mt. 16:16, p. 202
see note 5 at Jn. 1:41, p. 40
see note 5 at Mk. 1:1, p. 30
m Gk.-"asebes"- impious; without reverence for God; not merely irreligious, but acting in contravention (i.e. to come against) of God's demands (Vine)
see note 8 at Rom. 4:5, p. 675
Rom. 11:26
Ps. 1:1
1 Tim. 1:9
Ti. 2:12
2 Pet. 2:5-6
3:7
Jude 4, 15, 18
n Gk.-"molis"- with difficulty
Dict.- 1. by a small margin; just; barely; 2. almost not; hardly; 3. assuredly not
o Gk.-"dikaios"- equitable (in character or act); by impl. innocent; holy
p Gk.-"tacha"- shortly; i.e. (fig.) possibly
Trans. perhaps- once
peradventure- once
q Dict.- having positive or desirable qualities-
2 Sam. 18:27
Ps. 112:5
Acts 11:24
continued on center column

References continued from column 4

r Rom. 16:4
2 Sam. 18:3
23:14-17
s Gk.-"sunistao"- to show; prove; establish; exhibit (Thayer)
t Dict.- in the direction of-
1 Jn. 4:9-10
u Gk.-"hamartolos"- devoted to sin; a sinner; not free from sin; preeminently sinful; esp. wicked (Thayer)

Footnotes for Romans 5:4-8

11 (Rom. 5:4) The Greek word used for "experience" here is the word "dokime" and means "approved character; the quality of being approved as a result of test and trials" (Rienecker). Sanday and Headlam also defined this word in this verse as "the temper of the veteran as opposed to that of the raw recruit." Therefore, this verse is speaking of the character that is produced as a result of having fought battles and won.

12 (Rom. 5:4) Hope by itself will never give us victory. Many people have hoped for things and yet have never realized those hopes because they never moved into faith. Faith is the victory that causes us to overcome the world (1 Jn. 5:4). Yet faith won't work without hope.

Just as a thermostat activates the power unit on an air conditioner, so hope is what activates our faith. Faith only produces what we hope for (Heb. 11:1). Therefore, hope is the first step towards faith.

"To hope is to desire, usually with confidence in the likelihood of gaining what is desired" (Dict.) So, desiring the things of God with some expectation of obtaining them is the first step in walking in faith. Once this hope is present, then faith begins to bring the desired thing into manifestation. If a delay is encountered, patience completes the work (see note 10 at v. 3, p. 682).

In context, Paul is saying that our experience "worketh" (see note 9 at v. 3, p. 682) hope. However, he also said in this same epistle (Rom. 15:4) that hope came through the scriptures. Therefore, it is to be understood that the character that is developed through tribulations just adds to the hope that we have already received through scripture.

13 (Rom. 5:6) Notice the terms that Paul uses to describe us before the transformation of the new birth. We were weak (this verse), ungodly (this verse), sinners (v. 8), and enemies (v. 10). The Lord didn't save us because we deserved it. It was an act of grace.

As great as this truth is, Paul doesn't stop here. He continues on to make a comparison that if God loved us enough to die for us when we were weak, ungodly, sinners, and enemies, then much more now that we are justified (v. 9) and reconciled (v. 10), He is willing to save us in spite of our actions.

14 (Rom. 5:7) Paul is attempting to explain the great love of God shown to us through grace. He draws on the greatest expression of love known to man, which is laying down your life for another (Jn. 15:13), to illustrate this. However, he goes a step further.

It is possible to imagine someone giving up his life for someone else. That has happened many times. But it is inconceivable that someone would sacrifice his life for his enemy. Yet that is exactly what God did (v. 10). Since this is so, how could we ever doubt God's goodness to us now? On our worst day as a Christian, we love God infinitely more than our best day as an unbeliever.

15 (Rom. 5:8) This verse is commonly quoted to illustrate the unconditional love that God has towards sinners. While that is certainly true and this verse does clearly teach that, this is not the point that Paul is making. In context, Paul is talking to Christians about the grace of God. He is making a comparison and verses nine and ten are the point of his comparison. He is using this truth in verse eight about God commending His love towards us while we were still sinners as a step to another truth.

Not viewing this verse in context has caused many people to accept salvation by grace but then come back under the deception that they have to live good enough for God to use them as a Christian. While realizing one truth, they completely missed the whole point of what Paul was saying. These verses, taken in context, conclusively prove that we begin and continue our walk with God through faith in His grace (Col. 2:6).

ROMANS

THE BENEFITS OF JUSTIFICATION BY FAITH (continued)

a Eph. 2:13
Heb. 9:14, 22
1 Jn. 1:7
b see note 7 at Acts 2:21, p. 515
see note 8 at Acts 27:20, p. 645
see note 2 at Mt. 8:17, p. 68
c Gk.-"orge"- anger; wrath; indignation; retribution; punishment (Thayer)
see note 4 at Acts 12:23, p. 573
1 Th. 1:10
d Dict.- one who manifests malice or hostility toward, or opposes the purposes or interests of another; a foe; an opponent

CHAPTER 5

9 Much more[16] then, being now justified
by his blood,[a] we shall be saved[b] from
wrath[c] through him.
10 For if, when we were enemies,[d] we
were reconciled[e] to God by the death[f] of his
Son,[g] much more,[16] being reconciled[e] we
shall be saved[b] by his life.[h]
11 And not only *so,* but we also joy[i] in
God through our Lord Jesus Christ, by
whom we have now received the
atonement.[j]

e Dict.- to reestablish friendship between; to settle or resolve; as a dispute
see note 1 at Mt. 26:2, p. 410
2 Chr. 29:24
Dan. 9:24
2 Cor. 5:18-19, & 21
Eph. 2:16
Col. 1:20-21
Heb. 2:17
f Mt. 20:28
26:28
Jn. 1:29
Rom. 4:25
1 Cor. 5:7
15:3
Gal. 1:4
1 Tim. 2:6
1 Pet. 3:18
1 Jn. 4:10
continued on center column

References continued from column 4
g see note 5 at Mk. 1:1, p. 30
see note 4 at Rom. 5:2, p. 681
h see note 6 at Jn. 10:10, p. 242
i same Gk. word as "glory" in v. 3
Ps. 32:11
149:2
Isa. 61:10
Hab. 3:17-18
Gal. 5:22
Phil. 3:1,3
4:4
1 Pet. 1:8
j Gk.-"katallage"- exchange; i.e. restoration to (the divine) favor; Trans. reconciliation- 2 times
atonement- once
reconciling- once
see ref. h, this heading

Footnotes for Romans 5:9-11

16 (Rom. 5:9,10) The phrase "much more" that is used here and in verse 10 is amazing. It would have been wonderful to think that after salvation, God continued to love us with the same love that was manifested towards us through the death of His Son. But Paul is saying that once a person is justified by grace through faith, God loves him much more. Being loved the same would be great, more would have been awesome, but much more is beyond our ability to comprehend.

Many Christians accept the love of God for the sinner. They extend love towards a drunk or adulterer as long as they are lost, but if the drunk or adulterer receives the forgiveness of God and ever commits one of those sins again, they show no mercy. They are actually believing that God loves us much less now that we are saved. We got by with things before we were saved but now we have to be holy or else.

These verses clearly teach that is not the truth. God loves us much more now than He did before our salvation. And before our salvation, He loved us so much that He died for us. He loves us even more now.

Does this mean that living a holy life is not necessary? It means that our own holiness is not a requirement. We are accepted with God by grace through faith. But a person who is truly born again has had a change of heart. He wants to live holy (1 Jn. 3:3). However, we all fail to be as holy as we want to be. When we fail, this knowledge that God loves us more now than when He sent His Son to die for us, will keep us from being condemned and draw us back to serving God.

SIN AND DEATH CAME BY ADAM

a Rom. 5:19
Gen. 3:6
b see note 8 at Jn. 5:14, p. 96
see note 9 at Rom. 5:21, p. 687
see note 2 at Jn. 9:2, p. 237
see note 11 at Jn. 8:34, p. 232
see note 17 at Jn. 8:44, p. 234
see note 7 at Lk. 18:11, p. 320
c Dict.- to gain entry; to become an element in or a part of

CHAPTER 5

12 *Wherefore,[1] as by one man[a] sin[b]
entered[c] into the world, and death[d] by sin;[b]
and so death[d] passed upon all men,[a] for that
all have sinned:[e]

d see note 9 at Jn. 11:12, p. 308
see note 10 at Jn. 11:14, p. 308
see note 3 at Mk. 16:6, p. 484
Rom. 6:23
Gen. 2:17
3:19, 22-24
Ezek. 18:4
1 Cor. 15:21
Jas. 1:15
Rev. 20:14-15
e Rom. 3:23
Jas. 3:2
1 Jn. 1:8-10

PARALLEL SCRIPTURES FOR ROMANS 5:12

1 JOHN 1:8-10

8 *If we say that we have no sin, we deceive ourselves, and the truth is not in us.*

9 *If we confess our sins, he is faithful and just to forgive us* our *sins, and to cleanse us from all unrighteousness.*

10 *If we say that we have not sinned, we make him a liar, and his word is not in us.*

Footnotes for Romans 5:12

1 (Rom. 5:12) Paul had already made a strong case for salvation by grace through faith. He used a comparison which illustrated just how great God's grace is (see note 14 at Rom. 5:7, p. 683). He now uses another comparison to make this same point. He begins making this point in this verse but inserts a parenthetical phrase in verses 13-17. Therefore, to get the complete thought Paul is bringing it helps to skip from verse 12 to verse 18.

He is saying that in the same way that we inherited the sin nature independent of our actions, we also inherit God's righteous nature, not based on our actions, through the new birth. The reasoning is that if we became sinners through what one man did, then we can also become righteous through one man, the Lord Jesus Christ.

ROMANS

SIN AND DEATH CAME BY ADAM (continued)

f Dict.- up to the time of; before
g i.e. the Mosiac law
h Gen. 4:7-11 6:5-6, 11 13:13 19:32, 36
i see note 13 at Jn. 9:41, p. 240
j Rom. 4:15 1 Cor. 15:56 1 Jn. 3:4
k Dict.- none the less; however

CHAPTER 5

13 *(For[2] until[f] the law[g] sin[b] was in the world:[h] but sin[b] is not imputed[i] when there is no law.[j]

14 Nevertheless[k] death reigned[l] from Adam to Moses, even over them that had not sinned after the similitude[4m] of Adam's transgression,[n] who is the figure[5] of him that was to come.

l Gk.-"basileuo"- to rule Dict.- the exercise of sovereign power; dominance or widespread influence; to be predominant or prevalent- Rom. 5:17, 21
m Gk.-"homoioma"- resemblance
n Gk.-"parabasis"- violation; from - "parabaino"- to go contrary to; i.e. violate a command

PARALLEL SCRIPTURE FOR ROMANS 5:13

2 CORINTHIANS 5:19

19 To wit, that God was in Christ, reconciling the world unto himself, not imputing their trespasses unto them; and hath committed unto us the word of reconciliation.

Footnotes for Romans 5:13-14

2 (Rom. 5:13) Verses 13-17 are a parenthetical phrase. In verse 12, Paul begins likening imputed righteousness to imputed sin. He interrupts that thought to briefly explain how God dealt with the sin nature of man from the time of Adam until the time of the law of Moses. Therefore, the point that Paul is making can be received by skipping directly from verse 12 to 18. However, some very important information is revealed in this parenthetical phrase.

Paul said that until the time that the law was given, sin was not imputed unto men. As explained in note 6 at Romans 4:3, page 675, the most used Greek word for impute is "logizomai" which is an accounting term meaning that God was not entering men's sins in the account book. In this instance, there is a different Greek word used ("ellogeo"- used only one other time in N.T.—Phile. 18) but it has virtually the same meaning. This is a radical statement.

Most people have interpreted God's dealings with man after the sin of Adam to be immediate rejection and banishment from His presence. In other words, an immediate imputing of man's sins. However, Paul is stating just the opposite. God was not holding men's sins against them until the time that the law of Moses was given.

With this in mind, it should change the way we think about God's dealings with man between the fall and the giving of the law. Adam and Eve were not driven from the Garden of Eden because God could not stand them in His presence anymore. God's dealings with Adam and Eve and their children in Genesis 4 prove His presence was still with them. The reason He drove them from Eden is clearly stated in Genesis 3:22-23. It was to keep them from eating of the tree of life and living forever.

Instead of this being a punitive act, it was actually an act of mercy. It would have been terrible for man to live forever in a sinful body, subject to all the emotions and diseases that sin brings. God had a better plan through Jesus.

In accordance with what Paul was revealing here, God was merciful to the first murderer (Gen. 4:9-15), even to the point of placing a mark on his forehead and promising vengeance if anyone tried to kill him. In contrast, once the law was given, the first man to break the ordinance of the Sabbath was stoned to death for picking up sticks (Num. 15:32-36). That doesn't seem equitable. But the answer is that before the law God was not imputing men's sins unto them as He was after the giving of the law (see note 3 at v. 14, below).

It would appear that the destruction of Sodom and Gomorrah and the flood of Noah were two notable exceptions to this. Actually, these were not exceptions. While these two acts of judgment were punitive on the individuals who received the judgment, they were actually acts of mercy on the human race as a whole. In the same way as a limb or organ will sometimes be sacrificed to save a life, so God had to destroy these sinners to continue His mercy on the human race. The people in Noah's day and the inhabitants of Sodom and Gomorrah were so vile that they were like a cancer that had to be killed.

So, for the first 2,000 years after man's fall (approximate time between fall and the giving of the law) God was not holding men's sins against them. That is why Abram was not killed for marrying his half sister and Jacob for marrying his wife's sister (see note 3 at Rom. 4:15, p. 678).

Therefore, we can see that God's immediate reaction to man's sin was mercy and not judgment. It was over 2,000 years before God began to impute man's sins unto them and according to Galatians 3:19, 23-24, that was only a temporary way of dealing with sin until Jesus could come. Through Jesus, God is once again reconciling the world unto Himself, not imputing men's sins unto them (2 Cor. 5:19).

3 (Rom. 5:14) If God was not bringing judgment upon man's sins until the time of the law of Moses (see note 2 at v. 13, above), then why were men still dying? Isn't death the wage of sin (Rom. 6:23)? Why were men still dying if their sins weren't being counted against them?

Sin has a twofold effect. It is not only a transgression against God, worthy of His judgment, but it is also the inroad of Satan into our lives. Romans 6:16 says, *"Know ye not, that to whom ye yield yourselves servants to obey, his servants ye are to whom ye obey; whether of sin unto death, or of obedience unto righteousness?"* If we yield to sin, we also submit ourselves to Satan, the author of that sin.

This is why men were still dying even though God was not bringing His judgment on their sins. Satan was the one who had the power of death (Heb. 2:14), and it was Satan through sin who was causing men to die. As sin multiplied on the earth, the life span of man decreased, not because of God's judgment, but because of the effects of sin on the human race.

Therefore, we can see that even when God doesn't judge sin, sin is still deadly. This is why the New Testament believer should resist sin. God doesn't bring judgment on His children for their sins (see note 11 at Rom. 4:8, p. 676) but Satan will. The Christian doesn't live holy in order to avoid God's judgment, but so that our enemy won't have any access to us.

4 (Rom. 5:14) The people from Adam to Moses had not sinned in the same way that Adam had because they didn't have a direct commandment to violate as Adam did. They were living under their own conscience, which was enough to make them guilty (see note 2 at Rom. 1:18, p. 659). However, it was not until the time that God revealed the commandments through Moses that man once again began to violate direct commands of God (Rom. 4:15).

5 (Rom. 5:14) The Greek word translated "figure" here is "tupos" which means "a type; figure; pattern" (W.E. Vine). Paul is saying that Adam was a type of Jesus in the sense that in the same way sin entered the world through one man, so righteousness entered the world through one man, Jesus.

ROMANS

THE RESULTS OF BEING "IN ADAM" OR "IN CHRIST" CONTRASTED

CHAPTER 5

15 But[1] not as the offence,[a] so also[2] *is* the free gift.[3b] For if through the offence[a] of one[c] many[d] be dead,[e] much more[f] the grace[g] of God,[h] and the gift by grace,[g] *which is* by one man, Jesus[i] Christ,[j] hath abounded[k] unto many.[d]
16 And not as *it was* by one that sinned, *so is* the gift:[l] for the judgment *was* by one[4] to condemnation, but the free gift *is* of many offences unto justification.[m]
17 For if by one man's offence[a] death reigned[n] by one;[5] much more[f] they which receive[o] abundance[p] of grace[g] and of the gift of righteousness[q] shall reign[r] in life[s] by one, Jesus[i] Christ.[j])
18 Therefore[t] as by the offence[a] of one[u] *judgment*[v] *came* upon all[w] men[x] to condemnation;[y] even so[z] by the righteousness[aa] of one[bb] *the free gift came* upon all[cc] men unto justification[dd] of life.[ee]

a Gk.-"paraptoma"- a side-slip; i.e. error or transgression; Trans. fall; fault; sin; trespass; offence
b Gk.-"charisma"- a gift of grace; a gift involving grace on the part of God as the donor (Vine) see note 5 at Rom. 1:5, p. 655 Rom. 5:16-17 Jn. 4:10 3:16 But far greater is the gift than was the transgression (Con). But God's act of grace is out of all proportion to Adam's wrongdoing (NEB).
c i.e. Adam
d Dict.- a large, indefinite number of persons; the masses
e Rom. 5:12, 18, 21 Dan. 12:2 Mt. 20:28 26:28 Gen. 2:17 Ezek. 18:20 Rom. 6:23 1 Cor. 15:21-22 Jas. 1:15 Rev. 21:8
f Gk.-"mallon"- more (in a greater degree) or rather; Dict.- something that exceeds or surpasses expectation; to or in a greater extent or degree
g Gk.-"charis"- favour; kindness which bestows upon one what he has not deserved (Thayer) see note 5 at Rom. 1:5, p. 655 see note 1 at Lk. 16:16, p. 301 see note 5 at Acts 20:24, p. 618 Rom. 4:4 11:5-6

continued on column 4

continued from column 1
1 Cor. 15:10 Eph. 1:5-7 2:8 4:7
h see note 1 at Jn. 1:1, p. 2
i see note 2 at Acts 8:5, p. 545
j see note 2 at Mt. 16:16, p. 202 see note 5 at Jn. 1:41, p. 40 see note 5 at Mk. 1:1, p. 30
k Gk.-"perisseuo"- a thing comes in abundance or overflows, unto one; something falls to the lot of one in large measure; i.e. righteousness (Thayer)- Rom. 5:17, 20
l and the effect of the gift of God was greater than the effect of the offence of Adam (Lam)
m Judgment arose from one (i.e. Adam's) transgression that resulted in man's condemnation and punishment; on the other hand the gift of righteousness arose in the face of many transgressions resulting in justification see ref. dd, this heading see note 21 at Jn. 8:56, p. 234 see note 22 at Jn. 8:57, p. 234 see note 1 at Lk. 10:28, p. 253 see note 3 at Lk. 10:29, p. 253 see note 5 at Jn. 11:52, p. 312 Isa. 44:22 Acts 13:38-39 1 Cor. 6:9-11
n Gk.-"basileuo"- to rule; Trans. king; reign. The sin of this one man, Adam, caused

continued on center column

References continued from column 4
death to be king over all (Tay).
o Gk.-"lambano"- to take; to get hold of
p Dict.- a great quantity; plentiful amount; fullness to overflowing- Jn. 10:10 1 Tim. 1:14
q Gk.-"dikaiosune"- equity (of character or act); justification see ref. m, this heading Gen. 15:6 Ps. 32:2 Jer. 23:6 Acts 13:39 Rom. 3:22 4:5-8 9:30 1 Cor. 1:30 2 Cor. 5:21 Gal. 3:8, 24 Phil. 3:9 Ti. 3:7
r Dict.- the exercise of sovereign power; dominance or widespread influence see ref. n, this heading
s see note 6 at Jn. 10:10, p. 242
t Dict.- for that reason; consequently; hence
u i.e. Adam
v Dict.- a judicial decision
w Dict.- each and every one Rom. 5:12, 15, 19
x Gk.-"anthropos"- manfaced; i.e. a human being
y Gk.-"katakrima"- an adverse sentence (the verdict); Dict.- to pronounce judgment against; to sentence; to doom
z Gk.-"houto"- in this way (referring to what precedes or follows).
aa Gk.-"dikaioma"- an equitable deed; the righteous act of Christ in his giving himself up to death; opposed to the first sin of Adam (Strong; Thayer)
bb i.e. Jesus Christ
cc Jn. 12:32 1 Cor. 15:22 1 Tim. 2:4-6 Heb. 2:9 see ref. w, this heading
dd Gk.-"dikaiosis"- the act of God's declaring men free from guilt and acceptable to him; adjudging to be righteous (Thayer) see ref. m, this heading see note 2 at Lk. 1:6, p. 6 Rom. 3:22 9:30 10:6 Gal. 5:5 Phil. 3:9 Heb. 10:14
ee righteousness which bring life (TCNT) so through one righteous act there is for all men a justified life (Ber)

Footnotes Romans 5:15-18

1 (Rom. 5:15) Paul proceeds to make a series of comparisons about imputed righteousness through Christ being like imputed sin (see note 9 at Rom. 5:21, p. 687) through Adam. Five times Paul makes this comparison so that there should be no doubt that in the same way that all became sinners through Adam (see note 6 at v. 19, p. 687), all who put faith in Christ are made righteousness through Him.

The religious world has basically accepted this truth of inherited sin from Adam, but this truth of inherited righteousness through the new birth is still a mystery to many. Yet, Paul is saying that if one is true, then so is the other. These truths are like two sides of one coin. If you accept one truth, you have to accept the other.

2 (Rom. 5:15) These are five comparisons (vv. 15-19) but they are opposite comparisons. Adam's sin brought things from good to bad, but Jesus brought things from bad to good. The results are opposite extremes but the principle involved in both are the same. In the same way that Adam was able to pass sin (see note 9 at Rom. 5:21, p. 687) and its consequences on to his descendants, so Jesus is able to pass righteousness and all its benefits on to those who put faith in Him.

3 (Rom. 5:15) The gift by grace spoken of here and in verses 16 and 18 is clearly stated in verse 17. It is the gift of righteousness.

4 (Rom. 5:16) Adam's one sin produced a sin nature in all men (see note 9 at Rom. 5:21, p. 687) that in turn caused each person to commit individual acts of sin (see note 6 at v. 19, p. 687). However, Jesus not only dealt with the original sin that contaminated the human race, but He also dealt with each individual act of sin.

5 (Rom. 5:17) This comparison is repeated again in verse 21 (see note 9 at v. 5:21, p. 687).

ROMANS

THE RESULTS OF BEING "IN ADAM" OR "IN CHRIST" CONTRASTED (continued)

CHAPTER 5

19 For as by one man's[c] disobedience[ff] many[d] were made[gg] sinners,[6] so[7] by the obedience[hh] of one[bb] shall many[d] be made[gg] righteous.[ii]

20 Moreover[jj] the law[kk] entered,[ll] that[8] the offence might abound.[mm] But where sin[nn] abounded,[mm] grace did much more abound:[oo]

21 That as sin[nn] hath reigned unto death,[9] even so might grace[pp] reign[10] through[qq] righteousness[rr] unto eternal life[ss] by Jesus Christ our Lord.[tt]

ff Dict.- to refuse or fail to follow an order or rule- Gen. 2:17 3:6

gg Gk.-"kathistemi"- to place down (permanently) i.e. (fig.) to designate; constitute; convey

hh Gk.-"hupakoe"- attentive hearkening; i.e. (by impl.) compliance or submission

ii Gk.-"dikaios"- equitable (in character or act); by impl. innocent; holy- Isa. 53:10-12 2 Cor. 5:21 Eph. 1:6

jj Dict.- beyond what has been stated; further; besides

kk i.e. the Mosaic law

ll Gk.-"pareiserchomai"- to enter in addition; come in besides (Thayer)

mm Gk.-"pleonazo"- to do; make or be more; i.e. increase; to superabound

nn Gk.-"hamartia"- a failing to hit the mark; an error; a bad action; evil deed (Thayer)

oo Rom. 6:1 Eph. 1:7

pp Jn. 1:16-17 Ti. 2:11 Heb. 4:16 1 Pet. 5:10 see ref. g, this heading

qq Gk.-"dia"- a prim. preposition denoting the channel of an act

rr Rom. 5:17 4:13 2 Pet. 1:1 see ref. q, this heading

ss see note 3 at Jn. 3:36, p. 52 see note 94 at Jn. 17:3, p. 444 Rom. 6:23 Jn. 10:28 1 Jn. 2:25 5:11-13

tt Gk.-"kurios"- supreme in authority; i.e. (as noun) controller; by impl. Mr. (as a respectful title) Trans. God; Lord; Master; Sir see note 3 at Lk. 1:43, p. 12

Footnotes for Romans 5:19-21

6 (Rom. 5:19) Some people think it is our individual acts of sin that make us a sinner but that is not what Paul is saying in these verses. These scriptures clearly state that Adam's one sin made all men sinners (see note 17 at Jn. 8:44, p. 234). It is man's sin nature that produces sins, not his sins that produce a sin nature.

Therefore, anyone who is trying to obtain righteousness through their actions is totally missing the point. Even if an individual could stop all sins, he could not change his sin nature which he was born with. That's the reason we must be born again (see note 2 at Jn. 3:3, p. 48).

7 (Rom. 5:19) These scriptures should provide the ultimate argument for righteousness by faith to everyone who believes the scriptures to be inspired by God. Paul repeatedly says that believers are made righteous through faith in Christ, independently of their actions, in the same way that all were made sinners, not through their individual sins, but through Adam's one sin.

8 (Rom. 5:20) Paul was writing to Jewish Christians who had mistakenly thought that faith in Christ alone was not enough to produce justification. They thought one also had to fulfill a minimum standard of holiness by complying with certain commands of the Old Testament law. That's what occasioned Paul's whole teaching on justification by faith.

Paul had so conclusively proven justification by faith in Christ alone that he knew the legalistic Jews were wondering, "What was the purpose of the law then?" He states that purpose in this verse. **The law was given to make sin increase or superabound** (see ref. mm).

As explained in note 4 at Romans 3:19, page 671, the purpose of the law was not to strengthen us in our battle against sin, but to strengthen sin in its battle against us. Sin had already beat us and we didn't know it. The law brought that realization to us so that we would quit trusting in ourselves and call out to God for salvation.

So, the law made sin and all its devastating effects abound, but God's grace abounded even more. The law gave sin so much dominion against us that the grace of God is the only way out.

9 (Rom. 5:21) The sin that is being spoken of here is not the individual acts of sin that we commit, but rather the propensity for sin itself. The American Heritage dictionary defines "propensity" as "an innate inclination; tendency; bent." It is this inherited inclination to sin that Paul is speaking of.

The word "sin" is used 45 times in the book of Romans (Rom. 3:9, 20; 4:8; 5:12, 13, 20, 21; 6:1, 2, 6, 7, 10, 11, 12, 13, 14, 15, 16, 17, 18, 20, 22, 23; 7:7, 8, 9, 11, 13, 14, 17, 20, 23, 25; 8:2, 3, 10; 14:23). The plural "sins" is used four times (Rom. 3:25; 4:7; 7:5; 11:27).

Of this total of 49 times that "sin" or "sins" is used in Romans, these two English words come from three Greek words. One of these Greek words "hamartema" is only used once in Romans 3:25 and only three other times in all the New Testament (Mk. 3:28; 4:12; 1 Cor. 6:18). Of the remaining 48 times, the Greek word "hamartia" was used 47 times and "hamartano" just once (Rom. 6:15).

This is very significant because the Greek word "hamartia" is a noun while "hamartano" is a verb. A noun denotes a person, place, or thing, while verbs describe the action of nouns. Therefore, in all but one instance in the book of Romans, the words "sin" or "sins" describe man's tendency towards sin and not the individual acts of sins themselves. **If you think of the word sin in these chapters as denoting the act of sin, you will miss what Paul is saying.**

The believer's fight is not against individual acts of sin, but against the inner tendency to sin. If the propensity to sin can be broken, then the actions of sin will cease. Our individual acts of sin are only an expression or indication of how well we are doing in our war against this condition of the heart that causes us to sin.

Romans 5:12 says that this propensity to sin (or what many call the sin nature) entered the world through Adam. It is this sin nature that caused us to sin, not our individual acts of sin that gave us a sin nature (see note 17 at Jn. 8:44, p. 234; see note 3 at Rom. 7:9, p. 696; see note 6 at v. 19, above).

At salvation, our old man (Rom. 6:6) or sin nature died, but the tendency to sin remained through the thoughts and emotions that the old man left behind. The Christian no longer has a sin nature that compels him to sin, but he is simply dealing with the renewing of his mind.

10 (Rom. 5:21) Sin (see note 9 at v. 21, above) ruled like a king (see ref. n at v. 17, p. 686) through condemnation (v. 16) to bring death upon everyone. Condemnation is like the general of sin that enforced its power. Likewise, now God's grace rules like a king through righteousness to bring all who are in Christ into eternal life. Righteousness is the general of grace who defends us against all the wiles of the devil.

Sin would ultimately bring death to every individual whether they were condemned or not (Rom. 6:23). But to those individuals who are guilt ridden and condemned over their sins, sin has a particularly devastating effect. Likewise, those who put faith in Christ will ultimately experience God's eternal life. But those who understand righteousness as a gift to be received and not a wage to be earned are the ones who reign as kings in this life over sin and all its effects.

Remove guilt or condemnation and sin loses its strength to rule (1 Cor. 15:56). Remove the knowledge of righteousness by faith and grace loses its power to release eternal life in our daily lives.

ROMANS

DELIVERANCE FROM SIN BY UNION WITH CHRIST

CHAPTER 6

WHAT shall[1] we say then? Shall we
continue[a] in sin,[b] that grace[c] may abound?[d]
2 God forbid.[e] How[2f] shall we, that are
dead[3g] to sin,[b] live[h] any longer[i] therein?[j]
3 Know ye not,[k] that so many of us[4] as
were baptized[5l] into[m] Jesus[n] Christ[o] were
baptized[l] into[m] his death?[p]
4 Therefore[q] we are buried[r] with him by
baptism[s] into[m] death:[p] that like as[t] Christ[o]
was raised[u] up from the dead by the glory[v]
of the Father,[w] even so[x] we also[y] should[6]
walk[z] in newness[aa] of life.

References continued from column 4

v Gk.-"doxa"- the majesty of God as exhibited in deeds of power (Thayer) Jn. 2:11, 19-20 11:40 Col. 1:11
w see note 29 at Mt. 6:9, p. 79
x Gk.-"houto"- in this way (referring to what precedes or follows)
y Dict.-besides; in addition; likewise; too
z Gk.-"peripateo"- to tread all around; i.e. walk at large; fig. to live; deport oneself; follow (as a companion or votary)- Rom. 6:19 13:13-14 Gal. 6:15-16 Eph. 4:17 Eph. 4:22-24 5:8 Phil. 3:17-18 Col. 1:9-12 1 Jn. 2:6 Dict.- to conduct oneself or behave in a particular manner; to live (ref's cont'd on p. 689)

Footnotes for Romans 6:1-4

1 (Rom. 6:1) Paul had stated God's grace (see note 5 at Rom. 1:5, p. 655; see note 5 at Acts 20:24, p. 618) in such a way that it was inevitable that someone would ask, "Can we just keep on sinning since we are saved by grace?" Of course, that is not what Paul was saying at all. He had already answered this argument before (Rom. 3:8) and he does it again in Romans 6:15, making a total of three times in this epistle he had to overcome misunderstandings about his grace teaching encouraging sin.

Paul spoke this revelation of God's grace under the inspiration of the Holy Ghost with perfect balance, yet he was still misunderstood. Therefore, anybody teaching grace who does not encounter the same arguments and have to explain that they are not advocating a life of sin, has not preached grace the way that Paul did. If, in our efforts to prevent misuse, we present grace in such a way that no one ever accuses us of giving people a license to sin, then we haven't presented grace correctly.

2 (Rom. 6:2) Paul had so convincingly proven salvation by grace that there was not any theological argument left against it. Yet, the most common complaint against grace is not theological. It concerns the practical application. Most people can't handle grace because they think, "If I'm saved by grace, then why resist sin?" Paul answers this question in two ways in this chapter. First, Christians don't live a life of sin because they are dead to sin (see note 3 at this verse, below). This is the point Paul is making in verses 1-14. Secondly, although God is not imputing our sins unto us, Satan is. Beginning with verse 15, Paul clearly states that sin is an inroad of the enemy into our lives (see note 3 at Rom. 5:14, p. 685).

Therefore, Paul states that sin is still deadly and something to be resisted but he changes the motivation for living holy. No longer do we resist sin to try and be accepted with God, but we live holy lives because our nature has been changed and because actions of sin give place to the devil.

3 (Rom. 6:2) What does it mean that we are dead to sin? From the context and also from personal experience, we can easily see what it doesn't mean. It clearly doesn't mean that a Christian is incapable of committing sins.

Once again, the Greek word translated "sin" here is "hamartia" which is a noun describing the propensity for sin or what many call the sin nature (see note 9 at Rom. 5:21, p. 687). The NIV translation calls this the old self (see ref. ee at v. 6, p. 689). Our "old self" was the driving force behind our acts of sin. Paul is saying, that since our old self that loved to sin is dead, it is not the nature of a Christian to commit acts of sin as it was before they were born again (see note 2 at Jn. 3:3, p. 48). That's the number one reason that Christians don't sin. They don't want to sin.

However, by Paul saying that the part of us that compelled us to sin is dead, new questions are raised. If we no longer have a sin nature that compels us to sin, then why do we do it? Some Christians believe they are still driven to sin and quote Paul's statements in Romans 7 to justify this. Paul goes on to answer this question in verse 6 (see note 7 at Rom. 6:6, p. 689).

4 (Rom. 6:3) Our spirit is the part of us that got born again (see note 2 at Jn. 3:3, p. 48) and this is the part of us that Paul is referring to as being baptized into Jesus and His death (see note 3 at Mt. 26:41, p. 448). Our physical man is not dead and our soul is not dead. But our "old man" died with Christ (see note 8 at v. 6, p. 689).

5 (Rom. 6:3) The baptism that is being spoken of in verses three and four is not water baptism. Hebrews 6:2 speaks of the doctrine of baptisms (plural), clearly stating that there is more than one kind of baptism.

It is easy to see that there is a difference between the baptism of the Holy Spirit and the baptism into the body of Christ. When John the Baptist spoke of the baptism of the Holy Ghost in Matthew 3:11, he said that Jesus is the baptizer and the Holy Spirit is the one that we are being baptized with. But in 1 Corinthians 12:13, Paul says that the Holy Spirit is the baptizer and the body of Christ is what we are being baptized into. So, there are two different baptizers and two different elements that we are being baptized into, leaving no doubt that these are two different baptisms.

The mistake of always associating the word "baptism" with water baptism has led many people to incorrectly interpret Romans 6:3-4 as speaking of water baptism. Some have even attempted to use these verses to prove that water baptism is the act that causes salvation. However, that is not what Paul is saying, and in fact is the exact opposite of every point that he has been making in the book of Romans for salvation by grace through faith. This is not speaking of the sign of water baptism (see note 9 at Mk. 16:16, p. 505; see note 2 at Acts 2:38, p. 517).

Paul is speaking of the act where every person who puts saving faith in Jesus as their Lord is automatically and instantaneously baptized (immersed—see ref. l at this verse) into Jesus and all that He purchased for us (1 Cor. 12:13; Col. 2:12). He is simply stating that every believer has become dead to sin (v. 6) through the death of Jesus. Jesus didn't die for His sins, He had none. He died for our sins (1 Pet. 2:24). Therefore, His death was for us and all the benefits to be obtained through His death and resurrection are our benefits.

6 (Rom. 6:4) This verse states our death with Christ (see note 7 at v. 6, p. 689) as an accomplished fact and our resurrection with Christ as what should be the result of that death. That might lead some to speculate that our death with Christ to sin has already been accomplished while our resurrection with Him (in context—spiritual resurrection) has yet to be accomplished. Yet comparison with other scripture will reveal that is not so.

Footnotes for v. 4 continued on p. 689

a Gk.-"epimeno"- to stay over; i.e. remain; trans. abide (in); continue (in); tarry
b see note 9 at Rom. 5:21, p. 687
c see note 5 at Rom. 1:5, p. 655 see note 5 at Acts 20:24, p. 618 see note 1 at Lk. 16:16, p. 301 see note 2 at Lk. 9:55, p. 245 Jn. 1:16-17 Ti. 2:11 Heb. 4:16
d Gk.-"pleonazo"- to do, make, or be more; i.e. increase; trans. abound; abundant; make to increase; have over. Shall we persist in sin that the gift of grace may be more abundant? (Con) Are we to continue in sin that grace might increase? (NASV)
e see note 6 at Rom. 3:4, p. 668
f Gk.-"pos"- In what way? Also as exclamation, How much?
g Gk.-"apothnesko"- to die off (lit. or fig.); trans. be dead; death; die; lie-a-dying; be slain; from the Gk.-"apo"- off; i.e. away (from something near); in various senses (of place, time, or relation).
h Dict.- to conduct one's existence in a particular manner; to guide one's life by; see note 7 at Rom. 6:6, p. 689 2 Cor. 5:15 1 Pet. 1:14 4:1-2
i Gk.-"eti"- yet; still (of time or degree) Trans. yet- 51 times more- 17 times anymore- 5 times still- 4 times any further- 3 times continued on column 4

continued from column 1 further- 3 times moreover- 2 times yet more- 2 times also- once any longer- once even- once thenceforth- once longer- once
j Dict.- in that place or context
k Rom. 6:16 7:1 1 Cor. 3:16 5:6 6:2-3,9,15-16,19 9:13, 24 2 Cor. 13:5 Jas. 4:4
l Gk.-"baptizo"- to make whelmed (i.e. fully wet); from a prim. verb-"bapto"- to whelm; i.e. cover wholly with a fluid; hence, to dip- Rom. 6:4-5 Gal. 3:27
m Dict.- so as to be in or within
n see note 7 at Rom. 6:6, p. 689
o see note 2 at Mt. 16:16, p. 202 see note 5 at Jn. 1:41, p. 40 see note 5 at Mk. 1:1, p. 30
p Gk.-"thanatos"- death (lit. or fig.)
q Dict.- for that reason; consequently; hence
r Gk.-"sunthapto"- to inter in company with; i.e. (fig.) to assimilate spiritually (to Christ by a sepulture as to sin)- Col. 2:12-13 3:1-3
s Gk.-"baptisma"- from Gk."baptizo" see ref. a, this heading trans. baptism- 22 times
t Gk.-"hosper"- just as; i.e. exactly like
u see note 1 at Mt. 22:23, p. 378 1 Cor. 6:14 2 Cor. 13:4 Eph. 1:19-20 2:5-6
continued on center column

ROMANS

DELIVERANCE FROM SIN BY UNION WITH CHRIST (continued)

CHAPTER 6

5 For if we have been planted[bb] together
in the likeness[cc] of his death,[p] we shall be
also *in the likeness* of *his* resurrection:[u]
6 Knowing[dd] this,[7] that our old man[ee] is
crucified[ff] with *him,* that the body[8] of sin[gg]
might be destroyed,[hh] that henceforth[ii] we
should not serve[jj] sin.

ref's cont'd from p. 688

aa Gk.-"kainotes" this noun is found only here and in Rom. 7:6 (WMNT). It expresses the idea of life of a new quality; the believer being a new creation; newness of the Spirit (Rom. 7:6). said of the believer's manner of serving the Lord (Vine) new sphere of life (Mof) an entirely new life (Wey) a new kind of existence (Knox) we shall share a resurrection life like his (Williams)

bb Gk.-"sumphutos"- grown along with; i.e. (fig.) closely united to

cc Gk.-"homoioma"- resemblance Trans. likeness- 3 times shape- once similtude- once

dd Gk.-"ginosko"- to "know" in a great variety of applications and with many implications Trans. know- 196 times perceive- 9 times understand- 8 times allow- once be aware- once be aware of- once be resolved- once be sure- once be sure of- once can- once can speak- once feel- once have knowledge- once (Young)

ee i.e. old self (NIV)- Gal. 2:20 5:24 6:14 Eph. 4:22 Col. 3:5, 9-10

ff Gk.-"sustauroo"- to impale in company with (lit. or fig.) trans. crucify with- 5 times

gg the body, the stronghold of sin (TCNT)- Rom. 7:24 8:3, 13 Col. 2:11-12

hh Gk.-"katargeo"- to be (render) entirely idle (useless), lit. or fig. Trans. destroy- 5 times abolish- 3 times do away- 3 times make of none effect- 2 times cumber- once deliver- once bring to nought- once loose- once make void- once make without effect- once put away- once put down- once Rom. 7:24 8:3, 13 Col. 2:11-12

ii Dict.- from this forth; from now on

jj Gk.-"douleuo"- to be slave to (lit. or fig.; voluntarily or involuntarily)- Rom. 6:12 7:25 Jn. 8:34-36

Footnotes for Romans 6:4 cont'd from p. 688; Footnotes for Romans 6:5-6

Ephesians 2:5-6 states our spiritual resurrection with Christ as an accomplished fact that happens at salvation. Colossians 2:12-13 makes the same claim. In Colossians 3:1, Paul uses the reasoning that if we are risen with Christ, then we should seek those things which are above. Just as surely as all Christians are to seek heavenly things, likewise all Christians have been risen with Christ.

Our spirit (see note 3 at Mt. 26:41, p. 448) died to sin and is already resurrected with Christ unto newness of life. These things are already realities in our new spirit. Yet, to see these facts become realities in our physical lives we have to first know what happened to us in our spirit at salvation and then believe this good news. To the degree that we think, believe, and act like who we are in our spirit, to that degree we will experience the life of Christ in our flesh.

7 (Rom. 6:6) As explained in note 6 at Romans 6:4, page 688, our spirit has already died with Christ unto sin and is already resurrected unto newness of life. Yet, this newness of life which is a reality in our spirit does not automatically manifest itself in our flesh. Verse 6 makes it very clear that **we have to know some things before this resurrection life flows from our spirit into our flesh.**

Facts, whether spiritual or natural, don't govern our lives. **It's our knowledge or perception of truths that controls our physical emotions and experiences** (Prov. 23:7). If someone lied to you about a family member having just died, you would experience sorrow or other negative emotions even though there was no factual basis to feel that way. In the same way, if you were told that a family member had died and it was true, but you didn't believe the report, you would be spared those emotions.

Likewise, we have had the power of sin broken in our lives by our death to sin (see note 8 at this verse, below) and we have the resurrection power of Christ's life in our spirit. But these facts won't change our experiences until we know them and begin to act accordingly. All Christians are already blessed with all spiritual blessings (Eph. 1:3) but few Christians know that, and even fewer understand it to a degree that it impacts their life. *"My people are destroyed for lack of knowledge"* (Hosea 4:6).

8 (Rom. 6:6) Walking in resurrection power in our physical life is dependent on knowing (see ref. u at this verse) that our old man (NIV—old self) is crucified. If we don't believe that, then there won't be newness of life (v. 4) or victory for us (see note 7 at this verse, above).

As explained in note 6 at verse 4, our old self is already crucified. Yet some people have effectively voided the power of that truth (Mk. 7:13) by teaching that we still have an old self or sin nature which is constantly being resurrected from the dead. There is no scripture that mentions a daily or even periodical resurrection of our old man. Only Jesus has that power. Satan has no power to accomplish resurrection of any kind.

This common belief that we still have an old man or sin nature does not come from scripture but through observation. People observe a drive to sin and they assume that it is their old sin nature that drives them to it.

The scripture does teach that sin produced death (Gen. 2:17; Rom. 5:12, 15, 17; 6:23; Eph. 2:1) and therefore everyone was born with a spirit that was dead to (or separated from) God. This is the part of us that the Bible calls sin (see note 9 at Rom. 5:21, p. 687), or the old man (this verse). Therefore, the scriptures do teach that everyone was born with a sin nature or old man (see note 4 at Rom. 7:9, p. 697). But Paul is making a very clear presentation in these verses that for the Christian, the old man is dead. We do not have a nature that is driving us to sin (see note 2 at v. 2, p. 688).

If that is so, then why do we seem so bound to sin even after we experience the new birth? The reason is that our old man left behind what this verse calls a body. Just as a person's spirit and soul leave behind a physical body at death, so our old man left behind habits and strongholds in our thoughts and emotions. **The reason a Christian tends to sin is because of an unrenewed mind, not because of a sin nature.**

God made the mental part of us similar to a computer. We can program our minds so that certain actions and attitudes become automatic. For instance, when we were children, it was a major effort to tie our shoelaces or button our shirts, but as adults, we can now perform those duties without even thinking about what we are doing. It's like it is just a part of us, but in actuality it was an acquired trait.

Likewise, our old man ruled our thinking before we were born again. He taught us such things as selfishness, hatred, and fear, as well as placed within us the desire for sin. The old man is now gone, but these negative parts of his body remain. Just as a computer will continue to perform according to its programming until reprogrammed, so our minds continue to lead us on the course that our old man charted until renewed (Rom. 12:2).

Therefore, a Christian does not have a part of them that is still of the devil and is driving them to sin. Instead, the Christian has been liberated from the part of them that was dead in sin (i.e. old man—Eph. 2:1) and the rest of the Christian life is a renewing of the mind that results in the resurrection life of Jesus being manifest in our physical bodies (2 Cor. 4:11).

Someone might say, "What's the difference? Whether it's my old man or an unrenewed mind, I still struggle with the desire to sin." The difference is enormous! If we still have a sin nature, then we are doomed to a life of schizophrenia (lit.—split mind), but if it is just our unrenewed minds that cause the problem, then we can see the situation improve as we renew our minds.

If we retained a sin nature, even after the new birth, then a person who was bound by a particular sin before salvation would still be bound by it after salvation. They would just have to refrain from the physical act but in their heart they would continue to be guilty of committing that sin in thought (see note 12 at Mt. 5:22, p. 75). Yet, there are millions of examples of people who experience the new birth and are so changed, that the very sins that used to enslave them before salvation are now so repulsive to them that they have no desire to commit those acts. They can't even relate to the old self that did those things because they are a new person (2 Cor. 5:17) with a renewed mind.

It is truly liberating to learn that I don't have to commit sins, I chose to do so. Therefore, I can change through the renewing of my mind (Rom. 12:2) because there is no longer a part of me that is a sinner by nature. This is the point that Paul is making in this verse. To experience the resurrection life of Jesus, we have to know that our old man is dead, then through the renewing of our mind we destroy the body that the old man left behind, with the end result being that we will not serve sin any longer.

ROMANS

DELIVERANCE FROM SIN BY UNION WITH CHRIST (continued)

a Gk.-"dikaioo"- to render (i.e. show or regard as) just or innocent trans. justify- 37 times justifier- once be righteous- once free- once (Young)
b Rom. 6:3-5 2 Tim. 2:11
c Gk.-"suzao"- to continue to live in common with; i.e. co-survive (lit. or fig.) trans. live with- 3 times Jn. 14:19 2 Cor. 4:10,11-14 13:4 Col. 3:3-4
d Ps. 16:9-11 Acts 2:24-28 Heb. 7:16, 25 Rev. 1:18

CHAPTER 6

7 For he that is dead is freed[9a] from sin.
8 Now if we be dead with[b] Christ, we believe that we shall also live[c] with him:
9 Knowing[10] that Christ being raised[d] from the dead dieth no[11] more; death hath no more dominion[e] over him.[12]
10 For in that he died, he died unto sin once:[f] but in that he liveth, he liveth unto God.[g]

e Gk.-"kurieuo"- to rule Dict.- control or the exercise of control; rule; sovereignty trans. have dominion over- 4 times Lord- once be Lord of- once exercise Lordship over- once see note 3 at Mk. 16:6, p. 484
f Gk.-"ephapax"- upon one occasion (only); trans. once- 3 times at once- once once for all- once Heb. 9:26-28 1 Pet. 3:18
g Rom. 6:11 Lk. 20:38 2 Cor. 5:15

Footnotes for Romans 6:7-10

9 (Rom. 6:7) There is a difference between being "freed" and being "free." In the 1800's, President Lincoln issued the Emancipation Proclamation which "freed" the American slaves, but many slaves continued to serve their masters in slavery because the truth was hidden from them or in some cases, the slaves were afraid that they couldn't make it on their own.

Likewise, Christians have been "freed" from sin but that doesn't automatically mean all Christians experience that freedom. Through ignorance and deception, Satan continues to maintain mastery over those who have not yet realized their death and resurrection with Christ.

10 (Rom. 6:9) Our death to sin and resurrection to life with Christ is already a reality in our spirits (see note 7 at v. 6, p. 689) but it will only become a physical reality as we know and believe these truths (see note 8 at v. 6, p. 689). In this verse, Paul is stressing that this resurrection life is dependent on knowing that our death with Jesus to sin is a one time death that does not have to be repeated (see note 11 at this verse, below).

11 (Rom. 6:9) Much current theology believes that we died unto sin but that we resurrect unto sin every morning and therefore must continually repeat this process. That is not what happened to Jesus and these verses are comparing our death to sin with Jesus' death to sin (see note 3 at v. 11, below). It is true that we continually have to appropriate this death to sin but there is a big difference between dying over and over and over, and just renewing your mind with an accomplished fact.

12 (Rom. 6:9) In the same way that Jesus died unto sin once (v. 10) and now death has no more dominion over Him, the person who recognizes their death with Christ unto sin will not have sin rule over him anymore either (verse 14). Any Christian who is struggling with sin has not recognized that they are dead unto sin (see notes 7-8 at v. 6, p. 689).

DEAD TO SIN, ALIVE TO GOD

a Gk.-"logizomai"- see note 6 at Rom. 4:3, p. 675 Dict.- to count or compute; to consider as being; regard as- Rom. 8:18
b see note 3 at Rom. 6:2, p. 688 see note 6 at Rom. 6:4, p. 688 Rom. 6:5-10 Gal. 6:14 Col. 3:3 1 Pet. 2:24
c Dict.- without a doubt; certainly; truly; in fact; in reality; admittedly; unquestionably
d Gk.-"hamartia"- a missing of the mark; a principle or source of action, or an inward element producing acts (Vine)
e in a living state towards God; i.e. spiritually alive- continued on column 4

CHAPTER 6

11 Likewise[1] reckon[2a] ye also yourselves to be dead[b] indeed[c] unto sin,[d] but alive[3e] unto God[f] through[g] Jesus[h] Christ[i] our Lord.[j]

continued from column 1 see note 9 at Rom. 5:21, p. 687 Rom. 6:13 Gal. 2:20 Col. 3:3-4
f see note 1 at Jn. 1:1, p. 2
g Dict.- by way of; by the means or agency of- Rom. 5:1 16:27 Jn. 20:31 Eph. 2:7 Phil. 4:7 1 Pet. 4:11
h see note 2 at Acts 8:5, p. 545 see note 6 at Acts 4:12, p. 523
i see note 2 at Mt. 16:16, p. 202 see note 5 at Jn. 1:41, p. 40 see note 5 at Mk. 1:1, p. 30
j see note 3 at Lk. 1:43, p. 12

Footnotes for Romans 6:11

1 (Rom. 6:11) As already discussed in note 3 at Romans 6:2, page 688 and note 6 at Rom. 6:4, page 688, our "old man" is dead. However, because there is still a lust to sin present even after the new birth, many teach that the "old man" is constantly being resurrected. That's not so.

This verse makes it very clear that we are to reckon ourselves dead to sin in the same manner as Christ is dead to sin. The Greek word that was translated "likewise" in this verse is the word "houto" meaning "in this way (referring to what precedes or follows)." The dictionary defines "likewise" as, "in the same way; similarly." Therefore, we are dead to sin in the same way that Christ is dead to sin.

Of course, Jesus only died to sin once, so therefore, we only die to sin once (vv.9-10). After that, we simply reckon (see note 2 at Rom. 6:11, below) ourselves to be dead to sin and alive unto God.

2 (Rom. 6:11) In note 6 at Romans 4:3, page 675, the Greek word "logizomai" which was translated "reckon" here is explained in detail. The word conveys no causative meaning but rather only an inventory or assessment of a condition that already exists. Therefore, the state of being dead to sin already exists for the Christian, but we have to seize this benefit by reckoning it to be so. The use of the word "indeed" (see ref. c, this heading) in this verse, further establishes that this is already an accomplished work of Christ that we are simply appropriating.

3 (Rom. 6:11) Many people focus on the death to sin that is mentioned in this verse and omit, or at least put secondarily, the being alive unto God part. It is assumed that if we will just die to sin, then life with Christ comes automatically. That's no more so than physical death automatically producing physical resurrection. God doesn't need dead people. He needs people who have risen from the dead spiritually.

People who are preoccupied with dying to themselves will not experience their new life with Christ. This verse emphatically states that we are to believe unquestionably, without a doubt, that we are in fact, in reality (see definition of "reckon" at ref. a, this verse) already dead to sin (see note 2 at this verse, above) in the same way that Christ is already dead to sin (see note 1 at this verse, above).

As explained in note 9 at Romans 5:21, page 687, being dead to sin is not a struggle against or victory over sin that we are accomplishing, but it is deliverance from our "old man" (sin nature—note 9 at Rom. 5:21, p. 687) that enslaved us to sin. Our "old man" no longer exists and therefore no longer can dominate us if we know the truth (see note 7 at Rom. 6:6, p. 689).

Footnote for Romans 6:11 continued on p. 691

ROMANS

DEAD TO SIN, ALIVE TO GOD (continued)

CHAPTER 6

12 Let[4] not sin[d] therefore[5k] reign[l] in your mortal[m] body, that ye should obey[n] it[o] in the lusts[p] thereof.[q]

13 Neither yield[r] ye your members[s] *as* instruments[t] of unrighteousness[u] unto sin:[d] but yield[v] yourselves unto God,[f] as those that are alive[w] from the dead, and your members[s] *as* instruments[t] of righteousness[x] unto God.[f]

14 *For sin shall not have dominion[y] over you: for ye are not under[z] the law,[aa] but under[6] grace.[bb]

PARALLEL SCRIPTURES FOR ROMANS 6:14

JOHN 1:17

17 For the law was given by Moses, but *grace and truth came by Jesus Christ.*

ROMANS 3:20

20 Therefore by the deeds of the law there shall no flesh be justified in his sight: for by the law is *the knowledge of sin.*

ROMANS 5:20

20 Moreover the law entered, that the offence might abound. But where sin abounded, grace did much more abound:

ROMANS 7:4

4 Wherefore, my brethren, ye also are become dead to the law by the body of Christ; that ye should be married to another, even *to him who is raised from the dead, that we should bring forth fruit unto God.*

ROMANS 7:9

9 For I was alive without the law once: but when the commandment came, sin revived, and I died.

Footnote for Romans 6:11 (cont'd); Footnotes for Romans 6:12-14

It is wrong to teach that dying to sin is something that we still have to accomplish by acknowledging all our sinfulness and forsaking it. This actually causes people to focus on self (sinful self) more than ever before and therefore actually strengthen the hold of what's left of the "old man" (see note 8 at Rom. 6:6, p. 689) in our lives. The way to get rid of the residual effect of the "old man" in our lives is not to focus on our sins, but to focus on our resurrected union with Christ.

Therefore, according to the instruction of this verse, we are to unquestionably count on the fact that our "old man" is gone, and just as certainly reckon that our new man is alive with Christ, desiring only those things that please the Father. Doing this will transform us outwardly in our flesh, into a person who reflects on who we already are inwardly in our spirit.

4 (Rom. 6:12) If this sentence was to be diagrammed the way we were taught in school for the purpose of identifying the subject and verb, then the understood subject of this sentence would be "you." Paul is saying, "**You** let not sin therefore reign in your mortal body." **You** have the power to stop the reign of sin in your life or the Lord would not have given **you** this command.

A mistaken belief that we can't help but sin is one of the biggest reasons that we do sin. The power of sin (see note 9 at Rom. 5:21, p. 687) has been broken in our lives and the only reason a Christian sins is because he hasn't renewed his mind with the reality of his new life with Christ (see notes 7 and 8 at Rom. 6:6, p. 689).

5 (Rom. 6:12) The word "therefore" (see ref. o at Rom. 4:22, p. 680) makes our ability to end sin's reign in our lives that this verse speaks of, dependent on the truth that was just expressed in verse 11 (see note 3 at v. 11, p. 690). We have to know beyond any doubt that our "old man" is dead and gone, then and only then, will we be able to renew our minds and end the dictatorship of sin in our lives.

6 (Rom. 6:14) The "old man" (sin—see note 9 at Rom. 5:21, p. 687) is dead and gone. Yet there is a "residual old man", or the unrenewed mind and emotions, that the "old man" left behind (see note 8 at Rom. 6:6, p. 689). It is these lingering effects of the "old man" or sin to which Paul is referring.

Paul makes a very clear statement that the reason this sin shall not have dominion over us is because we are not under law (see note 3 at Rom. 3:19, p. 671) but under grace (see note 5 at Rom. 1:5, p. 655). However, most Christians today are still operating under the law, so it's no surprise that sin is still having dominion over them. Understanding our freedom from the Old Testament law is a prerequisite to breaking the dominion of sin in our lives.

The reason this is so is because the law strengthened sin by producing guilt that condemned us and killed us (see note 4 at Rom. 3:19, p. 671). The law also brought the wrath of God against our sin (see note 3 at Rom. 4:15, p. 678). However, once we accept the atonement of Christ for our sin, we no longer need to fear the wrath of God. That was placed on Jesus. We also don't need the law to condemn us and kill us. We have already come to Christ for salvation, which is what the law was designed to do (Gal. 3:24-25).

Knowing this (see note 7 at Rom. 6:6, p. 689) frees a person from sin, it doesn't free a person to sin. Every Christian continues to sin to some degree, not because we have to, but because we are still in the process of renewing our minds (see note 4 at v. 12, above). However, when we aren't condemned and feeling separated from God because of our sin, we are free to run to God for help instead of away from God in fear. Therefore, understanding God's grace and our freedom from the law is the key to breaking the dominance of sin in our lives.

k Dict.- for that reason; consequently; hence

l Gk.-"basileuo"- to rule (lit. or fig. trans. king; reign see note 10 at Rom. 5:21, p. 687 Rom. 5:21 Ps. 119:133

m Gk.-"thnetos"- liable to die Dict.- liable or subject to death- Rom. 8:11 1 Cor. 15:53-54 2 Cor. 4:11 5:4

n Gk.-"hupakouo"- to hear under (as a subordinate); i.e. to listen attentively; by impl. to heed or conform to a command or authority; trans. obey- 18 times be obedient to- 2 times hearken- once (Young)

o i.e. sin see ref. d at v.11

p Gk.-"epithumia"- a longing (esp. for what is forbidden); trans. lust- 31 times concupiscence- 3 times desire- 3 times Rom. 13:14 Gal. 5:16, 24 Eph. 2:3 4:22 1 Th. 4:5 2 Tim. 2:22 Ti. 2:12 3:3 Jas. 1:14-15 4:1-3 1 Pet. 1:14 2:11 4:2-3 1 Jn. 2:15-17 Jude 16, 18

q Dict.- of or concerning this, that, or it.

r Dict.- to give up; surrender; submit

s Gk.-"melos"- a limb or part of the body

t Gk.-"hoplon"- an implement or utensil or tool (lit. or fig., esp. offensive for war); trans. instrument- 2 times

continued on column 4

continued from column 1

armour- 2 times weapon- 2 times Dict.- a means by which something is done; agency; one used to accomplish some purpose

u Gk.-"adikia"- (legal) injustice; moral wrongfulness (of character, life, or act)- Rom. 1:29 2:8-9 2 Th. 2:12 2 Pet. 2:13-15 1 Jn. 1:9

v see ref. r at v. 13 Rom. 12:1 2 Chr. 30:8 Dan. 3:28 1 Cor. 6:20

w Rom. 6:11 Lk. 15:24, 32 Jn. 5:24 2 Cor. 5:15 Eph. 2:5 Col. 2:13 1 Pet. 2:24

x Gk.-"dikaiosune"- equity (of character or act); spec. (Christian) justification; trans. righteousness- 94 times

y Gk.-"kurieuo"- to rule; frans. have dominion over- 4 times exercise lordship over- once be Lord of- once Lord- once Dict.- control or the exercise of control; rule; sovereignty

z Dict.- subject to the authority, rule, or control of

aa see note 4 at Rom. 2:26, p. 666 see note 3 at Rom. 3:19, p. 671 see note 3 at Rom. 1:2, p. 655

bb see note 5 at Rom. 1:5, p. 655 see note 12 at Rom. 3:8, p. 669 see note 7 at Rom. 4:4, p. 675 see note 1 at Acts 15:1, p. 585

ROMANS

DEAD TO SIN, ALIVE TO GOD (continued)

CHAPTER 6

15 What then?[7] shall we sin,[a] because
we are not under the law, but under grace?
God forbid.[b]
16 Know ye not,[c] that to whom[8] ye yield
yourselves[d] servants[9e] to obey,[f] his servants
ye are to whom ye obey; whether[g] of sin
unto death,[h] or of obedience[f] unto
righteousness?
17 But God be thanked,[i] that ye were the
servants of sin,[j] but ye have obeyed[k] from
the heart[l] that form[m] of doctrine[n] which was
delivered you.
18 Being then made free[o] from sin, ye
became the servants[10] of righteousness.[p]
19 I speak after the manner of men[q]
because of the infirmity of your flesh:[r] for
as ye have yielded your members servants[s]
to uncleanness[t] and to iniquity[u] unto
iniquity;[u] even so now yield your members
servants[s] to righteousness unto holiness.[v]

a see note 2 at Lk. 9:55, p. 245; Gk.-"hamartano"- to miss the mark (and so not share in the prize), i.e. (fig.) to err, esp. (mor.) to sin; verb-form; see note 9 at Rom. 5:21, p. 687; Rom. 6:1-2; 2 Cor. 7:1; Ti. 2:11-14
b see note 6 at Rom. 3:4, p. 668
c Rom. 6:3; 7:1; 1 Cor. 3:16; 5:6; 6:2-3, 9,15-16,19; 9:13, 24; 2 Cor. 13:5; Jas. 4:4
d Rom. 6:13; Josh. 24:15; Mt. 6:24
e see note 1 at Rom. 1:1, p. 655
f Gk.-"hupakoe"- see note 6 at Rom. 1:5, p. 655
g Dict.- either
h Gk.-"thanatos"-in the widest sense, death that comprises all the miseries arising from sin, as well as physical death, to be followed by wretchedness in the lower world (Thayer)

i see note 1 at Rom. 1:21, p. 660; Rom. 1:8; Mt. 11:25-26; Acts 28:15; 1 Cor. 1:4; Eph. 1:16; Phil. 1:3-5; Col. 1:3-4; 1 Th. 1:2-3; 2 Th. 1:3; 2 Tim. 1:3-5; Phile. 4
j see note 9 at Rom. 5:21, p. 687; 1 Cor. 6:9-11; Eph. 2:1-5; 1 Tim. 1:13-16; Ti. 3:3-7; 1 Pet. 2:9; 4:2-5
k see ref. n at Rom. 6:12, p. 691; see note 6 at Rom. 1:5, p. 655; Rom. 1:5; 2:8; 15:18; 16:26; Ps. 18:44; 2 Cor. 10:5-6; Heb. 5:9; 11:8; 1 Pet. 1:22

continued on center column

References continued from column 4

l see note 3 at Mt. 12:34, p. 131; see note 10 at Mk. 7:21, p. 191; see note 6 at Mk. 11:23, p. 367; see notes 2-3 at Jn. 14:1, p. 431; see note 3 at Rom. 2:29, p. 667
m Gk.-"tupos"- the representation or pattern of anything; the metaphor is that of a cast or frame into which molten material is poured so as to take its shape; the gospel is the mould; those who are obedient to its teachings become conformed to Christ, whom it presents (Vine)-
n 2 Tim. 1:13; 3:16-17
o see note 9 at Rom. 6:7, p. 690; Jn. 8:36; Gal. 5:1; 1 Pet. 2:16
p Rom. 6:19-20, 22; Isa. 54:17
q Rom. 3:5; 1 Cor. 9:8; Gal. 3:5
r i.e. I speak in human terms so that you can more easily understand
s see ref. e, this page; see note 9 at Rom. 6:16, below
t Gk.-"akatharsia"- impurity
u Gk.-"anomia"- illegality; i.e. violation of law or wickedness
v see note 2 at Lk. 5:20, p. 89; see note 5 at Acts 9:13, p. 555

Footnotes for Romans 6:15-19

7 (Rom. 6:15) Paul had started this sixth chapter with a similar question as to whether or not his teaching was encouraging people to sin (see note 1 at Rom. 6:1, p. 688). He spent the first thirteen verses of this chapter explaining that Christians don't sin because they are dead to sin (see note 3 at Rom. 6:2, p. 688; see note 6 at Rom. 6:4, p. 688). Then in verse fourteen, he brings up our deliverance from the law again which prompts this similar question. He then goes on through the rest of this chapter to explain that the second reason Christians don't sin is because it gives Satan an inroad into our lives (see note 8 at v. 16, below).

8 (Rom. 6:16) This is the second argument that Paul presents in this chapter as to why Christians don't live in sin (see note 2 at Rom. 6:2, p. 688). The legalistic Jews were seeking a life without sin so that they could earn God's favor. Paul had conclusively proven that no one could keep the precepts of the law and that the law was never given for the purpose of justification (see note 4 at Rom. 3:19, p. 671; see note 14 at Rom. 3:31, p. 674). Therefore, he is explaining that Christians still seek to live holy but for different reasons.

This second reason Paul gives for holiness in the life of the believer is that when we obey sin, we yield ourselves to Satan, the author of that sin. Notice the use of the personal pronoun "whom" in this verse. Yielding to sin is yielding to a person, Satan. God doesn't impute the sin to us (see note 2 at Rom. 5:13, p. 685) but the devil does (see note 3 at Rom. 5:14, p. 685). Our actions either release the power of Satan or the power of God in us.

Therefore, although God is not imputing our sins unto us, we cannot afford the luxury of sin because it allows Satan to have access to us. When Christians do sin and allow the devil opportunity to produce his death in their lives, then the way to stop that is to confess the sin and God is faithful and just to take the forgiveness that is already present in our born-again spirit and release it in our flesh, thereby removing Satan and his strongholds (see note 11 at Rom. 4:8, p. 676).

9 (Rom. 6:16) The Greek word that was translated "servants" twice in this verse is "doulos" denoting a slave (see note 1 at Rom. 1:1, p. 655). Therefore, Paul is not speaking of an infrequent error on our part but rather a servile condition where one gives himself up wholly to another's will (Thayer). So, Paul is stating that a person who abandons himself to sin is in actuality becoming a slave of the devil (see note 8 at this verse, above) while a person who obeys righteousness is actually yielding himself to the Lord. This is the second reason in this chapter as to why a Christian should live holy.

10 (Rom. 6:18) Jesus said, *"No man can serve two masters: for either he will hate the one, and love the other; or else he will hold to the one, and despise the other. Ye cannot serve God and mammon"* (Mt. 6:24). We cannot become the servant of righteousness until we are made free from serving sin.

As discussed in note 9 at Rom. 6:16, the Greek word used for servant here denotes slavery. Christians still sin (1 Jn. 1:7,9) but they aren't the slaves of sin (see note 9 at Rom. 5:21, p. 687) anymore. Those who believe that the "old man" still lives and exerts mastery in their lives (see notes 1-3 at Rom. 6:11, p. 690) will not experience the joy of being servants to righteousness.

ROMANS

SERVANTS OF SIN NOW SERVANTS OF GOD

CHAPTER 6

20 For when ye were the servants[a] of
sin,[b] ye were free[1] from righteousness.[c]
21 What fruit[d] had ye then in those
things whereof ye are now ashamed?[e] for
the end[f] of those things *is* death.[g]
22 But now being made free[h] from sin,[b]
and become servants[i] to God,[j] ye have your
fruit[k] unto[2] holiness,[l] and the end[m]
everlasting life.[n]
23 For the wages[3] of sin[b] *is* death;[o] but
the gift[4] of God[j] *is* eternal life[n] through[p]
Jesus[q] Christ[r] our Lord.[s]

References continued from column 4

o Rom. 5:12, Gen. 2:17, 3:19, Isa. 3:11, Ezek. 18:4, 20, Gal. 6:7-8, Jas. 1:15, Rev. 21:8

p Dict.- by way of; by the means or agency of- Rom. 5:1, 16:27, Jn. 20:31, Eph. 2:7, Phil. 4:7, 1 Pet. 4:11

q see note 2 at Acts 8:5, p. 545, see note 6 at Acts 4:12, p. 523, see note 5 at Jn. 1:41, p. 40, see note 5 at Mk. 1:1, p. 30

r see note 2 at Mt. 16:16, p. 202

s see note 3 at Lk. 1:43, p. 12

Footnotes for Romans 6:20-23

1 (Rom. 6:20) Paul had just made a statement in the previous verse that we should serve the Lord with the same fervor that we served the devil with before we were born again. He continues that comparison through verse 22 and makes an amazing point. He is saying that in the same way that our good acts could not change our sinful nature before we were born again, likewise our sinful acts cannot change our righteous nature now that we have become a new creature in Christ Jesus.

In this verse, the phrase *"servants of sin"* is describing a person before they are born again. The phrase, *"free from righteousness"* is not saying that a lost man cannot do anything that is right, but rather, all of an individual's good acts aren't enough to change his nature. He must be born again (see note 2 at Jn. 3:3, p. 48).

Most Christians have accepted this truth unquestionably. They got saved by believing that. Yet this exact terminology is used again in verse 22 in a way that very few Christians accept. The same logic that was used in verse 20 is reversed in verse 22.

If *"servants of sin"* in verse 20 signified a person before salvation, then *"servants to God"* in verse 22 denotes just the opposite, a person who has been saved through faith in Christ. If *"free from righteousness"* in verse 20 described a lost man who was incapable of changing his sinful nature by his own good works, then *"free from sin"* in verse 22 describes a Christian as being unable to change his righteous nature through his sins.

This is a powerful truth. In the same way that our sinful nature could not be changed by our own actions, now our new, born-again spirit cannot be changed by our actions either. If we are going to accept one of these truths, we have to accept the other. We cannot honestly accept verse 20 and reject verse 22 when the exact same terminology is used in the same context.

Actions cannot produce the new birth and actions cannot destroy the new birth. We had to believe to receive salvation and we have to willfully reject that faith in Christ to become reprobate (see note 6 at Rom. 1:28, p. 661; see note 9 at Rom. 1:32, p. 662).

2 (Rom. 6:22) Notice that holiness is a fruit and not a root of salvation. That is to say that holiness is a by-product of relationship with God, it does not produce relationship with God (see note 21 at Mt. 23:26, p. 391).

3 (Rom. 6:23) The dictionary defines "wages" as "a fitting return; recompense; requital." Sin has a wage that it pays and no one can avoid "payday" without faith in Jesus.

As explained in note 9 at Romans 5:21, page 687, the sin spoken of here is not an individual act of sin, but rather the sin nature or "old man" itself. Anyone who does not receive the new birth (see note 2 at Jn. 3:3, p. 48) will be held liable for all the wrongs committed as a result of their sinful nature (see note 4 at Mk. 3:29, p. 128). However, for those who receive the new birth through faith in Jesus, they don't have a sin nature (see note 8 at Rom. 6:6, p. 689) and will therefore not receive this payment of death.

The physical death of our bodies is not really what is being spoken of here. Physical death as well as every result of the sin nature (i.e. sickness, depression, fear, etc.) are only by-products of the spiritual death that was already present on the inside of us. The Lord told Adam that in the day he ate of the forbidden tree, he would surely die (Gen. 2:17). Adam didn't die physically that day but he did die spiritually. Physical death came 930 years later for Adam (Gen. 5:5) as a by-product of spiritual death.

The wages (plural) of death that those who are not born again will receive, can be broken into two categories. The Bible speaks of a second death (Rev. 2:11; 20:6, 14; 21:8) which is banishment to the lake of fire (see note 4 at Mk. 3:29, p. 128) on judgment day. The first death is this separation from God (or spiritual death) which was inherited through Adam (see note 4 at Rom. 5:16, p. 686; see note 6 at Rom. 5:19, p. 687).

So this verse is specifically speaking of the spiritual death that was inherited through Adam and then the second death which is eternal banishment from God and torment in the lake of fire. However, any negative result of sin which was not a part of God's original plan for man can also be included in the term "death," since they are a direct result of this spiritual death.

4 (Rom. 6:23) Eternal life (see note 94 at Jn. 17:3, p. 444) is a gift. The dictionary defines gift as "something that is bestowed voluntarily and without compensation; a present." We have nothing to do with earning this gift. Eternal life would cease to be a gift if we earned it (Rom. 11:6). We simply receive it by faith.

a Gk.-"doulos"- see note 9 at Rom. 6:16, p. 692; see note 1 at Rom. 1:1, p. 655; Rom. 6:16-17; Jn. 8:34

b Gk.-"hamartia"- see note 9 at Rom. 5:21, p. 687

c When you were slaves to sin, you were free from the control of righteousness (NIV). When you were slaves of sin, you weren't free to serve righteousness as your master (Beck)

d Rom. 7:5; Prov. 1:31; Isa. 3:10; Jer. 17:10

e Dict.- shame - a painful emotion caused by a strong sense of guilt, embarrassment, unworthiness, or disgrace- Ezra 9:6; Job 40:4; Jer. 8:12; 31:19; Ezek. 16:61-63

f Dict.- the point in time at which an action, event, or phenomenon ceases or is completed; conclusion; a result; outcome

g Gk.-"thanatos"- in the widest sense, death that comprises all the miseries arising from sin, as well as physical death, to be followed by wretchedness in the lower world (Thayer)- Rom. 6:23; Prov. 14:12; Phil. 3:19; Jas. 1:15; 5:20; Rev. 20:14

h Gk.-"eleutheroo"- to liberate; see note 1 at Rom. 6:20, this page; Rom. 6:18; 8:2; Jn. 8:36; 2 Cor. 3:17; Gal. 5:13

i Gk.-"douloo"- to enslave (lit. or fig.); see note 9 at Rom. 6:16, p. 692; see note 1 at Rom. 6:20, this page; Gal. 1:10; Col. 4:12; Ti. 1:1; Jas. 1:1; 1 Pet. 2:16; Rev. 7:3

j see note 1 at Jn. 1:1, p. 2

k see note 50 at Jn. 15:4, p. 436; see note 46 at Jn. 15:1, p. 434; see note 47 at Jn. 15:2, p. 434; see notes 64-65 at Jn. 15:16, p. 438; Jn. 15:2, 16; Gal. 5:22-23; Eph. 5:9; Phil. 1:11; 4:17; Col. 1:10; see ref. d, this page

l Gk.-"hagiasmos"- consecration; purification; sanctification; see note 1 at Mt. 22:36, p. 382; see note 2 at Lk. 5:20, p. 89; see note 56 at Jn. 15:10, p. 436

m Rom. 6:21; Ps. 37:37-38; see ref. f, this page

n see note 3 at Jn. 3:36, p. 52; see note 9 at Jn. 5:24, p. 98; see note 94 at Jn. 17:3, p. 444

continued on center column

ROMANS

MAN UNDER LAW AND HIS DELIVERANCE THROUGH CHRIST

a Gk.-"agnoeo"- not to know (through lack of information or intelligence); by impl. to ignore (through disinclination)
Rom. 6:3, 16
1 Cor. 3:16
5:6
6:2-3, 9,15-16,19
9:13, 24
2 Cor. 13:5
Jas. 4:4

b Rom. 2:17-18
Ezra 7:25
Prov. 6:23
1 Cor. 9:8
Gal. 4:21

CHAPTER 7

KNOW ye not,[a] brethren,[1] (for I speak to
them that know the law,)[b] how that the law
hath dominion[c] over a man[d] as long as he
liveth?[2]

2 *For[3] the woman which hath an
husband[e] is bound[f] by the law to *her* husband
so long as he liveth; but if the husband be
dead, she is loosed[g] from the law of *her*
husband.

c Gk.-"kurieuo"- to rule; from same Gk. word used for Lord- see note 3 at Lk. 1:43, p. 12
Trans. have dominion over- 4 times
exercise Lordship over- once
be Lord of- once
Lord- once
Dict.- control or the exercise of control; rule; sovereignty

d i.e. mankind or human beings

e Gk. -"hupandros"- in subjection under a man; i.e. a married woman

f Dict.- under legal or moral obligation; under contract

g Gk.-"katargeo"- to be (render) entirely idle; lit. or fig.; same word was translated "deliver" in Romans 7:6

PARALLEL SCRIPTURES FOR ROMANS 7:2

DEUTERONOMY 24:1

WHEN *a man hath taken a wife, and married her, and it come to pass that she find no favour in his eyes, because he hath found some uncleanness in her: then let him write her a bill of divorcement, and give it in her hand, and send her out of his house.*

1 CORINTHIANS 7:39

39 The wife is bound by the law as long as her husband liveth; but if her husband be dead, she is at liberty to be married to whom she will; only in the Lord.

MATTHEW 19:5-9

5 And said, For this cause shall a man
leave father and mother, and shall cleave
to his wife: and they twain shall be one
flesh?
6 Wherefore they are no more twain,
but one flesh. What therefore God hath
joined together, let not man put asunder.
7 They say unto him, Why did Moses
then command to give a writing of
divorcement, and to put her away?
8 He saith unto them, Moses because
of the hardness of your hearts suffered
you to put away your wives: but from the
beginning it was not so.
9 And I say unto you, Whosoever
shall put away his wife, except it be *for*
fornication, and shall marry another,
committeth adultery: and whoso
marrieth her which is put away doth
commit adultery.

Footnotes for Romans 7:1-2

1 (Rom. 7:1) Remember that Paul wrote this epistle to all the saints in Rome (Rom. 1:7). Therefore, even though this term "brethren" can be used to designate fellow countrymen as in Romans 9:3, here it is specifying fellow believers, especially the Jewish believers who were knowledgeable of the law.

2 (Rom. 7:1) Paul is saying that the only way to get out from under the Old Testament law is through death. He had just taught that the old man is once and for all dead (see note 6 at Rom. 6:4, p. 688; see note 8 at Rom. 6:6, p. 689). Now he uses the natural illustration of marriage to further make this point.

In the same way that the marriage vow was intended by God to be binding until "death do us part" (see note 5 at Mt. 19:7, p. 324), so our bondage under the tyranny of the sin nature (see note 9 at Rom. 5:21, p. 687) was inescapable except through death. Therefore, this knowledge of our death to the old man is crucial to escaping the carnal life that the old man put in place in our lives.

3 (Rom. 7:2) Paul likens our death to sin, which he had explained in chapter six, to the laws governing a marriage relationship. The husband is our old man, the wife is the soul and body part of us, or our personality, and the binding civil and moral code that enforces a marriage is like the Old Testament law.

We, the wife, were enslaved to a wicked husband, the old man. In Old Testament times, the law gave the wife no option of divorce. The man could divorce his wife (Dt. 24:1) but the wife could not divorce her husband. Therefore, the only hope a woman could ever have of being delivered from that situation was that her "old man" would die. Then she was delivered from that moral and civil code that kept her from having relationship with someone else.

Likewise, we were in bondage to our old man. We wanted out of the relationship but we were by nature slaves to sin (Eph. 2:3). The Old Testament law only made the situation worse. It strengthened the control of the old man over us (see ref. v, v. 5, p. 695). The law actually empowered sin or our wicked husband against us (see note 4 at Rom. 3:19, p. 671).

Then Jesus entered the scene. He took our old man with him to the cross and when He died, our old man died too. But Jesus rose from the dead and our old man didn't. Now we are free from the old man and the law that bound us to him so that we can be married to Him who is risen from the dead.

ROMANS

MAN UNDER LAW AND HIS DELIVERANCE THROUGH CHRIST (continued)

h Gen. 2:24
Mk. 10:9
1 Cor. 7:10
Eph. 5:31-32
i Dict.- additional; a different one
j see note 6 at Mt. 19:9, p. 324
Ex. 20:14
Lev. 20:10
Dt. 22:22-24
Mt. 5:32
Mk. 10:6-12
Jn. 8:3-5
k Gk.-"eleutheros"- unrestrained; i.e. not a slave, exempt
l i.e. the law of marriage
m Rom. 7:4
Gen. 25:1
1 Sam. 25:39-42
n Rom. 7:6
6:14
Gal. 2:19-20
5:18
Eph. 2:15
Col. 2:14, 20
o i.e. through the (crucified) body of Christ (Amp)- see note 6 at Rom. 6:4, p. 688
see note 8 at Rom. 6:6, p. 689
Jn. 6:51-53
Gal. 3:13
Heb. 10:10
1 Pet. 2:24
p Hos. 2:19-20
Jn. 3:29
2 Cor. 11:2
Eph. 5:23-32
Rev. 19:7
21:9

CHAPTER 7

3 So then if, while *her* husband liveth,
she be married[h] to another[i] man, she shall
be called an adulteress:[j] but if her husband
be dead,[4] she is free[k] from that law;[l] so that
she is no adulteress,[j] though she be married[h]
to another[i] man.[m]
4 Wherefore, my brethren, ye also are
become dead[5] to the law[n] by the body of
Christ;[o] that ye should be married[p] to
another, *even* to him who is raised from the
dead, that we should[6] bring forth fruit[q]
unto[7] God.[r]
5 For when we were in[8] the flesh,[s] the
motions[t] of sins,[u] which were by[9] the law,[v]
did work[w] in our members[x] to bring forth
fruit[10q] unto death.[y]
6 But now[z] we are delivered[aa] from[11] the
law, that being dead wherein we were held;
that we should serve in newness of spirit,[12bb]
and not *in* the oldness of the letter.[cc]

q Gk.-"karpophoreo"- to be fertile (lit. or fig.) Dict.- conducive to productivity; producing results; profitable- Rom. 6:22
Jn. 15:8
Gal. 5:22-23
Phil. 1:11
4:17
Col. 1:6, 10
r see note 1 at Jn. 1:1, p. 2
s Gk.-"sarx"- the meat of an animal, or the body, or as the symbol of what is external, or human nature with its frailties and passions, or a human being- Rom. 8:8-9
Jn. 3:6
Gal. 5:24
Eph. 2:3
t Gk.-"pathema"- an emotion or influence
u see note 9 at Rom 5:21, p. 687
v see note 4 at Rom. 3:19, p. 671
see note 14 at Rom. 3:31, p. 674
see note 8 at Rom. 5:20, p. 687
Rom. 5:20
1 Cor. 15:56
Jas. 2:9-10
1 Jn. 3:4
continued on center column

References continued from column 4

w Gk.-"energeo"- to be active; efficient
6:13, 19
Col. 3:5
Jas. 4:1
x Gk.-"melos"- a limb or part of the body- Rom. 7:23
y Rom. 6:21
z Dict.- at the present time
aa same word was translated "loosed" in Rom. 7:2
bb Rom. 1:9
6:4
Ezek. 11:19
36:26
2 Cor. 3:6
5:17
Gal. 2:19-20
6:15
Phil. 3:3
Col. 3:10
cc i.e. that we should serve in the new way of the spirit and not in the old way of the letter or written code

Footnotes for Romans 7:3-6

4 (Rom. 7:3) In this comparison, it is clearly understood that a woman who has two husbands would be living in adultery. Likewise, Paul is saying that a Christian who has two natures would be living in adultery. A Christian who does not understand that our old man is dead will constantly feel the guilt of the Old Testament law that bound us to our first husband, the old man.

5 (Rom. 7:4) Through Jesus, not only is our old man dead, but we are dead to the law that enforced the tyranny of the old man over us. The law was only made for the old man (1 Tim. 1:9-10). Once he is dead, we are no longer under the law (see note 6 at Rom. 6:14, p. 691). Failure to understand this will produce the same end results as if our old man was not dead.

6 (Rom. 7:4) Christ didn't free us from the relationship to our first husband, the old man, so we could just run around and do whatever we want, but he freed us from that first marriage so we could marry Him. A Christian's freedom is not freedom to do "our own thing" but it is freedom from the old nature so that we can now serve Christ in newness of spirit (v. 6).

7 (Rom. 7:4) Just as it is normal for a physical marriage to produce children, so our marriage to Christ is intended to bring forth fruit (see note 47 at Jn. 15:2, p. 434).

8 (Rom. 7:5) A Christian is not **in** the flesh even though he walks **after** the flesh at times. There is a difference and Paul makes a major point concerning the difference between being **in** the flesh and **after** the flesh in chapter eight (see note 20 at Rom. 8:9, p. 703).

9 (Rom. 7:5) Notice that the emotions or influences (see ref. t, this verse) of sin were by the law. The law actually made sin come alive in us (see notes 3-4 at v. 9, pp. 696-697).

10 (Rom. 7:5) This is the same phrase that was used in the last part of verse four. In the same way that relationship with the old man produced death, now realizing our new relationship with Christ produces the fruit of holiness (see note 2 at Rom. 6:22, p. 693).

11 (Rom. 7:6) In these first six verses of Romans 7, Paul says we are *"loosed from the law"* (v. 2), *"free from the law"* (v. 3), *"dead to the law"* (v. 4), and *"delivered from the law"* (this verse). Romans 6:14 says that we *"are not under the law."* How could it be made any clearer that the law was not made for a born-again man (1 Tim. 1:9)?

12 (Rom. 7:6) The dictionary defines "spirit," when used as in this verse, as "the real sense or significance of something" (American Heritage Dict.). Just as Jesus taught against ritualistic observance of laws (see note 21 at Mt. 23:26, p. 391), so Paul is saying a Christian is someone who fulfills the real sense or significance of the law, not every detail. God is more pleased with someone who has a pure heart and yet fails Him in actions (example: Lk. 7:36-50) than someone who does the right things with an impure heart (1 Sam. 16:7). Second Corinthians 3:6 says, *"the letter killeth, but the spirit giveth life."*

True Christianity is not the observance of a different set of rules than some other religion. It is a change of the heart (2 Cor. 5:17; Ezek. 11:19; 36:26). Once a person's heart is changed, he will serve God, not because he has to but because he wants to.

ROMANS

SIN TAKING OCCASION BY THE LAW

a Rom. 3:5
4:1
6:15
b see note 6 at Rom. 3:4, p. 668
c see note 4 at Rom. 3:19, p. 671
Rom. 7:13
3:20
5:20
Gal. 3:19, 24
d Gk.-"epithumia"- a longing (esp. for what is forbidden)
Trans. lust- 31 times
concupiscence- 3 times
desire- 3 times
Rom. 7:8
1 Th. 4:5
e If it were not for the fact that the law had said . . .

CHAPTER 7

7 *What shall we say[a] then? *Is* the law
sin?[1] God forbid.[b] Nay, I had not known[2]
sin, but by the law:[c] for I had not known
lust,[d] except[e] the law had said,[f] Thou shalt
not covet.[g]
8 But sin,[h] taking occasion by the commandment,[i] wrought[j] in me all manner of
concupiscence.[d] For without the law sin[h]
was dead.[k]
9 For I was alive without the law once:
but when the commandment[i] came,[3] sin[h]
revived,[l] and I died.[4]

f Gk.-"lego"- to "lay" forth; i.e. relate in words
g Gk.-"epithumeo"- to set the heart upon; i.e. long for (rightfully or otherwise)- Ex. 20:17
h see note 9 at Rom. 5:21, p. 687
i Rom. 7:11,13,17
4:15
5:20
j Gk.-"katergazomai"- to work fully; i.e. accomplish
k Rom. 4:15
Jn. 15:22, 24
1 Cor. 15:56
l Gk.-"anazao"- to recover life (lit. or fig.)-
Rom. 3:19-20
7:11

PARALLEL SCRIPTURES FOR ROMANS 7:7

EXODUS 20:17

17 Thou shalt not covet thy neighbour's house, thou shalt not covet thy neighbour's wife, nor his manservant, nor his maidservant, nor his ox, nor his ass, nor any thing that is *thy neighbour's.*

DEUTERONOMY 5:21

21 Neither shalt thou desire thy neighbour's wife, neither shalt thou covet thy neighbour's house, his field, or his manservant, or his maidservant, his ox, or his ass, or any thing *that* is *thy neighbour's.*

Footnotes for Romans 7:7-9

1 (Rom. 7:7) Remember that in context, the sin that is being spoken of here is not an individual act of sin but rather the sin nature that compelled us to sin (see note 9 at Rom. 5:21, p. 687). Paul is saying, "Is it the law that compelled us to sin?" The answer to this is no.

Paul had just spoken of being "loosed from," "free from," "dead to," and "delivered from" the law (see note 11 at Rom. 7:6, p. 695). Now Paul is clarifying his statements so that someone doesn't think that he is saying that the law is the thing that drove us to sin. The law of God simply made clear to us that we already had a depraved nature. When the law said, *"thou shalt not covet,"* that commandment didn't make covetousness come, but it made the lust that was already present revive (v.9), and strengthened it (1 Cor. 15:56), so that we could not be deceived any longer into thinking that we could produce salvation on our own (see note 4 at Rom. 3:19, p. 671).

God's commandments are holy, just, and good (v. 12), but man apart from God is sinful. Therefore, it was impossible that a revelation of God's true standards could change our nature; only the new birth can do that. The law simply stripped our sinful nature of its disguise so that we could properly assess how bad the situation was.

2 (Rom. 7:7) As explained in note 2 at Romans 1:18, page 659, there is an intuitive knowledge of right and wrong inside every person. How does that harmonize with Paul's statement here? The answer is that the law brought sin into focus.

Every person has an intuitive picture of what sin is, but the hardness of our hearts caused this image to become blurred. Once the law comes to an individual, all blindness is removed and it is very clear what God's standard of right and wrong is.

3 (Rom. 7:9) Paul is stating that there was a time in his life when he (his soulish, emotional, or personality part) was not separated from God. This was before the law came. But the law of God was communicated thousands of years before Paul was born, so what does this mean?

When Paul speaks of the law coming, he is speaking of the time in every person's life when he recognizes that he is violating a command of God. A child may know he's been told not to do certain things and that if he does so he will be punished. However, there comes a time when he realizes that it is not just Mom or Dad or society that he is disobeying, but this is disobedience to God. That's when the law comes and God imputes that person's sins from that time. Prior to that time, the sin nature of that individual is not being imputed to him (see note 2 at Rom. 5:13, p. 685) and he can fellowship with God.

Footnotes for Romans 7:9 continued on p. 697

ROMANS

SIN TAKING OCCASION BY THE LAW (continued)

CHAPTER 7

10 And the commandment,[m] which *was ordained* to life,[n] I found *to be* unto death.[o]
11 For sin,[h] taking occasion[5p] by the commandment,[m] deceived[q] me, and by it slew[r] *me.*
12 Wherefore the law is holy, and the commandment holy, and just, and good.[s]
13 Was then that which is good[t] made death[6] unto me?[u] God forbid.[b] But sin,[h] that it might appear[v] sin, working[j] death in me by that which is good;[s] that sin[h] by the commandment[m] might become exceeding[w] sinful.[x]
14 For we know that the law is spiritual:[7y] but I am carnal,[z] sold[aa] under sin.[h]

m i.e. the O.T. law
n i.e. designed and intended to bring life . . . (Amp)- Gal. 3:21
o Rom. 7:13 2 Cor. 3:7
p Gk.-"aphorme"- a starting point; i.e. an opportunity
q Gk.-"exapatao"- to seduce wholly; "seduce"- to lead (a person) away from duty or proper conduct; entice into wrongful behavior; corrupt- Heb. 3:13
r Gk.-"apokteino"- to kill outright; fig. to destroy
s see note 14 at Rom. 3:31, p. 674 Rom. 7:14 Dt. 4:8 Neh. 9:13 Ps. 19:7-12 119:137,172 1 Tim. 1:8
t Dict.- having positive or desirable qualities
u But didn't the law cause my doom? How then can it be good? (Tay)
v Dict.- to come into view; become visible

w Dict.- to an advanced or unusual degree; extremely
x Gk.-"hamartolos"- devoted to sin; a sinner not free from sin; preeminently sinful, esp. wicked
y Gk.-"pneumatikos"- spiritual; emanating from the divine spirit, or exhibiting its effects and so its character; produced by the sole power of God Himself without natural instrumentality; supernatural (Thayer)
z Gk.-"sarkikos"- pertaining to flesh; i.e. bodily, temporal, or (by impl.) animal; unregenerate; I however am a creature of flesh (Rhm) but I am unspiritual, sold to sin (Wey)- Mt. 16:23 1 Cor. 3:1-3
aa Gk.-"piprasko"- to traffic; i.e. dispose of as merchandise or into slavery (lit. or fig.)

Footnotes for Romans 7:9 (cont'd); Footnotes for Romans 7:10-14

Notice that Paul said, *"when the commandment came, sin **revived**."* He did not say, "sin came." You cannot revive something that doesn't already exist. The sin nature already exists in every human at birth (see notes 1 and 4 at Rom. 5:15-16, p. 686), but until the law comes, that nature is dead (v. 8). That does not mean that it is not functional. Observation tells us that very young children have a functional sin nature. But God is not imputing sin unto us until the time that every person knowingly violates God's law.

This is why children can receive from God even before they are born again and it also explains why infants who die go to heaven. Until the time that Paul calls "when the commandment comes" or what many call "the age of accountability," the sin nature does exist but God is not imputing that sin. Therefore, they are not bearing God's judgment against sin. But once the commandment comes, then the wrath of God against sin is released (see note 3 at Rom. 4:15, p. 678) and unless they receive Jesus as their Savior, they will bear the eternal punishment of God (see note 4 at Mk. 3:29, p. 128).

It is impossible to fix a certain age when this accountability of children occurs. That varies from person to person and for some, such as in cases of retardation, it is possible that this age of accountability is never reached. We can be sure that our all-knowing God will be righteous in His judgment of each individual.

4 (Rom. 7:9) Every individual is born with a nature that is dead in trespasses and sin (Eph. 2:1-3), but until he reaches an understanding where he is accountable to God, that sin is not imputed unto him (see note 3 at this verse). Until that time people are alive in the sense that they can communicate with God without the barrier of sin. But once the law comes and sin is imputed, there is a separation (or death) from God which can only be remedied by the new birth (see note 2 at Jn. 3:3, p. 48) through faith in Jesus.

5 (Rom. 7:11) The ministry of the law actually gave sin (the sin nature—see note 9 at Rom. 5:21, p. 687) an occasion against us. The corrupt rebellious nature of man will always lust for what it cannot have. Forbid a man to do something that he was only mildly interested in before and he will develop an uncontrollable lust for that very thing.

This is how the law worked. Sin was already at work in man, but when the law came condemning their actions, sin came alive (v. 9) in comparison to what it was before. The reason God did this is because mankind had been blinded to what sin was and its consequences. Sin had already beaten and enslaved us and we didn't realize it. We thought we were good enough until the law came. Once we were forbidden to do and think certain ways, sin began to abound (Rom. 5:20) and we became aware that we were by nature children of the devil (Eph. 2:3) and needed a savior. That was the purpose and ministry of the Old Testament law (see note 4 at Rom. 3:19, p. 671).

Failure to understand this truth has led many well meaning religious people to attempt to get others to stop sinning through the proclamation of God's laws against, and punishments for, sin. That wasn't the purpose of the law. According to these verses, sin actually revives and gains an occasion against us when the law is used. The right use of the law is to give a knowledge of sin (Rom. 3:19) and convince us that we are doomed without a savior. The law is powerless to overcome sin. Only the grace of God can cause us to overcome sin (Rom. 6:14).

6 (Rom. 7:13) Even though the law was called *"the ministration of death"* (2 Cor. 3:7), the law itself was not death. Death was already at work in us through the sin nature (see note 9 at Rom. 5:21, p. 687). The law simply drew out what was already there so that we could see how sinful we were and realize that we needed a savior. The deceitfulness of sin evaporates in the presence of the law and sin becomes exceedingly sinful.

7 (Rom. 7:14) This is why the law could not produce life for us. It is because the law is spiritual, but we are carnal. Another way of saying this is, the law is perfect, but we aren't. If we could have lived up to every detail of the law, then we could have obtained salvation through it. But all have sinned and come short of God's perfect standard (Rom. 3:23). All except for one, and that is Jesus.

The law did provide life for one man, the man Christ Jesus, because He was the only man who was ever perfect. Jesus was without any sin whatsoever and therefore He deserved eternal life as a payment, not a gift. Those who put their faith in Jesus as their Savior benefit from His keeping of the law (Rom. 8:4).

ROMANS

THE EFFECTS OF TRYING TO LIVE BY LAW OR SELF-EFFORT

CHAPTER 7

15 For that[1] which I do[a] I allow not: for
what I would, that do[b] I not;[c] but what I
hate,[d] that do[e] I.[f]
16 If then I do that which I would not, I
consent[g] unto the law that *it is* good.[h]
17 Now then it is no more I that do it, but
sin[2i] that dwelleth[j] in me.
18 For I know that in me (that is, in my
flesh,)[3k] dwelleth[j] no good[l] thing:[m] for to
will is present with me; but *how* to perform
that which is good I find not.[n]

a Gk.-"katergazomai"- to work fully; i.e. accomplish; For that which I am working out I do not approve (Rhm)

b Gk.-"prasso"- to practice; i.e. perform repeatedly or habitually; by impl. to execute; accomplish

c Rom. 7:16, 19-20 Ps. 65:3 119:5 Eccl. 7:20 Gal. 5:17 Phil. 3:12-14 1 Jn. 1:7-10

d Gk.-"miseo"- to detest; Dict.- to loathe; detest; to dislike; wish to shun- Rom. 12:9 Prov. 8:13 13:5 Amos 5:15 Heb. 1:9

e Gk.-"poieo"- to make or to do

f notice the three different Gk. words used for the word "do" in this verse- see ref. a, this heading see ref. b, this heading see ref. e, this heading

g Gk.-"sumphemi"- to say jointly; i.e. assent to

h Gk.-"kalos"- beautiful, but chiefly good; i.e. valuable or virtuous- Rom. 7:12, 14, 22 Ps. 119:127-128

i Gk.-"hamartia"- a missing of the mark; a principle or source of action; or an inward element producing acts; a governing principle or power, acting through the members of the body (Vine) see note 9 at Rom. 5:21, p. 687 Rom. 7:20, 23

j Gk.-"oikeo"- to occupy a house; i.e. reside (fig. inhabit; remain; inhere); by impl. to cohabit- Rom. 7:20, 23

k Rom. 13:14 Gal. 5:19-21, 24

l Dict.- having positive or desirable qualities; not bad or poor

m Gen. 6:5 8:21 Ps. 51:5 Lk. 11:13

n I can will, but I cannot do, what is right (Gspd). For the wish to do right is there but not the power (Wey). No matter which way I turn I can't make myself do right. I want to but I can't (Tay).

Footnotes for Romans 7:15-18

1 (Rom. 7:15) Many debates have occurred over whether Paul was describing himself before his conversion in these verses or whether he was describing the carnality that still existed in him after all those years of walking with the Lord. Is Paul describing a condition that has already been taken care of through the new birth, or is he saying that even mature Christians are doomed to a life of schizophrenia (lit. split mind) where part of us wants to serve God and part of us wants to serve the devil?

Actually, Paul is not stating either one of those positions. He is expounding the impossibility of serving God in our own power, whether lost or saved. The flesh (see note 3 at v. 18, below) is unwilling and unable to fulfill the law of God, and if a Christian tries to fulfill the righteousness of the law through his own will power he will fail just the same as an unregenerate man. Paul is describing the futility of trying to obtain favor with God through our own goodness whether Christian or non-Christian. That has been the theme throughout the book of Romans.

Paul only used the term "spirit" once in Romans 7 (v. 6); a chapter that described the hopelessness of man to ever keep the righteousness of the law in his own strength. In contrast, the word "spirit" or "Spirit" is used 21 times in Romans 8; a chapter that gives the answer to the hopelessness of Romans 7.

In these verses of Romans 7 Paul is not describing a warfare that wages between the new man and the old man. He is contrasting the complete inability of man to save himself because of his corrupted flesh (see note 3 at v. 18, below) versus the life-transforming power of Christ described in chapter 8.

The apostle Paul was not living a life of constant failure where the good that he wanted to do, he was unable to accomplish, but the evil that he didn't want to do, he did. He wasn't living that kind of life because it was no longer him living, but Christ living in him (Gal. 2:20). Christ in Paul was manifesting a holiness in Paul's life that was second to none.

However, if he would have abandoned his dependency upon Christ and would have started trying to live the Christian life out of his own resources, then the condition described in Romans 7:15-24 would have been his experience.

Our flesh has been corrupted through sin, and though we can renew our minds through God's Word (Rom. 12:2), we can never elevate our flesh to a place where it can fulfill the law of God. Hence, the good news of Romans 8 that what the law couldn't do because of the weakness of our flesh (Rom. 8:3), God did for us, and all we have to do is receive by faith.

2 (Rom. 7:17) As already stated in note 9 at Romans 5:21, page 687, this sin is not speaking of an individual act of sin, but of the "old man" or "sin nature" itself. This looks like a direct contradiction of Paul's statements in Romans 6 about the old man being dead (see note 6 at Rom. 6:4, p. 688).

To harmonize these apparently opposite accounts, most people have said that the death spoken of in Romans 6 is not a one-time experience but an ongoing process. Experience and Paul's testimony here seem to bear that out.

However, Romans 6:9, 10, and 11 make a specific point of comparing our death to sin with Christ's death to sin. Verse 10 clearly states that Christ died unto sin **once** (see note 11 at Rom. 6:9, p. 690) and verse 11 says we should **likewise** reckon ourselves to be dead unto sin (see note 1 at Rom. 6:11, p. 690). To further strengthen this point, Paul begins Romans 7 with the illustration of marriage (see note 3 at Rom. 7:2, p. 694). In the same way that a woman cannot have two husbands, a Christian cannot have two natures (see note 4 at Rom. 7:3, p. 695).

So, in context, there is a very strong case for our old man being dead in the absolute sense. But, what about Paul's statements in verses 17 and 20 about sin dwelling in him? The key is in verse 23 where Paul speaks of a law (influence) of sin that dwelt in his members, not sin itself (see note 5 at Rom. 7:23, p. 699).

Therefore, this passage is referring to the force or influence of the old man, which does still exist, but not the old man himself. The argument for the complete abolishment of the sin nature is further strengthened in verse 24 (see note 2 at v. 24, p. 699) where Paul refers to *"the body of this death"* which is referring to the same thing that Paul spoke of in Romans 6:6 where he used the terminology *"the body of sin"* (see note 8 at Rom. 6:6, p. 689).

3 (Rom. 7:18) The term "flesh" comes from the Greek word "sarx." "Sarx" was translated "flesh" 147 times; "carnal" 2 times (Rom. 8:7 and Heb. 9:10); "carnally" 1 time (Rom. 8:6); and "fleshly" 1 time (Col. 2:18). There are many ways that the word "flesh" was used in the New Testament, but for simplification, we will group its usage into three main categories.

First, it can refer to the physical flesh of man (Lk. 24:39) or beasts (Ex. 1 Cor. 15:39). When used in that context, the term is descriptive of only the physical makeup of man and is neither good nor bad, as can be seen by the fact that Jesus was made "flesh" (Jn. 1:14).

Second, "flesh" can describe the weakness and frailty of man, or man apart from God. This is the way Paul used the term in Romans 8:3 when he said, *"For what the law could not do, in that it was weak through the flesh."* Paul is saying that man, without the quickening power of God in his life, was unable to keep the law. Paul described his own efforts at holiness without the power of Christ as works of the flesh (Phil. 3:3-9). *"The flesh* is *weak"* (Mt. 26:41).

Third, "flesh" can refer to all that is sinful in man. In Galatians 5:19-21, Paul describes the works of the flesh as *"adultery, fornication, uncleanness, lasciviousness, idolatry, witchcraft, hatred, variance, emulations, wrath, strife, seditions, heresies, envyings, murders, drunkenness, revellings, and such like."* In this sense, the term "flesh" can be used almost interchangeably with the sin nature of man when describing those who are not born again, or the effects of the residual old man (see note 6 at Rom. 6:14, p. 691) on those who are born again.

In this instance, when Paul used this parenthetical phrase, *"that is, in my flesh"* he was specifying the natural part of his person or the second category of "flesh" described above. He was stating that in himself, apart from his born-again spirit, there was no good thing. He had to include this explanation or his statement would not have been accurate, for in his spirit there was a good thing (i.e. Christ).

ROMANS

THE EFFECTS OF TRYING TO LIVE BY LAW OR SELF-EFFORT (cont'd)

CHAPTER 7

19 For the good[l] that I would[o] I do not:
but the evil[p] which I would not, that I do.[q]
20 Now if I do that I would not,[r] it is no
more I that do it,[s] but sin[i] that dwelleth[j] in
me.[t]

21 I find then a law,[4u] that, when I would
do good,[h] evil[p] is present[v] with me.
22 For I delight[w] in the law of God[x] after
the inward[y] man:
23 But I see another law[5] in my
members,[z] warring[aa] against the law[5] of my
mind, and bringing me into captivity[bb] to
the law[5] of sin[i] which is in my members.[z]

Footnotes for Romans 7:19-23

4 (Rom. 7:21) This law (force or influence—see note 5 at v. 23, below) was present, but Paul was not living under the dominance of it (Rom. 6:14). He clearly states in Romans 8:2 that the law of the Spirit of life in Christ Jesus had made him free from the law of sin and death (see note 1 at v. 15, p. 698).

5 (Rom. 7:23) The Greek word translated "law" three times in this verse is "nomos" meaning "a force or influence impelling to action" (Vines). So, these verses are not speaking of the "old self" or "sin nature" directly but rather of its influence.

In verse 22, this same Greek word was used to refer to the law of God. In that instance it is clear that this is speaking of the influence of God through His precepts and not the divine person Himself. Likewise, in verse 23, the influence of the "old man" is what is being spoken of.

As explained in note 8 at Romans 6:6, page 689, the "old self" is dead and gone, but it left behind a body. Attitudes and emotions, which still influence us until we renew our minds, are the body of the old man. We are not dealing directly with the "old sin nature" but with its influence that is still being exerted through our unregenerate flesh. So, the Christian life is a renewal of our minds to who we have become in Christ, not a hatred for who we are in our "old self."

o Gk.-"thelo"- to determine; i.e. choose or prefer, by impl. to wish; i.e. be inclined to
p Gk.-"kakos"- worthless; i.e. depraved or injurious;Trans.- bad; evil; harm; ill; noisome; wicked
q Gk.-"prasso"- to practice; i.e. perform repeatedly or habitually
r Now if my own will is against my deeds (Con) Well, if I act against my wishes (Mof)
s Clearly it is no longer I who am the agent (NEB)
t Rom. 7:17
u i.e. a principle- Rom. 7:23 8:2
v Gk.-"parakeimai"- to lie near; i.e. be at hand
w Gk.-"sunedomai"- to rejoice in with oneself; i.e. feel satisfaction concerning

x Job 23:12 Ps. 1:2 19:8-10 40:8 119:16, 24 Heb. 8:10
y Gk.-"eso"-inside- Rom. 2:29 2 Cor. 4:16 Eph. 3:16 1 Pet. 3:4
z Gk.-"melos"- a limb or part of the body- Rom. 7:5, 21 6:13,19 8:2 Gal. 5:17 Jas. 4:1
aa Gk.-"antistrateuomai"- to attack; i.e. (by impl.) destroy
bb Gk.-"aichmalotizo"- to make captive; Dict.- held as prisoner; one who is forcibly confined

GIVING UP AND ACCEPTING GOD'S PROVISION FOR DELIVERANCE

CHAPTER 7

24 O wretched[a] man[1] that I am! who
shall deliver[b] me from the body[c] of this
death?[2]
25 I[3] thank[d] God[e] through[f] Jesus[g] Christ[h]
our Lord.[i] So[4] then with the mind[j] I myself
serve[k] the law of God;[e] but with the flesh
the law of sin.[l]

Footnotes for Romans 7:24-25

1 (Rom. 7:24) Paul was not describing his spiritual condition when he said, *"O wretched man that I am!"* He was speaking of his flesh (see note 3 at Rom. 7:18, p. 698). He made this distinction clear in verse 18 when he said, *"I know that in me (that is, in my flesh) dwelleth no good thing."* So, as explained in note 1 at Romans 7:15, page 698, Paul was describing the absolute wretchedness of his flesh.

2 (Rom. 7:24) In context, Paul is summarizing his statements from verses 14 through 23. He didn't say, "who shall deliver me from this death," for the Christian has already been delivered from the death that is the wage of sin (see note 3 at Rom. 6:23, p. 693). He made special mention of the **body** of this death.

The terminology *"the body of this death"* corresponds to what Paul called *"the body of sin"* in Romans 6:6. He was not speaking of the sin nature itself, for a Christian no longer has a sin nature (see note 8 at Rom. 6:6, p. 689), but he is rather speaking of the "old man" or the lingering influence of the sin nature that still exerts itself through the unrenewed mind.

So, death, or the old man, is gone but the body that it left behind (i.e. the thoughts, attitudes, and emotions) still poses a problem to the Christian. How do we overcome this flesh (see note 3 at Rom. 7:18, p. 698)? The answer is stated in verse 25 and then explained in Romans 8.

3 (Rom. 7:25) Paul is not just stating that he is thanking God through Jesus Christ, but he is specifically thanking God for the deliverance from this body of death, which only comes through our Lord Jesus Christ.

4 (Rom. 7:25) Here is the conclusion of Paul's arguments from verses 14 through 24. He desires to serve the law of God but his flesh is incapable of doing so. How then can we overcome this frustration? The answer is given in Romans 8 as Paul explains how to escape the flesh and walk in the Spirit.

a Gk.-"talaiporos"- enduring trial; i.e. miserable Dict.- living in degradation and misery; miserable
b Gk.-"rhuomai"- to rush or draw (for oneself); i.e. rescue
c see note 8 at Rom. 6:6, p. 689 Rom. 7:23 8:2
d Rom. 6:17 1 Cor. 15:57 Eph. 5:20 Col. 3:17
e see note 1 at Jn. 1:1, p. 2
f Gk.-"dia"- a primary prep. denoting the channel of an act
g see note 2 at Acts 8:5, p. 545 see note 6 at Acts 4:12, p. 523

h see note 2 at Mt. 16:16, p. 202 see note 5 at Jn. 1:41, p. 40 see note 5 at Mk. 1:1, p. 30
i see note 3 at Lk. 1:43, p. 12
j Gk.-"nous"- the intellect; i.e. mind (divine or human; in thought, feeling, or will); by impl. meaning Trans. mind - 15 times minds - 2times understanding - 7 times
k Gk.-"douleuo"- to be a slave to (lit. or fig., invol. or vol.)
l see note 9 at Rom. 5:21, p. 687 Rom. 7:7, 20, 23 Gal. 5:17-24

ROMANS

WALKING AFTER THE SPIRIT, NOT AFTER THE FLESH

a Gk.-"katakrima"- an adverse sentence (the verdict)- Jn. 3:18-19 5:24
b Jn. 15:4, 7 1 Cor. 1:30 15:22 2 Cor. 5:17 12:2 Gal. 3:28 Phil. 3:9
c see note 20 at Rom. 8:9, p. 703
d see note 3 at Rom. 7:18, p. 698 Mt. 26:41 Gal. 5:16 Eph. 2:3 2 Pet. 2:10

CHAPTER 8

***THERE** is* therefore[1] now[2] no[3] condemnation[4a] to them which are in Christ Jesus,[b] who walk not after[c] the flesh,[d] but after the[5] Spirit.[e]

2 For the law[f] of the Spirit of life[g] in Christ Jesus[b] hath made me free[h] from the law[6f] of sin and death.[i]

e Gal. 5:16, 25
f see note 5 at Rom. 7:23, p. 699
g John 6:63 7:38-39 2 Cor. 3:6
h Gk.-"eleutheroo"- to liberate; Dict.- at liberty; not bound or constrained
i Rom. 6:18 6:22 7:24-25 2 Cor. 3:17

PARALLEL SCRIPTURE FOR ROMANS 8:1

JOHN 3:18

18 He that believeth on him is not condemned: but he that believeth not is condemned already, because he hath not believed in the name of the only begotten Son of God.

Footnotes for Romans 8:1-2

1 (Rom. 8:1) The dictionary defines the word "therefore" as "for that reason; consequently; hence." This word ties Paul's statement here in Romans 8:1 to the previous verses. Paul is now giving us the answer to the hopeless situation he described in Romans 7:14-24.

Prior to Romans 8, the Holy Spirit was only mentioned once in this epistle (Rom. 5:5). In this chapter alone, the Holy Spirit is referred to 19 times (comp. with note 1 at Rom. 7:15, p. 698). Paul is making the point that the only way to overcome the effects of sin in our lives is through the indwelling presence and power of the Holy Spirit.

2 (Rom. 8:1) There are eleven Greek words used in the New Testament that were translated "now." Some of these words simply provide a transition between thoughts. However, the Greek word translated "now" in this verse is "nun" which is "a primitive particle of present time; now" (Strong); "the immediate present" (W. E. Vine). Thus, Paul's use of this word makes it very clear that living with no condemnation is a present tense experience of the believer, not something reserved for the future.

3 (Rom. 8:1) The Greek word that was translated "no" in this verse is "ouden." This is an emphatic term meaning "none; not even one" (Strong). Wuest translated this as, "There is not even one bit of condemnation" (*Galatians in the Greek New Testament* by Kenneth S. Wuest).

4 (Rom. 8:1) The Greek word translated "condemnation" here is "katakrima" meaning "an adverse sentence (the verdict)." Paul is stating that God has no adverse sentence against us once we accept Him. All our punishment has been placed on Jesus and we don't bear it. A Christian who still walks in condemnation is being condemned by the devil or is condemning himself. It's not God who condemns us (Rom. 8:34).

Second Corinthians 3:9 called the law a *"ministration of condemnation."* It was the law that brought God's adverse sentence against us. Romans 3:19 says the law was given to make us guilty before God. Guilt is the emotional response to condemnation.

This can be illustrated by the way we condemn buildings. When the government condemns a building it is declared unfit for use and must be destroyed. Likewise, when Satan condemns us, he makes us feel unfit for use and ready to be destroyed. Since the Christian is no longer under the law (see note 3 at Rom. 4:15, p. 678), he should no longer be condemned or feel unfit for use. We have been accepted by the Father through Jesus (Eph. 1:6).

5 (Rom. 8:1) God placed the judgment that the law prescribed against us upon His Son. Therefore, those who accept Jesus as their Savior will not be condemned because Jesus was condemned for us (v. 3). This truth and the fact that this phrase, *"who walk not after the flesh but after the Spirit"* is not in some of the old Greek manuscripts has led many scholars to believe that this phrase does not belong here. They say it was borrowed from verse four by some scribe who was copying out the scriptures.

Condemnation still exists as any Christian knows. This verse has rightly portrayed that only those who are living in the power of the Holy Spirit escape that condemnation. Compare this to the law of gravity. Gravity is a law that never quits exerting its power, but it can be overcome. Through the laws of aerodynamics man can actually fly and send space ships beyond Earth's gravity. But it takes power to do this. If the power is shut off, the law of gravity is still at work and will cause the vehicle to fall.

Likewise, the law of sin and death still exists. If a Christian shuts off the power of the Spirit of life and begins to start walking in the power of his own flesh, Satan will use this law of sin and death to make sure he crashes and is condemned.

God convicts of sin but He doesn't condemn (Rom. 8:34). Conviction is solely for our profit with no malice while condemnation includes punishment (see note 4 at this verse, above). Satan is the one who condemns the Christian, but the Holy Spirit has given us the power to escape that condemnation.

6 (Rom. 8:2) Romans 7:15-24 described the hopelessness of anyone attempting to overcome the law (see note 5 at Rom. 7:23, p. 699) of sin and death in his own ability or holiness (see note 1 at Rom. 7:15, p. 698). But Romans 8, and specifically this verse, brings us the good news that what could not be done by human effort has been done through the power of the Holy Spirit. We are no longer slaves to the law of sin and death.

According to Romans 6:23, death is the wage of sin (see note 3 at Rom. 6:23, p. 693). Therefore, this phrase, *"the law of sin and death"* is referring to the influence of sin and the resulting wages of that sin. Another way of saying *"the law of sin and death"* is "the law that when we sin we receive death instead of life" or "when we sin we reap the curse instead of the blessing."

Deuteronomy 28:1-14 list the blessings that come if a person keeps the whole law. Verses 15-68 list all the curses that come as the wage of not keeping the law. Because the law of the Spirit of life has set us free from the law of sin and death, we no longer reap Deuteronomy 28:15-68, even though we haven't kept every precept of the law. Christ redeemed us from these curses of the law (Gal. 3:13). Praise God that we don't have to receive the wages of sin, which is death.

Not only have we been redeemed from the curses of Deuteronomy 28:15-68, but through Jesus we have the righteousness of the law fulfilled in us (see note 9 at v. 4, p. 701) so that the blessings of Deuteronomy 28:1-14 are now ours. So, through Christ, we receive what we don't deserve (the blessings of Dt. 28:1-14), and we don't receive what we do deserve (the curses of Dt. 28:15-68).

ROMANS

WALKING AFTER THE SPIRIT, NOT AFTER THE FLESH (cont'd)

CHAPTER 8

3 For what the law[7] could not do,[j] in that it was weak[k] through the flesh, God[l] sending his own Son[m] in the likeness[n] of sinful flesh,[o] and for sin,[p] condemned[q] sin[r] in the flesh:[8]

4 That the righteousness[s] of the law might be fulfilled[9] in us, who walk[10] not after[t] the flesh,[o] but after[t] the Spirit.

5 For[11] they that are after[t] the flesh do mind[u] the things of the flesh;[v] but they that are after the Spirit the things of the Spirit.[12w]

j Rom. 3:20; 7:5-11; Acts 13:39; Gal. 3:21; Heb. 7:19; 10:1-10
k Gk.-"astheneo"- to be feeble (in any sense)
l see note 1 at Jn. 1:1, p. 2
m see note 5 at Mk. 1:1, p. 30; Jn. 3:16; Gal. 4:4-5; 1 Jn. 4:10, 14
n Gk.-"homoioma"- resemblance; Trans. made like to; likeness; shape; similitude
o see note 3 at Rom. 7:18, p. 698
p for sin, or by a sacrifice for sin- 2 Cor. 5:21; Gal. 3:13
q Gk.-"katakrino"- to judge against; i.e. sentence see note 3 at Rom. 8:1, p. 700
r see note 9 at Rom. 5:21, p. 687
s Gk.-"dikaioma"- an equitable deed; by impl. a statute or decision; Trans. judgment; justification; ordinance; righteousness i.e. the outworked righteousness of the law- Gal. 5:22-24
t see note 20 at Rom. 8:9, p. 703
u Gk.-"phroneo"- to exercise the mind; i.e. entertain or have a sentiment or opinion; by impl. to be (mentally) disposed (more or less earnestly in a certain direction); intens. to interest oneself in (with concern or obedience)
v Rom. 8:6-7; Gal. 6:8; Phil. 3:19
w Col. 3:1-3; Gal. 5:22-25; Eph. 5:9

Footnotes for Romans 8:3-5

7 (Rom. 8:3) The law itself was not weak. In Romans 7:12 Paul said, *"the law* is *holy, and the commandment holy, and just, and good."* The law wasn't weak but our flesh (see note 3 at Rom. 7:18, p. 698) was. The law and our flesh were linked together like a chain, and a chain is no stronger than its weakest link. Our flesh was the weak link in the chain. Although the law was strong, it couldn't accomplish righteousness because of the weakness of our flesh.

8 (Rom. 8:3) This is speaking of the flesh of Jesus. God placed the condemnation that was directed towards us upon the flesh of His Son Jesus.

As stated in note 7 at this verse, the law was strong enough to produce life **if** anyone would have been able to keep it, but our human flesh rendered us impotent. This was a dilemma. The law was ordained to life (Rom. 7:10), but no one could keep it (Isa. 59:16). So, God Himself became flesh (Jn. 1:14; 1 Tim. 3:16). He did what no sinful flesh had ever done. He kept the law, thereby winning the life of God as the prize for keeping the law.

This granted Him eternal life, but before He could give it to us, we still had a debt that had to be paid. This is similar to someone receiving the death penalty for some hideous crime, then some billionaire leaves his whole estate to him. It would do the condemned man no good. But if that same billionaire could somehow take that man's place and die for him, then he could go free and enjoy his new wealth. That's what Jesus did for us. He took our sins and gave us His righteousness.

Jesus did much more than just obtain eternal life for us, He also paid all the wages of our sins (Rom. 6:23). God literally placed the condemnation, or judgment, that was against us upon His own Son. Jesus' perfect flesh was condemned so our defiled flesh could go free. What a trade!!

Since Jesus bore our sentence (condemnation), we don't have to bear it. The debt has already been paid. It would be double jeopardy if we also had to bear any condemnation.

9 (Rom. 8:4) This verse is saying that through the sacrificial death of Jesus, we can now fulfill the righteousness of the law. There are two ways that we need to understand this.

First, the righteousness of the law is now fulfilled in our new born-again spirit (see note 11 at Rom. 4:8, p. 676). Jesus fulfilled the law (Mt. 5:17) and has given us His righteousness (see note 10 at Rom. 3:26, p. 673). Every believer's spirit is righteous and truly holy.

Second, through the Holy Spirit, we are now empowered to live the holy lives outwardly in our actions that the law demanded but we were unable to do in our own strength. That's what Paul is referring to when he says, *"who walk not after the flesh, but after the Spirit."* It needs to be pointed out that although a Spirit-filled believer will live a holy life, he will never keep every detail of the law. It could not be done before salvation and it cannot be done after salvation.

In Luke 1:6, the same Greek word that was translated "righteousness" in Romans 8:4 was translated "ordinances" in that verse. Luke was speaking of Zacharias and Elisabeth that *"they were both righteous before God, walking in all the commandments and ordinances of the Lord blameless."* Notice that they were both righteous and blameless before the Lord, but not sinless (see note 2 at Lk. 1:6, p. 6). So, the righteousness of the law can be fulfilled without keeping every commandment.

The purpose of the law was to make us despair of saving ourselves and point us to a Savior (see note 4 at Rom. 3:19, p. 671). When a person comes to put faith in Jesus as his Savior, then that person is fulfilling the purpose of the law. So, this verse is speaking of the believer being empowered to live a holy life, but fulfilling the righteousness of the law is not the same as keeping every detail of the law (see note 12 at Rom. 7:6, p. 695).

Therefore, every Christian has fulfilled the righteousness of the law in his spiritual man through Jesus. But only those Christians who are under the control of the Spirit of God are fulfilling the spirit of the law in their actions.

10 (Rom. 8:4) The word "walk" in this phrase is translated from the Greek word "peripateo" meaning, "to tread all around, i.e. walk at large; figuratively to live, deport oneself, follow." The dictionary defines it as "to conduct oneself or behave in a particular manner; to live." Therefore, this phrase, *"who walk not after the flesh, but after the Spirit"* is speaking of those who do not conduct their lives according to the flesh but follow the leading of the Spirit.

The next verse goes on to further explain this and uses the terminology "mind the things of the flesh" to describe those who "walk after the flesh" and "mind the things of the Spirit" to describe those who "walk after the Spirit." So, "walking after the flesh" is simply having your mind focused on carnal things and "walking after the Spirit" is having your mind stayed on spiritual things (Jn. 6:63).

11 (Rom. 8:5) Verses 5-8 explain to us why only those who walk after the Spirit (see note 10 at Rom. 8:4, above) are seeing the righteousness of the law fulfilled in their lives (see note 9 at Rom. 8:4, above). It is because, whatever a person thinks on is what he is going to become or do (Prov. 23:7). Those who are after the flesh think on carnal things and therefore do carnal things. Thinking carnally can only produce death, while thinking spiritually (according to the Word—Jn. 6:63) can only produce life (see note 15 at v. 6, p. 702).

12 (Rom. 8:5) This verse gives us a test so we can determine if we are walking after the flesh or after the Spirit. Just judge what you are thinking about. If you are consistently thinking on the things of the Spirit (Jn. 6:63), then you are walking after the Spirit. If you are dominated with carnal thoughts (see note 13 at v. 6, p. 702), then you are walking after (see note 20 at Rom. 8:9, p. 703) the flesh (see note 3 at Rom. 7:18, p. 698).

ROMANS

WALKING AFTER THE SPIRIT, NOT AFTER THE FLESH (cont'd)

a Rom. 8:7 Eph. 2:3 4:17 Col. 1:21 2:18 Ti. 1:15
b But the mind of the (Holy) Spirit is life and soul-peace [both now and forever] (Amp)- Ps. 19:14 Isa. 26:3 Mt. 22:37 Rom. 12:2 Phil. 2:5 4:8 1 Tim. 4:15
c see note 13 at Rom. 8:6, this page
d Gk.-"phronema"-(mental) inclination or purpose

CHAPTER 8

6 For to be carnally[13] minded *is* death;[14a]
but to be spiritually minded *is* life[15] and
peace.[b]
7 *Because the carnal[16c] mind[17d] *is*
enmity[e] against God: for it is not subject to
the law of God,[f] neither indeed can[g] be.
8 So then they that are in[h] the flesh[i]
cannot please[18j] God.[19]

PARALLEL SCRIPTURES FOR ROMANS 8:7

GALATIANS 5:22-25

22 But the fruit of the Spirit is love,
joy, peace, longsuffering, gentleness,
goodness, faith,
23 Meekness, temperance: against
such there is no law.
24 And they that are Christ's have
crucified the flesh with the affections
and lusts.
25 If we live in the Spirit, let us also
walk in the Spirit.

e Gk.-"echthra"-hostility; by impl. a reason for opposition; Dict.- deep-seated hatred, as between rivals or opponents; antagonism; the feeling or expression of ill will; the ill will of one person or group toward another- Jas. 4:4
f Rom. 8:4 3:31 7:14, 22
g Gk.-"dunamai"-to be able or possible- Mt. 12:34 1 Cor. 2:14
h see note 20 at Rom. 8:9, p. 703
i see note 3 at Rom. 7:18, p. 698 Rom. 8:9 7:5 Jn. 3:3, 6
j Dict.- to give satisfaction or pleasure; be agreeable; make glad or contented

Footnotes for Romans 8:6-8

13 (Rom. 8:6) The same Greek word "sarx" that was translated "flesh" in verses 1, 3, 4, 5, and 8 was translated "carnally" in verse 6 and "carnal" in verse 7. So, these terms can be used interchangeably.

14 (Rom. 8:6) The death that is spoken of here is not only physical death, although that is included. It refers to all the effects or wages of sin (see note 3 at Rom. 6:23, p. 693). The Amplified Bible translates this verse, *"death that comprises all the miseries arising from sin, both here and hereafter."* Sickness, depression, loneliness, hatred, poverty, fear, and everything else that came as a result of sin would be included in this term "death."

15 (Rom. 8:6) This is a powerful statement. Being carnally minded doesn't just tend towards death, it **is** death. Likewise, being spiritually minded doesn't just tend towards life, it **is** life and peace. A person who says he is spiritually minded and yet is experiencing death (see note 14 at this verse, above) is deceived. If we would just dominate ourselves with the spiritual truths of God's Word, we would receive only life and peace.

16 (Rom. 8:7) This word "carnal" is translated from the same Greek word as "flesh" (see note 13 at Rom. 8:6, above). Just as with the word "flesh" (see note 3 at Rom. 7:18, p. 698), there is more than one way that the word "carnal" is used. All sin is carnal, but not all carnality is sin. Carnal can also refer to human ability or natural things.

Trying to live the Christian life from our own ability is carnal. In context, Paul is contrasting the hopeless struggle of the flesh to live holy, which he described in Romans 7:15-24, with the Spirit-filled life that he presents in this chapter. Therefore, he is portraying that trying to obtain holiness through the flesh is being carnal. It is inaccurate to think that only sin is carnal. All our self-righteousness is carnal too.

17 (Rom. 8:7) The carnal mind is hostile or opposed to God. The carnal mind hates the things of God (see ref. e, this page). Therefore, no one just naturally pleases God. It is impossible for the natural mind to think in the ways of God (1 Cor. 2:14). As Paul said in 1 Corinthians 2:14, *"But the natural man receiveth not the things of the Spirit of God: for they are foolishness unto him: neither can he know* them, *because they are spiritually discerned."* We have to deny our natural way of thinking and be led by the Spirit of God to walk pleasing to God.

18 (Rom. 8:8) Hebrews 11:6 says, *"without faith* it is *impossible to please* him.*"* This verse could also read, "So then they that are in the flesh cannot have faith" because faith is the only way to please God. Faith is a fruit of the Spirit (Gal. 5:22-23) and cannot be produced by human effort.

19 (Rom. 8:8) This is the sum of what Paul was saying in Romans 7:15-24 and the reason no one can ever trust in his own holiness to be justified in the sight of God. **The Christian life is not just hard to live; it is impossible to live in our own ability.** Christianity only works when the Spirit of God indwells and controls an individual, thereby giving him supernatural ability. Without the quickening power of the Holy Spirit, no one can believe God and receive salvation.

Many religions of the world believe in one God and some of them even worship the God of Abraham, but they don't believe in Jesus as their Savior. Without Jesus, they are in the flesh and cannot please God. They may even live a holier life than someone who has put faith in Jesus as his Savior, but their flesh will fail to be holy enough to earn salvation (see note 6 at Rom. 3:23, p. 672).

ROMANS

WALKING AFTER THE SPIRIT, NOT AFTER THE FLESH (cont'd)

CHAPTER 8

9 But ye are not in[20] the flesh, but in[20] the
Spirit,[k] if so be that the Spirit[21] of God
dwell[l] in you. Now if any man have not the
Spirit of Christ,[m] he is none of his.[22]
10 And if Christ[23] *be* in you,[n] the body
is dead because[24] of sin;[o] but the Spirit *is*
life because of righteousness.[p]
11 But if the Spirit of him that raised up
Jesus from the dead[q] dwell[l] in you, he that
raised up Christ from the dead[q] shall also
quicken[r] your mortal[s] bodies[25] by his Spirit
that dwelleth in you.[t]
12 Therefore,[u] brethren, we are
debtors,[26v] not to the flesh, to live after the
flesh.[w]
13 For if ye live after the flesh, ye shall
die:[27x] but if ye through the Spirit do
mortify[28] the deeds of the body, ye shall
live.[y]

k Rom. 8:2 Ezek. 11:19 36:26-27 Jn. 3:6
l Gk.-"oikeo"- to occupy a house; i.e. reside (fig. inhabit; remain; inhere); by impl. to cohabit- 1 Cor. 3:16 6:19 2 Cor. 6:16
m Gal. 4:6 Eph. 2:22 2 Tim. 1:14 1 Jn. 4:4 Phil. 1:19 1 Pet. 1:11
n Jn. 14:20 17:23 2 Cor. 13:5 Gal. 2:20 Eph. 3:17 Col. 1:27 Rev. 3:20
o although your bodies must die because of sin (Wms) though the body is a dead thing owing to Adam's sin (Mof) your body will die because of sin (LB)- Rom. 5:12 2 Cor. 4:11 5:1-4 2 Pet. 1:13-14
p see note 2 at Rom. 3:22, p. 672 see note 3 at Rom. 3:22, p. 672 see note 10 at Rom. 3:26, p. 673 Rom. 5:17 2 Cor. 5:21 Phil. 3:9

q see note 1 at Acts 1:3, p. 509 see note 2 at Acts 4:2, p. 522 see note 4 at Rom. 1:4, p. 655 Rom. 4:24 Acts 2:24 Eph. 1:19-20 Heb. 13:20 1 Pet. 1:21
r Gk.-"zoopoieo"- to (re-) vitalize (lit. or fig.) Trans. make alive; give life; quicken
s Gk.-"thnetos"- liable to die- Rom. 6:12 1 Cor. 15:53 2 Cor. 4:11 5:4
t Rom. 8:9 Jn. 7:38-39 14:17
u see note 1 at Rom. 8:1, p. 700
v Gk.-"opheiletes"- an ower; i.e. person indebted- Rom. 1:14
w see note 3 at Rom. 7:18, p. 698 Rom. 6:12-15 1 Cor. 6:19-20
x Rom. 8:6 6:21, 23 Rom. 7:5 Jas. 1:14-15
y Rom. 8:2 1 Cor. 9:27 Gal. 5:24 Col. 3:5-8 Ti. 2:11-12 1 Pet. 2:11

Footnotes for Romans 8:9-13

20 (Rom. 8:9) Paul makes a clear distinction between being "in" the flesh and "after" the flesh and "in" the Spirit and "after" the Spirit. A born-again person (see note 2 at Jn. 3:3, p. 48) cannot be "in" the flesh but they can walk (see note 10 at Rom. 8:4, p. 701) "after" the flesh. A lost person cannot be "in" the Spirit although he seeks to walk "after" the ways of the Spirit.

The word that was translated "in" here is the Greek word "en" and it "denotes a (fixed) position (in place, time or state)." In contrast, the word that was translated "after" in verses 1, 4, 5, 12, and 13 denotes "according to anything as a standard; agreeable to" (Thayer). Therefore, when Paul speaks of being "in" the flesh or Spirit, he is referring to a fixed position or state. When he speaks of being "after" the flesh or Spirit, he is referring to whatever we are using as a standard of conduct or whatever we are agreeing to at any given time.

A Christian can agree to or conduct his actions according to some standard other than God's and still keep his position in Christ (see note 1 at Rom. 6:20, p. 693). So, a Christian can walk "after" the flesh but he is never considered "in" the flesh.

21 (Rom. 8:9) According to Jesus' statement in John 14:17, no one can receive the Holy Spirit unless he has first received Jesus as his Savior (see note 27 at Jn. 14:17, p. 432). Therefore, anyone who has the Spirit of God dwelling in him is a born-again person (see note 2 at Jn. 3:3, p. 48) and is not in the flesh (see note 20 at this verse, above).

22 (Rom. 8:9) This passage makes an emphatic statement that every believer receives the Spirit of Christ at salvation. The supposition that the "Spirit of Christ" and the "Spirit of God" are synonymous terms has led many to believe that every Christian receives the Holy Spirit at salvation. However, this seems to be in contradiction to the examples given in the book of Acts (see note 6 at Acts 2:4, p. 512; see note 3 at Acts 8:16, p. 547; see note 1 at Acts 19:1, p. 609).

It is very likely that the phrase "Spirit of Christ" refers to the born-again spirit that every believer receives at salvation. The phrase "Spirit of God" possibly refers to the Holy Spirit that only indwells the believer if he receives the baptism of the Holy Spirit (see note 6 at Acts 2:4, p. 512).

23 (Rom. 8:10) Based on the previous verse as well as John 14:20, 2 Corinthians 13:5, and Colossians 1:27, Christ is in every born-again believer. Therefore, Paul is saying that for every Christian, our body is dead because of sin (see note 24 at this verse, below).

24 (Rom. 8:10) The body is dead "because" of sin but the Spirit is life "because" of righteousness. The Greek word translated "because" here is "dia" which "denotes the channel of an act; through." Therefore, our bodies are dead through or because of the influence of sin in our lives.

In the same way that some people who have recovered from the polio virus still have crippled bodies, so Christians who have been delivered from the old man (see note 9 at Rom. 5:21, p. 687) still have to deal with the corruption that the old man released into our physical bodies and minds. That's why no one can please God in his flesh. The flesh has been corrupted and is therefore dead or incapable of living up to God's standard.

To counter this, the Spirit of God is releasing life because of our new righteous spirit that we received through faith in Jesus. Sin has left its mark on our bodies but the Spirit of life within us is more than enough to overcome these problems. That's why it is imperative that the Christian learn how to walk after the Spirit and not after the flesh.

25 (Rom. 8:11) This verse is speaking of more than just the quickening of our bodies at the second return of Christ, although that is included. In the previous verse, Paul had spoken of the body being dead because of sin, but the Spirit being life because of righteousness. This is speaking of the current situation we face in this life.

Our flesh (see note 3 at Rom. 7:18, p. 698) has been rendered incapable of serving God correctly because of the effect sin had on it. But our situation isn't hopeless. God has given us His Spirit and we can overcome this deficit by letting Him live through us (Gal. 2:20). In this verse Paul is commenting on this quickening power of the Holy Spirit for this life as well as the ultimate victory when our physical bodies will be resurrected.

26 (Rom. 8:12) Paul is saying that our flesh (see note 3 at Rom. 7:18, p. 698) never helped us. It has been rendered powerless through sin (see note 24 at v. 10, above). It is only through the indwelling power of the Holy Spirit that the Christian has any hope of living in victory. Therefore, we are indebted to the Spirit and should yield to Him.

27 (Rom. 8:13) Paul is speaking of death in a figurative sense rather than a literal sense. He is addressing believers who have already received eternal life through the new birth (see note 2 at Jn. 3:3, p. 48) and he is not saying that they will lose their salvation if they walk "after" the flesh (see note 10 at Rom. 8:4, p. 701).

As explained in note 3 at Romans 6:23, page 693, death is a term that refers not only to physical death but it can also denote all the effects of sin in our lives. Therefore, Paul is speaking about experiencing defeat as we walk after the flesh compared to experiencing victory when we walk after the Spirit.

28 (Rom. 8:13) The word "mortify" was translated from the Greek word "thanatoo" meaning "to kill." The dictionary defines mortify as "to discipline (one's body and appetites) by self-denial." If we deaden ourselves to the flesh by self-denial and follow the leadership of the Holy Spirit, we will live.

ROMANS

WALKING AFTER THE SPIRIT, NOT AFTER THE FLESH (cont'd)

CHAPTER 8

14 For as many as are led[29] by the Spirit
of God,[a] they are the sons[30] of God.[b]
15 For ye have not received the spirit[31]
of bondage[c] again to fear;[d] but ye have
received the Spirit of adoption,[32e] whereby
we cry, Abba, Father.[f]
16 The Spirit itself beareth witness[33g]
with our spirit, that we are the children of
God:
17 And if children, then heirs;[h] heirs[h] of
God, and joint-heirs[34i] with Christ;[j] if so be
that we suffer[k] with *him,* that we may be
also glorified together.[l]

a Gal. 5:16,18, & 22-25 Eph. 5:9
b 2 Cor. 6:18 Gal. 3:26 Eph. 1:5 1 Jn. 3:1 Rev. 21:7
c Gk.-"douleia"- slavery- Heb. 2:15
d Ex. 20:19 Num. 17:12 Lk. 8:37 2 Tim. 1:7 Heb. 12:18-24 Jas. 2:19 1 Jn. 4:18
e Gk.-"huiothesia"- the placing as a son; i.e. (fig. Chr. sonship in respect to God)- Rom. 8:23 9:4 Gal. 4:5 Eph. 1:5
f see note 29 at Mt. 6:9, p. 79 Mk. 14:36 Lk. 11:2 22:42 Jn. 20:17
g Gk.-"summartureo"- to testify jointly; i.e. corroborate by (concurrent) evidence Trans. testify unto; bear witness
h Gk.-"kleronomos"- a sharer by lot; i.e. an inheritor; by impl. a possessor- Lk. 12:32 Acts 26:18 Gal. 3:29 4:7 Eph. 3:6 Ti. 3:7 Heb. 1:14 6:17 Jas. 2:5 1 Pet. 1:4
i Gk.-"sugkleronomos"- a co-heir; i.e. participant in common Trans. fellow heir- Eph. 3:6; heir together- 1 Pet. 3:7; heirs with- Heb. 11:9
j see note 2 at Mt. 16:16, p. 202 see note 5 at Jn. 1:41, p. 40 see note 5 at Mk. 1:1, p. 30
k Gk.-"sumpascho"- to experience pain jointly or of the same kind (spec. persecution; to "sympathize")- Acts 14:22 2 Cor. 4:8-18 Phil. 1:29 2 Tim. 2:10-13 3:12
l Gk.-"sundoxazo"- to exalt to dignity in company (i.e. similarly) with

Footnotes for Romans 8:14-17

29 (Rom. 8:14) Being led by the Spirit of God is the ultimate standard whereby we may know someone is a son of God. This raises the question, "If you aren't led by the Spirit of God, does that mean you are not born again?" It is true that everyone who is not born again is not led by the Spirit of God and everyone who is born again is led by the Spirit of God but that needs some explanation.

First, there are varying degrees of being led by the Holy Spirit. No believer is following the leading of the Lord as much as he could be, and, if an absolute standard was applied to this verse, no one would qualify to be a son of God. With this in mind, believers have been led by the Spirit to some degree, in making Jesus their Lord, if nothing else.

Second, being led by the Spirit does not cause us to be a son of God, but being a son of God causes us to be led of the Spirit. Every believer does have the Spirit of God to lead him, but that doesn't mean every believer heeds His leading (see note 3 at Jn. 10:3, p. 240). In context, Paul has just spoken about denying the flesh through the power and leading of the Holy Spirit. Now he is simply pointing out that every Christian has the leading of the Holy Spirit available to accomplish this.

30 (Rom. 8:14) Some people have tried to make a distinction between being a "child of God" and a "son of God." They say a "child of God" is any born-again believer, while a "son of God" refers only to a mature Christian. This looks good on the surface but further study will reveal there is no difference.

In Galatians 4, these same terms are used and "son" or "sons" is applied to all believers. Galatians 4:6 says, *"And because ye are sons, God hath sent forth the Spirit of his Son into your hearts, crying, Abba, Father"* and Romans 8:9 says, *". . .Now if any man have not the Spirit of Christ, he is none of his."* Since every believer has to have the Spirit of Christ (Rom. 8:9) and every son of God has the Spirit of God's Son in him crying, *"Abba, Father"* (Gal. 4:6), then we can clearly see that every born-again believer is a son of God. Therefore, these terms are used interchangeably and no doctrine about different levels of maturity can be drawn.

31 (Rom. 8:15) This "spirit of bondage" is a reference to the old sin nature (see note 9 at Rom. 5:21, p. 687). The fact that Paul says, *"ye have not received the spirit of bondage **again** . . ."* is a further testimony that our old sin nature is not just ceremonially dead but that it is totally gone in the life of the believer (see note 3 at Rom. 6:2, p. 688).

32 (Rom. 8:15) We are sons of God by adoption. Jesus was the Son of God by nature. As Jesus said to the Jews, we were of our father the devil (Jn. 8:44; Eph. 2:3), but Jesus purchased us and made us adopted sons of God.

33 (Rom. 8:16) First John 5:10 says, *"He that believeth on the Son of God hath the witness in himself."* John goes on to say in verse 13, *"These things have I written unto you that believe on the name of the Son of God; that ye may know that ye have eternal life."* So, the Spirit bearing witness with our spirit is to assure us that we are the children of God (1 Jn. 3:19).

34 (Rom. 8:17) We are not just heirs, we are joint-heirs with Christ. How wonderful it would be to inherit any amount of God's glory and power. But to think that we share equally with the one who has inherited everything God is and has is beyond comprehension. This is an awesome blessing, but it places a tremendous responsibility on us too.

In the same way that a check that is made out to two people cannot be cashed without the endorsement of both parties, so our joint-heirship with Jesus cannot be taken advantage of without our cooperation. Unaware of this, many Christians are just trusting that the Lord will produce the benefits of salvation for them. They are acutely aware that they can do nothing without Him, but don't realize that He will do nothing without us (Eph. 3:20).

The way we place our endorsement on the check is to believe and act like what God promised in His Word is true. Jesus has already signed His name to every promise in the Word. We aren't waiting for Him. He is waiting for us.

ROMANS

THE HOPE OF TOTAL SALVATION

CHAPTER 8

18 For I reckon[a] that the sufferings[b] of
this present time *are* not worthy *to be*
compared with the glory[c] which shall be
revealed[d] in[1] us.
19 For the earnest expectation[2] of the
creature[3][e] waiteth[f] for the manifestation[4] of
the sons of God.[g]
20 For the creature[5][e] was made subject[h]
to vanity,[6][i] not willingly,[j] but by reason of
him who hath subjected[h] *the same* in hope,[k]

a Gk.-"logizomai"- see note 6 at Rom. 4:3, p. 675
b Gk.-"pathema"- something undergone; i.e. hardship or pain; subj. an emotion or influence Trans. affection; affliction; motion; suffering- Mt. 5:11-12 Acts 20:24 2 Cor. 4:17-18 Heb. 11:25-26 & 35 1 Pet. 1:6-7 see note 3 at Acts 5:41, p. 532 see note 1 at Acts 8:1, p. 544 see note 67 at Jn. 15:19, p. 438 see note 69 at Jn. 15:20, p. 438 see note 73 at Jn. 16:4, p. 440 see note 2 at Acts 4:26, p. 526 see note 4 at Acts 9:4, p. 552 see note 3 at Acts 20:19, p. 618
c 2 Th. 1:7-12 2:14 1 Pet. 4:13 5:1 1 Jn. 3:2
d Gk.-"apokalupto"- to take off the cover; i.e. disclose
e see note 3 at Rom. 8:19, this page
f Gk.-"apekdechomai"- to expect fully; i.e. look for
g 2 Cor. 6:18 Gal. 3:26 Eph. 1:5 1 Jn. 3:1 Rev. 21:7
h Gk.-"hupotasso"- to subordinate; to obey
i to decay (Con) imperfection (TCNT) futility (Wey) not by choice (Rhm) not for some deliberate fault of its own (Knox)- Rom 8:22 Gen. 3:17-19 5:29 Isa. 24:5-6 Jer. 12:4
j not by its own choice (NEB) not of its own will (RSV)
k Gk.-"elpis"- from a prim. -"elpo"- (to anticipate, usually with pleasure); expectation or confidence- Rom. 4:18 5:2, 4-5 12:12 15:4, 13 1 Cor. 13:13

Footnotes for Romans 8:18-20

1 (Rom. 8:18) This is a very important statement. Paul did not say that this glory would be revealed "to us" but rather "in us." **The complete glory of God that Christians dream of receiving in eternity is already *in* us here on this earth!**

Paul said in 2 Thessalonians 2:14, *"he called you by our gospel, to the obtaining of the glory of our Lord Jesus Christ."* And in 1 Peter 5:1, Peter said he was a (present tense) partaker of this glory which shall be (future tense) revealed. Paul also prayed for the Ephesians that the Lord would grant them the spirit of wisdom and revelation in the knowledge of Him so they would see the glory of His inheritance which was already in the saints.

This leaves no doubt that the Christian's spirit is already complete. We don't need more faith, more power, or more anointing. We simply need to use more of what we have already received. Many Christians will be shocked when they stand before God and realize that all the things they prayed for were inside them from the time they believed (see note 3 at Mt. 26:41, p. 448).

2 (Rom. 8:19) The two English words "earnest expectation" were translated from the Greek word "apokaradokia." The word was only used twice in the New Testament (here and Phil. 1:20). This is a compound word meaning "intense anticipation" or as other scholars have translated it, "to strain forward" or literally, "await with outstretched head" (Sanday and Headlam); "to expect on and on, to the end" (Cremer). Fritz Rienecker says this word "denotes diversion from all other things and concentration on a single object."

Therefore, this verse makes it very clear that the whole creation is eagerly and intensely anticipating the day when the glory of God that is already deposited within God's saints (see note 1 at Rom. 8:18, above) will be revealed. That day won't completely arrive until the second return of the Lord, but it is logical to think that creation rejoices to some degree every time some saint manifests His glory here on this earth.

3 (Rom. 8:19) The Greek word "ktisis" was translated creature in verses 19-21. This same word was translated "creation" in verse 22. It literally means "that which is created."

4 (Rom. 8:19) The American Heritage Dictionary defines manifestation as, "the demonstration of the existence, reality, or presence of a person, object, or quality." You cannot manifest something that does not already exist. As the apostle John said, *"Beloved, now are we the sons of God and it doth not yet appear what we shall be . . ."* (1 Jn. 3:2). We are already the sons of God. This is not something that has yet to transpire. The whole creation is waiting for us to manifest what is already in us (see note 1 at Rom. 8:18, above).

5 (Rom. 8:20) Many people have thought that the part of creation that is being spoken of here is human beings. However, the contrast made in verses 22-23 clearly exempts the saints from this group. In verse 21 it speaks of the creature being *"delivered from the bondage of corruption into the glorious liberty of the children of God."* If "creature" were referring to unsaved people, then this would mean ultimate reconciliation of the human race to God, which is not the teaching of scripture. Therefore, it is most probable that the part of creation being spoken of here is all of creation, living and non-living, excluding humans. Paul is speaking of how all of creation did not choose to rebel against God. It was just mankind that sinned. Yet the Lord brought all the rest of creation against their choice into our cursed state with us so He could also redeem them with mankind.

Take, for example, the animal creation. Genesis 1:30 says that all the animals were given the green herbs of the field for their food. There were no carnivorous beasts. Yet after man's rebellion, parts of the animal creation began to devour one another as we see today. This was not God's original plan and it was not because of a specific sin on the animals' part that this happened. God subjected the animal creation to the same vanity (see note 6 at this verse, below) that man had come into, in the hope of redeeming them also.

The animal creation as well as the inanimate creation will be delivered from the corruption that we now see to walk in the glorious liberty of the children of God. It is not clear that every animal that has ever lived will be resurrected, but it is clear that the animal creation will be represented.

The scriptures declare this freedom for the creation when it speaks of the child playing with the snake (Isa. 11:8); the wolf and the leopard dwelling peacefully with sheep; and the lion and lamb, cow and bear dwelling together and eating straw like the ox (Isa. 11:6-7; also Isa. 65:25). We know that in heaven there are animals since the saints ride white horses at the second return of Jesus (Rev. 19:14).

So, in summary, the animal creation was plunged into the same degenerate state as mankind so that they could also be redeemed with us into liberty. Therefore, it can be expected that on the new earth where the saints will live for eternity (Rev. 21:1-7), there will be animals living in harmony with each other and mankind as God originally designed in His first creation.

6 (Rom. 8:20) The Greek word that was translated "vanity" here is the word "mataiotes" which means "emptiness as to results." In this verse it specifically means "failing of the results designed, owing to sin" (W.E. Vine). This is speaking of the non-human creation (see note 5 at this verse, above) being subjected to a corruption (v. 21) that was not God's original design.

ROMANS

THE HOPE OF TOTAL SALVATION (continued)

CHAPTER 8

21 Because[7] the creature[a] itself also
shall be delivered[b] from the bondage[c] of
corruption[d] into the glorious liberty of the
children of God.[e]
22 For we know that the whole creation[a]
groaneth[8] and travaileth in pain together
until now.[f]

23 And not only *they,* but ourselves
also, which have the firstfruits[g] of the Spirit,[9]
even we ourselves groan[h] within ourselves,
waiting[i] for the adoption,[10] *to wit,*[j] the
redemption[11] of our body.[k]
24 For we are saved[l] by hope:[12] but hope
that is seen[m] is not hope: for what a man
seeth,[m] why doth he yet hope[n] for?
25 But if we hope[n] for that we see[m] not,
then do we with patience[13o] wait[i] for *it.*

a see note 3 at Rom. 8:19, p. 705
b Gk.-"eleutheroo"- to liberate; i.e. to exempt Trans. deliver; make free
c Gk.-"douleia"- slavery
d Gk.-"phthora"- decay; i.e. ruin
e Rom. 8:19 Rev. 22:2-3
f It is plain to anyone with eyes to see that at the present time all created life groans of universal travail (Phil)
g Gk.-"aparche"- a beginning of sacrifice; i.e. the (Jewish) first-fruit (fig.). The first portion of the harvest, regarded both as an installment and as a pledge of the final delivery of the whole (Barrett).
continued on column 4

continued from column 1
The Holy Spirit is regarded as an anticipation of final salvation, and a pledge that we who have the Spirit shall in the end be saved (Barrett).
h Gk.-"stenazo"- to groan; sigh Trans. with grief; groan; grudge; sigh- Rom. 7:24 8:26 2 Cor. 5:2-4
i Gk.-"apekdechomai"- to expect fully Trans. look (wait) for- Rom. 8:19, 25
j Dict.- to know; that is to say; namely
continued on center column

References continued from column 4
k longing for the adoption that shall ransom our body from its bondage (Con) while we eagerly await our full adoption as sons, the redemption of our bodies (TCNT)- Lk. 21:28 Eph. 1:14 4:30 see note 7 at Mk. 10:45, p. 340 see note 1 at Mt. 26:2, p. 410
l see note 2 at Mt. 8:17, p. 68
m 2 Cor. 4:13 5:7 Heb. 11:1
n Gk.-"elpizo"- to expect or confide- Rom. 5:2 12:12 15:4, 13 Ps. 33:18, 22 42:5, 11 43:5 146:5 Jer. 17:7 1 Cor. 13:13 Gal. 5:5 Col. 1:5, 23, 27 1 Th. 5:8 2 Th. 2:16 Ti. 2:11-13 Heb. 6:18-19 1 Pet. 1:3, 21 1 Jn. 3:3
o Rom. 12:12 Ps. 37:7-9 62:1, 5-6 130:5-7 Lk. 8:15 21:19 Col. 1:11 1 Th. 1:3 2 Th. 3:5 Heb. 6:12, 15 10:36 12:1-3 Jas. 1:3-4 5:7-11 see note 3 at Lk. 21:19, p. 397

Footnotes for Romans 8:21-25

7 (Rom. 8:21) God made creation involuntarily subject to the same corruption that mankind voluntarily entered into so that He could reunite us through redemption back into the glorious creation He originally intended us to be.

8 (Rom. 8:22) Many times we are awestruck at the perfect balance that we see in all of nature. As glorious as it may seem, it is not God's best. Creation as we see it today has been corrupted and is far less than what God originally intended it to be. The whole creation is groaning and travailing together in pain and will not be relieved until the manifestation of the children of God (see note 4 at Romans 8:19, p. 705).

9 (Rom. 8:23) The Holy Spirit is called the "firstfruit" (see ref. g, this verse) of our salvation. Where there is a firstfruit, there has to be more fruit. Paul spoke of the Holy Spirit as being the earnest or down payment of our salvation with more to come (2 Cor. 5:5; Eph. 1:14).

As wonderful as our salvation is right here in this life, it is not complete. Our flesh (see note 3 at Rom. 7:18, p. 698) is a constant source of trouble and even victorious Christians groan for the time when we will be delivered from this flesh at the redemption of our body (2 Cor. 5:1-4).

10 (Rom. 8:23) The word "adoption" is used five times in the New Testament (Rom. 8:15, 23; 9:4; Gal. 4:5; Eph. 1:5). People draw many analogies from this term that have merit, but this verse makes it very clear that the term "adoption" is referring to the time when we will receive our glorified bodies.

11 (Rom. 8:23) Jesus purchased redemption for us—spirit, soul, and body. But our redemption is not completed yet. Our spirits are the only part of us that have experienced total redemption (see note 3 at Mt. 26:41, p. 448).

The English word "redemption" is translated from the Greek word "apolutrosis" which means "to ransom in full" (Strong). However, it is specifying more than just the payment of a ransom, but the releasing that comes as a result (W.E. Vine). So, Paul is speaking of the time when we will experience in our bodies what Jesus has already purchased for us.

This can be illustrated by the way we use trading stamps. First, the stamps have to be purchased, then they are redeemed for the desired product. The purchase is essential but so is the redemption. No one really wants the stamps. They want what the stamps can be redeemed for.

The purchase for our total salvation has already been made with the blood of Jesus, but our bodies are not redeemed yet. That is to say that we have not received all the benefits of that transaction in our physical bodies yet. That will take place at the second coming of the Lord when we receive our new glorified bodies (see note 3 at Lk. 24:49, p. 496).

12 (Rom. 8:24) Ephesians 2:8 says, *"For by grace are ye saved through faith."* Is there a contradiction between these two scriptures? Not at all. Putting faith in God's provision is what saves us, but hope is an important part of faith (see note 12 at Rom. 5:4, p. 683).

This verse makes it very clear that hope is not based on what is seen. Someone who says, "I have no reason to hope" doesn't understand what hope is. Hope comes directly from God (Rom. 15:13) through His Word (Rom. 15:4).

13 (Rom. 8:25) This verse definitely links patience and hope together. Hope produces patience. When we are in need of patience, we are in need of hope (see note 10 at Rom. 5:3, p. 682).

ROMANS

THE SPIRIT'S HELP IN WEAKNESS

CHAPTER 8

26 Likewise[1] the Spirit also helpeth[2a]
our infirmities:[3b] for we know not what we
should pray[c] for as we ought:[d] but the Spirit
itself maketh intercession[4e] for us with
groanings[f] which cannot be uttered.[5]
27 And he that searcheth[6] the hearts[g]
knoweth what *is* the mind[h] of the Spirit,
because he maketh intercession[i] for the
saints[j] according to *the will of* God.[k]

a Ps. 28:7; 33:20; 94:17; Isa. 41:10; 50:9; Acts 26:22; 27:17; Heb. 4:16; 13:6
b 2 Cor. 12:5-10; Heb. 4:15; 5:2
c Gk.-"proseuchomai"- to pray to God; i.e. supplicate; worship- Lk. 11:1; Jas. 4:3; see note 1 at Lk. 11:1, p. 256; see note 99 at Jn. 17:13, p. 444; see note 28 at Mt. 6:9, p. 79; see note 31 at Mt. 6:10, p. 79; see note 3 at Lk. 22:44, p. 449
d i.e. should
e Dict.- to plead on another's behalf; Latin-"intercedere"- to come between; "inter"- between + "cedere"- to go- Eph. 2:18; 6:18
f Dict.- to utter or convey with groaning; to voice a deep, wordless, prolonged sound expressive of pain, grief, annoyance, or disapproval; see note 2 at Jn. 13:21, p. 419; see note 16 at Jn. 11:33, p. 310
g 1 Chr. 28:9; 29:17; 2 Chr. 16:9; Ps. 7:9; 44:21; Prov. 17:3; Jer. 11:20; 17:10; 20:12; Acts 1:24; 15:8; 1 Th. 2:4; Heb. 4:12; Rev. 2:23; see note 10 at Mk. 7:21, p. 191; see note 3 at Mt. 12:34, p. 131
h Gk.-"phronema"- (mental) inclination or purpose
i Gk.-"entunchano"- primarily to fall in with, meet with in order to converse; then, to make petition, especially to make intercession; plead with a person, either for or against other (W.E. Vine)
j see note 5 at Acts 9:13, p. 555; see note 35 at Jn. 14:26, p. 434
k 1 Jn. 5:14-15

Footnotes for Romans 8:26-27

1 (Rom. 8:26) The word "likewise" is stressing that in the same way that hope helps us to endure until the redemption of our bodies (v. 23), so the Holy Spirit helps us through the frailties of our flesh by interceding for us.

2 (Rom. 8:26) The word "helpeth" was translated from the Greek word "sunantilambanomai" meaning "to take hold of opposite together; i.e. cooperate (assist)." It describes a union, not the Holy Spirit doing all the interceding for us. The Holy Spirit helps us as we are interceding, but He doesn't automatically do it for us.

3 (Rom. 8:26) The Greek word that was translated "infirmities" in this verse is "astheneia" meaning "feebleness (of body or mind); by implication malady; moral frailty" (Strong). This same word was translated "weakness" five times (1 Cor. 2:3; 15:43; 2 Cor. 12:9; 13:4; Heb. 11:34) so it is easy to see that this word is describing mental and moral weakness, not sickness.

Paul goes on to describe what these infirmities are when he says, *"for we know not what we should pray for as we ought."* The infirmities this scripture is speaking of are the weaknesses that come from not knowing how we should pray.

4 (Rom. 8:26) This has been an encouraging scripture for countless believers. It is certain that none of us knows exactly how to pray in every situation. Therefore, it is very comforting to know that the Holy Spirit is there to help us. However, as noted in note 2 at this verse, He helps us. He doesn't do the interceding for us but through us.

Even Jesus drew on this ministry of the Holy Spirit. It is written in John 11:33 and 38 that Jesus groaned in the Spirit twice when He raised Lazarus from the dead. What infirmity did Jesus have that He needed this ministry of the Holy Spirit? Jesus had no sin but He did have an infirmity. That was His physical mind. Even a sinless human mind could not comprehend raising a man from the grave after four days.

If Jesus needed the Holy Spirit to help Him when He didn't know how to pray, then certainly this should be an important ministry of the Holy Spirit in our lives.

5 (Rom. 8:26) This intercession of the Holy Spirit is with groanings that cannot be uttered. Some Spirit-filled Christians have said that this means groanings that cannot be uttered in our normal speech and therefore have said this is referring to speaking in tongues (see note 13 at Mk. 16:17, p. 507; see note 9 at Acts 2:4, p. 512). Yet this is referring to an intercession that is different from speaking in tongues.

In John 11:33 and 38, Jesus groaned in the Spirit twice. This is the exact terminology that is used here in Romans 8:26 and, in those cases, it is easy to see that there were no words uttered. It was exactly as the scripture states, a groaning **in the Spirit.**

Everyone who has the indwelling presence of the Holy Spirit has or will have this happen to them. Paul was referring to this in Galatians 4:19 when he spoke of travailing in birth for the Galatians. As explained in note 16 at John 11:33, page 310, this groaning of the Holy Spirit is not just a grief but a groan of anger and resistance against Satan's devices in our lives. Many times Christians don't discern this because they think that they are the only ones grieved with their situation. But this is the Holy Spirit desiring to get into intercession with us against our problems.

Although the groaning is unutterable, you can discern it and many times people react to this with audible groans or other outward acts. This has led to religious doctrines and traditions that are offensive to many people and unscriptural. There is nothing wrong with us reacting to the inner working of the Holy Spirit as long as we don't confuse our reactions with the Holy Spirit's actions. This intercession cannot be uttered.

Any counterfeits that religion may have produced only serve to illustrate that there has to be a genuine. The genuine groaning in the Spirit is priceless.

6 (Rom. 8:27) *"He that searcheth the hearts"* is a reference to God. God knows our hearts and He knows that the Holy Spirit will only intercede for the will of God to be done. The Holy Spirit is never at a loss as to how to convey our needs to the Father as we sometimes are. That's the reason this ministry of the Holy Spirit is so important. There is such oneness between the Father and the Holy Spirit that even His groanings are perfectly understood.

ROMANS

THE SPIRIT'S HELP IN WEAKNESS (continued)

CHAPTER 8

28 And[7] we know that all things work together[a] for good[b] to them that love God,[c] to them who are the called[d] according to *his* purpose.[e]

Footnote for Romans 8:28

7 (Rom. 8:28) This is a very powerful verse with a wonderful promise, but it has been greatly abused and misapplied. This verse is not saying that everything that happens to us is from God and is used by Him to accomplish His purposes in our lives. The Bible doesn't teach that.

Second Peter 3:9 makes a clear statement that the Lord is *"not willing that any should perish, but that all should come to repentance."* Yet many men and women are perishing because they have a choice. So, regarding salvation, God's will is not being done in the lives of many people.

Concerning physical healing, the Bible states that Jesus has already provided healing for us (Isa. 53:5; see note 2 at Mt. 8:17, p. 68; 1 Pet. 2:24) and that it is God's will for us to be healed (3 Jn. 2). Yet not everyone is healed and their sicknesses are not automatically working some redemptive purpose in their lives (see note 2 at Jn. 9:2, p. 237; see note 4 at Jn. 11:4, p. 306).

This twenty-eighth verse begins with the word "and." This means that the statement about everything working together for our good is made after Paul had spoken of the Holy Spirit making intercession for us. If we are not cooperating with the Holy Spirit so that He can make intercession for us (see note 4 at Rom. 8:26, p. 707), then everything will not work together for our good.

This verse also says this happens for those *"that love God, to them who are the called."* That means this doesn't apply to everyone. However, this verse has been used to try to convince even unbelievers that God is controlling the circumstances of their lives. That is not the message of this verse.

Also this verse did not say that everything that comes our way is from God but rather that the Lord can work it together for our good through the intercession of the Holy Spirit. Romans 6:16 clearly states that if we yield to the devil, we become his slaves. The false teaching that nothing happens to us but what God wills or allows has caused many people to yield to Satan's bondage instead of resisting him (Jas. 4:7).

People may cite experiences where they learned great lessons through tragedy and argue that these negative experiences are the only way the Lord could have accomplished His will in their lives. Again, that is not what the Bible teaches (see note 7 at Rom. 3:4, p. 668).

Second Timothy 3:16-17 says, *"All scripture* is *given by inspiration of God, and* is *profitable for doctrine, for reproof, for correction, for instruction in righteousness: That the man of God may be perfect, throughly furnished unto all good works."* Verse 17 says that God's Word will make us **perfect**, thoroughly furnished unto **all** good works. That means we don't have to learn through hardships. God's Word is for correction and reproof.

Although not ordained by God for our good, each of us will experience tribulation. Therefore, we can and should learn from trials, but God's Word could have taught us the same thing with less grief. Anyone who submits to his problems because he believes God has brought them to teach him something is making a great mistake. That mistake is allowing the devil to inflict much pain in his life.

Verse 28 is really promising that when we let the Holy Spirit intercede through us with these groanings that cannot be uttered, **then** we can rest assured that regardless of what the devil brings across our path, God can turn that situation around and work it together for our good.

a Gk.-"sunergeo"- to be a fellow-worker; i.e. co-operate
b Dict.- having positive or desirable qualities; not bad or poor; to one's benefit; for the best- Gen. 50:20 Rom. 5:3-4 8:35-39
c Ex. 20:6 Dt. 6:5 Neh. 1:5 1 Cor. 2:9 Jas. 1:12 2:5 1 Jn. 4:19 5:2-3
d Gk.-"kletos"- invited; i.e. appointed, or (spec.) a saint- Rom 8:30 1:6-7 9:11, 23-24 Acts 13:48 Gal. 1:15 2 Th. 2:13-14 1 Pet. 5:10 see note 11 at Jn. 12:39, p. 360
e Dict.- the object toward which one strives or for which something exists; goal; aim; a result or effect that is intended or desired; intention

GOD IS FOR US

CHAPTER 8

29 For whom he did foreknow,[1a] he also did predestinate[2b] *to be* conformed[c] to the image[d] of his Son,[e] that he might be the firstborn[3f] among many brethren.[g]

Footnotes for Romans 8:29

1 (Rom. 8:29) The word "foreknowledge" (see ref. a, this verse) refers to God knowing who would accept His offer of salvation in advance of them actually doing it. The scriptures teach that we (believers) were chosen in Christ before the foundation of the world (Eph. 1:4). That's how infinite God's ability is to know our choices in advance.

The scriptures also reveal that there are some things God does not know. Twice in the book of Jeremiah God said that the fact that people would offer their children as sacrifices to demon gods never even came into His mind (Jer. 19:5; 32:35). There are some things that God Himself said He had never foreseen.

It is most probable that the Lord has the ability to know everything in advance, but He simply doesn't choose to exercise that ability in every situation. He told us to be wise concerning that which is good and simple (or innocent) concerning that which is evil (Rom. 16:19). He also told us to think on things that are true, honest, just, pure, lovely, of good report, and things that have virtue and praise. That's the way He desires us to be because that's the way He is.

Therefore, when God acted surprised that Adam and Eve had eaten of the forbidden tree, He probably was. As we have already pointed out from Ephesians 1:4, God chose us in Christ before the foundation of the world. He knew there would be a transgression and a need for redemption before man was even created. But apparently, He did not utilize His foreknowledge to the extent that He knew every move that man was making. No reason is given for this, but certainly one reason is that an absolute use of God's foreknowledge would hinder His relationship with man.

Footnotes for Romans 8:29 continued on p. 709

a Gk.-"proginosko"- to know beforehand; i.e. foresee- Rom. 11:2 Jer. 1:5 2 Tim. 2:19 1 Pet. 1:2 see note 4 at Jn. 13:5, p. 416 see note 9 at Acts 18:10, p. 605
b Gk.-"proorizo"- to predetermine; decide beforehand; to foreordain; appoint beforehand- Eph. 1:5, 11 1 Pet. 1:20 see note 11 at Jn. 12:39, p. 360 see note 1 at Lk. 22:22, p. 421
c Gk.-"summorphos"- jointly formed; i.e. (fig.) similar; trans. conformed to; fashioned like unto
d Gk.-"eikon"- a likeness; i.e. statue, profile, or representation; resemblance- 1 Cor. 15:49 2 Cor. 3:18 Eph. 4:13 1 Jn. 3:2
e see note 5 at Mk. 1:1, p. 30
f Ps. 89:27 Col. 1:15-18 Heb. 1:5-6 Rev. 1:5-6
g Mt. 12:50 25:40 Jn. 20:17 Heb. 2:11-15

ROMANS

GOD IS FOR US (continued)

CHAPTER 8

30 Moreover[h] whom he did predestinate,
them he also called:[i] and whom he called,[i]
them he also justified:[j] and whom he
justified,[j] them he also glorified.[k]
31 What shall we then say to these
things? If God *be* for us,[4] who *can be*
against us?[l]
32 He that spared not his own Son,[m] but
delivered[n] him up for us all, how[5] shall he
not with him also freely give us all things?
33 Who[6] shall lay any thing to the
charge[o] of God's elect?[p] *It is* God that
justifieth.[q]
34 Who *is* he that condemneth?[r] *It is*
Christ[s] that died, yea rather, that is risen
again,[t] who is even at the right hand of
God,[u] who also maketh intercession[v] for
us.[7]

Footnotes for Romans 8:29 (cont'd); Footnotes for Romans 8:30-34

God sent two angels to Sodom and Gomorrah to see if their actions were really as bad as had been reported to Him (Gen. 18:20-19:29). The Lord tested Abraham (Gen. 22:1-10). After the test He said, *"For now I know that thou fearest God, seeing thou hast not withheld thy son, thine only* son *from me"* (Gen. 22:12). The Lord repented for choosing Saul to be king when He saw the way he turned out (1 Sam. 15:11). There are many other examples in scripture.

God's ability to know all things in advance is limitless, but God does not know every detail by His choice. Understanding foreknowledge provides the foundation for understanding predestination (see note 2 at this verse, below), calling (v. 30), and election (1 Pet. 1:2).

2 (Rom. 8:29) This verse provides the key for unlocking the answer to the doctrine of predestination. Predestination (see ref. b at this verse, p. 708) is dependent on foreknowledge (see note 1 at this verse, p. 708).

The word, "predestinate" means "to predetermine." "Predestinate" and its variant "predestinated" are only used four times in the New Testament (Rom. 8:29-30; Eph. 1:5, 11). Men have interpreted this doctrine as saying that God predetermines everything in an individual's life, including whether he will be saved or lost. This interpretation is not consistent with other doctrines or examples in scripture. This belief will destroy a person's motivation to fight evil and do good. If God predetermines everything that happens in your life, then everything that happens to you is God's will—even sin. That is not true.

This verse limits God's predestination to only those who He foreknew. This means that only those people who God knew would accept his offer of salvation have been predestined. He does not predestine people to be saved or lost. Those who He foreknew in Christ have been predestined to be conformed to the image of Christ. As we can tell by observation, God doesn't even force that to happen. With some Christians, this will not occur until they receive their glorified bodies, but it will occur.

God gave every individual a free will, and God will not violate that free will except in judgment. Even in judgment, God is only enforcing the choices that each individual has already made of his own free will. Each person has a God-given right to go to hell if he wants to.

Just as in the previous verse, Romans 8:28, God works everything together for good for those who already love Him. And even then He does not take away our free will. Everything that happens to us is not good, and it is not from God. However, God in His infinite wisdom can work it together for good (see note 7 at Rom. 8:28, p. 708). Verse 29 is simply continuing to develop the truth that God is for us and has predetermined that those who have come to Him for salvation will be saved to the uttermost.

Understood correctly, this verse provides great reassurance to the believer that God is for them and working with them to bring them to the complete stature of the Lord Jesus Christ (Eph. 4:13).

3 (Rom. 8:29) This English word "firstborn" was translated from the Greek word "prototokos." This is a compound Greek word comprised of "protos" meaning "foremost" (in time, place, order or importance) and "tikto" meaning "to produce" (from seed). Therefore, this word "firstborn" could refer to either first in order or importance. Both of these applications are true of Jesus.

Although others were raised from the dead before Jesus (see note 3 at Mk. 16:6, p. 484), Jesus was the first one to be raised from the dead, never to die again. Jesus was also the firstborn in the sense of importance, since His resurrection made all other resurrections possible.

In context, Paul is stressing that we are predestined to be just like Jesus, then he draws from scripture that prophesied Jesus being the firstborn (Ps. 89:27). Therefore, the point that is being made is the extent that we will be conformed to the image of Jesus. There are other children who will become just like Jesus, and it is in this sense that "firstborn" is used here.

4 (Rom. 8:31) The eighth chapter of Romans came as the answer to the hopelessness of the flesh ever pleasing God that Paul declared in the seventh chapter. The eighth chapter is full of victory through the indwelling presence and power of the Holy Spirit.

Paul had just spoken of the Holy Spirit making intercession for us (vv. 26-27), God working all things together for our good (v. 28), and us being predestined to be conformed to the image of Jesus (v. 29). Now he is drawing a conclusion from all these things. If God be for us (which is exactly what he has been saying) then no one can successfully be against us. This is an exclamation of victory for the Spirit-controlled life which Paul continues through the end of this chapter.

5 (Rom. 8:32) Paul had already used this same reasoning in Romans 5:6-10 (see ref. f at this verse).

6 (Rom. 8:33) If Almighty God has dropped all charges against us because of our faith in Christ, then why should we let the accusations of others bother us?

7 (Rom. 8:34) Jesus is making intercession for us. Therefore, Jesus couldn't be the one ministering condemnation to us. Intercession and condemnation are opposites.

h Dict.- beyond what has been stated; further; besides
i Rom. 8:28
1:6
9:23-24
Eph. 1:18
4:4
Isa. 41:9
1 Cor. 1:2, 9
Heb. 9:15
1 Pet. 2:9
2 Pet. 1:10
Rev. 17:14
19:9
j see note 2 at Lk. 1:6, p. 6
see note 55 at Mt. 7:21, p. 85
see note 1 at Lk. 10:28, p. 253
see note 3 at Lk. 10:29, p. 253
see note 5 at Jn. 11:52, p. 312
see note 1 at Mt. 26:2, p. 410
see note 2 at Acts 15:1, p. 585
see note 7 at Rom. 3:24, p. 673
see note 13 at Rom. 3:30, p. 674
see note 3 at Rom. 4:3, p. 675
see note 8 at Rom. 4:5, p. 675
see note 2 at Rom. 4:10, p. 677
see note 3 at Rom. 4:10, p. 677
k Rom. 8:17-18
Jn. 17:22, 24
2 Th. 1:10-12
2:14
1 Pet. 5:10
l Josh. 10:42
1 Sam. 14:6
17:45-47
Ps. 118:6
Isa. 54:17
Jer. 1:19
1 Jn. 4:4
m see note 14 at Rom. 5:7, p. 683
see note 16 at Rom. 5:9-10, p. 684
Gen. 22:12
Isa. 53:10
Jn. 3:16
2 Cor. 5:21
1 Jn. 4:10
n Gk.-"paradidomi"- to surrender; i.e. yield up; intrust; transmit-
Rom. 4:25

o Gk.-"egkaleo"- to call in (as a debt or demand); i.e. bring to account (charge, criminate, etc.); trans. accuse; call in question; implead; lay to the charge-
Rev. 12:10-11
p Gk.-"eklektos"- select; by impl. favorite; trans. chosen; elect-
Isa. 42:1
Mt. 24:24
Lk. 18:7
1 Th. 1:4
Ti. 1:1
1 Pet. 1:2
q see ref. j, this heading
Rom. 3:26
Gal. 3:8
r Gk.-"katakrino"- to judge against; i.e. sentence; trans. condemn; damn
see note 4 at Rom. 8:1, p. 700
Rom. 8:1
Ps. 109:31
s see note 5 at Jn. 1:41, p. 40
see note 2 at Mt. 16:16, p. 202
see note 3 at Acts 4:26, p. 526
t Rom. 4:25
Heb. 1:3
10:12
12:2
1 Pet. 3:18
see note 4 at Rom. 1:4, p. 655
u see note 6 at Mk. 10:37, p. 339
Mk. 16:19
Acts 7:56
Col. 3:1
Heb. 8:1
1 Pet. 3:22
v Gk.-"entugchano"- to chance upon; i.e. (by impl.) confer with; by extens. to entreat (in favor or against); trans. deal with; make intercession-
Rom. 8:27
Isa. 53:12
Heb. 7:25
1 Jn. 2:1-2
see note 97 at Jn. 17:9, p. 444

ROMANS

GOD IS FOR US (continued)

CHAPTER 8

35 Who[8] shall separate us from the love
of Christ?[a] *shall* tribulation,[b] or distress,[c] or
persecution,[d] or famine,[e] or nakedness, or
peril, or sword?
36 *As it is written, For thy sake we are
killed all the day long; we are accounted as
sheep for the slaughter.[f]
37 Nay,[g] in all these things we are more
than conquerors[9] through him that loved[a]
us.
38 For I am persuaded,[h] that neither
death, nor life, nor angels,[i] nor principalities,[j] nor powers,[k] nor things present,
nor things to come,[l]
39 Nor height, nor depth, nor any other
creature,[m] shall be able to separate[n] us from
the love of God, which is in Christ Jesus our
Lord.[o]

O.T. SCRIPTURE CITED IN ROMANS 8:36

PSALM 44:22

22 Yea, for thy sake are we killed all the day long; we are counted as sheep for the slaughter.

a Rom. 8:39 Jer. 31:3 Jn. 13:1 2 Th. 2:16 see note 4 at Jn. 13:35, p. 424 see note 8 at Jn. 9:27, p. 238 see note 4 at Lk. 11:11, p. 256
b Gk.-"thlipsis"- pressure (lit. or fig.) Trans. afflicted (-tion); anguish; burdened; persecution; tribulation; trouble see note 7 at Rom. 5:3, p. 682 Mt. 13:21 2 Cor. 1:4 7:4 1 Th. 1:6 1 Pet. 4:12-14
c Gk.-"stenochoria"- narrowness of room; i.e. (fig.) calamity; trans. anguish; distress- 2 Cor. 4:8
d 2 Tim. 3:12 see note 7 at Mt. 5:10, p. 73 see note 1 at Lk. 17:2, p. 305 see note 4 at Acts 9:4, p. 552

e Gk.-"limos"- a scarcity of food; trans. dearth; famine; hunger
f Isa. 53:7 Jn. 16:2
g Dict.- 1. no; 2. and moreover; used to introduce a more precise or emphatic expression than the one first made
h Dict.- to cause (someone) to do something by means of argument, reasoning, or entreaty; to win over (someone) to a course of action by reasoning or inducement; to make (someone) believe something; convince- Rom. 4:21 2 Tim. 1:12 Heb. 11:13
i see note 12 at Mt. 24:31, p. 401 see note 7 at Acts 12:10, p. 571 see note 13 at Acts 12:15, p. 572

continued on center column

References continued from column 4

j Gk.-"arche"- a beginning; government; rule; is used of supramundane beings who exercise rule, called "principalities." (a) of holy angels; (b) of evil angels (W.E. Vine)- Eph. 3:10 6:12 Col. 1:16 2:15 Ti. 3:1
k Gk.-"dunamis"- force (lit. or fig.); spec. miraculous power
l neither what happens today or what may happen tomorrow (Phi)
m nor any other created thing (Knox)
n Dict.- to set or keep apart; divide; disunite
o see note 3 at Lk. 1:43, p. 12

Footnotes for Romans 8:35-39

8 (Rom. 8:35) Neither people nor things external can separate us from the love of Christ. The only way for a believer to be exempted from the love of Christ is to deny his faith in Christ (see note 5 at Acts 5:5, p. 528; see note 4 at Acts 12:23, p. 573).

9 (Rom. 8:37) How can you be more than a conqueror? A conqueror has the victory and the spoils of war, but he has to fight to get them. We are more than conquerors because we have victory and all the spoils of war, but we didn't do the fighting. Jesus fought and won this battle for us and all we have to do is receive the benefits. That's being more than a conqueror.

PAUL'S PERSONAL FEELINGS FOR LOST ISRAEL

CHAPTER 9

I SAY the truth in Christ,[a] I lie[1] not,[b] my
conscience[c] also bearing me witness in the
Holy Ghost,[d]
2 That I have great heaviness[e] and
continual[2] sorrow[f] in my heart.[g]

a see note 5 at Jn. 1:41, p. 40 see note 2 at Mt. 16:16, p. 202 see note 3 at Acts 4:26, p. 526
b Rom. 1:9 2 Cor. 1:23 11:31 Gal. 1:20 Phil. 1:8 1 Tim. 2:7
c see note 9 at Rom. 2:15, p. 665 see note 4 at Acts 24:16, p. 634 see note 1 at Acts 23:1, p. 628 Rom. 2:15 2 Cor. 1:12 1 Tim. 1:5 1 Jn. 3:19-21

d my conscience [enlightened and prompted] by the Holy Spirit, bearing witness with me (Amp)
e Gk.-"lupe"- sadness Trans. grief- once grievous- once heaviness- 2 times sorrow- 11 times (Young)
f Gk.-"odune"- grief (as dejecting) Trans. sorrow- 2 times- Rom. 10:1 Ps. 119:136

continued on center column

References continued from column 4

Jer. 13:17 Lam. 3:48-49, 51 Lk. 19:41-44 Phil. 3:18
g see note 3 at Mt. 12:34, p. 131 see note 10 at Mk. 7:21, p. 191 see note 14 at Rom. 4:21, p. 680

Footnotes for Romans 9:1-2

1 (Rom. 9:1) Paul is going to great lengths to verify that what he is saying is the truth. This needs to be stated because Paul's statement in verse 3 would certainly have been interpreted as a hyperbole (exaggeration) if there had not been some clarification.

2 (Rom. 9:2) This is not a contradiction to other statements by Paul (2 Cor. 7:13; Gal. 5:22-23; Phil. 1:4,18; 2:2,18; 4:4; Col. 1:24; 1 Th. 3:9; 5:16; Phile. 1:7). Paul did operate in the joy of the Holy Ghost just as he told others to do. However, there was this continual heaviness and sorrow in his heart when it came to the unbelieving Jews.

This is comparable to someone who has lost a loved one who is very dear to him. In the process of time, he "gets over it" to the point that he may be considered a very joyful person. But there is always that vacancy in his heart. Similarly, Paul was rejoicing in the Lord but he always had this great longing in his heart for the salvation of the Jews.

ROMANS

PAUL'S PERSONAL FEELINGS FOR LOST ISRAEL (continued)

a Dict.- a desire longing, or strong inclination for some specific thing
b Gk.-"anathema"- a (religious) ban or (concr.) excommunicated (thing or person) Dict.- under a curse; doomed
c Gk.-"suggenes"- a relative (by blood); by extens. a fellow countryman- Rom. 11:1 Est. 8:6 Acts 7:23-26 13:26
d Rom. 9:6 Gen. 32:28 Ex. 19:3-6 Ps. 73:1 Isa 41:8 Jn. 1:47

CHAPTER 9

3 For I could wish[a] that myself were
accursed[b] from Christ for my brethren,[3] my
kinsmen[c] according to the flesh:
4 Who are Israelites;[d] to whom
pertaineth the adoption,[e] and the glory,[f]
and the covenants,[g] and the giving of the
law,[h] and the service[i] *of God,* and the
promises;[j]
5 Whose *are* the fathers,[k] and of whom
as concerning the flesh Christ *came,*[l] who is
over all,[m] God blessed for ever.[n] Amen.

e Gk.-"huiothesia"- the placing as a son; i.e. adoption (fig. chr. sonship in respect to God) see note 29 at Mt. 6:9, p. 79 Ex. 4:22 Jer. 31:9 Hos. 11:1
f 1 Sam. 4:21-22 1 Ki. 8:11 Ps. 63:2 Isa. 60:19
g Gk.-"diatheke"- a disposition; i.e. (spec.) a contract (esp. a devisory will)- Gen. 15:18 17:2, 7, 10 Ex. 24:7-8 34:27 Ps. 89:3, 34 Jer. 31:33 33:20-25 Acts 3:25 Heb. 8:6-10 continued on center column

References continued from column 4
h Rom. 3:2 Neh. 9:13-14 Ps. 147:19 Ezek. 20:11-12 Jn. 1:17
i Gk.-"latreia"- ministration of God; i.e. worship-
Ex. 12:25
j Gk.-"epaggelia"- an announcement (for information, assent, or pledge; esp. a divine assurance of good) Trans. message; promise- Lk. 1:69-75 Acts 2:39 13:32-33 Eph. 2:12 Heb. 6:13-17
k Rom. 11:28 Dt. 10:15
l Rom. 1:3 Gen. 12:3
m Ps. 45:6 103:19 Isa. 9:6-7 Jer. 23:5-6 Mic. 5:2 Jn. 1:1-3 10:30 Phil. 2:6-11 Col. 1:16 Heb. 1:8-13
n Rom. 1:25 Ps. 72:19 2 Cor. 11:31 1 Tim. 6:15

Footnote for Romans 9:3-5

3 (Rom. 9:3) What a statement! Paul is saying that he would go to hell in the place of the Jews if that would accomplish their salvation. This is nothing less than the perfect "agape" love (see note 4 at Jn. 13:35, p. 424) that Jesus demonstrated when He died for our sins.

Although this desire is commendable on Paul's part, there is nothing that he could accomplish that Jesus hadn't already accomplished completely. Paul was specifically commissioned by the Lord to go to the Gentiles, yet we see him repeatedly going to the Jews, even after he said he wouldn't do that any more (see note 2 at Acts 13:14, p. 577). Paul even went to Jerusalem apparently against the instruction of the Holy Ghost (see note 4 at Acts 21:4, p. 621) and was more than willing to lay down his life for the sake of the Jews (Acts 21:13). This illustrates his great love for the Jewish people that he is describing here.

ELECTION ACCORDING TO GRACE

a see note 4 at Rom. 3:3, p. 668 see note 5 at Lk. 4:4, p. 37
b Rom. 3:3 Num. 23:19 Isa. 55:11 Mt. 24:35 Jn. 10:35 2 Tim. 2:13
c Rom. 2:28-29 4:12-16 Gal. 3:16 6:16

CHAPTER 9

6 Not as though the word of God[a] hath
taken none effect.[b] For they *are* not all
Israel, which are of Israel:[1c]
7 *Neither, because they are the seed of
Abraham, *are they* all children:[d] but, In
Isaac shall thy seed be called.[e]

d see note 10 at Jn. 8:33, p. 232 see note 14 at Jn. 8:37, p. 232 see note 1 at Rom. 4:13, p. 678 see note 5 at Rom. 4:16, p. 678 Lk. 3:8 Jn. 8:37-45 Phil. 3:3
e Heb. 11:18

O.T. SCRIPTURE CITED IN ROMANS 9:7

GENESIS 21:12

12 And God said unto Abraham, Let it not be grievous in thy sight because of the lad, and because of thy bondwoman; in all that Sarah hath said unto thee, hearken unto her voice; for in Isaac shall thy seed be called.

Footnote for Romans 9:6-7

1 (Rom. 9:6) Paul had just expressed a compassion for the Jewish race that was so strong that he was willing to be damned in their place if that would have produced their salvation (see note 3 at Rom. 9:3, this page). As he said in verse 2, this produced "great heaviness and continual sorrow."

According to verses 4 and 5, one of the reasons he longed for the salvation of the Jews so intensely is because he himself was a Jew and he was acutely aware that Christ was the Jewish Messiah. How ironic it was that Jesus came unto His own and His own received Him not (Jn. 1:11). Now he begins to relate the reasoning that had enabled him to cope with the Jews' tragic rejection of Jesus.

The promises made to Abraham and his descendants were not made to his physical descendants, but to his spiritual seed (vv. 6-8). Therefore, the true people of God have not rejected their Messiah. There is a body of believers comprised of believing Jews and Gentiles which are the true Israel of God. To back this up, Paul cites the two Old Testament examples of Isaac (v. 9) and Jacob (vv. 10-13) to illustrate how the blessing of God was not passed on through the normal method of inheritance but through election.

Paul had expressed some of these same thoughts twice before in this epistle and he used the same reasoning in his letter to the Galatians (see ref. c, this verse).

ROMANS

ELECTION ACCORDING TO GRACE (continued)

a Rom. 4:11-16 Gal. 4:22-31 see ref. d, this heading
b Gk.-"sperma"-something sown; i.e. seed (includ. the male "sperm"); by impl. offspring; spec. a remnant-Ps. 22:30 Jn. 1:13 Gal. 3:26-29 4:28 1 Jn. 3:1-2
c Gen. 18:10 21:2 Heb.11:11-12,17
d Dict.- a result or effect that is intended or desired; intention-Rom. 8:28-30 Isa. 14:24, 26-27 23:9 46:10-11 Jer. 51:29 Eph. 1:9-11 3:11 2 Tim. 1:9

CHAPTER 9

8 That is,[2] They which are the children of the flesh, these *are* not the children of God:[a] but the children of the promise are counted for the seed.[b]
9 *For this *is* the word of promise, At this time will I come, and Sarah shall have a son.[c]
10 *And not only *this*; but when Rebecca also had conceived by one, *even* by our father Isaac;
11 *(For *the children* being not yet born,[3] neither having done any good or evil, that the purpose[d] of God according to election[4e] might stand, not of works,[f] but of him that calleth;)[g]
12 *It was said unto her, The elder shall serve the younger.[5]

e Gk.-"ekloge"- (divine) selection-Rom. 11:5-7 Eph. 1:4-5 1 Th. 1:4 2 Pet. 1:10 see note 11 at Jn. 12:39, p. 360 see note 1 at Lk. 22:22, p. 421
f see note 2 at Rom. 4:2, p. 674 see note 1 at Rom. 4:1, p. 674 see note 7 at Rom. 4:4, p. 675 Rom. 11:6 Eph. 2:8-9 Ti. 3:4-5
g Dict.- to summon Rom. 8:28 1 Th. 2:12 2 Th. 2:13-14 1 Pet. 5:10 Rev. 17:14

O.T. SCRIPTURES CITED IN ROMANS 9:9

GENESIS 17:21

21 But my covenant will I establish with Isaac, which Sarah shall bear unto thee at this set time in the next year.

GENESIS 18:14

14 Is any thing too hard for the LORD? At the time appointed I will return unto thee, according to the time of life, and Sarah shall have a son.

O.T. SCRIPTURES CITED IN ROMANS 9:10-12

GENESIS 25:21-23

21 And Isaac intreated the LORD for his wife, because she was *barren: and the LORD was intreated of him, and Rebekah his wife conceived.*
22 And the children struggled together within her; and she said, If it be *so, why* am *I thus? And she went to enquire of the LORD.*
23 And the LORD said unto her, Two nations are *in thy womb, and two manner of people shall be separated from thy bowels; and* the one *people shall be stronger than* the other *people; and the elder shall serve the younger.*

Footnotes for Romans 9:8-12

2 (Rom. 9:8) Paul cites six Old Testament references to make his point that God's promises to Abraham and his "seed" were made to the spiritual offspring of Abraham, not the physical.

First, Isaac was not the firstborn son of Abraham entitled to the birthright and blessing, yet he obtained both because he was chosen by God. Next, Jacob was not the firstborn either, yet he was chosen by God. These two examples confirm that God's promise was not inherited by birth.

Paul also points out that before Jacob and his twin brother Esau were born, God told Rebecca that the elder would serve the younger. They weren't even born yet, so they had not done any good or evil that caused God to make this choice. This meant that the blessing of Abraham was not obtained by individual performance either, but was based solely on God's choosing by grace.

3 (Rom. 9:11) Paul is citing these Old Testament examples to show that those who were considered the children of Abraham were not his physical descendants, but they were chosen by God, in this case, before they were born. This proves God's election is not based on birth or performance (see note 2 at v. 8, above).

However, some people have interpreted this verse and the quotation from Malachi 1:2-3 in verse 13 as an example of extreme predestination. They reason that Esau was hated by God before he was born (see note 5 at v. 12, below). Therefore, some people are predestined by God for damnation while some are elected to salvation before they are ever born. This means a person has no choice in the matter. That is not what these verses are saying.

As explained in note 2 at Romans 8:29, page 709, God's predestination is based on His foreknowledge (see note 1 at Rom. 8:29, p. 708). Only those who God foreknew would accept Him have been elected and predestinated. God did not force Jacob and Esau to make the choices they made. But through His foreknowledge He was able to foresee who would respond to Him and that is the one He chose.

4 (Rom. 9:11) The doctrine of election is based on God's foreknowledge (see note 1 at Rom. 8:29, p. 708) the same way that predestination is based on God's foreknowledge (see note 2 at Rom. 8:29, p. 709). This can be clearly seen in 1 Peter 1:2, which says we are, *"Elect according to the foreknowledge of God the Father. . . "* God does not choose an individual independent of his free will. Instead, through His foreknowledge, He knows who will choose Him and those are the individuals He elects to be His own.

5 (Rom. 9:12) There is no record in scripture that the individual Esau ever served the individual Jacob. However, Esau's posterity (Edomites–Gen. 32:3) did serve Jacob's posterity (1 Chr. 18:13). Although Paul is making reference to the actual birth of these two individuals, the prophecy given to Rebecca and its fulfillment are referring to the nations which came from these men.

ROMANS

ELECTION ACCORDING TO GRACE (continued)

h Dt. 32:4
2 Chr. 19:7
Job. 34:10-12
Ps. 92:15
145:17
Rev. 15:3-4
16:7
i Gk.-"me genoito"- Lit., 'let it not be'; in Paul's epistles it is almost entirely used to express the apostle's repudiation of an inference which he apprehends may be drawn from his argument (W.E. Vine)- Rom. 3:6, 31
6:2, 15
7:7, 13
11:1
1 Cor. 6:15
Gal. 2:17
3:21
see note 6 at Rom. 3:4, p. 668

CHAPTER 9

13 *As it is written, Jacob have I loved,
but Esau have I hated.[6]
14 What shall we say then? *Is there*
unrighteousness with God?[h] God forbid.[7i]

15 *For he saith to Moses, I will have
mercy on whom I will have mercy, and I
will have compassion on whom I will have
compassion.[j]
16 So then *it is* not of him that willeth,
nor of him that runneth,[8] but of God that
sheweth mercy.[k]

j Rom. 9:16, 18-19
Ex. 34:6-7
Isa. 27:11
Mic. 7:18
k Rom. 9:11
Isa. 65:1
Mt. 11:25-26
Jn. 1:12-13
1 Cor. 1:26-31
Ti. 3:3-5

O.T. SCRIPTURES CITED IN ROMANS 9:13

MALACHI 1:2-3

2 I have loved you, saith the LORD. Yet ye say, Wherein hast thou loved us? Was *not Esau Jacob's brother? saith the LORD: yet I loved Jacob,*
3 And I hated Esau, and laid his mountains and his heritage waste for the dragons of the wilderness.

O.T. SCRIPTURE CITED IN ROMANS 9:15

EXODUS 33:19

19 And he said, I will make all my goodness pass before thee, and I will proclaim the name of the LORD before thee; and will be gracious to whom I will be gracious, and will shew mercy on whom I will shew mercy.

Footnotes for Romans 9:13-16

6 (Rom. 9:13) God did not hate Esau and love Jacob while they were still in their mother's womb. He did choose Jacob over Esau as the inheritor of Abraham's blessing before they were born, but Esau could have walked with God and have been blessed by God if he would have chosen to do so.

The scripture from Malachi 1:2-3 that says, *"I loved Jacob, and I hated Esau . . ."* was written in approximately 557-525 B.C., thousands of years after the birth of Esau and Jacob. So, this is not speaking of God hating Esau at birth. There is not any mention in scripture that God hated the individual Esau. This reference to Esau is referring to the nation of Edom (Esau's descendants) in the same way that the term Israel often referred to the entire nation of Israel, not the individual. So, God is saying that He had rejected the nation of Edom and had chosen the nation of Israel.

Paul quotes from Malachi, not to show that God hated Esau and loved Jacob while they were still in their mother's womb, but rather to confirm that the choice God made before they were born, based on His foreknowledge (see note 1 at Rom. 8:29, p. 708), was the right choice. Jacob went on to become a mighty man of God and Esau despised the things of God. God's choice of Jacob didn't cause this to happen. This quotation from Malachi simply confirms that God's foreknowledge was accurate.

Jacob was called to a higher position than his brother Esau before they were born, but that does not display any rejection of Esau on God's part. That is comparable to God choosing one person to be a pastor while another is called to be a deacon. The deacon is not inferior to the pastor. They are simply called to different positions. Jacob and Esau were called to different positions before they had done any good or evil to illustrate that election was not based on performance but choice.

7 (Rom. 9:14) Paul is seeking to stop anyone from interpreting his statements in a way that would make it look like God was unfair in his dealings with man. God can extend mercy to an individual without treating others unjustly. Just as in the parable that Jesus gave in Matthew 20:1-16, God treats everyone fairly but to some He chooses to give extra mercy. Does that mean He was unjust? Not at all.

If God chooses to call an individual to account for his actions and choices he has made of his own free will, He is completely justified to do that at any time. In Luke 13:1-9, Jesus mentioned the people who Pilate had killed and mingled their blood with the sacrifices, and the people on whom the tower in Siloam fell and who were killed. He raised the question, "Were these people worse sinners than others to suffer this judgement?" He answered His own question by saying that all of them deserved such judgment, but God in His mercy had spared them (see note 2 at Lk. 13:2, p. 274).

He then immediately follows with the parable about the man with an unproductive tree in his vineyard. He was going to cut down this dead tree and replace it, but the vine dresser interceded for the tree and the owner gave him some extra time to see if he could revive it (see note 1 at Lk. 13:6, p. 276). Likewise, we all deserve judgment but through things such as the intercession of others, God will sometimes show extra mercy to certain individuals.

However, if He chose not to extend mercy to anyone and He called all of our accounts due, He would be completely justified in doing so. It's His choice. God has never brought judgment on anyone without being righteous in doing so. Likewise, He has never extended mercy to any individual that made His treatment of someone else unfair.

8 (Rom. 9:16) There is a very subtle trap which many people who have been used of God fall into. They see what God has accomplished through them and they begin reasoning, "God must use me because of my great faithfulness." But that is not the case. God has never had anyone qualified working for Him yet. God is a lot more merciful than we are faithful.

ROMANS

ELECTION ACCORDING TO GRACE (continued)

a Est. 4:14
Isa. 45:1-3
Jer. 27:6-7
Dan. 4:22
5:18-21
b Ex. 10:1-2
14:17-18
15:14-15
18:10-11
Josh. 2:9-10
9:9
1 Sam. 4:8
Prov. 16:4
c see note 1 at Rom. 5:1, p. 681
d Gk.-"eleeo"- to be compassionate (by word or deed, spec. by divine grace)
e Ex. 4:21
7:13
Dt. 2:30
Josh. 11:20
Mt. 13:14-15
Acts 28:26-28
Rom. 1:24-28
11:7-8
2 Th. 2:10-12
see note 3 at Mt. 13:15, p. 136
see note 10 at Mk. 6:52, p. 179
see note 1 at Mt. 16:8, p. 198
see note 3 at Mk. 8:17, p. 199

CHAPTER 9

17 *For the scripture saith unto Pharaoh,[9]
Even for this same purpose have I raised
thee up,[a] that I might shew my power in
thee, and that my name might be declared
throughout all the earth.[b]
18 Therefore[c] hath he mercy[d] on whom
he will *have mercy,* and whom he will he
hardeneth.[e]
19 Thou wilt say then unto me,[10] Why
doth he yet find fault?[f] For who hath resisted
his will?[g]
20 *Nay but, O man, who art thou that
repliest against[h] God?[11] Shall the thing
formed say to him that formed *it,* Why hast
thou made me thus?

O.T. SCRIPTURE CITED IN ROMANS 9:17

EXODUS 9:16

16 And in very deed for this cause *have I raised thee up, for to shew* in *thee my power; and that my name may be declared throughout all the earth.*

PARALLEL SCRIPTURES FOR ROMANS 9:20

ISAIAH 29:16

16 Surely your turning of things upside down shall be esteemed as the potter's clay: for shall the work say of him that made it, He made me not? or shall the thing framed say of him that framed it, He had no understanding?

ISAIAH 45:9-10

9 Woe unto him that striveth with his Maker! Let *the potsherd* strive *with the potsherds of the earth. Shall the clay say to him that fashioneth it, What makest thou? or thy work, He hath no hands?*

10 Woe unto him *that saith unto his father, What begettest thou? or to the woman, What hast thou brought forth?*

f Gk.-"memphomai"- to blame; trans. find fault
g 2 Chr. 20:6
Dan. 4:35
Acts 4:27-28
h Gk.-"antapokrinomai"- to contradict or dispute-
Job 33:13
36:23
38:2-3, 18
40:2, 5, 8
42:2-6
Ti. 2:9
1 Cor. 1:20

Footnotes for Romans 9:17-20

9 (Rom. 9:17) Some people have taken this word from God about Pharaoh and have made a paragraph out of it. They have drawn conclusions that God predetermines everything in our lives to the degree that our free will doesn't exist. That is not what the Lord is speaking of here.

We can be assured that Pharaoh had already had ample opportunity to respond to God prior to the time that God began to harden his heart. Since Pharaoh had already made his choice, even to the point that he proclaimed himself to be deity and commanded the Egyptians to worship him, God was not unrighteous in bringing him into judgment for this.

God did not make Pharaoh the way he was, but God used the way Pharaoh had chosen to be for His glory. God exalted Pharaoh and gave him leadership of the nation, knowing full well how he would respond to His demands to let His people go. Since Pharaoh had already hardened his heart towards God, God was not unjust in continuing to harden his heart further until His glory was manifest completely.

This verse is depicting God as using Pharaoh's hardened heart for His glory, but Pharaoh had already had his chance. God simply upheld his choice and received glory through His triumph over Pharaoh and all his host.

10 (Rom. 9:19) The argument that Paul is refuting here is not a correct interpretation of what he had said. This is comparable to his statement in Romans 6:1 where he said, *"What shall we say then? Shall we continue in sin, that grace may abound?"* Just as he knew someone would interpret his teaching on grace to be an advocation of sin, therefore, he spoke their wrong conclusion and then refuted it; likewise here, he states an abusive interpretation of his statements and then proceeds to counter it.

11 (Rom. 9:20) The truth that Paul is expressing here is the overall point that is made in the book of Job. God never did explain Himself to Job as Job had insisted that He do. Instead, God rebuked Job for his "know it all" attitude (Job 38:18). God basically asked Job what right he had to maintain his own integrity at the expense of God's (Job 40:8). Job got the message when God spoke to him from a whirlwind and he humbled himself (Job 42:2-6). Paul's message should bring the same response from us.

ROMANS

ELECTION ACCORDING TO GRACE (continued)

CHAPTER 9

21 *Hath not the potter[12] power over the
clay,[i] of the same lump to make one vessel
unto honour,[j] and another unto dishonour?[k]
22 **What* if God, willing to shew *his*
wrath,[l] and to make his power[m] known,
endured with much longsuffering[n] the
vessels of wrath[o] fitted to destruction:[p]
23 *And that he might make known the
riches of his glory on the vessels of mercy,[q]
which he had afore prepared unto glory,[r]
24 Even us, whom he hath called,[s] not of
the Jews only,[13] but also of the Gentiles?[t]

i Rom. 9:11, 18; Prov. 16:4; Isa. 64:8; Jer. 18:3-6
j Acts 9:15; 2 Tim. 2:20-21
k Rom. 9:22-23; Jer. 22:28; Hos. 8:8
l Rom. 1:18; 2:4-5; Ps. 90:11; Rev. 6:16-17; see note 4 at Jn. 3:36, p. 52; see note 4 at Acts 12:23, p. 573
m Rom. 9:17; Ex. 9:16
n Dict.- patiently enduring wrongs or difficulties; patient endurance- Num. 14:11, 18; Eccl. 8:11-12; Lam. 3:22-23; 1 Pet. 3:20; 2 Pet. 3:8-9, 15; Rev. 6:9-11
o Rom. 9:21; 1 Th. 5:9; 2 Tim. 2:20
p Gk.-"apoleia"- ruin or loss (physical, spiritual, or eternal)
q Eph. 2:4, 7
r Col. 1:12; 2 Th. 2:13-14; 1 Pet. 1:2-5
s Dict.- summon- Rom. 8:28-30; 1 Cor. 1:9; Heb. 3:1; 1 Pet. 5:10; Rev. 17:14; 19:9
t Rom. 3:29-30; 4:11-12; 10:12; 11:11-13; 15:8-16; Ps. 22:27; Acts 13:47-48; 15:14; 21:17-19; Gal. 3:28; Eph. 2:11-13; 3:6-8; Col. 3:11

PARALLEL SCRIPTURES FOR ROMANS 9:21-23

JEREMIAH 18:1-10

***THE** word which came to Jeremiah*
from the LORD, saying,
2 Arise, and go down to the potter's
house, and there I will cause thee to hear
my words.
3 Then I went down to the potter's
house, and, behold, he wrought a work
on the wheels.
4 And the vessel that he made of clay
was marred in the hand of the potter: so
he made it again another vessel, as
seemed good to the potter to make it.
5 Then the word of the LORD came to
me, saying,
6 O house of Israel, cannot I do with
you as this potter? saith the LORD.
Behold, as the clay is *in the potter's*
hand, so are *ye in mine hand, O house of*
Israel.
7 At what *instant I shall speak*
concerning a nation, and concerning a
kingdom, to pluck up, and to pull down,
and to destroy it;
8 If that nation, against whom I have
pronounced, turn from their evil, I will
repent of the evil that I thought to do
unto them.
9 And at what *instant I shall speak*
concerning a nation, and concerning a
kingdom, to build and to plant it;
10 If it do evil in my sight, that it obey
not my voice, then I will repent of the
good, wherewith I said I would benefit
them.

Footnotes for Romans 9:21-24

12 (Rom. 9:21) Paul is drawing an illustration from an Old Testament passage of scripture from Jeremiah 18:3-6 (see Parallel Scriptures, above). In that passage, God sent Jeremiah to the potter's house to learn a lesson. The potter was making a vessel and it was marred, so he remade it. The Lord spoke to Jeremiah and said, *"O house of Israel, cannot I do with you as this potter?... Behold, as the clay* is *in the potter's hand, so* are *ye in mine hand, O house of Israel."*

From this illustration, some people have drawn a wrong conclusion that the Lord creates some people evil and predestined to a life of damnation, not by their choice, but by God's. However, a closer look at the passage in Jeremiah and its context will show that is not the case.

First of all, the potter started to create a good vessel but the clay was marred. Whose fault was that? It wasn't the potter's fault. The clay was faulty. So, the potter took this imperfect clay and, instead of discarding it, he refashioned it into another vessel that may not have been worth nearly as much as his original design, but was still useful.

Likewise, the Lord does not create certain individuals for destruction. However, some do become marred by their own choice, not due to any fault of the Creator. Instead of just removing them from the earth, the Lord will endure (v. 22) their atrocities. He may even put them in great positions of authority, such as He did with Pharaoh, so that He may manifest His great power through His victory over them and their devices. God can still use someone who has rejected Him, in the same way that a potter can take a marred piece of clay and find some use for it.

It can be clearly seen, by continuing to read the context of Jeremiah's experience with the potter, that the Lord does not do these things against the will of the individual. In verses 7-10, the Lord says that when He purposes evil or good against a nation, if that nation repents, then God will change His plans for them. That undeniably states that our choice influences God's choice.

13 (Rom. 9:24) Paul had started explaining in verse six that there was a true people of God, not based on nationality, but on faith in God. He now gives four quotes from two Old Testament prophets to show that this is not a new concept, but it had been prophesied hundreds of years before (see ref. a at v. 30, p. 717).

ROMANS

ELECTION ACCORDING TO GRACE (continued)

a i.e. Hosea
b see note 8 at Rom. 1:7, p. 656
c 1 Pet. 2:10

CHAPTER 9

25 *As he saith also in O´see,[a] I will call
them my people, which were not my people;
and her beloved,[b] which was not beloved.[c]
26 *And it shall come to pass, *that* in the
place where it was said unto them, Ye *are*
not my people; there shall they be called
the children of the living God.
27 *E-sai´as[d] also crieth concerning
Israel, Though the number of the children
of Israel be as the sand of the sea, a remnant[14]
shall be saved:
28 For he will finish the work, and cut
it short in righteousness: because a short
work will the Lord make upon the earth.
29 *And as E-sai´as[d] said before, Except
the Lord of Sab´a-oth had left us a seed, we
had been as Sod´o-ma, and been made like
unto Go-mor´rha.[e]

d i.e. Isaiah-Isa. 6:13
e Lam. 3:22-23
4:6
2 Pet. 2:6
Jude 7

O.T. SCRIPTURE CITED IN ROMANS 9:25

HOSEA 2:23

23 And I will sow her unto me in the earth; and I will have mercy upon her that had not obtained mercy; and I will say to them which were *not my people, Thou* art *my people; and they shall say,* Thou art *my God.*

O.T. SCRIPTURE CITED IN ROMANS 9:26

HOSEA 1:10

10 Yet the number of the children of Israel shall be as the sand of the sea, which cannot be measured nor numbered; and it shall come to pass, that *in the place where it was said unto them, Ye* are *not my people,* there *it shall be said unto them,* Ye are *the sons of the living God.*

O.T. SCRIPTURE CITED IN ROMANS 9:27

ISAIAH 10:22

22 For though thy people Israel be as the sand of the sea, yet *a remnant of them shall return: the consumption decreed shall overflow with righteousness.*

O.T. SCRIPTURE CITED IN ROMANS 9:29

ISAIAH 1:9

9 Except the LORD of hosts had left unto us a very small remnant, we should have been as Sodom, and *we should have been like unto Gomorrah.*

Footnote for Romans 9:25-29

14 (Rom. 9:27) This verse could read, "**only** a remnant shall be saved." That is the point that Paul is making. His next reference from Isaiah (v. 29) complements this one, and it is clearly stressing that there will be very few Jews who are truly God's people.

ROMANS

RIGHTEOUSNESS OF LAW VS. RIGHTEOUSNESS OF FAITH

a see note 45 at Mt. 6:32, p. 83; see note 2 at Lk. 2:32, p. 22; see note 3 at Lk. 7:9, p. 117; see note 3 at Acts 10:45, p. 564; see note 3 at Acts 14:27, p. 584
b Rom. 10:20
c see note 3 at Acts 28:28, p. 653
d see note 2 at Lk. 1:6, p. 6; see note 3 at Rom. 1:17, p. 658; see notes 2-3 at Rom. 3:22, p. 672; see note 10 at Rom. 3:26, p. 673; see note 7 at Rom. 5:19, p. 687; Rom. 4:9, 11, & 13, 22; 5:1; 10:10; Gal. 3:8; 5:5; Phil. 3:9; Heb. 11:7

CHAPTER 9

30 *What shall we say then?[1] That the Gentiles,[a] which followed not[b] after righteousness, have attained[2] to righteousness,[c] even the righteousness which is of faith.[d]

31 But Israel, which followed after the
law of righteousness,[e] hath not attained to
the law of righteousness.[f]
32 Wherefore?[3g] Because *they sought it*
not by faith, but as it were by the works[4] of
the law.[h] For they stumbled at that
stumblingstone;[5i]

PARALLEL SCRIPTURE FOR ROMANS 9:30

ISAIAH 65:1

***I AM** sought of* them that *asked not* for me*; I am found of* them that *sought me not: I said, Behold me, behold me, unto a nation* that *was not called by my name.*

e Rom. 9:30-32; 10:2-4; Gal. 3:21; Phil. 3:6
f Rom. 3:20; 4:14-15; 11:7; Gal. 3:10-11; 5:3-4; Jas. 2:10-11
g Dict.- for what purpose or reason; why
h see note 4 at Rom. 3:19, p. 671; see note 14 at Rom. 3:31, p. 674; see note 1 at Rom. 3:21, p. 672; see note 1 at Acts 15:1, p. 585; see note 3 at Rom. 1:2, p. 655; see note 4 at Rom. 2:26, p. 666; Acts 15:1, 5, 11; Gal. 2:16; 3:10; Ti. 3:5
i Rom. 11:11; Mt. 13:57; 15:12-13; Lk. 2:34; 7:23; 1 Cor. 1:23

Footnotes Romans 9:30-32

1 (Rom. 9:30) Paul is saying that this is the conclusion or the summary of his point in this chapter.

2 (Rom. 9:30) This is another one of Paul's radical statements. How can it be that people who are not seeking to be righteous can become righteous? The answer to this question lies in God's grace.

By grace, God has provided righteousness for everyone, regardless of their actions. If a person will believe and receive this gift, God will reckon him righteous. This is what happened to the Gentiles. They had a reputation for not seeking God (Eph. 4:17-19; 1 Pet. 4:3) and yet the Gentiles as a whole accepted God's gift of salvation while the Jews as a whole, who were seeking after God, rejected His gift. The reason for this is given by Paul in verses 32-33 (see note 5 at v. 32, below).

People who don't understand God's grace will always be confused and unbelieving that a person who hasn't lived a morally good life can be righteous in the sight of God while a morally good person can be unrighteous in His sight. Righteousness is based on faith, not actions (see ref. d, this verse).

3 (Rom. 9:32) Why is it that a person who is seeking so hard to please God can be rejected, while a person who has not sought God at all can come into a righteous relationship with Him? This is an important question and its answer is one of the most profound doctrines in scripture.

Paul gives the answer to his own question. The answer is faith and its object. The Jews were zealous (Rom. 10:2) for the things of God, but their faith was in themselves. They were trusting that they could earn God's favor by their acts of righteousness. On the other hand, the Gentiles had no holiness to trust in. So, when they heard the gospel that Jesus paid our debt for us, they readily accepted His "gift" of salvation while the religious Jews could not abandon their trust in themselves for salvation.

This same problem exists today. Millions of church people are trying to live holy lives, but they do not have a true faith in Jesus as their Savior. If they were to stand before God and He was to ask them what they had done to deserve salvation, they would immediately start recounting all their acts of holiness; church attendance, giving receipts, etc. Regardless of how good our actions are compared to others, they always come short of the perfect standard of God (see notes 5 and 6 at Rom. 3:23, p. 672). The only response to this kind of question that would grant us entrance to heaven is to say, "my only claim to salvation is faith in Jesus as my Savior." Anything more or less is damned.

4 (Rom. 9:32) There is a difference between works of faith (1 Th. 1:3; 2 Th. 1:11) and works of the law (Gal. 2:16; 3:2, 5, 10). The difference is not in the action but in the attitude. A work of the law is some act of righteousness or holiness that is being done to earn the favor of God. A work of faith may be the same act of righteousness or holiness but it is done as a labor of love (1 Th. 1:3). It is done not to obtain favor, but in gratitude for the favor that has already been extended to us in Christ. Works of the law and faith in Jesus are opposites (Rom. 11:6).

5 (Rom. 9:32) Jesus is the stumblingstone that Paul is speaking of. God has placed Jesus directly in the path of every person. Those who fail to put their complete trust in Jesus because they are trusting in themselves will stumble and fall into hell, while those who believe in Him will never be ashamed (v. 33).

ROMANS

RIGHTEOUSNESS OF LAW VS. RIGHTEOUSNESS OF FAITH (cont'd)

a Ps. 118:22
Mt. 21:42, 44

CHAPTER 9

33 *As it is written, Behold, I lay in Sion
a stumblingstone and rock of offence:[6a]
and whosoever believeth on him shall not
be ashamed.[7b]

b Rom. 10:11
Ps. 25:3, 20
Isa. 45:17
Joel 2:26-27
Phil. 1:20
2 Tim. 1:12

O.T. SCRIPTURES CITED IN ROMANS 9:33

ISAIAH 8:14

14 And he shall be for a sanctuary; but for a stone of stumbling and for a rock of offence to both the houses of Israel, for a gin and for a snare to the inhabitants of Jerusalem.

ISAIAH 28:16

16 Therefore thus saith the Lord GOD, Behold, I lay in Zion for a foundation a stone, a tried stone, a precious corner stone, *a sure foundation: he that believeth shall not make haste.*

PARALLEL SCRIPTURE FOR ROMANS 9:33

ISAIAH 54:4

4 Fear not; for thou shalt not be ashamed: neither be thou confounded; for thou shalt not be put to shame: for thou shalt forget the shame of thy youth, and shalt not remember the reproach of thy widowhood any more.

PARALLEL SCRIPTURES FOR ROMANS 9:33

1 PETER 2:6-8

6 Wherefore also it is contained in the scripture, Behold, I lay in Sion a chief corner stone, elect, precious: and he that believeth on him shall not be confounded.

7 Unto you therefore which believe he is *precious: but unto them which be disobedient, the stone which the builders disallowed, the same is made the head of the corner,*

8 And a stone of stumbling, and a rock of offence, even to them *which stumble at the word, being disobedient: whereunto also they were appointed.*

JOEL 2:32

32 And it shall come to pass, that *whosoever shall call on the name of the LORD shall be delivered: for in mount Zion and in Jerusalem shall be deliverance, as the LORD hath said, and in the remnant whom the LORD shall call.*

Footnotes for Romans 9:33

6 (Rom. 9:33) Those who are offended at Jesus are the ones who are trusting in themselves. They feel they will be accepted with God because they are holy enough on their own. It is humbling to admit that all of of our righteousness is as filthy rags (Isa. 64:6). This is why the religious people have always been the persecutors of true Christians (see note 6 at Mk. 15:10, p. 465).

7 (Rom. 9:33) This quotation does not appear in the Old Testament in these exact words. It is most probable that Paul is quoting the last part of Isaiah 28:16 (see O.T. Scripture cited for v. 33). If so, Paul substituted the words "be ashamed" for Isaiah's words "make haste." In the context of war, making haste is descriptive of a person who has been shamed in battle.

ROMANS

RIGHTEOUSNESS OF LAW SAYS "DO," RIGHTEOUSNESS OF FAITH SAYS "DONE"

CHAPTER 10

BRETHREN, my heart's[a] desire and prayer
to God for Israel[b] is, that they might be
saved.[c]
2 For I bear them record[d] that they have[1]
a zeal[e] of God, but not according to
knowledge.[f]
3 For they being ignorant[g] of God's
righteousness,[h] and going about to establish
their own[i] righteousness, have not
submitted[j] themselves unto the
righteousness of God.[2]
4 For Christ *is* the end[3] of the law[k] for
righteousness[l] to every one that believeth.[4m]

Footnotes for Romans 10:1-4

1 (Rom. 10:2) This scripture goes contrary to many religious teachings. Many people believe that it's not necessary to believe the right thing— just as long as we believe something, we'll be all right. However, Paul disproves this kind of thinking in this passage by saying that their zeal was without knowledge and therefore they were not saved (v. 2).

The Jews were very zealous about their religion, but that wasn't enough. It's not enough just to believe; we have to believe the truth. Even a person who is sincere can be sincerely wrong. Jesus said, *"And you shall know the truth, and the truth shall make you free"* (Jn. 8:32).

2 (Rom. 10:3) This verse describes the condition of much of the church today. Most people are unaware that there are two kinds of righteousness. Only one type of righteousness is acceptable to God.

One form of righteousness that Paul describes here is our own righteousness (also Phil. 3:9). These are the acts of holiness that we do in an attempt to fulfill the commands of the Old Testament law. This is an imperfect righteousness because human nature is imperfect and incapable of fulfilling the law (see note 7 at Rom. 8:3, p. 701). Therefore, our own righteousness, which is according to the law, is inadequate. Isaiah said it this way in Isaiah 64:6, *". . .all our righteousnesses are as filthy rags. . ."*

In contrast, God's righteousness is perfect. Also, God's righteousness is not something that we do, but something that we receive as a gift through faith in Christ (see note 5 at Rom. 10:5, p. 720).

Paul makes it very clear in this verse that it's not possible to trust in our own righteousness and in God's righteousness also. A person who believes that he must earn God's acceptance by his holy actions cannot be believing in God's righteousness, which is a gift. It has to be one or the other; we cannot mix the two. Righteousness is not what Jesus has done for us plus some minimum standard of holiness that we have to accomplish (Rom. 11:6).

3 (Rom. 10:4) The Greek word that was translated "end" here is "telos," which means "the point aimed at as a limit; i.e. (by implication) the conclusion of an act or state (termination)."

This verse does not say that Christ is the end of the law, but rather that Christ is the end of the law for the purpose of righteousness. This means that no one any longer becomes righteous, or justified in the sight of God, by how well he perform the deeds of the law (see note 2 at Lk. 1:6, p. 6). However, there are still useful purposes of the law to the New Testament believer.

The Old Testament law still reveals to us God's holiness, which we should seek to emulate. It must be understood however, that our failure to comply does not bring the punishments pronounced in the law since Jesus bore those for us (Gal. 3:13). Our compliance does not earn the blessings of God either; those only come by faith in Christ (Rom. 4:8-13). We also need to be acquainted with the Old Testament law so we will better understand our new covenant and God's historical dealings with mankind.

Also, Paul said to Timothy, *"But we know that the law* is *good, if a man use it lawfully"* (I Tim. 1:8). He then says that the law was not made for a righteous man (i.e. a Christian — 2 Cor. 5:21), but rather for an unbeliever (1 Tim. 1:9-10). So, a Christian can still use the law when ministering to unbelievers to show them their sin and their need for a savior (see note 4 at Rom. 3:19, p. 671).

As Christians, we should not discard the Old Testament law. When understood in the light of the new covenant, the old covenant provides us with invaluable revelation of God. Paul is simply stressing that the time when anyone sought to be justified through the keeping of the Old Testament law is over. Now, everyone must put his faith in Christ, and Christ alone, for salvation.

Someone might ask, "Was anyone ever justified by the keeping of the law?" The answer is, "Yes." One person did become righteous through his keeping of the Old Testament law. That person was Jesus. One of the reasons the Old Testament law was given was so that Jesus could legally earn man's redemption. Now that the purchase has been completed, that function of the law is over.

4 (Rom. 10:4) This phrase, *"to every one that believeth"* limits this benefit only to believers (Christians). To those who do not receive God's gift of salvation, the law is still in effect (see note 4 at Jn. 3:36, p. 52). A person who fails to believe on Jesus will have to answer to God for each and every one of his transgressions of the law.

a see note 3 at Mt. 12:34, p. 131; see note 10 at Mk. 7:21, p. 191; see note 6 at Mk. 11:23, p. 367; see note 3 at Rom. 2:29, p. 667; see note 14 at Rom. 4:21, p. 680
b Rom. 9:1-3; Ex. 32:10, 13; 1 Sam. 12:23; Lk. 13:34; 1 Cor. 9:20-22
c see note 3 at Rom. 9:3, p. 711; see note 5 at Lk. 13:28, p. 284; see note 2 at Rom. 2:29, p. 667
d Gk.-"martureo"- to be a witness; i.e. testify (lit. or fig.)- 2 Cor. 8:3; Gal. 4:15; Col. 4:13
e Dict.- enthusiastic and diligent devotion in pursuit of a cause, ideal, or goal; fervent adherence or service; ardor; fervor- 2 Ki. 10:16; Jn. 16:2; Acts 21:20; 22:3; Gal. 1:14; 4:17-18; Phil. 3:6
f Hos. 4:6; Rom. 10:3; 9:31-32; Prov. 19:2; 2 Cor. 4:4, 6; Phil. 1:9; 2 Pet. 1:3
g Gk.-"agnoeo"- not to know (through lack of information or intelligence); by impl. to ignore (through disinclination)
h i.e. God's way of justifying men- Rom. 1:17; 3:22, 26; 5:19; 9:30; Jer. 23:5-6; 2 Cor. 5:21; 2 Pet. 1:1
i Dict.- belonging to oneself- Isa. 64:6; Lk. 18:9-12; Phil. 3:9
j Gk.-"hupotasso"- to arrange under; to subordinate; to subject; put in subjection; to obey (Thayer)
k Rom. 3:21-22; 6:14; 7:4, 6; Gal. 3:24-25; Eph. 2:15; Col. 2:14-17; Heb. 9:10-11
l i.e. as a means of achieving righteousness; see note 2 at Lk. 1:6, p. 6
m see note 3 at Rom. 1:17, p. 658; see notes 2-3 at Rom. 3:22, p. 672; see note 7 at Rom. 5:19, p. 687; see note 13 at Rom. 3:30, p. 674; see note 15 at Rom. 4:23, p. 680

ROMANS

RIGHTEOUSNESS OF LAW SAYS "DO," RIGHTEOUSNESS OF FAITH SAYS "DONE" (continued)

a Phil. 3:9
b Neh. 9:29
Ezek. 20:11, 13, & 21
Gal. 3:12
c Rom. 3:21-22
4:13
9:30
Phil. 3:9
see ref. o, p. 721

CHAPTER 10

5 *For Moses describeth the righteousness which is of the law,[a] That the man
which doeth[5] those things shall live[6] by
them.[b]

6 *But the righteousness which is of
faith[c] speaketh on this wise,[7] Say not in
thine heart, Who shall ascend into heaven?[d]
(that is, to bring Christ down *from above:*)[e]
7 *Or, Who shall descend into the
deep?[f] (that is, to bring up Christ again
from the dead.)[g]

d Prov. 30:4
e Eph. 4:8-10
f Gk.-"abussos"-depthless; i.e. "abyss"
g 1 Pet. 3:18, 22
see note 1 at Acts 1:3, p. 509
see note 4 at Rom. 1:4, p. 655

OT. SCRIPTURE CITED IN ROMANS 10:5

LEVITICUS 18:5

5 Ye shall therefore keep my statutes, and my judgments: which if a man do, he shall live in them: I am *the LORD.*

Footnotes for Romans 10:5-7

5 (Rom. 10:5) In verses 5-9, Paul contrasts those who seek righteousness by the law with those who seek the righteousness of God as a gift (see note 2 at v. 3, p. 719). Those who seek to earn righteousness through keeping the law are consumed with "doing" (this verse), while those who receive righteousness by faith are simply confessing what has already been done (v. 9).

This is a simple and yet profound difference. If we are still "doing" acts of holiness to get God to move in our lives, then we are still operating under a "law" mentality that is not faith (Gal. 3:12). When we simply believe and confess what has already been provided through Christ, then that's grace.

A person who is living under the law and a person who lives under grace should have very similar actions of holiness, but their motivations are completely opposite. The legalist has his attention on what he must do, while the person living by faith has his attention on what Christ has already done for him.

For instance, the scriptures teach us to confess with our mouth and believe with our heart and we will receive from God (Rom. 10:9-10; Mk. 11:23-24). The legalist thinks, "That means I can get God to heal me by confessing 'By his stripes I am healed.'" However, the person who understands God's grace will not confess the Word to get healed. He will confess, "By his stripes I am healed," because he really believes it has already been done.

Analyzing our "mind set" is the simplest way of discerning whether we are operating in true Bible faith or a legalistic counterfeit. If the motive for our actions is to be accepted with God, then that's legalism. If we live holy out of faith and gratefulness for what God has already done, then that's grace.

6 (Rom. 10:5) The Greek word that was translated "live" here is "zao," which means "to live." However, that definition by itself doesn't fully convey Paul's intent in quoting this Old Testament passage from Leviticus 18:5. It is clear from the context that Paul is contrasting the effort to keep the Old Testament law with the New Testament faith in Christ. He is concluding that the observance of the Old Testament law for producing righteousness (see note 3 at v. 4, p. 719) is inferior to the New Testament method of obtaining righteousness by putting faith in Jesus as our Savior.

This quote from Moses is intended to illustrate the harshness of living by the Old Testament law. Paul quotes this same Old Testament passage in Galatians 3:12, and so does Nehemiah in Nehemiah 9:29. In each case, the context clearly reveals that the writer was quoting this verse to speak of the negative effects of living by the law.

The word "live" in the English language can mean many different things, as can be seen by the multiple definitions of this word in any dictionary. In the American Heritage Dictionary, there is one meaning that communicates Paul's meaning here. The word "live" can mean "to continue to remain alive."

Using this definition, this quote from Leviticus 18:5 is saying that once a man starts trying to fulfill the law to earn righteousness, he will have to subsist, or remain alive, by his continued adherence to the precepts of that law. In other words, once you decide to "earn" right standing with God, then God is going to give you what you deserve. The thing that is dreadfully wrong with this thought is that no one really deserves righteousness. **We don't need justice. We need mercy!**

This is what Paul is communicating when he quotes this scripture from Leviticus. Trying to achieve righteousness by keeping the law doesn't bring peace because it puts the burden of salvation on our shoulders (see note 2 at Rom. 5:1, p. 681). In contrast, salvation by grace through faith places the burden on Jesus, and allows us to walk free.

7 (Rom. 10:6) Paul is saying that failure to understand justification by grace produces an attitude that, in effect, denies Christ's substitutionary work for us. A person who still believes that his performance is essential for salvation is denying that Christ is in heaven making intercession for us (Rom. 8:34). That dethrones Christ from His present position. It is like denying that Christ has ascended into heaven for us.

Likewise, a belief that we have to bear the punishment for our sins is like denying that Christ's death was sufficient by itself. If we are to be punished for our sins, then Christ might as well not have died for us.

All of this is continuing the contrast that Paul began in verse 5 between the doing of the Old Testament law and the believing of the New Testament grace (see note 5 at Rom. 10:5, above). The law mentality puts us under an unbearable load of performance to obtain righteousness; faith just receives the righteousness that has already been provided through Christ.

ROMANS

RIGHTEOUSNESS OF LAW SAYS "DO," RIGHTEOUSNESS OF FAITH SAYS "DONE" (continued)

CHAPTER 10

8 *But what saith it? The word is nigh thee, *even* in thy mouth, and in thy heart: that is, the word of faith,[h] which we preach;[8i]

9 That if thou shalt confess[j] with thy mouth the Lord[k] Jesus, and shalt believe[9] in thine heart that God hath raised him from the dead,[l] thou shalt be saved.[m]

10 For with the heart[n] man believeth unto righteousness;[o] and with the mouth[10] confession[j] is made unto salvation.[p]

O.T. SCRIPTURES CITED IN ROMANS 10:6-8

DEUTERONOMY 30:11-14

11 For this commandment which I command thee this day, it is not *hidden from thee, neither* is *it far off.*

12 It is *not in heaven, that thou shouldest say, Who shall go up for us to heaven, and bring it unto us, that we may hear it, and do it?*

13 Neither is *it beyond the sea, that thou shouldest say, Who shall go over the sea for us, and bring it unto us, that we may hear it, and do it?*

14 But the word is *very nigh unto thee, in thy mouth, and in thy heart, that thou mayest do it.*

h Rom. 10:17; 1:16-17; Acts 10:43; 13:38-39; 16:31; Gal. 3:2, 5
i see note 3 at Mt. 5:2, p. 73; see note 1 at Mt. 10:8, p. 165; see note 3 at Acts 8:6, p. 545; see note 2 at Acts 14:4, p. 581; see note 2 at Acts 20:7, p. 615
j Gk.-"homologeo"- to agree; to confess; to proclaim. As a judicial term, the word indicates the binding and public declaration which settles a relationship with legal force (*An Die Römer Handbuch Zum Neuen Testament* by Ernst Käsemann; TDNT) Dict.- to acknowledge belief or faith in – Mt. 10:32-33; Lk. 12:8; Jn. 9:22; 12:42-43; Phil. 2:11; 1 Jn. 4:2-3; 2 Jn. 1:7
k see note 3 at Lk. 1:43, p. 12
l Jn. 20:26-29; 1 Cor. 15:14-18; 1 Pet. 1:21
m see note 8 at Acts 27:20, p. 645; see note 2 at Mt. 8:17, p. 68
n Lk. 8:15; Heb. 3:12; 10:22; see ref. a, this heading
o Gen. 15:6; Rom. 1:16-17; 3:21-22; 4:3, 5, 11, 13; 9:30; Gal. 3:6-7; Phil. 3:9; Heb. 11:7
p Gk.-"soteria"- denotes deliverance; preservation; salvation. The spiritual and eternal deliverance granted immediately by God to those who accept His conditions of repentance and faith in the Lord Jesus (Vine) see note 7 at Acts 2:21, p. 515; see note 3 at Acts 16:31, p. 597; see note 1 at Acts 10:44, p. 564; see note 2 at Acts 16:30, p. 597; see note 1 at Rom. 4:9, p. 676; see note 4 at Rom. 4:16, p. 678

Footnotes for Romans 10:8-10

8 (Rom. 10:8) In verses 6-8, Paul was again quoting from Moses, this time from Deuteronomy 30:11-14. However, in this verse, he adds, *"that is, the word of faith, which we preach,"* which provides us with a commentary on Moses' statements.

A reading of Deuteronomy 30:11-14 by itself might lead someone to suggest that Moses was saying that the law was not hard to keep. Yet that is against everything that Paul taught and the context of this verse in particular. Paul was saying that Moses' statements in this quotation were actually prophesying the day of justification by faith that Paul was preaching.

Paul revealed in Galatians 3:22-25 that the purpose of the Old Testament law was to shut us up *"unto the faith which should afterwards be revealed."* The law was our schoolmaster to bring us unto Christ. From Paul's use of Moses' statements to make his point, it is possible that Moses had revelation of the day when faith in Christ would supersede the law (Dt. 18:15-18).

9 (Rom. 10:9) Remember that in context, Paul had been contrasting two types of righteousness (see note 2 at Rom. 10:3, p. 719). The righteousness of the law binds a person up in "doing" while the righteousness of faith just receives what Christ has already done (see note 5 at Rom. 10:5, p. 720).

This verse is stressing the simplicity of receiving righteousness by faith, as opposed to the bondage of trying to produce our own righteousness that is by the law (Phil. 3:9). An attempt to amplify on the conditions of this verse too much would counter the point that Paul is making. However, in the light of other scriptures, some explanation needs to be given.

This verse is not saying that anyone who just says the words, "Jesus is Lord" and believes that He rose from the dead is born again (see note 2 at Jn. 3:3, p. 48). As explained in note 1 at Mark 1:24, page 66, the Greek word "homologeo" that was translated "confesseth" here means more than just saying words. It literally means, "to assent; i.e. covenant; acknowledge." By looking at Jesus' statement in Luke 6:46, a true confession of Jesus as Lord has to be heartfelt enough to involve a person's actions (see note 2 at Rom. 1:16, p. 658).

There are some groups that interpret the word "Lord" in a way that denies the deity of Jesus (see note 3 at Lk. 1:43, p. 12; see note 8 at Jn. 5:23, p. 98). This confession of Jesus as Lord has to be a declaration of faith in Jesus as God manifest in the flesh (1 Tim. 3:16). A Jesus who is less than God could not provide salvation for the whole human race.

Therefore, this verse is a promise to those who believe on Jesus to the extent that they are willing to change their actions accordingly and confess Him as Lord (God) with their mouths so that they might be saved.

10 (Rom. 10:10) For true salvation to take place, there must be confession with the mouth and belief from the heart. People tend to major on one or the other of these requirements, but that fails to obtain the desired results.

Confession is scriptural, but it is a result of faith in the heart. Only when a person has already believed with his heart will confession release the power of God. Confession without sincere belief in the heart is dead works (Heb. 9:14). Likewise, faith without works is dead (Jas. 2:17). When a person really believes in his heart, he will speak what he believes (Mt. 12:34; Lk. 6:45). A faith that won't confess what is believed is not God's kind of faith (see note 6 at Rom. 4:17, p. 679).

Failure to properly combine these two truths has caused some people to fail in their attempts to receive from God and reject "faith teaching" or "confession teaching." However, if one of these truths was presented without the proper emphasis on the other, then it wasn't scriptural teaching. The truths of faith and confession will work when used according to the instructions in this verse.

ROMANS

RIGHTEOUSNESS OF LAW SAYS "DO," RIGHTEOUSNESS OF FAITH SAYS "DONE" (continued)

a see note 7 at Rom. 9:33, p. 718; Rom. 9:33; Isa. 28:16; 49:23; 1 Pet. 2:6
b or Gentile- Rom. 3:22, 29-30; 4:11-12; 9:24; Acts 10:34-35; 15:8-9; Gal. 3:28; Eph. 2:18-22; 3:6; Col. 3:11
c see note 3 at Lk. 1:43, p. 12; Rom. 14:9; 15:12; Phil. 2:11; Rev. 17:14; 19:16

CHAPTER 10

11 For the scripture saith, Whosoever[11] believeth on him shall not be ashamed.[a]

12 For there is no difference[12] between the Jew and the Greek:[b] for the same Lord[c] over all is rich[d] unto all that call upon him.[e]
13 *For whosoever[f] shall call upon the name of the Lord shall be saved.[13g]

d Dict.- (as used here) abundant- Rom. 2:4; 9:23; Eph. 1:7; 2:4, 7; 3:8, 16; Phil. 4:19; Col. 1:27; 2:2-3
e Ps. 86:5; 145:18; Isa. 55:6; Acts 9:14; 1 Cor. 1:2
f see note 11 at Rom. 10:11, this page
g see note 7 at Acts 2:21, p. 515

O.T. SCRIPTURE CITED IN ROMANS 10:13

JOEL 2:32

32 And it shall come to pass, that *whosoever shall call on the name of the LORD shall be delivered: for in mount Zion and in Jerusalem shall be deliverance, as the LORD hath said, and in the remnant whom the LORD shall call.*

Footnotes for Romans 10:11-13

11 (Rom. 10:11) The emphasis here, as well as in verse 13, is on the word "whosoever." In the first chapter of Romans, Paul had started making the point that Gentiles did not have to become Jews to be saved (Rom. 1:16). He developed that truth all the way through this epistle and is making it once again.

12 (Rom. 10:12) The differences between Jew and Gentile do not mean much to the Christian church today. Therefore, many church people may feel that they agree with this verse. However, Paul is speaking of more than just racial differences.

Paul is saying that there is no difference between moral and immoral people. There is no difference in the sight of God between the religious and the non-religious. Everyone is a sinner and in need of the same salvation. This point still aggravates the religious people today as much as it did in the days of Paul.

13 (Rom. 10:13) Paul is quoting from Joel 2:32 (see O.T. Scripture cited in v. 13, above). Paul used the word "saved" for the word "delivered" that Joel used. There is no contradiction. Salvation includes deliverance (see note 7 at Acts 2:21, p. 515).

THE GOSPEL HEARD BUT REJECTED

a see note 14 at Acts 12:16, p. 572; see note 14 at Rom. 4:21, p. 680

CHAPTER 10

14 How then shall they call on him in whom they have not believed?[a] and how shall they believe in him of whom they have not heard?[1] and how shall they hear[2] without a preacher?[b]

b see note 2 at Acts 8:5, p. 545; Mk. 16:15; Lk. 24:47; 2 Tim. 4:17; Ti. 1:3

Footnotes for Romans 10:14

1 (Rom. 10:14) Paul had just conclusively proven that salvation was not according to a person's performance but according to his acceptance of God's grace by faith in Christ Jesus. This was great news! Yet this great news will not do anyone any good if they don't know it. The gospel has to be heard to release its power (Rom. 1:16).

2 (Rom. 10:14) Verses 14 and 15 show a number of things that must happen in order for a person to be born again. The individual must believe, but he needs to have something or someone to believe in. Therefore, someone has to share the gospel with him. But in order for that to happen, others have to send the ministers to the uttermost parts of the earth.

So there are three areas of responsibility for salvation. An individual has to believe, someone has to preach, and others have to send. Satan works on all three of these areas to stop people from receiving God's gift of salvation.

Satan tries to harden a person's heart through the deceitfulness of sin (Heb. 3:13) to the point that the gospel will not penetrate. If people are faithful to the two other responsibilities, salvation still will not occur if the individual rejects the good news.

Yet many times people are hungry and ripe for salvation, and still there is no one to share the good news with them. If Satan can stop people from preaching the gospel, because of a lack of preachers or a lack of people who will send them, then he can stop the individual from being saved.

As Christians we cannot take responsibility for people's reaction to the gospel, but we must take the responsibility of preaching the gospel and giving so others can preach the gospel.

ROMANS

THE GOSPEL HEARD BUT REJECTED (continued)

c see note 4 at Acts 10:5, p. 560; Mt. 9:38; 10:5-6; 28:18-20; Lk. 10:1; Jn. 20:21; Acts 9:15; 13:2-4; 22:21
d Nah. 1:15
e Lk. 2:14; Eph. 6:15; 2:17; Acts 10:36; see note 5 at Acts 20:24, p. 618; see note 1 at Rom. 1:16, p. 658; see note 10 at Rom. 2:16, p. 665
f Isa. 40:9; 61:1; Lk. 2:10; 8:1
g Gk.-"hupakouo"- to hear under (as a subordinate); i.e. to listen attentively; by impl. to heed or conform to a command or authority. Trans. hearken; be obedient to; obey- Rom. 1:5; 2:8; 3:3; 6:17; 16:26; Acts 28:24; Gal. 3:1; 5:7; 2 Th. 1:8; Heb. 5:9; 11:8; 1 Pet. 1:22

CHAPTER 10

15 *And how shall they preach,[b] except
they be sent?[c] as it is written,[d] How
beautiful[3] are the feet of them that preach[b]
the gospel of peace,[e] and bring glad tidings[f]
of good things!
16 *But they have not all obeyed[g] the
gospel.[e] For E-sai´as[h] saith, Lord, who hath
believed[4] our report?
17 So then faith[5i] *cometh* by hearing,[6j]
and hearing[j] by the word of God.[k]
18 But I say, Have they not heard? Yes
verily, their sound went into all the earth,[l]
and their words unto the ends of the world.[m]
19 *But I say, Did not Israel know?[7]
First Moses saith, I will provoke you to
jealousy by *them that are* no people, *and* by
a foolish nation I will anger you.[n]

h i.e. Isaiah- Jn. 12:38-40
i see note 4 at Rom. 3:3, p. 668; see note 8 at Rom. 4:18, p. 679; see note 13 at Rom. 4:21, p. 680; see note 14 at Jn. 14:8, p. 430; see note 9 at Rom. 4:19, p. 680; see note 2 at Mt. 21:22, p. 367; see note 3 at Mk. 11:22, p. 367
j see note 8 at Lk. 16:31, p. 302; Mk. 4:24; Lk. 8:21; 11:28; 16:29-31; see note 2 at Acts 13:47, p. 580
k see note 4 at Jn. 20:29, p. 498
l Rom. 1:8; Ps. 19:4; Mt. 24:14; Acts 2:5-11; 26:20; Col. 1:6, 23
m Ps. 22:27; 98:3; Isa. 49:6; 52:10; Jer. 16:19
n Hos. 2:23; 1 Pet. 2:10

O.T. SCRIPTURE CITED IN ROMANS 10:15

ISAIAH 52:7

7 How beautiful upon the mountains are the feet of him that bringeth good tidings, that publisheth peace; that bringeth good tidings of good, that publisheth salvation; that saith unto Zion, Thy God reigneth!

O.T. SCRIPTURE CITED IN ROMANS 10:16

ISAIAH 53:1

***WHO** hath believed our report? and to whom is the arm of the LORD revealed?*

O.T. SCRIPTURE CITED IN ROMANS 10:19

DEUTERONOMY 32:21

21 They have moved me to jealousy with that which is *not God; they have provoked me to anger with their vanities: and I will move them to jealousy with* those which are *not a people; I will provoke them to anger with a foolish nation.*

Footnotes for Romans 3:15-19

3 (Rom. 10:15) When a person understands that sharing the gospel is just as important a part of salvation as the individual's acceptance of the message, then he will rejoice with Isaiah about the beauty of the person who shares this good news.

4 (Rom. 10:16) Contrary to popular belief, an anointed messenger with an anointed message is not always well received. This quotation from Isaiah shows that not everyone received his message about the coming Messiah. The same thing was true of many other prophets that the Lord sent to Israel including Jeremiah, Ezekiel, and even Jesus.

A misbelief that if we really minister in the power of the Holy Spirit, we will always succeed in converting the hearers has brought undeserved condemnation on many Christians. We cannot take responsibility for other people's actions.

5 (Rom. 10:17) Faith comes by hearing God's Word because God's Word is His faith (see note 4 at Rom. 3:3, p. 668). A person cannot be born again (see note 2 at Jn. 3:3, p. 48) through human faith. He has to use God's supernatural faith (see note 2 at Mt. 8:10, p. 116; see note 4 at Jn. 20:29, p. 498; see note 6 at Rom. 4:17, p. 679) to receive God's supernatural gift of salvation.

The only place to obtain God's kind of faith is from God's Word. Therefore, we cannot compromise God's Word. It must be proclaimed boldly to make God's faith available to those who choose to believe.

6 (Rom. 10:17) Notice that this verse says faith comes by "hearing," not by "having heard." A person cannot rest on a revelation he received from God years ago, unless he is still hearing the Lord speak that same truth to him now.

It is not the Lord who fails to speak; it is us who fail to hear. Therefore, anyone can keep his faith in the present tense if he will open his spiritual ears to hear what God's Word is saying (Prov. 4:20-22; see note 10 at Mk. 6:52, p. 179; see note 3 at Mk. 8:17, p. 199).

7 (Rom. 10:19) What was it that Israel knew? Paul is saying that Israel knew the gospel of salvation by faith which he had expounded in this epistle. One way this truth was revealed in the Old Testament was through the prophecies concerning the Gentiles becoming the people of God. If God was going to embrace nationalities that didn't adhere to the rites and ceremonies that were delivered to the Jews, then it should have been evident that these things were not prerequisites to salvation.

Paul quotes a prophesy of Moses and two additional passages from Isaiah to verify that this truth was revealed in the Old Testament. The truth was there but the Jewish heart had become so hardened through legalism that it couldn't perceive this truth (see note 3 at Mk. 8:17, p. 199).

ROMANS

THE GOSPEL HEARD BUT REJECTED (continued)

a Prov. 28:1 Eph. 6:19-20
b Isa. 49:6 55:4-5 Mt. 22:9-10
c Isa. 65:2-5 Mt. 22:3-7 23:34-37

CHAPTER 10

20 *But E-sai´as is very bold,[a] and saith,
I was found of them that sought me not; I
was made manifest unto them that asked
not after me.[b]
21 *But to Israel he saith, All day long
I have stretched forth my hands[c] unto a
disobedient[d] and gainsaying[e] people.

d Dt. 9:13 31:27 Neh. 9:26 Acts 7:51-52 1 Pet. 2:8
e Dict.- to be contrary to; oppose; contradict

O.T. SCRIPTURES CITED IN ROMANS 10:20-21

ISAIAH 65:1-2

I AM sought of them that *asked not* for me; *I am found of* them that *sought me not: I said, Behold me, behold me, unto a nation* that *was not called by my name.*

2 I have spread out my hands all the day unto a rebellious people, which walketh in a way that was *not good, after their own thoughts;*

A REMNANT ACCORDING TO GRACE

a 1 Sam. 12:22 Ps. 89:31-37 94:14 Jer. 33:24-26
b see note 6 at Rom. 3:4, p. 668 Lk. 20:16
c Rom. 9:3 Acts 22:3 26:4 2 Cor. 11:22 Phil. 3:5
d see note 1 at Rom. 8:29, p. 708 see note 4 at Jn. 13:5, p. 416 see note 9 at Acts 18:10, p. 605 Rom. 9:6, 23 Acts 13:48 15:18 1 Pet. 1:2
e Dict.- archaic; first and third person singular present tense of wit (to know)
f i.e. Elijah

CHAPTER 11

I SAY then, Hath God cast away[1] his
people?[a] God forbid.[b] For I also am an
Israelite, of the seed of Abraham, *of* the
tribe of Benjamin.[c]
2 God hath not cast away his people
which he foreknew.[d] Wot[e] ye not what the
scripture saith of E-li´as?[f] how he maketh
intercession[g] to God against Israel, saying,
3 *Lord, they have killed thy prophets,[h]
and digged down[i] thine altars;[j] and I am left
alone, and they seek my life.
4 *But what saith the answer of God
unto him? I have reserved to myself seven
thousand men, who have not bowed the
knee[k] to *the image of* Baal.[l]

g Dict.- to plead on another's behalf Latin- "intercedere"- to come between; "inter"- between + "cedere"- to go
h see note 2 at Lk. 7:26, p. 121 see note 1 at Acts 11:27, p. 569
i Gk.-"kataskapto"- to undermine; i.e. (by impl.) destroy Trans. dig down; ruin
j 1 Ki. 18:30
k 1 Ki. 19:18 Ex. 20:5
l Num. 25:3 Dt. 4:3 Jud. 2:13 1 Ki. 16:31 2 Ki. 10:19-20 Jer. 19:5 Hos. 2:8 13:1 Zeph. 1:4

O.T. SCRIPTURES CITED IN ROMANS 11:3

1 KINGS 19:10,14

10 And he said, I have been very jealous for the LORD God of hosts: for the children of Israel have forsaken thy covenant, thrown down thine altars, and slain thy prophets with the sword; and I, even *I only, am left; and they seek my life, to take it away.*

14 And he said, I have been very jealous for the LORD God of hosts: because the children of Israel have forsaken thy covenant, thrown down thine altars, and slain thy prophets with the sword; and I, even *I only, am left; and they seek my life, to take it away.*

O.T. SCRIPTURE CITED IN ROMANS 11:4

1 KINGS 19:18

18 Yet I have left me *seven thousand in Israel, all the knees which have not bowed unto Baal, and every mouth which hath not kissed him.*

Footnote for Romans 11:1-4

1 (Rom. 11:1) Paul's message of grace and his announcement that Gentiles could now become a part of the true Israel of God through the new birth, without becoming Jews, was a startling revelation. Paul had systematically dealt with objections that a legalistic Jew would have to such a message. Now, he answers the criticism that this would mean God has forsaken the Jewish nation.

Basically Paul is saying that Jews are not excluded, they just aren't favored over the Gentiles. He cites himself as an example of a believing Jew and compares the status of Israel to that of the Jewish nation in the days of Elijah. In the same way that there were 7,000 true worshipers of God left in Israel in Elijah's day (1 Ki. 19:18), so there was a remnant of believing Jews in Paul's day.

The rest of this chapter is Paul's explanation of Israel's current relationship to God during the church era.

ROMANS

A REMNANT ACCORDING TO GRACE (continued)

CHAPTER 11

5 Even so then at this present time also
there is a remnant[m] according to the election[n]
of grace.[o]
6 And[2] if by grace, then *is it* no more of
works:[p] otherwise grace is no more grace.
But if *it be* of works,[p] then is it no more
grace: otherwise work is no more work.[q]

m Dict.- something left over; a remainder; a small remaining group of people- Rom. 9:27
n see note 4 at Rom. 9:11, p. 712 Rom. 11:28
o see note 5 at Acts 20:24, p. 618 see note 5 at Rom. 1:5, p. 655 see note 8 at Rom. 3:24, p. 673 see note 7 at Rom. 4:4, p. 675 Rom. 4:4-5 5:20-21 1 Cor. 15:10 continued on column 4

continued from column 1 Gal. 2:21 5:4 Eph. 2:4-9 2 Tim. 1:9
p Gk.-"ergon"- from a prim. (but obsol.) "ergo"- (to work); toil (as an effort or occupation); by impl. an act Trans. deed; doing; labour; work see note 7 at Rom. 4:4, p. 675 see note 1 at Rom. 4:1, p. 674 see note 2 at Rom. 4:14, p. 678 continued on center column

References continued from column 4
see note 3 at Acts 9:36, p. 558
q If it be gained by works, it is no longer the gift of grace; for work claims wages, and not gifts (Con)

Footnote for Romans 11:5-6

2 (Rom. 11:6) Paul stated the doctrine of justification by grace through faith so clearly in his writings that any person who claims to believe the Bible has to acknowledge this truth. However, one of Satan's cleverest deceptions is to take a truth and add to it until it is no longer the truth. Lest that happen with this doctrine of grace, Paul states emphatically that we cannot combine anything with God's grace as a requirement for salvation.

In the same way that gasoline and water don't mix, so grace and works will not mix. Justification has to be all works or all grace, but not a combination of the two.

In this epistle, Paul had repeatedly made his point of justification by grace through faith. He had repeatedly stressed that faith is the only requirement on our part. He is repeating that point once again in perhaps his clearest words yet. Still, there are an abundance of religious people today who cannot accept the fact that all we have to do is to believe to receive God's grace (Rom. 5:2). This verse leaves no alternatives.

ISRAEL'S FALL AND BLINDING

CHAPTER 11

7 What then?[a] Israel hath not obtained
that which he seeketh[b] for; but the election[c]
hath obtained it, and the rest[d] were blinded[e]
8 (According as it is written,[1] God hath
given them the spirit of slumber, eyes that
they should not see, and ears that they
should not hear;) unto this day.[f]
9 *And David saith,[2] Let their table be
made a snare,[g] and a trap, and a
stumblingblock,[h] and a recompence[i] unto
them:[j]
10 *Let their eyes be darkened, that they
may not see,[k] and bow down[l] their back
alway.[m]

a What are we to infer from this? (Mof)- Rom. 3:9 6:15 1 Cor. 10:19 Phil. 1:18
b Dict.- to endeavor to obtain or reach; to try see note 3 at Rom. 9:32, p. 717 Rom. 9:31 10:3 Prov. 1:28
c Gk.-"ekloge"- (divine) selection Trans. chosen; election see note 4 at Rom. 9:11, p. 712 see ref. e at Rom. 9:11, p. 712 Rom. 11:5 8:28-30 9:23 Eph. 1:4 2 Th. 2:13-14 1 Pet. 1:2
d Gk.-"loipoy"- remaining ones
e Gk.-"poroo"- from "poros" (a kind of stone); to petrify; i.e. (fig.) to indurate (render stupid or callous) Trans. blind; harden see note 10 at Mk. 6:52, p. 179 Isa. 44:18 Mt. 13:14-15 continued on column 4

continued from column 1 Jn. 12:40 2 Cor. 3:14 4:4 2 Th. 2:10-12
f Isa. 29:10 6:9 Dt. 29:4 Jer. 5:21 Ezek. 12:2 Mk. 4:11-12 Lk. 8:10 Acts 28:26
g Dict.- a trapping device; to entrap (someone)
h Dict.- an obstacle or impediment
i Gk.-"antapodoma"- a requital- Dt. 32:35 Ps. 28:4 Heb. 2:2
j Let their good food and other blessings trap them into thinking all is well between themselves and God. Let these things boomerang on them (LB)
k Rom. 11:8 1:21
l Gk.-"sugkampto"- to bend together; i.e. (fig.) to afflict
m Gk.-"diapantos"- through all time; i.e. (adv.) constantly

PARALLEL SCRIPTURES FOR ROMANS 11:9-10

PSALM 69:22-23

22 Let their table become a snare before them: and that which should have been *for* their *welfare,* let it become *a trap.*

23 Let their eyes be darkened, that they see not; and make their loins continually to shake.

Footnotes for Romans 11:7-10

1 (Rom. 11:8) This appears to be a paraphrase of a Bible truth that is expressed in many scriptures. See reference f at this verse for a listing of possible scriptures that Paul was referring to.

2 (Rom. 11:9) This quotation from David comes from Psalm 69:22-23 (see Parallel Scripture, above). In this Psalm, David was prophesying about the suffering of Christ in the first person as if David himself was actually describing his own suffering. However, there are seven very clear references to Christ in this chapter which were quoted in the New Testament as having a direct fulfillment in Jesus: (1) Psalm 69:4—fulfilled in John 15:25; (2) Psalm 69:9a—fulfilled in John 2:17; (3) Psalm 69:9b—fulfilled in Romans 15:3; (4) Psalm 69:21a—fulfilled in Matthew 27:34, Mark 15:23, Luke 23:36; (5) Psalm 69:21b—fulfilled in Matthew 27:48, Mark 15:36, John 19:28-30; (6) Psalm 69:22—fulfilled in Romans 11:9; (7) Psalm 69:25—fulfilled in Acts 1:20. Also Psalm 69:8 was certainly fulfilled in Jesus (Jn. 7:5), although this passage was not quoted in the New Testament.

Therefore, Psalm 69 is a prophetic psalm where Christ, through David, is describing His earthly ministry and crucifixion. The denunciation of Psalm 69:22-23 is given by Christ against those who crucified him. When understood in this context, it is easy to see that this blindness and deafness didn't cause the Jews' rejection, but it was the Jews' rejection that caused this pronouncement.

All of this is to say that God is not unjust and has never taken away a person's freedom of choice unless that individual or nation had already exercised that choice against Him (see note 9 at Rom. 9:17, p. 714).

ROMANS

ISRAEL'S FALL AND BLINDING (continued)

CHAPTER 11

11 I say then, Have they stumbled[a] that
they should fall?[3] God forbid:[b] but *rather*
through their fall salvation *is come* unto the
Gentiles,[c] for to provoke them to jealousy.[d]
12 Now if the fall of them *be* the riches
of the world,[e] and the diminishing[f] of them
the riches of the Gentiles; how much more
their fulness?[g]

Footnotes for Romans 11:11-12

3 (Rom. 11:11) The Greek word translated "fall" here is "pipto" signifying "a complete irrevocable fall" (Rienecker). Paul is saying, "Is this rejection of Jesus by the Jews irrevocable?" The answer is "No."

The Amplified Bible reads, *"So I ask, have they stumbled so as to fall — to their utter spiritual ruin, irretrievably? By no means!"* The New International Version reads, *"Again I ask: Did they stumble so as to fall beyond recovery? Not at all!"*

Paul then begins to relate how the Jews can still be saved during this "church age" and he cites Old Testament scriptures to declare a future time when the whole nation of Israel will once again come back into God's fold (vv. 26-27).

a Gk.-"ptaio"- to trip; i.e. (fig.) to err; sin; fail (of salvation)
b Gk.-"me genoito"- Lit. 'Let it not be' see note 6 at Rom. 3:4, p. 668 Rom. 3:6, 31 6:2, 15 7:7, 13 9:14 11:1, 11 1 Cor. 6:15 Gal. 2:17 3:21
c see note 45 at Mt. 6:32, p. 83 Rom. 11:12, 31 Acts 13:42,46-48 18:6 22:18-21 28:24-28
d Rom. 11:14 10:19
e Rom. 11:15 9:23 Col. 1:27
f Gk.-"hettema"- a deterioration; i.e. (obj.) failure or (subj.) loss
g Rom. 11:25 Isa. 60 66:8-20 Zech. 2:11 8:20-23

THE SAVING OF THE NATIONS THROUGH ISRAEL'S FALL

CHAPTER 11

13 For I speak to you Gentiles,[a] inasmuch
as I am the apostle[b] of the Gentiles,[c] I
magnify mine office:
14 If by any means I may provoke[d] to
emulation *them which are* my flesh,[e] and
might save[f] some of them.
15 For if the casting away[g] of them *be*
the reconciling[h] of the world, what *shall*
the receiving *of them be,* but life[1] from the
dead?[i]
16 For if the firstfruit[j] *be* holy,[k] the lump
is also *holy*: and if the root *be* holy, so *are*
the branches.[l]
17 And if some of the branches be
broken off,[m] and thou, being a wild olive
tree, wert graffed in[n] among them, and with
them partakest of the root and fatness[o] of
the olive tree;
18 Boast[2] not[p] against the branches. But
if thou boast, thou bearest not the root, but
the root thee.[q]
19 Thou wilt say then, The branches
were broken off, that I might be graffed in.[r]
20 Well; because of unbelief[s] they were
broken off, and thou standest by faith.[t] Be
not highminded,[u] but fear:[v]

References continued from column 4

q Remember that you do not support the root, but the root supports you (TCNT)
r Rom. 11:11-12, 17 Rom. 11:23-24
s Rom. 9:30-32 Gal. 3:7, 26 Heb. 11:6
t Rom. 5:1-2 2 Chr. 20:20 Isa. 7:9 1 Cor. 16:13 2 Cor. 1:24 Col. 2:7
u Gk.-"hupselophroneo"- to be lofty in mind; i.e. arrogant Rom. 11:18 Prov. 16:18 Ps. 138:6 Isa. 2:11 Hab. 2:4 Lk. 18:14 Jas. 4:6 1 Pet. 5:5-6
v Prov. 28:14 Heb. 4:1 1 Pet. 1:17

Footnotes for Romans 11:13-20

1 (Rom. 11:15) Paul had conclusively proven that the Jews did not have a monopoly on God. The Gentiles could now come directly to God without becoming Jews. He had also stated that the Jewish nation as a whole had rejected God because they denied the concept of a savior. They had become their own savior (see note 3 at Rom. 9:32, p. 717).

This could leave some Jews wondering if the Jews had been forsaken by God. Paul answers this question in this chapter (see note 1 at Rom. 11:1, p. 724). There was still a remnant of Jews who were heirs through faith (Rom. 11:5).

In this passage of scripture, Paul draws a conclusion. "If the Jews' rejection of Christ opened up salvation to the rest of the world, then what will happen when the Jews turn back to God? It will be resurrection from the dead!" Paul's statement that the return of the Jews to their God will be life from the dead could be an analogy. That is, Paul could be comparing the Jews' return to God to the joy and blessing that would come from seeing a friend raised from the dead. Or Paul could be speaking literally that the time the Jews return to God will be at the end of the world and the return of Christ when the dead shall be raised.

In either case, Paul is stressing the facts that there will be a future spiritual restoration of Israel (see note 3 at Rom. 11:26, p. 727) and great blessing on the world as a result.

2 (Rom. 11:18) Paul is warning the Gentiles against gloating in the fact that salvation had now been opened unto them as though it happened because of some goodness on their part. It wasn't earned. It was God's grace. Paul explains that the Jews' unbelief (v. 20) caused them to be broken off and that the same thing could happen to the Gentiles (v. 21) if they didn't stand strong through faith.

a see note 45 at Mt. 6:32, p. 83 see note 2 at Lk. 2:32, p. 22 see note 1 at Jn. 12:23, p. 359 see note 1 at Acts 11:22, p. 568 see note 3 at Acts 28:28, p. 653
b see note 2 at Lk. 6:13, p. 109 see note 3 at Acts 14:4, p. 581 1 Tim. 2:7 2 Tim. 1:11
c Rom. 15:16-19 Acts 9:15 13:2 22:21 26:17-18 Gal. 1:16 2:2, 7-9 Eph. 3:8
d Gk.-"parazeloo"- to stimulate alongside; i.e. excite to rivalry- Rom. 11:11
e Rom. 9:3
f Gk.-"sozo"- see note 7 at Acts 2:21, p. 515 see note 8 at Acts 27:20, p. 645 see note 2 at Mt. 8:17, p. 68
g Rom. 11:1-2, & 11-12
h Rom. 5:10 Dan. 9:24 2 Cor. 5:18-20 Col. 1:20-21 see note 1 at Mt. 26:2, p. 410
i When the Jews come to Christ, it will be like dead people coming back to life (LB)
j Ex. 22:29 23:16, 19 Lev. 23:10 Num. 15:17-21 Dt. 18:4 26:10 Neh. 10:35-37 Prov. 3:9 Ezek. 44:30 Jas. 1:18 Rev. 14:4
k Gk.-"hagios"- sacred (physically pure; morally blameless; ceremonially consecrated)- Ex. 19:6 Lev. 20:26 Dt. 14:2 Rom. 12:1 1 Cor. 3:17 2 Cor. 7:1 Col. 1:22 1 Th. 3:13 4:3-4, 7 2 Pet. 3:11
l Rom. 11:17 Gen. 17:7 Jer. 2:21
m Jer. 11:16-17 Ezek. 15:6-8 Mt. 21:43 Jn. 15:6
n Eph. 2:11-13 3:6
o Gk.-"piotes"- plumpness; i.e. (by impl.) richness (oiliness)
p Rom. 11:20 Prov. 16:18
continued on center column

ROMANS

THE SAVING OF THE NATIONS THROUGH ISRAEL'S FALL (cont'd)

CHAPTER 11

21 For if God spared not the natural branches, *take heed* lest he also spare not thee.[w]

22 Behold[3] therefore the goodness[x] and severity[y] of God: on them which fell, severity; but toward thee, goodness, if thou continue in[z] *his* goodness:[x] otherwise thou also shalt be cut off.[aa]

Footnote for Romans 11:21-22

3 (Rom. 11:22) Even in the midst of God's judgment there is mercy. The people who suffered destruction during Noah's flood and the overthrow of Sodom and Gomorrah experienced the severity of God. But these judgments were actually an act of mercy upon the world as a whole. During those times, sin was so rampant in the earth that it was like a cancer. God did radical surgery on mankind by removing these vile sinners and therefore allowed the human race as a whole to survive.

Likewise, God's turning from the Jewish nation to the Gentiles had both severity and goodness in it. It had severe consequences for the Jews, but it blessed the rest of the world.

w 2 Pet. 2:4-9 Jude 1:5 1 Cor. 10:1-12
x Gk.-"chrestotes"- usefulness; i.e. moral excellence (in character or demeanor) Trans. gentleness; good (-ness); kindness
y Dict.- extreme strictness; rigid conformity; strict justice of God (Phi) The term "severity" denotes excision; cutting off; continued on column 4

continued from column 1 as the gardener cuts off, with a pruning knife, dead boughs, or luxuriant stems (TSK)
z Rom. 2:7 Lk. 8:15 Jn. 8:31 15:4-10 Acts 11:23 14:22 1 Cor. 15:2 Gal. 6:9 1 Th. 3:5 Heb. 3:6, 14 10:23, 35-39 1 Jn. 2:19
aa Mt. 3:9-10 Jn. 15:2 Rev. 2:5

ISRAEL RESTORED; GOD'S MERCY SHOWN TO ALL

CHAPTER 11

23 And they also, if they abide[a] not still in unbelief, shall be grafted in:[b] for God is able[1] to graff them in again.

24 For if thou wert cut out of the olive tree which is wild by nature, and wert graffed contrary to nature into a good olive tree: how much more shall these, which be the natural *branches,* be graffed into their own olive tree?[c]

25 *For I would not, brethren, that ye should be ignorant[d] of this mystery,[e] lest ye should be wise in your own conceits;[f] that blindness[g] in part is happened to Israel, until the fulness of the Gentiles[2] be come in.[h]

26 *And so all[3] Israel shall be saved:[i] as it is written,[j] There shall come out of Sion the Deliverer,[k] and shall turn away ungodliness from Jacob:[l]

PARALLEL SCRIPTURE FOR ROMANS 11:25

LUKE 21:24

24 And they shall fall by the edge of the sword, and shall be led away captive into all nations: and Jerusalem shall be trodden down of the Gentiles, until the times of the Gentiles be fulfilled.

O.T. SCRIPTURE CITED IN ROMANS 11:26

ISAIAH 59:20

20 And the Redeemer shall come to Zion, and unto them that turn from transgression in Jacob, saith the LORD.

Footnotes for Romans 11:23-26

1 (Rom. 11:23) God is not only "able" to restore the Jewish nation, but Paul goes on to say in verse 26 that all Israel "will" be saved (see note 3 at Rom. 11:26, below).

2 (Rom. 11:25) This phrase *"fulness of the Gentiles"* is only used here. A similar expression, *"times of the Gentiles"* is used in Luke 21:24 (see Parallel Scripture for this verse). There are two obvious ways this phrase could be interpreted.

First, the fulness of the Gentiles could be referring to all the Gentiles who are foreordained (see note 2 at Rom. 8:29, p. 709) to come to Christ experiencing salvation. Then there would be a wonderful move of God among the Jews in which the Jewish nation as a whole would come to the Lord (v. 26). The Amplified Translation would lend itself to this interpretation: *". . . a hardening (insensibility) has **[temporarily]** befallen a part of Israel **[to last]** until the full number of the ingathering of the Gentiles has come in."*

This phrase could also be referring to the time when the Gentiles would no longer be dominating the Jewish nation, specifically referring to the occupation of Jerusalem by the Gentiles. This is apparently what Luke 21:24 is referring to. If so, then there will have to be a future fulfillment of the scriptures that prophesied the end of Gentile control of Jerusalem since Israel has physically possessed Jerusalem since the Israel-Arab War of 1967 and yet, the nation as a whole has not come to God.

3 (Rom. 11:26) There are an abundance of Old Testament prophecies that speak of the Jewish nation being restored to its former status both physically and spiritually (see ref. i, this verse). It must be understood that when Paul says "all" Israel shall be saved, he is using a figure of speech (see note 6 at Mk. 1:5, p. 32). The Jewish nation as a whole will return to God but there will be individual Jews who do not.

a Gk.-"epimeno"- to stay over; i.e. remain (fig. persevere) Trans. abide (in); continue (in); tarry
b Rom. 11:11-12, & 17, 23-24
c Rom. 11:17-18, & 30
d Gk.-"agnoeo"- not to know (through lack of information or intelligence); by impl. to ignore (through disinclination) Trans. (be) ignorant (-ly); not know; not understand; unknown- 1 Cor. 10:1 12:1 2 Pet. 3:8
e Gk.-"musterion"- a hidden or secret thing; not obvious to the understanding; a hidden purpose or counsel (Thayer)- Col. 1:26-27 Rom. 16:25 Eph. 3:3-4, 9 Rev. 10:7

f Dict.- too high an opinion of one's abilities, worth, or personality; vanity- Rom. 12:16 Prov. 3:5-7 26:12, 16 Isa. 5:21
g i.e. blindness or hardness see note 3 at Mk. 8:17, p. 199 Rom. 11:7-8 2 Cor. 3:14-16
h Ps. 22:27 Isa. 2:1-8 60:1-22 66:18-23 Mic. 4:1-2 Zech. 8:20-23 Rev. 7:9
i Isa. 11:11-16 45:17 54:6-10 Jer. 3:17-23 30:17-22 31:31-37 32:37-41 33:24-26 Ezek. 34:22-31 37:21-28 39:25-29 Hos. 3:5 Amos 9:14-15 Zech. 10:6-12
j Isa. 59:20 Ps. 14:7
k Dict.- to release or rescue from bondage, danger, or evil of any kind; set free
l Mt. 1:21 Acts 3:26 Ti. 2:14

ROMANS

ISRAEL RESTORED; GOD'S MERCY SHOWN TO ALL (continued)

CHAPTER 11

27 *For this *is* my covenant[a] unto them,
when I shall take away their sins.[b]
28 As concerning the gospel,[c] *they are*
enemies[d] for your sakes: but as touching
the election,[e] *they are* beloved for the
fathers' sakes.[f]
29 For the gifts[g] and calling[4] of God *are*
without repentance.[h]
30 For as ye in times past have not
believed[i] God, yet have now obtained
mercy[j] through their unbelief:
31 Even so have these also now not
believed, that through your mercy they
also may obtain mercy.[k]
32 For God hath concluded them all in
unbelief, that he might have mercy upon
all.[l]

O.T. SCRIPTURES CITED IN ROMANS 11:27

JEREMIAH 31:31-34

31 Behold, the days come, saith the
LORD, that I will make a new covenant
with the house of Israel, and with the
house of Judah:
32 Not according to the covenant
that I made with their fathers in the day
that I took them by the hand to bring
them out of the land of Egypt; which my
covenant they brake, although I was an
husband unto them, saith the LORD:
33 But this shall be the covenant that
I will make with the house of Israel;
After those days, saith the LORD, I will
put my law in their inward parts, and
write it in their hearts; and will be their
God, and they shall be my people.
34 And they shall teach no more
every man his neighbour, and every man
his brother, saying, Know the LORD:
for they shall all know me, from the least
of them unto the greatest of them, saith
the LORD: for I will forgive their iniquity,
and I will remember their sin no more.

a Gk.-"diatheke"- a disposition; i.e. (spec.) a contract (esp. a devisory will) Trans. covenant; testament- Isa. 55:3 59:21 Jer. 31:31-34 32:38-40 Heb. 8:8-12 10:16
b Isa. 43:25 Jer. 50:20 Ezek. 36:25-29 Jn. 1:29
c see note 3 at Rom. 1:2, p. 655 see note 7 at Mt. 24:14, p. 396 see note 5 at Acts 20:24, p. 618 see note 1 at Rom. 1:16, p. 658
d Acts 13:45-46 14:2 18:6 1 Th. 2:15-16
e Gk.-"ekloge"- (divine) selection Trans. chosen; election see note 4 at Rom. 9:11, p. 712 Rom. 11:7 Isa. 41:8-9 42:1 Mt. 24:24 Lk. 18:7 1 Th. 1:4 Ti. 1:1 1 Pet. 1:2
f But from the standpoint of God's selection, they are dear to Him on account of the Patriarchs (TCNT) But in His elective purpose He still welcomes them, for the sake of their Father (Knox)
g Gk.-"charisma"- a gift of grace; a favor which one receives without any merit of His own (Thayer)
h Num. 23:19 Hos. 13:14 Mal. 3:6
i Gk.-"apeitheo"- to disbelieve (willfully and perversely) Trans. not believe; disobedient; obey not; unbelieving- Eph. 2:2, 12 Col. 3:7 Ti. 3:3-7
j Rom. 11:31 2 Cor. 4:1 1 Pet. 2:10
k But some day they will share in God's mercy upon you (Tay)- Rom. 11:15, 25
l For God has bound all men over to disobedience so that He may have mercy on them all (NIV)

Footnote for Romans 11:27-32

4 (Rom. 11:29) In context, this is speaking about the future restoration of the Jewish nation. Paul is saying that even though the Jews had rejected God, the Lord was still going to bring His promises to the Jews to pass. This is an act of total grace on the Lord's part (see note 5 at Rom. 1:5, p. 655).

This scripture has a broader application too. Any calling, or gift to accomplish that calling, that the Lord gives an individual is without repentance. It means that, regardless of what an individual does, God doesn't withdraw His gifts and callings. This is why some ministers who fall into sin can still see the supernatural gifts of God flow in their ministries.

That is not to say that living a life separated unto God is not important. It is very important. People who are living in sin are going to have their faith made shipwreck through their conscience (1 Tim. 1:19). They will begin to lose effectiveness. However, as much as they can operate in faith, the gifts and callings of God that they have received are still there and they will function.

Anything that you've ever received from God is still there; it just needs to be activated by faith.

ROMANS

A PRAISE TO GOD FOR HIS WISDOM

CHAPTER 11

33 O the depth[a] of the riches[b] both of the wisdom[c] and knowledge[d] of God! how unsearchable[e] *are* his judgments,[f] and his ways[g] past finding[h] out!

34 *For who hath known the mind of the Lord?[i] or who hath been his counsellor?[j]

35 Or who hath first given[k] to him, and it shall be recompensed[l] unto him again?

36 For of him, and through him, and to him, *are* all things: to whom *be* glory for ever.[m] Amen.[n]

O.T. SCRIPTURE CITED IN ROMANS 11:34

ISAIAH 40:13

13 Who hath directed the Spirit of the LORD, or being *his counsellor hath taught him?*

PARALLEL SCRIPTURE FOR ROMANS 11:34

1 CORINTHIANS 2:16

16 For who hath known the mind of the Lord, that he may instruct him? But we have the mind of Christ.

a Gk.-"bathos"- profundity; i.e. (by impl.) extent; (fig.) mystery Trans. deep (-ness) things; depth Dict.- "profundity"- great depth; depth of intellect, feeling, or meaning; something profound or abstruse
b Rom. 2:4 9:23 Eph. 1:7 2:7 3:8,16 Col. 1:27 2:2-3
c Gk.-"sophia"- insight into the true nature of things (W.E. Vine) Dict.- understanding of what is true, right, or lasting; common sense; sagacity; good judgment- Ps. 104:24 Prov. 3:19 continued on column 4

continued from column 1 Dan. 2:20 Mt. 13:54 1 Cor. 1:25 Col. 2:3 Jas. 1:5
d Dict.- The state or fact of knowing- 1 Sam. 2:3 Ps. 69:5 139:2, 12 Isa. 40:13-14 Dan. 2:22 Heb. 4:13
e Dict.- beyond research; inscrutable; imponderable- Job 5:9 Eccl. 3:11
f i.e. His decisions
g i.e. His ways; His methods; His paths! (Amp)
h Gk.-"anexichniastos"- not tracked out; i.e. (by impl.) untraceable
i see note 3 at Lk. 1:43, p. 12 continued on center column

References continued from column 4
j Gk.-"sumboulos"- a consultor; i.e. advisor; adviser- 1 Cor. 2:16
k Gk.-"prodidomi"- to give before the other party has given
l Dict.- payment in return for something given or done- Job 35:7 41:11 1 Cor. 4:7
m Everything is from Him, by Him, and for Him; to Him be glory forever. Amen (Beck)- Rom. 16:27 Phil. 4:20 1 Tim. 1:17 Heb. 13:21 1 Pet. 5:11 2 Pet. 3:18 Jude 25 Rev. 1:5-6
n Num. 5:22 Dt. 27:15-26 1 Chr. 16:36 Neh. 5:13 1 Cor. 14:16

PRESENTING OUR BODIES AND RENEWING OUR MINDS

CHAPTER 12

I BESEECH[a] you therefore, brethren,[1] by the mercies[2b] of God, that ye[3] present[c] your bodies a living[4] sacrifice,[d] holy, acceptable[e] unto God, *which is* your reasonable[5] service.[f]

a Dict.- to address an earnest or urgent request to; implore Syn.- beg- Rom. 15:30 1 Cor. 1:10 2 Cor. 5:20 6:1 10:1 Eph. 4:1 1 Th. 4:1,10 5:12 Heb. 13:22
b Gk.-"oiktirmos"- emotions; longings; manifestations of pity (Thayer)- Rom. 11:30-31
c Dict.- to offer for acceptance; to make a gift of; bestow- Rom. 6:13, 16, 19 1 Cor. 6:13-20 Phil. 1:20
d Ps. 69:30-31 Hos. 14:2 1 Cor. 5:7 Phil. 2:17 Heb. 13:15-16 1 Pet. 2:5
e Rom. 11:2 15:16 Ps. 19:14 Isa. 56:7 Eph. 5:10 Phil. 4:18 1 Tim. 2:3 5:4 1 Pet. 2:5, 20
f Gk.-"latreia"- ministration of God; i.e. worship Trans. (divine) service

Footnotes for Romans 12:1

1 (Rom. 12:1) Paul was speaking to Christians. It is possible to commit one's life to the Lord for the purpose of salvation, and yet not be yielded to the Lord in our daily lives. It is only when we make the total sacrifice of every area of our lives that we begin to see God's perfect will manifest through our lives.

2 (Rom. 12:1) Paul uses the mercies of God to encourage these Romans to give themselves totally to God. Today, most preachers use the wrath of God to try and drive men to God. There are some people who need the condemnation of the law to make them aware of their need for a Savior, but as a whole, we could "draw more flies with honey than with vinegar." It's the goodness of God that leads men to repentance (Rom. 2:4).

3 (Rom. 12:1) Notice that we are the ones who have to make this presentation of our bodies to the Lord. He will not do it for us. Many people pray, "Lord, you do what you have to do to make me serve you." That is not a proper prayer. You cannot have someone lay hands on you to impart this commitment to you. You cannot just rebuke the flesh and expect it to disappear. You have to give your bodies to God as a living sacrifice daily (see note 4 at this verse, below).

4 (Rom. 12:1) This sounds like a contradiction of terms. How can we be a living sacrifice when sacrifices are always dead? This is speaking of the fact that offering ourselves to God is not just a one-time deal. We have to die to our own desires daily. This has to be a living, on going commitment to the Lord.

The Apollo spacecraft traveled to the moon, but it was not just as simple as blasting off and landing on the moon. There were course corrections made every ten minutes or so for the entire trip. And then, they only landed a few feet inside the targeted landing area of 500 miles. Yet the missions were a success.

Likewise, there has to be a starting place for this decision to be a living sacrifice. We have to blast off or start our journey sometime. But we don't ever "arrive" in this life. We just leave and start toward the goal (Phil. 3:12-13). We may be making course corrections every ten minutes for the rest of our lives.

You see, living sacrifices have a tendency to keep crawling off the altar. Every minute of every day, we have to reaffirm this decision to be totally separated unto God. This is what Paul is referring to by the term "living sacrifice."

5 (Rom. 12:1) Many Christians think that living a totally consecrated life to God is something that only preachers or a few lay people do. They see it as "extra" and not "normal" Christianity. However, Paul says this level of commitment is our reasonable service. Jesus died for each one of us. Each one of us ought to live for Him.

ROMANS

PRESENTING OUR BODIES AND RENEWING OUR MINDS (cont'd)

CHAPTER 12

2 And[6] be not conformed[7] to this world:[a] but be ye transformed[8] by the renewing[b] of your mind,[9c] that ye may prove[10d] what *is* that good,[11] and acceptable,[e] and perfect,[f] will[g] of God.[12]

a Dt. 18:9 Jn. 15:19 17:14 2 Cor. 6:14-17 Gal. 1:4 Eph. 2:2 4:17-20 Jas. 1:27 4:4 2 Pet. 1:4 2:20 1 Jn. 2:15-17 5:19

b Gk.-"anakainosis"- renovation Dict.- to become new again; to start over

c Gk.-"nous"- the intellect; i.e. mind (divine or human; in thought, feeling, or will); by impl. meaning Trans. mind; understanding

d Gk.-"dokimazo"- to test; by impl. to approve- Eph. 5:10

e Gk.-"euarestos"- fully agreeable

f Gk.-"teleios"- complete

g i.e. desire; pleasure

Footnotes for Romans 12:2

6 (Rom. 12:2) Many people would think that if we fulfill the conditions of verse one then everything else would automatically work out. Yet Paul goes on to state that we also have to renew our minds. There have been many people who have had a genuine commitment to the Lord but they didn't renew their minds through God's Word and they needlessly suffered many problems.

7 (Rom. 12:2) The Greek word that was translated "conformed" here is the word "suschematizo" meaning "to fashion alike, i.e. conform to the same pattern." This scripture is telling us that we should be different than the unbelievers. Most Christians recognize this but they seem at a loss of how to accomplish it. This verse goes on to give us the answer. The key is our minds. *"For as he thinketh in his heart, so is he. . ."* (Prov. 23:7).

If we think on the same things that the world thinks on, we are going to get the same results. If we keep our minds stayed upon God through the study of His Word and fellowship with Him, then we'll have perfect peace (Isa. 26:3). It's that simple.

8 (Rom. 12:2) The Greek word that was translated "transformed" here is the word "metamorphoo" and is the same word that we get our word "metamorphosis" from. It is describing a complete change, like that of a caterpillar changing into a butterfly. This word is also the same word that was used to describe Jesus' transformation when His garments became white as the light (Mt. 17:2).

Making our thinking line up with God's Word will affect this complete transformation in our lives.

9 (Rom. 12:2) When anyone gets born again (see note 2 at Jn. 3:3, p. 48), he becomes a totally new creation in his spirit. His spiritual salvation is complete. He doesn't need any more faith, joy, or power. He is complete in Him (Col. 2:9-10; see note 3 at Mt. 26:41, p. 448).

However, it is not God's will that we only be changed on the inside. He wants to manifest this salvation in our physical lives also. That takes place through the renewing of our minds.

Man is a spirit, soul, and body (1 Th. 5:23). Our spirits are as perfect as they will ever be in heaven (see note 1 at Rom. 8:18, p. 705). If we will change our thinking so that we believe what God says in His Word about who we are and what we have, then this agreement between our spirit and soul forms a majority and our flesh will experience the life of God that has been deposited in our spirits.

If we fail to renew our minds, we can live our entire time on this earth without experiencing the abundant life that Jesus provided for us (Jn. 10:10).

10 (Rom. 12:2) The dictionary defines "prove" as "to establish the truth or validity of by evidence or argument; to be shown to be; turn out." Therefore, this is speaking of how to physically display God's will in our lives. This is a promise that if we fulfill the requirements of these two verses, we will prove (not **might** prove, but **will** prove) the good, and acceptable, and perfect will of God.

Finding God's will for our lives is not hard when we do what these verses instruct us to do. As a matter of fact, it would be impossible to miss God's will once we commit ourselves to God as a living sacrifice and begin to renew our minds. Finding God's will for our lives only becomes hard if we are not totally committed to God.

11 (Rom. 12:2) There is a difference of opinion among scholars as to whether Paul is using "good, and acceptable, and perfect" to describe the will of God or if Paul is saying that there are stages in walking in the will of God (i.e. good, then acceptable, then the perfect will of God). Either of these cases would be doctrinally correct.

God's will certainly is good and acceptable and perfect. It is also true that no one moves immediately into everything that God has for him, but there is always growth into the things of God.

12 (Rom. 12:2) This is a wonderful promise that we can prove God's will in our lives (see note 10 at this verse, above). The first step is to make a total commitment of our lives to the Lord (a living sacrifice—v. 1). Actually this is the will of God for everyone. Our vocation is secondary. God's will for every individual is to be a living sacrifice to Him. Once that is accomplished, more specific direction will come as we renew our minds.

If we try to find God's vocation for us, but don't present ourselves to God as a living sacrifice, then we are frustrating God's plan. God doesn't just want our service, He wants us. Once He gets us, He'll get our service.

ROMANS

PRESENTING OUR BODIES AND RENEWING OUR MINDS (cont'd)

h see note 5 at Rom. 1:5, p. 655
see note 8 at Rom. 3:24, p. 673
see note 15 at Rom. 5:8, p. 683
Rom. 11:6-8
1:5
15:15-16
1 Cor. 3:10
15:10
Gal. 2:8-9
Eph. 3:2-4, 7-8
4:7-12

CHAPTER 12

3 For[13] I say, through the grace[h] given unto me, to every man that is among you, not to think[14] *of himself* more highly[i] than he ought to think; but to think soberly,[j] according[15] as God hath dealt[k] to every man the[16] measure of faith.[l]

i Gk.-"huperphroneo"- to esteem oneself overmuch; i.e. be vain or arrogant-
Rom. 11:20
Prov. 16:18-19
25:27
26:12
Mt. 18:1-4
Lk. 18:11
Gal. 6:3
Phil. 2:3-8
Jas. 4:6
1 Pet. 5:5
3 Jn. 1:9
continued on center column

References continued from column 4

j i.e. with a sane estimate (Phi)-Ti. 2:2, 4, 6, 12
1 Pet. 1:13

k Gk.-"merizo"- to part; i.e. to apportion; bestow; share; or to disunite; differ Trans. deal; be difference between; distribute; divide; give part

l see note 3 at Lk. 17:5, p. 305

Footnotes for Romans 12:3

13 (Rom. 12:3) Paul begins this sentence with the conjunction "for." That means, the point he is making in verse 3 is a continuation or result of what was said in verse 2. Many times the word "because" can be used interchangeably with "for."

Paul had just admonished them about humility and submission (a living sacrifice) being the way to true success. He now continues that thought by giving these people another reason for humility: the fact that every man has been dealt *"the measure of faith"* (see note 15 at this verse, below).

In other words, every believer has a perfect plan for his life which he can "prove" (see note 10 at v. 2, p. 730) if he will totally yield himself to God. We may have a different gift, but it is not a better gift than someone else's. He then continues in verse 4 with the word "for" again, and draws a comparison from the way our bodies have different parts but they all work together to make one body.

14 (Rom. 12:3) Religion has interpreted this verse to say that we should think of ourselves in a lowly manner, but that is not what Paul is saying. It would be proper to say that we shouldn't think of ourselves more highly or more lowly than we ought to think. We need to remember that any good thing that we have is a gift from God (1 Cor. 4:7). Paul is admonishing us to have the correct viewpoint, not a lowly viewpoint.

15 (Rom. 12:3) The dictionary defines "according as" as "in proportion to." Paul is saying that we need to remember that God has given every believer "the" measure of faith (see note 14 at this verse, above). This sobers us up because we recognize that what we have is a gift from God that every child of God possesses. Some live up to more of their potential than others, but it's only God's mercy that makes it possible for any of us to accomplish anything.

16 (Rom. 12:3) God has dealt to every man "the" measure of faith, not "a" measure of faith. There are not different measures with God. The Lord doesn't give one person great faith while another person is given small faith. We were all given an equal amount of faith at salvation. The problem is not that we don't have faith, but rather we don't know how to use our faith because of a lack of renewing our minds.

Peter said we had "like precious faith" with him (2 Pet. 1:1). The same faith that he used to raise Dorcas from the dead (Acts 9:36-42) is in us, too. The same faith that Peter used is the same faith that we have.

Paul said he was living his Christian life by the faith of the Son of God (Gal. 2:20). Since we all have been given "the" measure of faith, then that means we all have the faith of the Son of God in us. Our faith is sufficient. The problem we're experiencing is a result of our **minds** not knowing what we have.

In the same way that a car battery transfers its power to the starter through battery cables, so our minds are the thing that allows this faith of God that is in our spirits to flow into our bodies. If our minds are not renewed, then it's like having corroded cables. The power is there but it won't flow. Likewise, every believer has the same faith that Jesus has, but it won't flow through us until we renew our minds through the Word of God.

ROMANS

THE EXERCISING OF GOD'S GRACE GIFTS

a Gk.-"melos"- a limb or part of the body- Eph. 4:15-16

CHAPTER 12

4 *For[1] as we have many members[a] in one body, and all members[a] have not the same office:[b]
5 *So we, *being* many, are one body in Christ, and every one members one of another.[c]

b Gk.-"praxis"- practice; i.e. an act; by extens. a function Trans. deed; office; work- 1 Cor. 12:4

c 1 Cor. 10:17 Eph. 1:23 4:25 5:30 Col. 1:24 2:19

PARALLEL SCRIPTURES FOR ROMANS 12:4-5

1 CORINTHIANS 12:12-27

12 For as the body is one, and hath many members, and all the members of that one body, being many, are one body: so also is *Christ.*
13 For by one Spirit are we all baptized into one body, whether we be *Jews or Gentiles, whether* we be *bond or free; and have been all made to drink into one Spirit.*
14 For the body is not one member, but many.
15 If the foot shall say, Because I am not the hand, I am not of the body; is it therefore not of the body?
16 And if the ear shall say, Because I am not the eye, I am not of the body; is it therefore not of the body?
17 If the whole body were *an eye, where* were *the hearing? If the whole* were *hearing, where* were *the smelling?*
18 But now hath God set the members every one of them in the body, as it hath pleased him.
19 And if they were all one member, where were *the body?*
20 But now are they *many members, yet but one body.*
21 And the eye cannot say unto the hand, I have no need of thee: nor again the head to the feet, I have no need of you.
22 Nay, much more those members of the body, which seem to be more feeble, are necessary:
23 And those members *of the body, which we think to be less honourable, upon these we bestow more abundant honour; and our uncomely* parts *have more abundant comeliness.*
24 For our comely parts *have no need: but God hath tempered the body together, having given more abundant honour to that* part *which lacked:*
25 That there should be no schism in the body; but that *the members should have the same care one for another.*
26 And whether one member suffer, all the members suffer with it; or one member be honoured, all the members rejoice with it.
27 Now ye are the body of Christ, and members in particular.

Footnote for Romans 12:4-5

1 (Rom. 12:4) This verse starts with the word "for," which is a conjunction just as in verse 3 (see note 13 at v. 3, p. 731). This is linking Paul's following statements with his previous statements.

Paul had encouraged these people to experience the perfect will of God (v. 2) through humbling themselves (being a living sacrifice). This was vastly different than the world's formula for success and needed some further explanation. Therefore, in verse 3, Paul explains that every believer has been given the same opportunity for success through "the" measure of faith.

Now in verse 4, Paul continues to explain that although every believer has been given "the" measure of faith, not every believer has been given the same job in the body of Christ. He uses our physical bodies to illustrate this.

We have many different parts of our body and they all have a different purpose or function. Yet, it takes all the parts operating in unity to make one body. Likewise, it takes all the different people in the church performing their different functions to make up Christ's body.

So, in verses 1-2, Paul gave a "fool-proof" formula for success. However, to keep anyone from gloating at the tremendous potential of these promises, he makes it clear in verse 3 that everyone has been given the same potential. And in verses 4-8 he reveals that we all have different functions, and we all need each other.

ROMANS

THE EXERCISING OF GOD'S GRACE GIFTS (continued)

CHAPTER 12

6 *Having then gifts[2d] differing[e] according to the grace[f] that is given to us, whether prophecy,[3g] *let us prophesy* according to the proportion of faith;[h]

7 Or ministry,[4i] *let us wait* on *our* ministering: or he that teacheth,[j] on teaching;[5j]

8 Or he that exhorteth,[6k] on exhortation:[k] he that giveth,[l] *let him do it* with simplicity;[7] he that ruleth,[8m] with diligence;[n] he that sheweth mercy,[o] with cheerfulness.[9]

PARALLEL SCRIPTURE FOR ROMANS 12:6

1 PETER 4:11

11 If any man speak, let him speak *as the oracles of God; if any man minister,* let him do it *as of the ability which God giveth: that God in all things may be glorified through Jesus Christ, to whom be praise and dominion for ever and ever. Amen.*

d Gk.-"charisma"- a gift of grace; a favor which one receives without any merit of his own; extraordinary powers, distinguishing certain Christians and enabling them to serve the church of Christ; the reception of which is due to the power of divine grace operating in their souls by the Holy Spirit (Thayer) see note 5 at Rom. 1:5, p. 655
e 1 Cor. 12:4-11, & 28-31 1 Pet. 4:10
f see note 5 at Rom. 1:5, p. 655 see note 8 at Rom. 3:24, p. 673 see note 15 at Rom. 5:8, p. 683
g see note 7 at Acts 13:2, p. 574 see note 10 at Acts 27:22, p. 646 Acts 2:17 21:9 1 Cor.12:10 13:2 14:1, 3-5, 24, 31 1 Th. 5:20
h Rom. 12:3
i Rom.15:25, 31 Acts 6:1-3 11:29 2 Cor. 8:4
j see note 3 at Mt. 5:2, p. 73 see note 5 at Mt. 28:19, p. 504 Acts 13:1 18:11, 25 28:31 1 Cor. 12:28 Gal. 6:6 Eph. 4:11 Col. 1:28 1 Tim. 2:7 3:2 2 Tim. 2:2, 24
k Acts 13:15 15:32 20:2 1 Cor. 14:3 1 Th. 2:3 1 Tim. 4:13 Heb. 10:25 13:22
l Gk.-"metadidomi"- to give over; i.e. share Trans. give; impart- Rom. 12:13 Dt. 15:8-11, 14 Job 31:16-20 Ps. 112:9 Prov. 22:9 Isa. 58:7-11 Mt. 6:2-4 25:40 Lk. 21:1-4 Acts 2:44-46 4:33-35 11:28-30 2 Cor. 8:1-9, 12 1 Pet. 4:9-10
m i.e. leadership, managing, administering, or presiding- Acts 20:28 1 Cor. 12:28 1 Th. 5:12-14 1 Tim. 3:4-5 5:17 Heb. 13:7, 17, 24 1 Pet. 5:2-3
n i.e. with earnestness; eagerness; not half-hearted
o Gk.-"eleeo"- be compassionate (by word or deed; spec. by divine grace) Trans. have compassion (pity on); have (obtain; receive; shew) mercy (on) Dict.- kind and compassionate treatment of an offender, enemy, prisoner, or other person under one's power; clemency; a disposition to be kind and forgiving see note 2 at Mk. 1:41, p. 86 Ps. 37:21

Footnotes for Romans 12:6-8

2 (Rom. 12:6) It must be remembered that Paul is not teaching on the function and administration of these seven gifts that he mentions here as he taught on the nine gifts of the Spirit in 1 Corinthians 12-14. He is simply mentioning these gifts to illustrate his point that different people in the body of Christ have different positions or functions. However, there are some truths concerning these gifts that we can glean from these scriptures.

First, it needs to be pointed out that all believers can operate in the gifts listed here, but that doesn't mean that is their ministry. For instance, we can and should be able to teach others but that doesn't make us a teacher. Paul said we could all prophesy one by one (1 Cor. 14:31) but he also made it clear that we are not all called to be prophets (1 Cor. 12:29). It is definite that we should all show mercy and be givers, but there are some people who are given a supernatural gift in these areas which Paul is describing here.

Concerning the gift of giving, Paul says that we should do our giving with simplicity (see note 7 at v. 8, below). He that rules should be diligent about it (see note 8 at v. 8, below), and the person who has the gift of mercy should administer it with cheerfulness.

3 (Rom. 12:6) The Greek word that was translated "prophecy" here is "propheteia," which "signifies the speaking forth of the mind and counsel of God" (W.E. Vine). This originally applied to Old Testament prophets who were predicting future events, but it came to apply to any messenger who was inspired by God as he spoke. This would apply to a preacher today if he is speaking under the anointing of the Holy Spirit.

This verse is saying essentially the same thing that Peter said in 1 Peter 4:11 (see Parallel Scripture, above). If we are going to prophesy, let's do it according to the ability that God gave us—the measure of faith (see note 16 at v. 3, p. 731).

4 (Rom. 12:7) The Greek word that was translated "ministry" here is "diakonia" and means "attendance (as a servant, etc.)." It is a variation of the Greek word "diakonos" where we get our English word "deacon" from.

This same Greek word was translated "serving" in Luke 10:40; "service" (referring to charitable giving) in Romans 15:31; "relief" in Acts 11:29; and "office" in Romans 11:13. The Amplified Bible translates this verse as *"[He whose gift is] practical service, let him give himself to serving . . . ."*

Therefore, we can surmise from these things that this is referring to those who have been given a ministry of serving others as Paul described the house of Stephanas (1 Cor. 16:15). This gift is not often recognized and even more often not appreciated, but it is listed in good company. Paul mentions this between prophecy and teaching, two gifts which are recognized and accepted.

5 (Rom. 12:7) The ministry gift of a teacher was placed third in authority in the church, behind the ministry of the apostle and prophet (1 Cor. 12:28). The basic difference between a teacher and a preacher is that a preacher proclaims and a teacher explains.

6 (Rom. 12:8) The Greek word for "exhorteth" is "parakaleo." It was translated "beseech" in Romans 12:1; 15:30; and 16:17. It can also mean "to comfort or encourage" and it is probably used that way here.

Our English word "exhort" comes from the Latin "exhortari." This is a compound word comprised of "ex" meaning "completely" and "hortari" meaning "to encourage." Therefore, the word "exhort" literally means "to completely encourage." One of the purposes of prophesy is exhortation (1 Cor. 14:3). Exhortation is also a part of preaching the Word (2 Tim. 4:2). However, this verse shows that there are individuals who have a special ministry of encouraging people. This is a supernatural gift.

7 (Rom. 12:8) The Greek word used here is "haplotes" and means "sincerity, uprightness, or frankness," but it can also mean "generosity or liberality." Most scholars agree that in this case it is expressing "generosity or liberality." Therefore, Paul is saying that those who have a ministry of giving should be generous in their giving.

8 (Rom. 12:8) The Greek word that was translated "ruleth" here is "proistemi" and it means "to stand before, i.e. (in rank) preside." The Amplified Bible translates this phrase as *". . .he who gives aid* and *superintends, with zeal* and *singleness of mind. . . ."* This could be speaking of any one of many positions of authority in the church. This does reveal that although everyone has some degree of authority, there are individuals who are given a ministry gift of ruling, or what might be commonly called administration today.

9 (Rom. 12:8) The Greek word that was translated "cheerfulness" here is "hilarotes" and means "cheerfulness." It comes from the Greek word "hilaros" which is where we get our word "hilarious." Therefore, Paul is admonishing those who show mercy to be hilarious in their administration of this gift.

ROMANS

THE PRACTICAL LIVING OF CHRIST'S LIFE

CHAPTER 12

9 *Let* love[a] be without dissimulation.[1b]
Abhor[2c] that which is evil;[d] cleave[e] to that
which is good.[f]
10 *Be* kindly affectioned[g] one to another
with brotherly love;[3h] in honour[i] preferring[4]
one another;[j]

a see note 4 at Jn. 13:35, p. 424
b 2 Sam. 20:9-10 Ps. 55:21 Ezek. 33:31 Mt. 26:49 Jn. 12:6 2 Cor. 8:8 1 Th. 2:3 1 Tim. 1:5 Jas. 2:15-16 1 Pet. 1:22 4:8 1 Jn. 3:18-20
c Ps. 97:10 101:3 119:104, 163 Amos 5:15
d Dict.- anything that causes displeasure, injury, pain, suffering, etc.; moral depravity; wickedness; anything morally bad or wrong
e Gk.-"kollao"- to glue; i.e. to stick Trans. cleave; join (self); keep company- Acts 11:23
f Gk.-"agathos"- describes that which, being good in its character or constitution, is beneficial in its effect . . . morally honourable; pleasing to God, and therefore beneficial (W.E. Vine)
g Gk.-"philostorgos"- fond of natural relatives; i.e. fraternal towards fellow Christians- Acts 4:32 Gal. 5:6, 13 Col. 1:4 1 Th. 4:9 2 Th. 1:3 Heb. 13:1 1 Pet. 1:22 1 Jn. 2:10 3:11, 14-18, 23 4:11, 20-21 5:2
h Ps. 133:1
i Gk.-"time"- a value; i.e. money paid, or valuables; by anal. esteem (esp. of the highest degree), or the dignity itself Trans. honour; precious; price; some
j Eager to show one another honor (Gspd) A willingness to let the other man have the credit (Phi) Give preference to one another in honor (NASB) Outdo one another in showing respect (Beck)- Gen. 13:9 Mt. 20:26 Lk. 14:10 Phil. 2:3-5 1 Pet. 5:5

Footnotes for Romans 12:9-10

1 (Rom. 12:9) The dictionary defines "dissimulate" as "to disguise under a feigned appearance." The Greek word that was used was "anupokritos" meaning "without hypocrisy, unfeigned." This Greek word was only used six times in all the New Testament. In James 3:17 it was translated "without hypocrisy" and four times it was translated "unfeigned" (2 Cor. 6:6; 1 Tim. 1:5; 2 Tim. 1:5; 1 Pet. 1:22).

Paul is still talking about love when he said, *"Abhor that which is evil, cleave to that which is good."* Part of true love is hatred (see note 2 at this verse, below). If we don't hate the things that oppose the one we love, then it is not God's kind of love. If we don't hate evil, then our love for God is with dissimulation. It is hypocritical.

It has become customary in our society to conceal our real feelings behind a hypocritical mask. Although we should be tactful and not purposely say things to offend people, there is a time and a place for speaking the truth, even if it isn't popular.

In Leviticus 19:17, the Lord said, *"Thou shalt not hate thy brother in thine heart: thou shalt in any wise rebuke thy neighbour, and not suffer sin upon him."* That verse is saying that if we fail to rebuke our brother when we see sin approaching, then we hate him. Many people have concealed their true feelings about evil under the pretense of "I just love them too much to hurt their feelings." The truth is, they just love themselves too much to run the risk of being rejected. That's hypocrisy.

This scripture **commands** us to abhor (see note 2 at this verse, below) that which is evil. We need to love the sinner, but hate the sin. We need to be outspoken on what is right and wrong. Jesus illustrated this scripture when He drove the moneychangers out of the temple with a whip (Jn. 2:14-17).

2 (Rom. 12:9) The Greek word that was translated "abhor" here is "apostugeo" meaning "to detest utterly."

Sometimes people have misunderstood and misapplied God's kind of love so that they no longer hate evil. However, Proverbs 8:13 says, *"The fear of the LORD is to hate evil. . . ."* Those who love the Lord hate evil (Ps. 97:10). Only the wicked don't abhor evil (Ps. 36:4).

Jesus got angry (see notes 5-6 at Mk. 3:5, p. 104) and the scriptures say His hatred for sin was the reason God anointed Him with gladness above His fellows (Ps. 45:7; Heb. 1:9). It is impossible to truly love someone with God's kind of love without hating anything that comes against that person. There is a righteous type of anger which is not sin (Eph. 4:26).

3 (Rom. 12:10) The word that was translated "brotherly love" here in Romans 12:10 is "philadelphia" meaning "fraternal affection" and comes from the Greek word "phileo." The Greek word that was translated "kindly affectioned" in this verse is a compound of "phileo" and "storge" meaning "cherishing one's kindred."

There is much confusion on the subject of love today because we have only one English word (love) to describe a broad aspect of meanings. For example, if I said, "I love my wife, I love apple pie, and I love my dog," obviously I am not talking about love in the same degree or definition.

In the New Testament, there were three major Greek words that described the various kinds of love. One of these words, "eros," was not actually used in the New Testament, but it was alluded to. The following is a brief definition of these three major words.

EROS–sexual passion; arousal, its gratification and fulfillment. The Greek word is not used in the New Testament, probably because its origin came from the mythical god Eros, the god of love. It is inferred in many scriptures and is the only kind of love that God restricts to a one-man, one-woman relationship within the bounds of marriage (Heb. 13:4; Song 1:13; 4:5-6; 7:7-9; 8:10; 1 Cor. 7:25; Eph. 5:31).

PHILEO–friendly love based on feelings or emotions. We could describe "phileo" love as "tender affection, delighting to be in the presence of; a warm or good feeling towards someone that may come and go with intensity."

This verb with its other related Greek words are found around 72 times in the New Testament. Although "phileo" love is encouraged in the scripture, it is never a direct command. God never commands us to "phileo" love anyone, since this type of love is based on feelings. Even God did not "phileo" the world. He operated in "agape" love towards us.

The following are some scriptures in which "phileo" or a form of it is used (Jn. 5:20; 11:3, 36; 12:25; 16:27; 20:2; Acts 28:2; Rom. 12:10 [kindly affection]; 1 Tim. 6:10; 2 Tim. 3:4; Ti. 2:4; 3:4; Heb. 13:1; 3 Jn. 9; Rev. 3:19).

AGAPE–God's type of love; the highest kind of love. "Agape" is "seeking the welfare or betterment of others even if there is not affection felt" (a paraphrase of *Happiness Explained* by Bob Rigdon). "Agape" love does not have the primary meaning of affection, nor of coming from one's feelings.

Jesus displayed this "agape" kind of love by going to the cross and dying even though He didn't feel like dying. He prayed, *"O my Father, if it be possible, let this cup pass from me: nevertheless, not as I will, but as thou wilt"* (Mt. 26:39; Mk. 14:36; Lk. 22:41-43; Jn. 18:11). Jesus sought the betterment of you and me, regardless of His feelings.

We too can "agape" love our enemies, even though we don't have a warm feeling of affection for them (Lk. 6:35). If they are hungry we can feed them; if they thirst we can give them a drink (Rom. 12:20-21). We can choose to seek the betterment and welfare of others regardless of how we feel.

The Apostle John said, *". . . let us not love in word, neither in tongue; but in deed and in truth"* (1 Jn. 3:18). Jesus referred to His love for others (Jn. 13:34; 15:9,12), but He never directly told anyone, "I love you."

4 (Rom. 12:10) The dictionary defines "preferring" as "to choose as more desirable; like better." That means this verse is admonishing us to desire the welfare of others more than our own, to like others better than ourselves. That is an awesome command that is only obtainable through God's supernatural love.

If this very simple yet very profound truth could be understood and applied, then strife would cease (Prov. 13:10), the world would see Christianity as never before (see note 3 at Jn. 13:35, p. 425), and we would discover the true joy that comes from serving someone besides ourselves (Mt. 10:39; 16:25).

ROMANS

THE PRACTICAL LIVING OF CHRIST'S LIFE (continued)

CHAPTER 12

11 Not slothful[5k] in business;[l] fervent[m]
in spirit;[6] serving[7] the Lord;[n]
12 Rejoicing in hope;[o] patient[p] in
tribulation;[q] continuing instant[r] in prayer;
13 Distributing to the necessity of
saints;[s] given to hospitality.[t]
14 *Bless[u] them which persecute you:
bless,[u] and curse[8v] not.
15 Rejoice[9] with them that do rejoice,[w]
and weep with them that weep.[x]

PARALLEL SCRIPTURES FOR
ROMANS 12:14

MATTHEW 5:44

44 But I say unto you, Love your enemies, bless them that curse you, do good to them that hate you, and pray for them which despitefully use you, and persecute you;

1 CORINTHIANS 4:12

12 And labour, working with our own hands: being reviled, we bless; being persecuted, we suffer it:

References continued from column 4

u Gk.-"eulogeo"- to speak well of; i.e. to bless– Mt. 5:44 Lk. 6:28 Acts 7:60 1 Cor. 4:12-13 Jas. 4:11 1 Pet. 3:9

v Gk.-"kataraomai"- to curse; doom; imprecate evil on (Thayer) Lk. 1:58 15:5-10 1 Cor. 12:26 Phil. 2:17-18, 28

w Isa. 66:10-14

x Job 2:11 Ps. 35:13-14 Jer. 9:1 Jn. 11:19, 33-36

Footnotes for Romans 12:11-15

5 (Rom. 12:11) There are many scriptures against slothfulness or laziness (see ref. k, this verse). Paul even went so far as to say, *". . .this we commanded you, that if any would not work, neither should he eat"* (2 Th. 3:10).

It is interesting that Paul speaks about not being slothful right after he mentions brotherly love and preferring one another. This adds a very important balance to brotherly love which many today are missing. While it is true that we have a responsibility to help others, it is also true that a handout doesn't help a lazy person.

When we support those who are living in direct disobedience to God's instructions regarding slothfulness, we are hurting that person. Charity should be reserved for those who need it, not those who abuse it.

6 (Rom. 12:11) The Amplified translation of this verse indicates that the "spirit" that is being spoken of here is the Holy Spirit (*"Never lag in zeal* and *in earnest endeavor; be aglow* and *burning with the Spirit, serving the Lord"*). The New American Standard (*"not lagging behind in diligence, fervent in spirit, serving the Lord"*) and the New International Version (*"Never be lacking in zeal, but keep your spiritual fervor, serving the Lord"*) refer to "spirit" as our attitude.

The Greek word that was translated "spirit" is "pneuma." This word was used to distinguish the Holy Spirit many times (Examples: Mt. 3:16; 10:20; 12:28; Lk. 4:18; 11:13; Jn. 7:39; Acts 2:4) but it was also translated "spirit" when the context clearly indicates it is speaking of our attitude (Mt. 5:3; 1 Cor. 4:21; 2 Cor. 4:13; Eph. 1:17; 4:23; Phil. 1:27; 1 Tim. 4:12; Rev. 19:10).

"Pneuma" can mean "mental disposition." In this application "spirit" is speaking of our attitude. The American Heritage Dictionary defines spirit as "a prevailing mood or attitude."

7 (Rom. 12:11) This same point was made in Ephesians 6:6-7 where Paul said, *"Not with eyeservice, as menpleasers; but as the servants of Christ, doing the will of God from the heart; with good will doing service, as to the Lord, and not to men."* Paul is emphasizing that even in our business endeavors, we are serving the Lord and not man. He repeated this same thought in Colossians 3:23 when he said, *"And whatsoever ye do, do* it *heartily, as to the Lord, and not unto men."*

8 (Rom. 12:14) Many people think of a curse only in relation to witchcraft. However, it should go without saying that a Christian should not practice witchcraft against someone who has done them harm. That is not the type of curse that is being spoken of here.

The Greek word used for "curse" is "kataraomai" meaning "to execrate; by analogy to doom." The word "execrate" means "to protest vehemently against; denounce." W.E. Vine says "kataraomai" means "to pray against; to wish evil against a person or thing."

Therefore, our vicious talk about others is actually a curse. Without realizing it, many Christians curse others and thereby allow the devil access to the lives of those they are denouncing.

Proverbs 18:21 says, *"Death and life* are *in the power of the tongue: and they that love it shall eat the fruit thereof."* Every word we speak either releases life or death. Our negative talk releases death. When we speak against others, we are actually releasing Satan against them.

Once a person understands this it should make us pray this prayer with David, *"Set a watch, O LORD, before my mouth; keep the door of my lips"* (Ps. 141:3).

9 (Rom. 12:15) A self-centered person will not rejoice at someone else's prosperity. He will be jealous instead. Likewise, a selfish person will not weep with those that weep because he really doesn't care about anyone but himself. The Lord is continuing the thought about preferring one another (see note 4 at Rom. 12:10, p. 734).

k Dict.- aversion to work or exertion; lazy; indolent; sluggish- Prov. 6:6-9 10:26 13:4 18:9 22:29 24:30-34 26:13-16 Eccl. 9:10 Mt. 25:26 Acts 20:34-35 Eph. 4:28 1 Th. 4:11-12 2 Th. 3:6-12 1 Tim. 5:13 Heb. 6:10-12

l i.e. earnestness, diligence, or work

m Gk.-"zeo"- to boil with heat; be hot; fervent in spirit (said of zeal for what is good) (Thayer)- Acts 18:25 Col. 4:12-13 Jas. 5:16 1 Pet. 1:22 4:8

n Ex. 23:25 Dt. 10:12 Eph. 6:7 Col. 3:24 4:1 Heb. 12:28

o see note 5 at Rom. 5:2, p. 681 see note 7 at Rom. 4:18, p. 679 see note 12 at Rom. 5:4, p. 683 see note 12 at Rom. 8:24, p. 706 see note 13 at Rom. 8:25, p. 706 Rom. 5:2-3 15:13 Ps. 16:9-11 Lam. 3:24-26 Heb. 3:6 1 Pet. 1:3-8

p Gk.-"hupomeno"- to stay under (behind); i.e. remain; fig. to undergo; i.e. bear (trials); have fortitude; persevere see note 9 at Rom. 5:3, p. 682 see note 3 at Lk. 21:19, p. 397 Rom. 5:3-4 8:25 Col. 1:11 2 Th. 1:4 Heb. 6:12,15 10:36 Jas. 1:3-4 5:10-11 1 Pet. 2:19-20

q Gk.-"thlipsis"- pressure (lit. or fig.) Trans. afflicted (-tion); anguish; burdened; persecution; tribulation; trouble see note 7 at Mt. 5:10, p. 73 see note 3 at Acts 5:41, p. 532 see note 4 at Acts 9:4, p. 552 see note 2 at Acts 4:26, p. 526 see note 3 at Acts 20:19, p. 618 see note 1 at Acts 14:3, p. 581

r Gk.-"proskartereo"- to be earnest towards; i.e. to persevere; be constantly diligent, or to attend assiduously all the exercises, or to adhere closely to- Ps. 55:16-17 109:4 Jer. 29:12-13 Lk. 11:5-13 18:1 Acts 1:14 2:42 6:4 12:5 Eph. 6:18 Phil. 4:6-7 Col. 4:2, 12 1 Th. 5:17 Jas. 5:15-16 1 Pet. 4:7

s Rom. 15:25-28 Ps. 41:1 Acts 4:35 9:36-41 10:4 20:34-35 1 Cor. 16:1-2 2 Cor. 8:1-4 9:1, 12 Gal. 6:10 Heb. 6:10 13:16 1 Jn. 3:17

t Gen. 18:2-8 19:1-3 1 Tim. 3:2 5:10 Ti. 1:8 Heb. 13:2 1 Pet. 4:9

continued on center column

ROMANS

THE PRACTICAL LIVING OF CHRIST'S LIFE (continued)

CHAPTER 12

16 *Be of the same mind one toward
another.[a] Mind not high things, but
condescend[b] to men of low[10] estate.[c] Be not
wise in your own conceits.[d]
17 Recompense[e] to no man evil for
evil.[11] Provide things honest[f] in the sight[12]
of all men.
18 If it be possible,[13] as much as lieth in
you, live peaceably[g] with all men.

PARALLEL SCRIPTURES FOR ROMANS 12:16

1 PETER 3:8

8 *Finally,* be ye *all of one mind, having compassion one of another, love as brethren,* be *pitiful,* be *courteous:*

1 CORINTHIANS 1:10

10 Now I beseech you, brethren, by the name of our Lord Jesus Christ, that ye all speak the same thing, and that *there be no divisions among you; but* that *ye be perfectly joined together in the same mind and in the same judgment.*

a Be of one mind amongst yourselves (Con) Live in harmony with one another (Gspd)- Rom. 15:5-6 2 Chr. 30:12 Jer. 32:39 Acts 4:32 1 Cor. 1:10 Phil. 1:27 2:2-3 3:16 4:2 1 Pet. 3:8

b Dict.- to agree to do something one regards as beneath one's rank or dignity

c Do not be haughty, but associate with the lowly (RSV) Don't become snobbish, but take a real interest in ordinary people (Phi) Avoid being haughty; mingle with the lowly (Nor)- Lk. 6:20 14:13 Phil. 4:11-13 Jas. 2:5-6

d too high an opinion of oneself Do not be wise in your own estimation (NASB) Do not think too highly of yourselves (TCNT)

e Dict.- to award compensation to; to reward; pay; make a return for- Lev. 19:18 Prov. 20:22 24:29 Mt. 5:39 1 Th. 5:15 1 Pet. 3:9

f Dict.- not characterized by deception or fraud- Lev. 19:35-36 Dt. 16:20 25:13-16 Prov. 11:1 12:22 Acts 24:16 2 Cor. 8:21 Phil. 4:8 1 Th. 4:11-12 Heb. 13:18

g see notes 37-39 at Jn. 14:27, p. 434 see notes 90-91 at Jn. 16:33, p. 442 see note 2 at Lk. 24:38, p. 496 see note 2 at Rom. 5:1, p. 681

Footnotes for Roman 12:16-18

10 (Rom. 12:16) This is not saying that Christians should never occupy a prominent position. If that were true, then Paul would not need to admonish these people to be willing to associate with those of low estate. They wouldn't have any other choice.

Many Bible people were people of renown, even among the nonbelievers (Examples: Abraham, Isaac, Joseph, David, Solomon, Paul—Acts 28:7, John—Jn. 18:15). Paul is just saying that we shouldn't seek out prestigious people and snub those who the world doesn't consider important. God doesn't evaluate people the way that the world does. Those who are greatest in His kingdom are the greatest servants.

We will miss some of the most beautiful people who could bless our lives if we judge people by the world's standards. We also run the risk of destroying our faith when we seek the honor that comes from man (see note 22 at Jn. 5:44, p. 100).

11 (Rom. 12:17) There is an unwritten but widely understood code in human relations that says we should treat people the way they treat us. Jesus taught just the opposite (see note 1 at Lk. 23:34, p. 475) and Paul is reaffirming that same teaching. If we are to be Christ-like, then we cannot give people what they deserve.

12 (Rom. 12:17) It is not enough to just be honest in the sight of God. This scripture commands us to also have integrity in the sight of man. This corresponds to *"abstain from all appearance of evil"* (1 Th. 5:22). We not only need to be right, but we need to appear right as much as possible.

13 (Rom. 12:18) This verse is advocating living peaceably with all men. Yet, the very wording reveals that this is not always possible. We are not responsible for other people's actions. We must pursue peace, even when we are not at fault, but the other person does have a choice. Be sure that you are at peace with all men. Whether or not they are at peace with you is their decision.

ROMANS

THE PRACTICAL LIVING OF CHRIST'S LIFE (continued)

h Rom. 12:17 Lev. 19:18 1 Sam. 25:33 Prov. 24:17-19, & 29
i Leave a place for divine retribution (NEB) i.e. let God take care of the situation (*Word Meanings in N.T.*)
j Ps. 94:1 Heb. 10:30

CHAPTER 12

19 *Dearly beloved, avenge[14] not yourselves,[h] but *rather* give place unto wrath:[i] for it is written,[j] Vengeance[k] *is* mine; I will repay, saith the Lord.[l]
20 *Therefore if thine enemy hunger, feed him; if he thirst, give him drink:[m] for in so doing thou shalt heap coals of fire on his head.[15]
21 Be not overcome[n] of evil, but overcome[n] evil with good.[16]

k Dict.- the act or motive of punishing another in payment for a wrong or injury he has committed; retribution- Nah. 1:2
l see note 3 at Lk. 1:43, p. 12
m Ex. 23:4-5 1 Sam. 24:16-19 Prov. 25:21-22 Mt. 5:44
n Gk.-"nikao"- to subdue (lit. or fig.) Trans. conquer; overcome; prevail; get the victory

PARALLEL SCRIPTURE FOR ROMANS 12:19

DEUTERONOMY 32:35

35 To me belongeth *vengeance, and recompence; their foot shall slide in* due *time: for the day of their calamity* is *at hand, and the things that shall come upon them make haste.*

PARALLEL SCRIPTURES FOR ROMANS 12:20

PROVERBS 25:21-22

21 If thine enemy be hungry, give him bread to eat; and if he be thirsty, give him water to drink:
22 For thou shalt heap coals of fire upon his head, and the LORD shall reward thee.

Footnotes for Romans 12:19-21

14 (Rom. 12:19) Verses 19-21 are humanly impossible. It takes the supernatural power of God's faith at work in the heart to fulfill these scriptures. Letting God be the one who defends us is a matter of faith. If there is no God who will bring men into account for their actions, then turning the other cheek would be the worst thing we could do (see note 22 at Mt. 5:44, p. 77). But if there is a God who promised that vengeance is His, and He will repay, then taking matters into our own hands shows a lack of faith in God and His integrity.

15 (Rom. 12:20) These coals of fire are not coals of punishment or torment, but rather conviction. If this was urging us to be kind to our enemies because that would hurt them more than anything else, then that would be violating the context of this verse. Paul is telling us to live peaceably with all men (v. 18) and to render to no man evil for evil (v. 17). God's kind of love is being promoted, not some scriptural way to hurt those who hurt you.

When we walk in love towards those who hurt us, it heaps conviction on them. They know what their reaction would be if they were in our place, and to see us walk in love under adverse circumstances shows them that we have something special that they don't have.

Paul should know. He saw Stephen forgive and pray for the very people who stoned him to death. When Jesus appeared to him on the road to Damascus, He told Paul that it was hard to kick against the pricks. The Lord was saying it was hard for Saul to resist the conviction that had come to him through Stephen's witness (see note 6 at Acts 9:5, p. 553).

16 (Rom. 12:21) We cannot fight evil with evil. Evil has to be overcome with good. It is frustrating to see the schemes of Satan and his kingdom. However, we must never let our frustration drive us to using their tactics. The wrath of man does not accomplish the righteousness of God (Jas. 1:20). Instead of cursing the darkness, turn on a light.

ROMANS

SUBMISSION TO GOVERNING AUTHORITY

CHAPTER 13

LET every soul be subject[1] unto the higher
powers.[a] For there is no power but of God:
the powers that be are ordained[2] of God.[b]

a rulers or governing authorities-Dt. 17:12 Ti. 3:1 1 Pet. 2:13-17 2 Pet. 2:10-11 Jude 8

b 1 Chr 28:4-5 Ps. 62:11 75:6-7 Prov. 8:15-16 21:1 Jer. 27:5-8 Dan. 2:21 4:32 5:18-23 Jn. 19:11

Footnotes for Romans 13:1

1 (Rom. 13:1) The subject of submission to authority is a very basic Bible doctrine. Some of the major areas of submission commanded in the scriptures are: (1) submission to God (Eph. 5:24; Jas. 4:7); (2) submission to civil or governmental authority (Rom. 13:1-7); (3) submission to the church or religious authority (Heb. 13:17); (4) wives are to submit to husbands (Eph. 5:22-24; Col. 3:18); (5) children are to submit to their parents (Eph. 6:1; Col. 3:20); (6) slaves are to submit to masters—today's equivalent would be employees submit to employers (1 Pet. 2:18); (7) the younger are to submit to the older (1 Pet. 5:5); and (8) we are all supposed to submit to each other in love (Eph. 5:21; 1 Pet. 5:5).

The Greek word translated "subject" here, as well as 14 other times in the New Testament is "hupotasso." This was a military term meaning "to rank under." Although in most cases, obedience is a part of submission, these terms are not synonymous. Just as an enlisted man in the army has limits to his obedience to an officer, so we only obey men as long as their commands do not oppose God.

A failure to understand the difference between submission and obedience has given birth to many false teachings that have caused some people to obey others in matters of sin. That is never commanded in the word of God.

One of the easiest ways to see that a person can submit without obeying an ungodly command is to look at the life of Peter. Peter made some striking statements in 1 Peter 2:13-14 when he said, *"Submit yourselves to **every** ordinance of man for the Lord's sake: whether it be to the king, as supreme; Or unto governors, as unto them that are sent by him for the punishment of evildoers, and for the praise of them that do well."*

This is the same Peter who refused to obey the chief priests when they commanded him to not speak or teach anymore in the name of Jesus (Acts 4:18-19). When Peter and the other apostles continued their teaching and preaching about Jesus, the high priest and the elders of the Jews imprisoned them. However, they were supernaturally freed from prison by an angel of the Lord who told them to go back to the temple and preach again (Acts 5:17-20). This command was a direct contradiction to the commands of the Jews.

The Jews again arrested Peter and the other apostles and said, *"Did not we straitly command you that ye should not teach in this name?"* (Acts 5:28). Peter responded by saying, "*We ought to obey God rather than men*" (Acts 5:29). This is always the bottom line. We never obey any man if that would cause us to disobey God.

Yet, we are to submit to every ordinance of man (1 Pet. 2:13). Submission is an attitude, not an action. It will express itself through actions, but a person can have a submissive attitude and yet disobey an ungodly command.

If a government official commanded us to not preach Jesus, we should follow the example of Peter and not obey him. But we should also not rebel at his authority, in the same way that Peter and the other apostles did not rebel at the authority of the Jews.

When the apostles were beaten for their obedience to God, they didn't criticize or form a revolt. They praised God and kept right on preaching the gospel (Acts 5:41-42). They didn't obey ungodly commands but they didn't become ungodly either by cursing those who had hurt them (see note 8 at Rom. 12:14, p. 735). They submitted to the authority over them to the point that they took a beating without one complaint, but they never did do what the Jews commanded them.

If a man commanded his wife not to go to church anymore, she should not obey that command. The Bible clearly says not to forsake the assembling of ourselves together (Heb. 10:25). However, there is a submissive way and a rebellious way of doing that.

If she said, "You old reprobate. You never have liked me going to church. Well, I'm going to show you that you can't tell me what to do. I'm going anyway and I don't care what you say," that would be a rebellious attitude.

Yet, a woman in the same circumstance could affirm her love to her husband and state that she really wants to comply as much as possible. But in this instance, she has to obey God over her husband. If that was her attitude, she would be in submission to her husband even though she didn't do what he said.

Submission is also a voluntary thing. You cannot make another person submit. You can make people obey you, but that doesn't mean they've submitted. Their attitude is totally a matter of choice on their part. This is the reason that a man cannot hear a teaching on submission and go home and make his wife submit. She has to choose to submit.

The book of Daniel has two examples of civil disobedience done through a commitment to God's higher laws (Dan. 3:8-18; 6:10-17). And yet, this disobedience was accomplished with respect and submission to the civil authority. Moses' parents did not obey Pharaoh's command to kill their son and God blessed them for their actions.

Submission is an essential part of true Christianity. However, it is a missing ingredient in most Christians' lives. The root of all lack of submission in our lives lies in pride (1 Pet. 5:4-6).

2 (Rom. 13:1) This sentence has perplexed many people. Is Paul saying that God wills that there be oppressive governments like the Nazis or even the Roman government that Paul was under? Definitely not. Even though He has used corrupt rulers and governments to punish offenses, their governmental authority was not created by God to be oppressive. They were ordained to be ministers of God to us for good (v. 4).

In the same way that God ordains people to the ministry, and yet they fail to fulfill that call as God intended, likewise, God ordains governments, but doesn't ordain everything that they do. There are countless scriptural examples of rebukes and punishments by God upon civil leaders because they did not submit to His will.

God's original government over man was directly administered by God Himself. Man answered only to his Creator. Even after the fall of man, God worked in cooperation with the conscience of man to refrain him from evil. In the beginning, this was effective, as can be seen through Cain's statement, *"My punishment* is *greater than I can bear"* (Gen. 4:13).

However, man seared his conscience (1 Tim. 4:2) through repeated sin. Therefore, since man was no longer responsive to his Creator, God ordained man to begin to police themselves. He told Noah, *"Whoso sheddeth man's blood, by man shall his blood be shed: for in the image of God made he man"* (Gen. 9:6). This responsibility of corporate man to avenge the wrongs of individual men continued to develop until, through the giving of the Old Testament law, God gave detailed instructions on how mankind was to treat each other and prescribed punishments for failure to do so.

Footnote 2 for Romans 13:1 continued on p. 739

ROMANS

SUBMISSION TO GOVERNING AUTHORITY (continued)

CHAPTER 13

2 Whosoever therefore resisteth the
power,[3] resisteth the ordinance of God:[c]
and they that resist shall receive to
themselves damnation.[4]
3 For rulers are not a terror[5] to good
works, but to the evil.[d] Wilt thou then not
be afraid of the power? do that which is
good, and thou shalt have praise of the
same:[e]
4 For he is the minister[6f] of God to thee
for good. But if thou do that which is evil,
be afraid; for he beareth not the sword[g] in
vain:[7] for he is the minister of God, a
revenger[h] to *execute* wrath[i] upon him that
doeth evil.

c Hence anyone who resists authority is opposing the divine order (Mof)- 1 Pet. 2:13

d for civil authorities are not a terror to [people of] good conduct, but to [those of] bad behavior (Amp)- Rom. 13:4 Dt. 25:1 Prov. 14:35 20:2 Jer. 22:15-18

e Do you want to have no dread of the civil authorities then practice doing right, and you will be commended for it (Wms)- 1 Pet. 2:13-14 3:13-14

f Gk.-"diakonos"- one who executes the commands of another, esp. of a master; a servant, attendant, minister; a deacon; a waiter (Thayer)- Rom. 13:6 2 Chr. 19:6 Ps. 82:2-4 Prov. 31:8-9 Isa. 1:17

g Gk.-"machaira"- a knife; i.e. dirk; fig. war, judicial punishment

h Gk.-"ekdikos"- carrying justice out; i.e. a punisher- Rom. 12:19 Ezek. 25:14

i Nah. 1:2 Rom. 1:18 2:5 4:15 Eph. 5:6 Col. 3:6

Footnote 2 for Romans 13:1 cont'd from p. 738; Footnotes for Romans 13:2-4

So, in that context, God did ordain all government. But in more cases than not, governments are not any more responsive to Him than are individuals. However, we are to submit to them and obey them as long as we don't have to violate a clear command of God. **Even bad government is superior to anarchy.**

The governor himself may not be of God, but civil government is definitely of God.

3 (Rom. 13:2) Notice specifically Paul's choice of words here. *"Whosoever therefore **resisteth** the **power**. . . ."* The word "resist" implies "to actively fight against." As discussed in note 1 at Romans 13:1, page 738, you can refuse to comply with ungodly edicts without resisting the government that issued them. And the word "power" is referring directly to the authority of the government itself, not just its directives.

Therefore, Paul is instructing us to not fight against the authority of the government we live under. That doesn't mean we have to comply with any law that is in direct opposition to God's laws. But, when we oppose the order of government, we are opposing God's order.

The early Christians were great examples of this. They lived under one of the most corrupt and ruthless governments of all time. The Roman emperors even proclaimed themselves as gods. Yet, nowhere in scripture was there any instruction given to the believers to subvert that government and replace it. On the contrary, Paul commanded the believers to pray for their governmental leaders (1 Tim. 2:1-4). Peter commanded the believers to submit to every ordinance of the king and his governors (1 Pet. 2:13-14).

The early Christians never brought any political pressure to bear on the Roman government or encouraged revolt. Yet in a relatively short period of time, Christianity overwhelmed the pagan Roman government and was adopted as the official state religion. Although this was one of the worst things that ever happened to Christianity, it does illustrate how we can overcome evil with good (Rom. 12:21).

4 (Rom. 13:2) The word that was translated "damnation" here is the Greek word "krima." This same word was translated "judgment" 13 times; "damnation" 7 times; "condemnation" 5 times; "be condemned" once; "go to law" once; and "avenge" once. It means "judgment; i.e. condemnation of wrong; the decision (whether severe or mild) which one passes on the faults of others: in a forensic sense, the sentence of a judge."

In this case, this is not speaking of the eternal damnation or judgment of God. This is saying that if a person resists the power of government, he will come under the judgment of that government.

5 (Rom. 13:3) There are certainly scriptural exceptions to this statement. The Egyptian government turned on the Israelites (Ex. 1:8-22), not because of any sin on their part but because of the insecurities and fears of the Pharaoh. James the apostle was killed by Herod just because it pleased the Jews (Acts 12:2). John the Baptist was imprisoned and beheaded by Herod, and Jesus Himself commented on the innocence of John (Mt. 11:9-11).

However, there is a truth that, as a whole, even corrupt governments do not bother those who are doing good. Paul was an example of this. Many times the Roman government actually came to his defense (Examples: Acts 18:12-16; 19:35-41; 21:31-36; 23:23-24; 25:1-5; 27:42-44). In the book of Daniel, Daniel and his three friends were repeatedly honored even though the governmental system was corrupt and unjust. Joseph prospered in Egypt despite the injustices some people did to him.

With few exceptions, governments are established to protect the good and punish the evil. If we do good, we have nothing to fear.

6 (Rom. 13:4) This is the same Greek word that was translated "deacon, servant, minister" (see ref. f, this verse). Government officials, including police and army, were ordained by God to minister to us. The Lord uses this civil authority to protect us and execute His wrath on the ungodly. Knowing this gives us added assurance when we pray for justice to be done through the judicial system (1 Jn. 5:14-15).

When an individual fails to respond to the conviction of the Holy Spirit, we can pray that the Lord will use the legal system to stop his evil ways. Those in the legal system are ministers of God. Many thousands of prisoners have praised God for the prison term that finally stopped them and made them come to grips with the real problems of their lives.

7 (Rom. 13:4) The sword that is being spoken of here is symbolic of power to restrain or kill. That is what swords were used for. God has delegated some of His power to rule to governments, even to the extent of taking life.

The Lord told Noah that any man who murdered another man had to die at the hand of mankind (Gen. 9:5-6; see note 2 at v. 1, p. 738). Likewise, this verse shows that God has given government the right to use force and execute His wrath, which would include capital punishment. Even some wars can be justified on the basis of this scripture (see note 6 at Jn. 18:36, p. 462).

Therefore, Christians can serve as police officers or soldiers as long as they are enforcing what is right.

ROMANS

SUBMISSION TO GOVERNING AUTHORITY (continued)

a see note 9 at Rom. 2:15, p. 665
see note 1 at Acts 23:1, p. 628
1 Sam. 24:5-6
Acts 24:16
Rom. 14:23
1 Cor. 10:29
Heb. 13:18
1 Pet. 2:19
3:16
b Gk.-"phoros"- a load (as borne); i.e. a tax-
Ezra 4:13, 20
6:8
Neh. 5:4
Mt. 17:24-27
22:17-21

CHAPTER 13

5 Wherefore *ye* must needs be subject,
not only for wrath, but also for conscience[a]
sake.[8]
6 For for this cause[9] pay ye tribute[b] also:
for they are God's ministers, attending
continually upon this very thing.[c]
7 Render therefore to all their dues:[d]
tribute to whom tribute *is due*; custom to
whom custom; fear to whom fear; honour
to whom honour.[e]

c The authorities are God's servants, and it is their duty to take care of these matters (Contemporary English Version [CEV])
d pay them all what is due them (Gspd)
e whether it is taxes and fees or respect and honor (CEV)

Footnotes for Romans 13:5-7

8 (Rom. 13:5) In the first four verses of this chapter, Paul had given two reasons for being subject to civil government, which he now summarizes. First, we need to be subject to them because the government has the power to punish us if we aren't. Secondly, since God has ordained government, we have to submit or have our conscience condemn us for violating the instruction of God.

Therefore, even if we could break the laws of government and get away with it, we shouldn't because we are also violating God's Word. So, laws that are not in direct opposition to God's Word should be kept, whether or not we will get caught, or whether or not we think they are important.

In the next verse, Paul specifically mentions taxes as one of those laws that we should comply with (see note 9 at v. 6, below). This could be updated to include speed limits, local ordinances, and a host of other things that many of us may disagree with, but we cannot say they are directly against God's Word. The government has a God-given right and responsibility to regulate and establish order and we should comply for consciences' sake. Our submission to government and our submission to God are intertwined.

9 (Rom. 13:6) Paul had commanded being subject to the laws of the government we live under as long as they don't cause us to sin against God (see note 1 at v. 1, p. 738). In verse 5, Paul said we not only need to do this because of the power of government to punish us, but even if we never got caught, we need to submit because of our submission to God (see note 8 at v. 5, above). Then he mentions taxes.

Many Christians feel that taxes and serving God are two different things. But the Lord commanded us to pay our taxes. We cannot be a true servant of God and refuse to obey Him in this area. Jesus as the Creator was not obligated to pay taxes to His creation, but He did (see note 1 at Mt. 17:25, p. 215). He paid taxes to a corrupt system where much of the tax money went straight into the pocket of the tax collector.

In the United States of America, we are given certain tax deductions for charitable gifts and other exemptions. There is nothing wrong with taking advantage of these, or even using the political process to try and change taxation laws that we feel are wrong. Our government guarantees us those rights. But no Christian has any scriptural ground for refusing to pay taxes. Whether or not we can get away with it is immaterial. God commands us to submit, even in the area of taxes. Failure to do so is rebellion against God.

LOVE—THE FULFILLING OF THE LAW

a Rom. 13:7
Dt. 24:14-15
Prov. 3:27-28
Mt. 7:12
22:39-40
b see note 3 at Jn. 13:35, p. 425
see note 4 at Jn. 13:35, p. 424
see note 4 at Lk. 11:11, p. 256
see note 54 at Jn. 15:9, p. 436
see note 55 at Jn. 15:9, p. 436
see note 56 at Jn. 15:10, p. 436
see note 111 at Jn. 17:23, p. 446
see note 1 at Lk. 23:34, p. 475
continued on column 4

CHAPTER 13

8 *Owe[1] no man any thing, but to love[2]
one another:[a] for he that loveth[b] another
hath fulfilled[3c] the law.

continued from column 1
see note 10 at Jn. 21:15, p. 500
see note 8 at Rom. 1:7, p. 656
see note 14 at Rom. 5:7, p. 683
see note 16 at Rom. 5:9, p. 684
see note 3 at Rom. 12:10, p. 734
c Dict.- to measure up to; satisfy
Syn.- perform
see note 59 at Jn. 15:12, p. 436
see note 2 at Jn. 13:34, p. 425
Rom. 13:10

Footnotes for Romans 13:8

1 (Rom.13:8) In context, Paul is speaking about paying our taxes, respect, and honor (v. 7). However, this principle holds true in every area of our lives. We are to pay our bills.

Some people have interpreted this verse as forbidding a Christian to go in debt. It can be shown in scripture that purchasing on credit is not a blessing but a curse (Dt. 28:12, 44); therefore, it is not God's best. However, it is not a sin to borrow money. Many scriptures speak of lending money and place restrictions on who we should lend to. The Lord would not have us help someone sin.

Therefore, being in debt is not a sin. But failure to pay our bills or payments on loans that we have given our word on, is wrong.

2 (Rom. 13:8) Notice that Paul speaks of love for our fellow man as a debt. This is not optional. We are commanded to love one another. Indeed, this is the royal law of God (Jas. 2:8).

3 (Rom. 13:8) Mankind as a whole had misunderstood the purpose of the law. They thought that God was giving us a list of what we must do to be accepted by Him. But the law was given to convince man that he didn't have a chance of saving himself; he needed a savior (see note 4 at Rom. 3:19, p. 671).

However, the law was accurate, and a perfect description of what God created man to be. The law portrayed what a person who was walking in God's kind of love would do. We still can't keep the law perfectly in our flesh (see note 9 at Rom. 8:4, p. 701) but the New Testament believer can now fulfill the spirit of the Old Testament law as an Old Testament man never could.

ROMANS

LOVE—THE FULFILLING OF THE LAW (continued)

d Dt. 5:16-21
Mt. 19:18-19
Mk. 10:19
Lk. 18:20
e see note 6 at Mt. 19:9, p. 324
Lev. 18:20
Prov. 2:16-19
5:3-4
6:24-29, 32-33
7:5-23
9:13-18
22:14
23:27
Mt. 5:28, 32
15:19
Acts 15:20
Rom. 7:3
1 Cor. 6:15-16,18
Gal. 5:19
f i.e. murder
see note 3 at Mt. 19:18, p. 329
Gen. 4:9-12
9:5-6
Ex. 20:13
Num. 35:16-22, & 30-31
Dt. 5:17
Prov. 6:16-17
28:17
Mt. 5:21-22
15:19
Gal. 5:19-21
1 Tim. 1:9
1 Jn. 3:15
Rev. 21:8
22:15
g Ex. 20:15
21:16
22:1-4
Lev. 19:11
Dt. 5:19
Prov. 6:30
21:7
Zech. 5:3
Mt. 15:19
Mk. 11:17
15:27

CHAPTER 13

9 *For this,[d] Thou shalt not commit
adultery,[e] Thou shalt not kill,[f] Thou shalt
not steal,[g] Thou shalt not bear false witness,[h]
Thou shalt not covet;[i] and if *there be* any
other commandment, it is briefly
comprehended[j] in this saying, namely, Thou
shalt love thy neighbour as thyself.[k]
10 *Love worketh no ill to his neighbour:[l]
therefore love[b] *is* the fulfilling[4] of the law.[c]

h Gk.-"pseudomartureo"- to be an untrue testifier; i.e. offer falsehood in evidence-
Ex. 20:16
23:1
Prov. 24:28
25:18
i i.e. desire or want what belongs to others-
Ex. 20:17
Ps. 10:3
119:36
Prov. 15:27
Isa. 57:17
Jer. 8:10
Ezek. 33:31
Mt. 6:19-21
Mk. 7:21-23
Lk. 12:15
Rom. 1:29
1 Cor. 5:11
Eph. 5:3
Col. 3:5
1 Tim. 3:3
6:10
2 Tim. 3:2
Heb. 13:5
1 Jn. 2:15-16
j Gk.-"anakephalaiomai"- to sum up
k Lev. 19:34
Mt. 22:39
Mk. 12:31
Lk. 10:27
Jas. 2:8-9
l i.e. love never harms or wrongs others

PARALLEL SCRIPTURES FOR ROMANS 13:8-10

GALATIANS 5:14

14 For all the law is fulfilled in one word, even *in this; Thou shalt love thy neighbour as thyself.*

1 TIMOTHY 1:5

5 Now the end of the commandment is charity out of a pure heart, and of *a good conscience, and* of *faith unfeigned:*

JAMES 2:8

8 If ye fulfil the royal law according to the scripture, Thou shalt love thy neighbour as thyself, ye do well:

PARALLEL SCRIPTURES FOR ROMANS 13:9

EXODUS 20:13-17

13 Thou shalt not kill.
14 Thou shalt not commit adultery.
15 Thou shalt not steal.
16 Thou shalt not bear false witness against thy neighbour.
17 Thou shalt not covet thy neighbour's house, thou shalt not covet thy neighbour's wife, nor his manservant, nor his maidservant, nor his ox, nor his ass, nor any thing that is *thy neighbour's.*

LEVITICUS 19:18

18 Thou shalt not avenge, nor bear any grudge against the children of thy people, but thou shalt love thy neighbour as thyself: I am *the LORD.*

Footnote for Romans 13:10
4 (Rom. 13:10) Instead of focusing on all the do's and don'ts, all we have to do is let God's kind of love rule in our hearts and we will automatically meet the requirements of the law.

ROMANS

CAST OFF THE WORKS OF DARKNESS AND PUT ON CHRIST

CHAPTER 13

11 *And that, knowing the time,[a] that
now *it is* high time[1] to awake out of sleep:[b]
for now *is* our salvation[c] nearer than when
we believed.[d]
12 *The night is far spent, the day is at
hand: let us therefore cast off[e] the works of
darkness,[f] and let us put on the armour of
light.[g]
13 *Let us walk honestly, as in the day;[h]
not in rioting[i] and drunkenness, not in
chambering[j] and wantonness,[2k] not in strife[l]
and envying.[m]
14 *But put ye on the Lord Jesus Christ,[n]
and make not provision[o] for the flesh,[3] to
fulfil the lusts *thereof.*[p]

PARALLEL SCRIPTURE FOR
ROMANS 13:11-14

LUKE 21:34

34 And take heed to yourselves, lest at any time your hearts be overcharged with surfeiting, and drunkenness, and cares of this life, and so that day come upon you unawares.

a Mt. 16:3 Lk. 21:8 1 Cor. 7:29 1 Th. 5:1-3 1 Pet. 4:7
b Gk.-"hupnos"- sleep; i.e. spiritual torpor- Mt. 25:5-7 26:40-41 Mk. 13:35-37 1 Cor. 15:34 Eph. 5:14
c Gk.-"soteria"- rescue or safety see note 7 at Acts 2:21, p. 515
d wake up, for the coming of the Lord is nearer now than when we first believed (LB)- Lk. 21:28 1 Pet. 4:7 2 Pet. 3:13-15 Rev. 22:12, 20 see note 28 at Mk. 13:32, p. 401 see note 15 at Mt. 24:38, p. 403 see note 16 at Mt. 24:40, p. 403 see note 17 at Mt. 24:43, p. 403 see note 18 at Mt. 24:44, p. 403 see note 20 at Mt. 25:1, p. 405 see note 21 at Mt. 25:14, p. 405

e Gk.-"apotithemi"- to put away; fling away (Amp)- Ezek. 18:31-32 Eph. 4:22 Col. 3:8-9 Jas. 1:21 1 Pet. 2:1
f Jn. 3:19-21 Eph. 5:11 1 Th. 5:5-8 1 Jn. 1:5-7 2:8-9 see note 11 at Jn. 8:34, p. 232 see note 8 at Rom. 6:16, p. 692 see note 3 at Rom. 6:23, p. 693
g Rom. 13:14 2 Cor. 6:7 Eph. 6:11-18 Col. 3:10-17 1 Th. 5:8
h so behave properly, as people do in the day (CEV)- Acts 2:15 1 Th. 5:7

continued on center column

References continued from column 4

i Gk.-"komos"- a revel; carousal; used generally of feasts and drinking parties that are protracted till late at night and indulge in revelry (Thayer)- Prov. 23:20 Isa. 22:12-13 28:7-8 Lk. 17:27-28 1 Cor. 6:10 Gal. 5:21 Eph. 5:18 1 Pet. 2:11 4:3-5
j Gk.-"koite"- a bed; esp. the marriage bed; denotes, in Rom. 13:13, illicit intercourse (W.E. Vine)- 1 Cor. 6:9 Gal. 5:19 Eph. 5:3-5 Col. 3:5 1 Th. 4:3-5
k 2 Pet. 2:18-20
l Gk.-"eris"- contention; strife; wrangling (Thayer) see note 2 at Acts 4:17, p. 524 Prov. 3:30 6:16-19 10:12 13:10 15:18 16:28 17:1, 14, 19 20:3 22:10 26:17, 20-21 28:25 29:22 30:33 1 Cor. 3:3 Gal. 5:19-20 Jas. 3:16
m Gk.-"zelos"- an envious and contentious rivalry; jealousy (Thayer)- Prov. 14:30 23:17 24:1 27:4 Song 8:6 Jas. 3:16
n Let the Lord Jesus Christ be as near to you as the clothes you wear (CEV) But clothe yourselves with the Lord Jesus Christ (Con)- Gal 3:27 Eph. 4:24 Col. 3:10-12
o Gk.-"pronoia"- forethought; i.e. provident care or supply
p Rom. 8:12-13 Gal. 5:16-17, 24 Col. 3:5-8 1 Pet. 2:11 1 Jn. 2:15-17

Footnotes for Romans 13:11-14

1 (Rom. 13:11) Paul had commanded submission to government and had used two reasons for compliance (see note 8 at Rom. 13:5, p. 740). The most important reason was not just to avoid being caught and punished by government, but to have a good conscience towards God. He is continuing that thought in this verse.

He is saying that the time left before the Lord's return is growing short and we must therefore be even more sensitive to God. This is the same reasoning that the Lord Jesus used in the parables of the ten virgins and of the stewards and their talents (Mt. 25).

The message of these four verses (vv. 11-14) can be summed up in the words of Jesus from Luke 21:34 (see Parallel Scripture for these verses, above). The issue of the Lord's imminent return adds even more importance to us walking in love.

2 (Rom. 13:13) The dictionary defines "wanton" as "(1) immoral or unchaste; lewd; (2) maliciously cruel; merciless; (3) sensual; (4) extravagant; excessive; and (5) unrestrained; frolicsome."

3 (Rom. 13:14) Paul is using the term "flesh" here as referring to the part of man that has not been changed by Christ, i.e. our sinful appetites and desires (see note 3 at Rom. 7:18, p. 698). These sinful lusts cannot dominate us if we don't make provision for them. Paul is saying to cut off the flesh's rations and starve it to death.

Many Christians have mistakenly believed that during our life here on the earth, we are doomed to have ungodly lusts and desires. But it doesn't have to be that way. The sin nature that enslaved our flesh is gone, and to the degree that we renew our minds through God's Word, we can experience victory over the flesh (see note 9 at Rom. 5:21, p. 687). The reason the flesh seems so strong in many people's lives is because they are continually feeding it.

Temptation is linked to what we think on. If we don't think on things that engender temptation, then we won't be tempted and we won't sin (see note 9 at Rom. 4:19, p. 680).

ROMANS

CHRISTIAN LIBERTY AND QUESTIONABLE THINGS

a Gk.-"astheneo"- to be feeble (in any sense) Trans. be diseased; impotent folk; sick; weak- Rom. 14:21 4:19 15:1 1 Cor 8:7-13 9:22
b Dict.- to greet or welcome- Rom. 15:7 Mt. 10:40-42 18:5 Jn. 13:20 Phil. 2:29 3 Jn. 8-10

CHAPTER 14

HIM[1] that is weak[2a] in the faith receive[b] ye, *but* not to doubtful[c] disputations.[3d]

c Dict.- subject to or tending to cause doubt; uncertain; unclear; of uncertain outcome; undecided
d Dict.- the act of disputing; a debate- Rom. 14:2-5 1:29 2 Cor. 12:20 Ti. 3:9

Footnotes for Romans 14:1

1 (Rom. 14:1) Paul wrote this epistle to the saints in Rome. There was a big argument between the Jewish Christians and the Gentile Christians over the issue of grace and works. Paul spent the majority of this letter dealing with the mistaken teaching that Gentiles who became Christians had to keep the Old Testament laws in order to be saved.

The main Old Testament requirement Paul had dealt with up to this point was circumcision (Rom. 4). He conclusively proved that circumcision, or any other point of the law, was unnecessary for salvation (see notes 1-5 at Rom. 4:9-12, pp. 676-677). The only thing that God requires for the born-again experience is faith in what Jesus Christ did for us (see note 2 at Rom. 4:14, p. 678).

In this chapter, Paul brings up two more points of the law which were a real stumbling block to Jewish Christians. These are the issues of eating meats which the law declared unclean and observing special days such as the Sabbath and the feast days. The Jewish Christians were saying that the Gentile Christians had to keep these laws. The Gentile Christians felt no obligation to old Jewish rituals.

Paul stated that the Gentile Christians were correct doctrinally (v. 20), but he warns them against despising their weak Jewish brethren who could not eat meat or skip the observance of special days in good conscience. Therefore, Paul established a principle that those who have the greater revelation of their freedom in Christ have an obligation to try not to display that freedom in a way that offends their weak brethren.

2 (Rom. 14:1) Who is the weak brother referred to here? It is the religious Jew who was converted to Christianity. Verse two refers to the weak one as the one who is eating herbs. This is a reference to the Jewish Christian who had not totally realized his freedom from the Old Testament dietary laws.

The Old Testament law forbade Jews from eating certain meats (Lev. 11) and blood (Gen. 9:4; Lev. 3:17; 7:26-27; 17:10-14; Dt. 12:16, 23-25; 15:23). Because the Jews who were in Rome could not always be certain of what type of meat they were buying or if it had been killed properly to drain the blood, many of them had become vegetarians to avoid any possible contamination.

This is very interesting that Paul would cite the religious person as the weak brother. Most religious people think all their religious convictions make them superior to those who come to Christ without any religious background. But that wasn't Paul's assessment.

There is no bondage like religious bondage. A simple pagan background is easy to overcome in comparison to a heritage of legalistic religion. Paul ought to know. He was the Pharisee of the Pharisees.

3 (Rom. 14:1) Paul is saying that we shouldn't be critical of, or discriminate against, those who are weak in their convictions. This has been interpreted by some as inconsistent with some of Paul's actions.

Right here in this epistle, Paul had called the legalistic Jewish Christians impenitent and hardhearted (Rom. 2:5). In dealing with the same subject in the letter to the Galatians, Paul was very uncompromising, saying that they had been bewitched (Gal. 3:1) and that they were fallen from grace if they trusted in circumcision (Gal. 5:2-4). He also said in Galatians 2:5 that he didn't give any place to the legalistic Jews who were advocating circumcision for salvation.

How do Paul's actions harmonize with what he is teaching here?

There are some doctrinal points that are non-negotiable and others that are not. When it came to the doctrine of grace for salvation, Paul didn't compromise. He even said, *"But though we, or an angel from heaven, preach any other gospel unto you than that which we have preached unto you, let him be accursed"* (Gal. 1:8).

If these Jewish believers had taught abstinence from meats and observance of special days as essential for salvation, Paul would not have tolerated that. But if these Jewish Christians were professing righteousness with God solely on the work of Christ, yet they had a personal conviction about these things, that was okay.

The thought or the motive behind the action is what must be judged.

Paul didn't object to circumcision. Paul objected to faith in circumcision instead of faith in Christ. He even circumcised Timothy to keep from offending the Jews (Acts 16:3). Yet when the legalistic Jews tried to pressure Paul about the circumcision of Titus (Gal. 2:3-5), Paul would not bend.

Likewise, we cannot compromise on the matter of salvation by grace through faith (Eph. 2:8). Yet there should be room for Christians to dwell together and yet have different ways of conduct.

ROMANS

CHRISTIAN LIBERTY AND QUESTIONABLE THINGS (cont'd)

CHAPTER 14

2 *For one[4] believeth that he may eat all things:[a] another, who is weak, eateth herbs.[b]
3 *Let[5] not him that eateth despise[6c] him that eateth not; and let not him which eateth not judge[d] him that eateth: for God hath received[e] him.
4 *Who art thou that judgest[d] another man's servant?[7] to his own master[f] he standeth or falleth. Yea, he shall be holden[g] up: for God is able to make him stand.[h]
5 *One man esteemeth[i] one day above another: another esteemeth every day *alike*. Let every man be fully persuaded[j] in his own mind.[8]
6 *He that regardeth[k] the day,[9] regardeth *it* unto the Lord;[f] and he that regardeth not the day, to the Lord he doth not regard *it*. He that eateth, eateth to the Lord, for he giveth God thanks;[l] and he that eateth not, to the Lord he eateth not, and giveth God thanks.[l]

PARALLEL SCRIPTURES FOR ROMANS 14:2-6

COLOSSIANS 2:16-17

16 Let no man therefore judge you in meat, or in drink, or in respect of an holyday, or of the new moon, or of the sabbath days:

17 Which are a shadow of things to come; but the body is *of Christ.*

GALATIANS 4:9-10

9 But now, after that ye have known God, or rather are known of God, how turn ye again to the weak and beggarly elements, whereunto ye desire again to be in bondage?

10 Ye observe days, and months, and times, and years.

a Rom. 14:14; 1 Cor. 10:25; 1 Tim. 4:4; Ti. 1:15; Heb. 9:10; 13:9
b Gk.-"lachaino"- (to dig); a vegetable. The Gk. word comes from a verb meaning "to dig" - so something that comes out of the ground (WMNT)- Gen. 1:29; 9:3; Dan. 1:12, 16
c Dict.- to regard with contempt or disdain; from Latin-"despicere"- to look down on- Mt. 18:10; Lk. 18:9
d Dict.- to pass sentence upon; condemn; make a critical determination or appraisal- Rom. 14:10, 13; Mt. 7:1-2; 1 Cor. 10:29-30; Col. 2:16-17
e Gk.-"proslambano"- to take to oneself; i.e. use (food); lead (aside); admit (to friendship or hospitality) Dict.- to greet or welcome
f Gk.-"kurios"- see note 3 at Lk. 1:43, p. 12
g i.e. made to stand (ASV)
h Rom. 11:23; 8:31-39; 16:25; Ps. 37:17, 24, 28; 119:116-117; Heb. 7:25; Jude 24
i Dict.- to regard as of a high order; think of with respect; prize; to judge to be; regard as; consider
j or assured- 1 Jn. 3:19-21
k or observeth- Gal. 4:10
l Gk.-"eucharisteo"- to be grateful; i.e. to express gratitude (towards); spec. to say grace at a meal see note 1 at Rom. 1:21, p. 660; Mt. 15:36; 1 Cor. 10:30-31; 1 Tim. 4:3-5

Footnotes for Romans 14:2-6

4 (Rom. 14:2) This verse is speaking of the Gentile Christian who didn't have any convictions about eating certain meats and the Jewish Christian who would only eat herbs for fear of breaking an Old Testament dietary law (see note 2 at v. 1, p. 743).

5 (Rom. 14:3) Paul is preaching a tolerance for other believers who have differing views that could appear contradictory to his own actions. However, as explained in note 3 at verse 1, on page 743, these are not believers who are putting faith in these actions for salvation; they wouldn't be true Christians if they were. These people were justified by faith but they had a personal conviction about keeping the ceremonial law of their Jewish heritage.

These people are different from the ones that Paul spoke of in his letter to Timothy. In 1 Timothy 4:3, Paul said those who commanded others to abstain from meats were speaking a doctrine of devils. The key difference is the word "command." Those in 1 Timothy 4 were demanding compliance for salvation. The people that Paul is saying to receive in this verse are people who are not judging others for their own personal convictions.

6 (Rom. 14:3) Notice that Paul instructs those who have the revelation of their freedom in Christ not to despise those who don't. He also instructs those who are still emphasizing works to not judge those who aren't.

Paul is revealing that the danger for those who have a revelation of God's grace is to become insensitive to and impatient with their brethren who haven't yet come to that knowledge. We have to temper our freedom in Christ with love for our fellow Christians. *". . .Knowledge puffeth up, but charity edifieth"* (1 Cor. 8:1).

Those who have not yet renewed their minds to their freedom from the Old Testament law tend to be judgmental of others who don't have their standard of holiness. Passing judgment on others is a sure sign of a legalistic mentality (see note 46 at Mt. 7:1, p. 83).

7 (Rom. 14:4) We are all servants, not judges. We should let the Lord be the judge. The only thing that we are supposed to judge is ourselves—that we aren't a stumbling block to anyone (v. 13).

8 (Rom. 14:5) On other occasions Paul called it bondage to observe special days (Gal. 4:9-10). Once again, this must be denoting people who were observing certain days as a mere conviction and not a command (see note 3 at v. 1, p. 743). Personal convictions and doctrinal truth are two different things.

9 (Rom. 14:6) This verse verifies that these observances of certain days and abstinence from meats were not done in a legalistic manner that caused the individual to think he was earning salvation. They were doing these things as unto the Lord.

ROMANS

CHRISTIAN LIBERTY AND QUESTIONABLE THINGS (cont'd)

CHAPTER 14

7 For none of us liveth to himself, and
no man dieth to himself.[m]
8 For whether we live, we live unto the
Lord;[n] and whether we die, we die unto the
Lord:[o] whether we live therefore, or die, we
are the Lord's.[p]
9 For to this end[q] Christ both died,[r] and
rose, and revived,[s] that he might be Lord[t]
both of the dead and living.
10 But why dost thou judge[d] thy brother?
or why dost thou set at nought thy brother?[u]
for we shall all stand before the judgment
seat of Christ.[v]

PARALLEL SCRIPTURES FOR
ROMANS 14:2-6

1 CORINTHIANS 10:23-31

23 All things are lawful for me, but all things are not expedient: all things are lawful for me, but all things edify not.

24 Let no man seek his own, but every man another's wealth.

25 Whatsoever is sold in the shambles, that *eat, asking no question for conscience sake:*

26 For the earth is *the Lord's, and the fulness thereof.*

27 If any of them that believe not bid you to a feast, *and ye be disposed to go; whatsoever is set before you, eat, asking no question for conscience sake.*

28 But if any man say unto you, This is offered in sacrifice unto idols, eat not for his sake that shewed it, and for conscience sake: for the earth is *the Lord's, and the fulness thereof:*

29 Conscience, I say, not thine own, but of the other: for why is my liberty judged of another man's *conscience?*

30 For if I by grace be a partaker, why am I evil spoken of for that for which I give thanks?

31 Whether therefore ye eat, or drink, or whatsoever ye do, do all to the glory of God.

1 CORINTHIANS 8:4-13

4 As concerning therefore the eating of those things that are offered in sacrifice unto idols, we know that an idol is *nothing in the world, and that* there is *none other God but one.*

5 For though there be that are called gods, whether in heaven or in earth, (as there be gods many, and lords many,)

6 But to us there is but *one God, the Father, of whom* are *all things, and we in him; and one Lord Jesus Christ, by whom* are *all things, and we by him.*

7 Howbeit there is *not in every man that knowledge: for some with conscience of the idol unto this hour eat* it *as a thing offered unto an idol; and their conscience being weak is defiled.*

8 But meat commendeth us not to God: for neither, if we eat, are we the better; neither, if we eat not, are we the worse.

9 But take heed lest by any means this liberty of yours become a stumblingblock to them that are weak.

10 For if any man see thee which hast knowledge sit at meat in the idol's temple, shall not the conscience of him which is weak be emboldened to eat those things which are offered to idols;

11 And through thy knowledge shall the weak brother perish, for whom Christ died?

12 But when ye sin so against the brethren, and wound their weak conscience, ye sin against Christ.

13 Wherefore, if meat make my brother to offend, I will eat no flesh while the world standeth, lest I make my brother to offend.

m Rom. 14:9; 1 Cor. 6:19-20; 2 Cor. 5:15; Gal. 2:19-20; Phil. 1:20-24; 1 Th. 5:10
n Lk. 20:38; 2 Cor. 5:15; Gal. 2:20; Phil. 1:21; 1 Jn. 4:9
o Acts 20:24; 21:13; Phil. 2:30
p 1 Cor. 6:19-20; 7:23
q Gk.-"telos"- the point aimed at as a limit; i.e. the conclusion of an act or state; result
r see note 7 at Mk. 10:45, p. 340; see note 1 at Mt. 26:2, p. 410
s Gk.-"anazao"- to recover life; Trans. live again; revive; see note 1 at Acts 1:3, p. 509; see note 4 at Rom. 1:4, p. 655; Acts 2:24; Eph. 1:19-20; Heb. 13:20; 1 Pet. 1:21
t Gk.-"kurieuo"- to rule; Trans. have dominion over; lord; be lord of; exercise lordship over; see note 3 at Lk. 1:43, p. 12; Acts 2:36; Rom. 10:9, 13; 1 Cor. 12:3; Rev. 19:16
u i.e. why do you look down upon or despise your brother? (Amp)- Rom. 14:3-4
v Jn. 5:22; 1 Cor. 4:5; 2 Cor. 5:10

ROMANS

CHRISTIAN LIBERTY AND QUESTIONABLE THINGS (cont'd)

CHAPTER 14

11 *For it is written, *As* I live, saith the
Lord, every knee shall bow to me, and
every tongue shall confess[a] to God.[10]
12 So then every one of us shall give
account[b] of himself to God.
13 Let us not therefore judge[c] one
another any more: but judge this[11] rather,
that no man put a stumblingblock[d] or an
occasion to fall[e] in *his* brother's way.
14 I know, and am persuaded by the
Lord Jesus, that *there is* nothing unclean[12f]
of itself: but to him that esteemeth[g] any
thing to be unclean,[f] to him *it is* unclean.[f]
15 But if thy brother be grieved with *thy*
meat,[h] now walkest thou not charitably.[13i]
Destroy[j] not him with thy meat, for whom
Christ died.
16 Let not then your good be evil spoken
of:[k]

PARALLEL SCRIPTURES FOR ROMANS 14:11

ISAIAH 45:22

22 Look unto me, and be ye saved, all the ends of the earth: for I am *God, and* there is *none else.*

PHILIPPIANS 2:10

10 That at the name of Jesus every knee should bow, of things *in heaven, and* things *in earth, and* things *under the earth;*

a Rom. 10:9; 15:9; Mt. 10:32; 1 Jn. 4:15; 2 Jn. 7; see note 1 at Mk. 1:24, p. 66; see note 10 at Rom. 10:10, p. 721

b Dict.- to hold answerable for- Eccl. 11:9; Mt. 12:36; 18:23; 1 Pet. 4:5

c Dict.- to pass sentence upon; condemn; see note 46 at Mt. 7:1, p. 83; Rom. 14:4,10; Jas. 2:4; 4:11

d Gk.-"proskomma"- to stumble; i.e. strike one's foot against (WMNT)- Rom. 9:32-33; 11:9; Lev. 19:14; 1 Cor. 8:9-13; 10:32; 2 Cor. 6:3; Phil. 1:10; Rev. 2:14

e Gk.-"skandalon"- this word originally meant the bait stick on a trap or snare and then the trap or snare itself (WMNT)

f i.e. profane; defiled; impure; intrinsically unholy (Rhm, ABUV, Wey, Phi)- Acts 10:14-15; 11:8-9; 1 Tim. 4:4; Ti. 1:15

g Dict.- to judge to be; regard as; consider

h If your brother is being pained or his feelings hurt or if he is being injured by what you eat (Amp); If your habit of unrestricted diet seriously upsets your brother (Phi)

i see note 4 at Jn. 13:35, p. 424; see note 3 at Rom. 12:10, p. 734; Rom. 13:10; 15:2; Gal. 5:13

j i.e. cause the ruin (Amp); to tamper with conscience (WWS)- 1 Cor. 8:11

k 1 Cor. 10:30; 1 Th. 5:22

Footnotes for Romans 14:11-16

10 (Rom. 14:11) Paul is citing this Old Testament verse to show that each individual is accountable to God (v. 12). Therefore, we don't have to judge our brethren. God will do it.

11 (Rom. 14:13) We are not supposed to judge our brother (see note 46 at Mt. 7:1, p. 83). Instead, we are supposed to judge ourselves to make sure that we are not causing others to stumble in their faith through our actions.

12 (Rom. 14:14) This is quite a statement! Nothing is unclean. It is how we use things that makes them unclean.

The Old Testament law declared many animals unclean (Lev. 11), not because there was anything wrong with the animals, but the Lord was making a point. In the New Testament, Paul reveals that every creature of God is good and nothing to be refused if it is received with thanksgiving (1 Tim. 4:4). Every creature of God was always good, even during Old Testament times. But the Lord wanted His people to be a holy people, separated unto Him even in the things they ate.

Therefore, He gave them dietary laws that pronounced certain animals as unclean so that they would be reminded, even as they ate, that they were not free to do just whatever they wanted to do. They were bought with a price (1 Cor. 6:20) and they were to glorify God in every area of their lives (1 Cor. 10:31).

Colossians 2:16-17 makes it very clear that these dietary laws were shadows of things that are now realities in Christ. Yet, just as with so many other Old Testament truths, the Jews had become engrossed in the observance of the ritual with no understanding as to what it symbolized. Likewise today, some Christians still hold to Old Testament ritual without any idea that the ritual has become reality in Christ (see note 1 at Jn. 5:16, p. 97).

In Colossians 2:16-17, Paul said these things were **shadows** of things to come. If I were walking towards you but the corner of a building blocked your view, then my shadow could be very significant. It could show you I was coming and how close I was. But once I came around the corner and was in view, it would be unthinkable that you would fall down and embrace my shadow. My shadow is meaningful only because it represents me. Once you could talk to me, my shadow would be meaningless.

Likewise, Old Testament rituals were significant before Christ came. They illustrated truths that were not yet in full view. But now that Christ has come, the rituals are meaningless and can be oppressive if they are wrongfully thought to be requirements for acceptance with God.

13 (Rom. 14:15) This ties all of this teaching back in with Romans 13:8-10. Paul had summarized all our duty to mankind as loving our neighbor as ourself (see note 4 at Rom. 13:10, p. 741). If we ignore the influence our actions have on others, we are not walking in this law of love.

ROMANS

CHRISTIAN LIBERTY AND QUESTIONABLE THINGS (cont'd)

CHAPTER 14

17 For the kingdom[14] of God[l] is not
meat[m] and drink;[n] but righteousness,[o] and
peace,[p] and joy[q] in the Holy Ghost.[r]
18 For he that in these things serveth
Christ *is* acceptable[s] to God, and approved[t]
of men.
19 Let us therefore follow after the
things which make for peace,[u] and things
wherewith one may edify[v] another.
20 For meat destroy not the work of
God.[w] All things indeed *are* pure;[x] but *it is*
evil[15] for that man who eateth with offence.
21 *It is* good[16] neither to eat flesh, nor to
drink wine,[y] nor *any thing* whereby thy
brother stumbleth,[z] or is offended,[aa] or is
made weak.[bb]
22 Hast thou faith?[17] have *it* to thyself
before God. Happy *is* he that condemneth
not himself in that thing which he alloweth.[cc]
23 And he that doubteth[dd] is damned[18] if
he eat, because *he eateth* not of faith: for
whatsoever[19] *is* not of faith is sin.[ee]

l see note 3 at Jn. 3:3, p. 48
see note 30 at Mt. 6:10, p. 79
see note 1 at Lk. 17:21, p. 317
see note 4 at Acts 1:7, p. 509
m Gk.-"brosis"- the act of eating; that which is eaten; food; aliment (Thayer)-
1 Tim. 4:3
n Rom. 14:20-21
Jn. 2:9-10
Eph. 5:18
1 Tim. 5:23
o Gk.-"dikaiosune"- equity (of character or act); spec. (Christian) justification; righteousness here is used in its practical ethical sense, as shown in moral rectitude toward men (Vincent)
p see notes 38-39 at Jn. 14:27, p. 434
see note 90 at Jn. 16:33, p. 442
see note 2 at Lk. 24:38, p. 496
see note 2 at Rom. 5:1, p. 681
q see notes 57-58 at Jn. 15:11, p. 436
see note 91 at Jn. 16:33, p. 442
see note 1 at Lk. 24:4, p. 485
r i.e. through the presence of the Holy Spirit (TCNT)

s Gk.-"euarestos"- well-pleasing, acceptable (Wuest)
t Dict.- to regard favorably; commend by word or action; consider right or good
u i.e. let us keep on pursuing the things of peace (WMNT)
v Lit. upbuild-
Rom. 15:2
1 Cor. 14:12, 26
Eph. 4:29
1 Th. 5:11
1 Tim. 1:4
w Mt. 18:6
1 Cor. 6:12-13
8:8, 13
10:31
x Rom. 14:14
Mt. 15:11
Acts 10:15
1 Tim. 4:3-5
Ti. 1:15
y Rom. 15:1-2
1 Cor. 8:13
z Rom. 14:13
Mal. 2:8
Rev. 2:14
aa Mt. 16:23
18:7-10
Lk. 17:1-2
Phil. 1:10
bb Rom. 15:1
1 Cor. 8:7-12
9:22
cc see note 9 at Rom. 2:15, p. 665
see note 4 at Acts 24:16, p. 634
see note 1 at Acts 23:1, p. 628
dd Gk.-"diakrino"- to be divided in one's mind; to hesitate; doubt (LNT)-
1 Cor. 8:7
ee Dt. 32:20
Mk. 16:14
Heb. 3:12
4:11

Footnotes for Romans 14:17-23

14 (Rom. 14:17) Man usually focuses his attention on external things such as meat and drink, but God is always concerned with the heart of man (1 Sam. 16:7). God deals with our actions because they indicate the condition of our hearts. But it is always the spiritual condition of our inner man that God is seeking to change.

Paul is saying that we need to be like God and focus on the inner condition of our brothers in Christ. Then we will be able to tolerate minor differences in their actions.

15 (Rom. 14:20) Prior to this verse, Paul had encouraged the believers to consider their weaker brothers based on their obligation to love one another (see note 2 at Rom. 13:8, p. 740). Now he strengthens that argument by revealing how damaging it could be if the weaker brother follows our actions with a defiled conscience. It is evil for him (v. 20); it will offend him and make him weak (v. 21); it will damn him, and it is sin for him (v. 23).

16 (Rom. 14:21) A casual reading of Paul's instructions here might leave a person with the impression that Paul is only suggesting that we not offend the weak brother in this area. However, this is not the case.

The Jerusalem church had already issued a command to the Gentile Christians that they abstain from meat that had been offered to idols (Acts 15:20, 28-29). Paul agreed with this mandate and became one of the messengers who delivered this decree to the churches (Acts 15:25, 30).

Paul also commented on this same subject in 1 Corinthians 8 and 10. In chapter eight Paul said, *"But when ye sin so against the brethren, and wound their weak conscience, ye sin against Christ"* (v. 12). That doesn't sound optional. He also gave a direct command in 1 Corinthians 10:28, not to eat meat sacrificed to idols for the sake of the weak brother.

However, the greatest proof that this abstinence from meat offered to idols was not optional are the comments of Jesus Himself. In Revelation 2:14 and 20, the Lord rebuked two churches for allowing individuals to teach in those churches that the people could eat meats sacrificed to idols.

Therefore, even though these scriptures do explain that the actual eating of meats sacrificed to idols is not wrong in itself, it does not give the believers the right to indulge. They are strictly to abstain because of the effect their actions would have upon the weaker Christian's conscience.

17 (Rom. 14:22) This is specifically speaking of having faith that they could eat meat sacrificed to idols. *The Epistles of Paul* by W. J. Conybeare renders this verse, *"hast thou faith [that nothing is unclean]: Keep it for thine own comfort before God."* Therefore, Paul is stating that if anyone has a clear conscience about eating meat sacrificed to idols, he should keep that faith to himself and not practice it openly lest he offend the weaker brother.

18 (Rom. 14:23) The Greek word that was translated "damned" here is "katakrino," meaning "to judge against; sentence." This differs from the Greek word "krino" that is used in 2 Thessalonians 2:12 to designate eternal damnation. "Katakrino," as used in this verse, actually means "to condemn" and is translated that way 17 other times in the New Testament. In contrast, "krino" is only translated as "condemn" once (Jn. 3:17), "condemned" twice (Jn. 3:18), and "condemning" once (Acts 13:27). Therefore, this verse is not saying that any Christian who does something with a defiled conscience is eternally damned. Paul is stating that any Christian who violates his conscience is going to come under condemnation.

19 (Rom. 14:23) This verse provides us with a definition of sin that is applicable to all people of all cultures and different religious backgrounds. Any action is sin for us if we don't have faith in its correctness. Until we can settle our doubts, we aren't to do it. This would provide an infallible system for determining right and wrong for any individual.

ROMANS

BEARING OTHERS' WEAKNESSES AND NOT PLEASING OURSELVES

CHAPTER 15

WE THEN that are strong[a] ought[1] to bear[2]
the infirmities[3] of the weak,[b] and not to
please[4] ourselves.[c]
2 Let every one of us please *his* neighbour
for *his* good to edification.[d]
3 *For even Christ[5] pleased not himself;[e]
but, as it is written, The reproaches[f] of them
that reproached[f] thee fell[g] on me.
4 For whatsoever things were written
aforetime were written for our learning,[6h]
that we through patience[7i] and comfort of
the scriptures[j] might have hope.[k]
5 Now the God of patience[i] and
consolation[l] grant you to be likeminded[m]
one toward another according[8] to Christ
Jesus:[n]
6 That ye may with one mind *and* one
mouth[o] glorify God, even the Father[p] of our
Lord Jesus Christ.
7 Wherefore receive ye one another,[q]
as[9] Christ also received us[r] to the glory of
God.[s]

PARALLEL SCRIPTURES FOR ROMANS 15:1

GALATIANS 6:2, 5

2 Bear ye one another's burdens, and so fulfil the law of Christ.

5 For every man shall bear his own burden.

O.T. SCRIPTURE CITED IN ROMANS 15:3

PSALM 69:9

9 For the zeal of thine house hath eaten me up; and the reproaches of them that reproached thee are fallen upon me.

a i.e. strong in faith, understanding our freedom in Christ- Rom. 4:20 1 Cor. 4:10 1 Jn. 2:14
b Rom. 14:1 1 Cor. 9:22 12:22-24 1 Th. 5:14
c Let's please the other fellow, not ourselves . . . and thus build him up (LB)- Rom. 15:3 Jn. 8:29 Rom. 14:21 1 Cor. 8:13
d see note 4 at Acts 9:31, p. 557 Rom. 14:19 1 Cor. 8:1 10:23 14:26 2 Cor. 12:19 Eph. 4:29 1 Th. 5:11 1 Tim. 1:4
e Mt. 26:39 Jn. 5:30 6:38
f Gk.-"oneidizo"- to defame; i.e. rail at; chide; taunt- Ps. 69:20 89:50-51 Mt. 10:25
g Gk.-"epipipto"- to embrace or seize
h i.e. for our instruction- Rom. 4:23-24 1 Cor. 9:9-10 10:11 2 Tim. 3:16-17
i see note 9 at Rom. 5:3, p. 682 see note 3 at Lk. 21:19, p. 397 Col. 1:11 1 Th. 1:3 1 Tim. 6:11 Ti. 2:2 Heb. 6:12 12:1 Jas. 1:4 5:7-8 2 Pet. 1:6 Rev. 3:10
j i.e. encouragement drawn from the scriptures (TCNT) Dict.- comfort; consolation; solace; help; assistance; aid
k see note 7 at Rom. 4:18, p. 679 see note 5 at Rom. 5:2, p. 681 see note 6 at Rom. 5:2, p. 681 see note 12 at Rom. 5:4, p. 683 see note 1 at Rom. 8:26, p. 707 see note 12 at Rom. 8:24, p. 706 see note 13 at Rom. 8:25, p. 706
l see note 73 at Jn. 16:4, p. 440 Jn. 14:26 Acts 9:31 2 Cor. 1:3-4 7:6 Phil. 2:1 2 Th. 2:16-17
m Rom. 12:16 2 Chr. 30:12 Jer. 32:39 Ezek. 11:19 Acts 4:32 1 Cor. 1:10 2 Cor. 13:11
n according to, or, after the example of- Rom. 15:3 Eph. 5:2 Phil. 2:4-5
o Rom. 15:9-11 Zeph. 3:9 Acts 4:24, 32
p see note 29 at Mt. 6:9, p. 79 2 Cor. 1:3 11:31 Eph. 1:3 1 Pet. 1:3
q Rom. 14:1-3 Mt. 10:40 Mk. 9:37 Lk. 9:48
r Mt. 11:28-30 Lk. 15:2 Jn. 6:37
s Rom. 15:9 Eph. 1:6 2 Th. 1:10-12

Footnotes for Romans 15:1-7

1 (Rom. 15:1) This verse is the summary of Paul's teaching in chapter 14. He explained that the Christian who is strong in grace and realizes that it is all right to eat meat sacrificed to idols is technically correct. But just because it's lawful doesn't mean it is the correct thing to do (1 Cor. 6:12; 10:23). He clearly states that the strong believer is supposed to bear the infirmities of his weak Christian brother.

2 (Rom. 15:1) This word "bear" was translated from the Greek word "bastazo," meaning "to lift." This gives the picture of the Christian with the weak conscience being burdened down with guilt or condemnation. We that are strong are supposed to help him lift that load. We do that by not offending his weak conscience.

3 (Rom. 15:1) The word that was translated "infirmity" here is the Greek word "asthenema," which means "a scruple of conscience." This is saying that the stronger brother needs to help lift the burden (see note 2 at this verse, above) of the brother that has a weak conscience.

4 (Rom. 15:1) Paul is summing up his instructions given in chapter 14 on how to get along with a brother who has convictions differing from yours (see note 1 at this verse, above). It all comes back to love. Love thinks of the other person first. Love is not selfish (1 Cor. 13). If we would seek the pleasure of others more than our own pleasure, we would kill strife. *"Only by pride cometh contention. . ."* (Prov. 13:10).

5 (Rom. 15:3) As always, Jesus is the supreme example of God's kind of love. Jesus submitted to things that He didn't have to as God. However, He became a man and submitted Himself lest He should offend people (Mt. 17:27). If Jesus did this for us, how can any of us justify not bearing the infirmities of our weak brother?

6 (Rom. 15:4) All the Old Testament scriptures were written for our instruction so that we would not make the same mistakes. A person who does not heed the lessons of the Old Testament is like a person who is trying to re-invent the wheel. People have already made mistakes and the Old Testament scriptures were faithful to report the consequences of those sins. We don't have to learn the same lessons by "hard knocks." We can learn at their expense instead of our own.

7 (Rom. 15:4) Patience, comfort, and hope do not come to us by begging and pleading with God. You cannot have a lasting measure of these things just by having someone lay hands on you. They come through the scriptures (see notes 12-13 at Rom. 8:24-25, p. 706)

Some people have also mistakenly thought that problems produced patience because of a misunderstanding of scriptures like Romans 5:3 and James 1:3. However, this verse makes it clear that patience is a product of the scriptures. If tribulations produced patience, then **every** Christian would be patient. We have all had tribulation.

Patience comes through God's Word, but problems cause us to exercise or use our patience and thereby become stronger (see note 8 at Rom. 5:3, p. 682).

8 (Rom. 15:5) Paul is referring back to verse 3 where he used Christ as an example of bearing the infirmities of those who are weak. He is praying that the Lord would work this same grace in us that was displayed in Christ Jesus.

9 (Rom. 15:7) How do we determine what doctrines are negotiable and which ones are not? If an individual has been truly born again by Christ receiving him, then **we** should receive that person also, regardless of our differences. If Jesus is able to overlook the doctrinal errors of an individual, who are we to refuse that person?

ROMANS

CHRIST THE SAVIOUR OF JEW AND GENTILE

CHAPTER 15

8 Now I say that Jesus Christ was a minister[1] of the circumcision[a] for the truth of God, to confirm[b] the promises[c] *made* unto the fathers:[d]

9 *And that the Gentiles[e] might glorify God for *his* mercy;[f] as it is written,[2] For this cause I will confess to thee among the Gentiles,[e] and sing[g] unto thy name.

10 *And again he saith, Rejoice, ye Gentiles, with his people.

11 And again,[h] Praise[i] the Lord,[j] all ye Gentiles;[e] and laud[k] him, all ye people.

12 *And again, E-sai´as[l] saith, There shall be a root of Jesse,[m] and he that shall rise to reign[n] over the Gentiles;[e] in him shall the Gentiles trust.[o]

13 Now the God of hope[p] fill you with all joy[q] and peace[r] in believing,[s] that ye may abound in hope,[p] through the power[t] of the Holy Ghost.

O.T. SCRIPTURES CITED IN ROMANS 15:9

2 SAMUEL 22:50

50 Therefore I will give thanks unto thee, O LORD, among the heathen, and I will sing praises unto thy name.

PSALM 18:49

49 Therefore will I give thanks unto thee, O LORD, among the heathen, and sing praises unto thy name.

O.T. SCRIPTURE CITED IN ROMANS 15:10

DEUTERONOMY 32:43

43 Rejoice, O ye nations, with *his people: for he will avenge the blood of his servants, and will render vengeance to his adversaries, and will be merciful unto his land,* and *to his people.*

O.T. SCRIPTURE CITED IN ROMANS 15:12

ISAIAH 11:10

10 And in that day there shall be a root of Jesse, which shall stand for an ensign of the people; to it shall the Gentiles seek: and his rest shall be glorious.

PARALLEL SCRIPTURE FOR ROMANS 15:12

MATTHEW 12:21

21 And in his name shall the Gentiles trust.

Footnotes for Romans 15:8-13

1 (Rom. 15:8) In Romans 15:7, Paul concluded his remarks about walking in love towards brethren who had different convictions. He judged that on certain issues that were not critical to salvation (see note 3 at Rom. 14:1, p. 743), the stronger should bear with the weak (see note 1 at Rom. 15:1, p. 748).

Now, lest someone should try to cite Jesus' exclusion of the Gentiles during His earthly ministry as proof that we can reject those who don't conform to Jewish traditions, Paul explains why Jesus ministered nearly exclusively to the Jews. He was fulfilling God's promises to the Jews. Jesus could not become the Savior of the Gentiles until He had been the Messiah to the Jews.

Paul then goes on to cite a number of Old Testament scriptures that make it very clear that Jesus' present ministry embraces the Gentiles without converting them to Judaism.

2 (Rom. 15:9) Paul briefly verifies a point that he has already made in this book to the Romans. He quotes four Old Testament scriptures (see O.T. Scriptures Cited, above) to verify that Christ opened up the door of salvation to the Gentiles.

This is done to make it clear that Gentiles do not have to become Jews to be saved. Salvation to Gentiles as Gentiles does not fall into the category of one of those "non-essential" doctrines (see note 3 at Rom. 14:1, p. 743) that Paul discussed in chapter 14, on which we compromise for the sake of our weak brother.

a Mt. 10:5-6; 15:24; Acts 3:25-26; Rom. 3:1-2; i.e. a minister to the Jews
b Dict.- to assure the certainty or validity of
c Gk.-"epaggelia"- an announcement (for information, assent, or pledge; esp. a divine assurance of good)
d Gen. 12:1-3; 17:5-7; 22:18; 26:3-4; 28:13-14
e see note 45 at Mt. 6:32, p. 83; see note 2 at Lk. 2:32, p. 22; see note 3 at Lk. 7:9, p. 117; see note 1 at Jn. 12:23, p. 359; see note 3 at Acts 28:28, p. 653
f see note 7 at Rom. 9:14, p. 713; Lam. 3:22-23; Mic. 7:18; Lk. 1:50; Eph. 2:4; Ti. 3:5
g Heb. 2:12
h Ps. 117:1
i see note 2 at Lk. 19:40, p. 356; see note 3 at Mt. 21:16, p. 364; see note 2 at Acts 16:24, p. 595; see note 4 at Acts 16:25, p. 596; see note 5 at Acts 16:26, p. 596; see note 11 at Rom. 4:20, p. 680
j see note 3 at Lk. 1:43, p. 12
k Dict.- to give praise or express devotion to; glorify
l i.e. Isaiah
m see note 2 at Lk. 18:39, p. 343
n Gk.-"archo"- to be first (in political rank or power); Trans. reign (rule) over; see note 3 at Jn. 3:3, p. 48; see note 30 at Mt. 6:10, p. 79
o Eph. 1:12-13
p see note 7 at Rom. 4:18, p. 679; see note 5 at Rom. 5:2, p. 681; see note 6 at Rom. 5:2, p. 681; see note 12 at Rom. 5:4, p. 683; see note 12 at Rom. 8:24, p. 706; see note 13 at Rom. 8:25, p. 706; Joel 3:16; 1 Tim. 1:1
q see note 57 at Jn. 15:11, p. 436; see note 58 at Jn. 15:11, p. 436; see note 91 at Jn. 16:33, p. 442; see note 1 at Lk. 24:4, p. 485
r see notes 37-39 at Jn. 14:27, p. 434; see note 90 at Jn. 16:33, p. 442; see note 2 at Lk. 24:38, p. 496; see note 2 at Rom. 5:1, p. 681
s see note 5 at Lk. 17:10, p. 304; see note 8 at Rom. 4:18, p. 679; see note 9 at Rom. 4:19, p. 680; see note 13 at Rom. 4:21, p. 680; see ref. q at Lk. 17:5, p. 305
t see note 5 at Acts 1:8, p. 509; see note 2 at Acts 8:18, p. 547; Rom. 15:19

ROMANS

MINISTERING CHRIST TO THE NATIONS

CHAPTER 15

14 And I myself also am persuaded of
you, my brethren, that ye also are full of
goodness,[a] filled with all knowledge,[b] able[c]
also to admonish[d] one another.
15 Nevertheless, brethren, I have written
the more boldly unto you in some sort,[e] as
putting you in mind,[f] because of the grace[g]
that is given to me of God,
16 That I should be the minister of Jesus
Christ to the Gentiles,[h] ministering the
gospel of God,[i] that the offering up of the
Gentiles might be acceptable, being
sanctified[1] by the Holy Ghost.[j]
17 I have therefore whereof I may
glory[2k] through Jesus Christ in those things
which pertain to God.
18 For I will not dare to speak of any of
those things which Christ hath not wrought
by me,[l] to make the Gentiles obedient,[m] by
word and deed,[n]
19 Through mighty signs[3] and wonders,[o]
by the power[p] of the Spirit of God; so that
from Jerusalem,[q] and round about unto
Illyr´i-cum,[4] I have fully[5] preached[r] the
gospel of Christ.[i]

a Gal. 5:22 Eph. 5:9 2 Th. 1:11 see note 3 at Acts 10:38, p. 564
b 1 Ki. 3:9 Ps. 119:66 Prov. 1:7 8:10 12:1 18:15 24:5 Lk. 11:52 1 Cor. 8:7, 10 Phil. 3:8 see note 9 at Jn. 8:32, p. 232
c Dict.- having sufficient ability or resources
d Gk.-"noutheteo"- to put in mind; i.e. (by impl.) to caution or reprove gently Dict.- to reprove mildly or kindly, but seriously- Col. 3:16 2 Th. 3:15 Heb. 8:5
e But I have written very boldly to you on some points (NASB)
f 1 Tim. 4:6 2 Tim. 1:6 2:14 Ti. 3:1 2 Pet. 1:12-15 3:1-2
g see note 5 at Rom. 1:5, p. 655 see note 8 at Rom. 3:24, p. 673 see note 15 at Rom. 5:8, p. 683 Rom. 1:5 12:3, 6 1 Cor. 3:10 15:10 Gal. 1:15-16 2:9 Eph. 3:7-8 1 Tim. 1:11-14 1 Pet. 4:10
h Rom. 11:13 Acts 9:15 22:21 26:17-18 Gal. 2:7-8 Eph. 3:1 1 Tim. 2:7 2 Tim. 1:11

i see note 7 at Mt. 24:14, p. 396 see note 5 at Acts 20:24, p. 618 see note 3 at Rom. 1:2, p. 655 see note 1 at Rom. 1:16, p. 658 see note 10 at Rom. 2:16, p. 665 see note 1 at Rom. 10:14, p. 722 see note 3 at Rom. 10:15, p. 723 Rom. 1:1 Acts 20:24 1 Th. 2:2, 9 1 Tim. 1:11
j Acts 11:15-18
k Gk.-"kauchesis"- boasting
l For I will not venture to speak thus of any work except what Christ has actually done through me as an instrument in His hands (Amp)- Prov. 25:14 2 Cor. 10:13-18
m Gk.-"hupakoe"- attentive hearkening; i.e. (by impl.) compliance or submission- Rom. 1:5 6:17 16:26 Mt. 28:18-20 Heb. 5:9 11:8
n Col. 3:17
o see note 2 at Lk. 2:12, p. 18 Mk. 16:17, 20 Jn. 20:30 Acts 2:22, 43 4:30 5:12 14:3 2 Cor. 12:12 Heb. 2:4 continued on center column

References continued from column 4

p see note 5 at Acts 1:8, p. 509 see note 4 at Mt. 28:19, p. 504 see note 9 at Acts 4:14, p. 524 see note 2 at Acts 5:14, p. 529 see note 4 at Acts 8:13, p. 546
q see note 1 at Jn. 5:1, p. 95
r see note 3 at Mt. 5:2, p. 73 see notes 2-3 at Acts 8:5-6, p. 545 see note 2 at Acts 14:4, p. 581 see note 2 at Acts 20:7, p. 615

Footnotes for Romans 15:14-19

1 (Rom. 15:16) We cannot just worship God any way we want to. Our worship has to be sanctified by the Holy Ghost. Until a person makes Jesus his Lord, the Holy Spirit does not intercede for him. Paul is saying that through his preaching of the gospel and the Gentiles' reception of salvation, the Holy Spirit was then free to work on their behalf.

2 (Rom. 15:17) Paul brought the gospel to the Gentiles, which granted salvation to those who received it. Therefore, he had quite a bit to boast about (see ref. k at v. 17, this page). However, he said his boasting was through Christ Jesus, which clarifies that this was not done in arrogancy or pride.

3 (Rom. 15:19) Paul was known primarily for his preaching of the gospel of God's grace (see note 5 at Acts 20:24, p. 618). But Paul had the miraculous power of God working in him too. Indeed, this should be true of all true ministers of the gospel (see note 4 at Acts 4:30, p. 526).

Paul struck Elymas the sorcerer with blindness, causing the conversion of Sergius Paulus (Acts 13:6-12). In Lystra, Paul healed a man who had been a cripple from birth (Acts 14:8-10). In Philippi, Paul cast a spirit of divination out of a girl (Acts 16:16-18), and he was also delivered from prison in that city by a miraculous earthquake (Acts 16:25-26).

In Ephesus, the Lord accomplished "special miracles" through Paul by healing and delivering people as they came in contact with handkerchiefs or aprons that Paul had touched (Acts 19:11-12). In Troas, Paul raised Eutychus from the dead (Acts 20:9-12). And while shipwrecked on the island of Melita, Paul miraculously survived a bite from a poisonous snake (Acts 28:3-6).

Paul was also delivered from death at the hands of the Romans and Jews many times, including one time when he may actually have been raised from the dead (see note 3 at Acts 14:20, p. 583). Paul's life, as well as the lives of everyone on his ship, was spared from death at sea through God's intervention (Acts 27:21-26, 43-44).

Paul also wrote to the Corinthians that the signs of an apostle were wrought among them by him (2 Cor. 12:12). Yet there is no record in Acts of a single miracle performed by Paul during his visits to Corinth (Acts 18:1-17 and Acts 20:2-3).Therefore, it can be concluded that there were many miraculous things accomplished by Paul that were not recorded, just as in the case of our Lord Jesus (Jn. 20:30; 21:25).

4 (Rom. 15:19) Ancient Illyricum occupied the territory that is modern day Albania and Yugoslavia, just north of Macedonia where Thessalonica and Berea were located. There is no record of Paul preaching in this area, so it can be supposed that he is referring to ministering up to the border of this province.

5 (Rom. 15:19) Some people have interpreted Paul's statement here to mean that he had covered all the area of Asia (see note 3 at Acts 16:6, p. 592; see note 4 at Acts 19:10, p. 609), Macedonia (see note 1 at Acts 16:9, p. 593) and Achaia (see note 11 at Acts 18:12, p. 605) with the gospel. The following few verses would lend itself to that interpretation.

However, the immediate context of this verse specifically mentions *"mighty signs and wonders, by the power of the Spirit of God."* This would lead us to believe that Paul "fully" preaching the gospel referred to the confirmation of the Word through demonstration of God's miraculous power (see note 2 at Mk. 16:20, p. 506).

Therefore, Paul could be making a distinction between just preaching the gospel and fully preaching the gospel. A minister hasn't fully preached the gospel unless there are accompanying signs and wonders (see note 4 at Acts 4:30, p. 526). This must be where the phrase "full gospel" came from.

ROMANS

MINISTERING CHRIST TO THE NATIONS (continued)

s Dict.- to exert much effort or energy
t 2 Cor. 10:14-16

CHAPTER 15

20 Yea, so have I strived[s] to preach[6r] the
gospel,[i] not where Christ was named,[t] lest
I should build upon another man's
foundation:[u]
21 *But as it is written, To whom he was
not spoken of, they shall see: and they that
have not heard shall understand.[v]

u 1 Cor. 3:9-15
2 Cor. 10:13-16
Eph. 2:20-22
v Isa. 65:1

O.T. SCRIPTURE CITED IN ROMANS 15:21

ISAIAH 52:15

15 So shall he sprinkle many nations; the kings shall shut their mouths at him: for that *which had not been told them shall they see; and* that *which they had not heard shall they consider.*

Footnote for Romans 15:20-21
6 (Rom. 15:20) Paul had a burning desire to reach the unreached. Yet the greatest legacy that Paul left us are his epistles written to those he led to the Lord. This reflected an attitude that Paul had that we should have also. Paul didn't just evangelize, he discipled people (see note 5 at Mt. 28:19, p. 504).

PAUL'S DESIRE IS TO VISIT ROME

a Gk.-"egkopto"- to cut into; impede one's course by cutting off his way; to hinder; to detain (Thayer) see note 11 at Rom. 1:13, p. 657
Rom. 1:13
1 Th. 2:17-18
b see note 1 at Rom. 15:22, this page
c Rom. 15:32
1:10-12
d i.e. be aided or assisted on my journey by you-
Acts 15:3
1 Cor. 16:6
2 Cor. 1:16
3 Jn. 6

CHAPTER 15

22 For which cause[1] also I have been
much hindered[a] from coming to you.
23 But now having no more place in
these parts,[b] and having a great desire these
many years[2] to come unto you;[c]
24 Whensoever I take my journey into
Spain,[3] I will come to you: for I trust to see
you in my journey, and to be brought on my
way[4] thitherward by you,[d] if first I be
somewhat filled with your *company.*[e]
25 But now I go unto Jerusalem[f] to
minister[g] unto the saints.[h]

e After I have enjoyed your company for a while (Mof)-
Rom. 1:12
1 Cor. 16:5-7
f see note 1 at Jn. 5:1, p. 95
Acts 19:21
20:16, 22
24:17
g Rom. 15:26-31
1 Cor. 16:1-3
Gal. 2:10
h see note 5 at Acts 9:13, p. 555
Rom. 1:7
1 Cor. 1:2
Eph. 1:1
Phil. 1:1
Col. 1:2
Heb. 6:10

Footnotes for Romans 15:22-25
1 (Rom. 15:22) The cause that Paul is referring to is his desire to preach the gospel to everyone who had not heard. He had wanted to go to Rome, but he felt it was necessary to preach the gospel to everyone in the areas he had already been first. This is what he refers to in the next verse when he says, *"now having no more place in these parts."* He was saying there was no place left in those parts that hadn't heard the gospel. Therefore, he was ready to depart for new, unreached areas.
2 (Rom. 15:23) In Acts 19:21, Paul purposed in his spirit to visit Rome after he had gone back through Macedonia (see note 1 at Acts 16:9, p. 593) and Achaia (see note 11 at Acts 18:12, p. 605). This happened while he was in Ephesus from A.D. 54 to 57 (see note 2 at Acts 18:23, p. 607).
Paul was writing this epistle around A.D. 57-58 from Corinth (see Date and Place of Writing in Introduction to the Book of Romans, p. iv). Therefore, Paul's "many years" is referring to a two- to three-year period of time.
3 (Rom. 15:24) Paul mentions his intentions to travel to Spain twice in this chapter (this verse and v. 28). These are the only two times in scripture that this is mentioned. There is no scriptural account that Paul ever made it to Spain. Some have speculated that Paul went to Spain after his imprisonment in Rome. There are traditions that support that but no fact.
4 (Rom. 15:24) Paul is referring to the Romans helping him with his expenses for his planned trip to Spain. This is also what this terminology means in the scriptures listed in reference d at this verse.

ROMANS

PAUL'S DESIRE IS TO VISIT ROME (continued)

CHAPTER 15

26 For it hath pleased them of
Macedonia[a] and A-chai´a[b] to make a certain
contribution[5] for the poor[c] saints which are
at Jerusalem.
27 It hath pleased them verily; and their
debt-ors they are.[d] For if the Gentiles[e] have
been made partakers[f] of their spiritual
things, their duty is also to minister unto
them in carnal[6g] things.
28 When therefore I have performed
this, and have sealed to them this fruit,[h] I
will come by you into Spain.[i]
29 And I am sure[7] that, when I come
unto you, I shall come in the fulness of the
blessing of the gospel[j] of Christ.
30 Now I beseech[8] you, brethren, for the
Lord[k] Jesus Christ's sake,[l] and for the love[m]
of the Spirit, that ye strive together[n] with
me in *your* prayers[o] to God[p] for me;
31 That I may be delivered[9] from them
that do not believe[10q] in Judæa;[r] and that my
service which *I have* for Jerusalem may be
accepted[s] of the saints;[t]
32 That I may come unto you with joy[u]
by the will of God,[v] and may with you be
refreshed.[w]
33 Now the God of peace[x] *be* with you
all.[y] Amen.[z]

a see note 1 at Acts 16:9, p. 593
b see note 11 at Acts 18:12, p. 605
c Dict.- lacking money or means for an adequate existence- Lev. 19:9-10 25:35 Ps. 41:1-3 Prov. 14:21, 31 19:17 21:13 1 Cor. 16:1-4 Gal. 2:10
d They were very glad to do this, for they feel that they owe a real debt to the Jerusalem Christians (Tay)
e see note 45 at Mt. 6:32, p. 83
f Gk.-"koinoneo"- to share with others
g Gk.-"sarkikos"- pertaining to flesh; i.e. bodily; temporal- 1 Cor. 9:11
h i.e. delivered the contribution for the poor saints at Jerusalem- Rom. 15:26 Phil. 4:17
i see note 3 at Rom. 15:24, p. 751 Rom. 15:24
j see note 7 at Mt. 24:14, p. 396 see note 3 at Acts 8:4, p. 544 see note 2 at Acts 8:12, p. 546 see note 5 at Acts 20:24, p. 618 see note 3 at Rom. 1:2, p. 655 see note 1 at Rom. 1:16, p. 658
k see note 3 at Lk. 1:43, p. 12
l Acts 9:16 1 Cor. 4:10 2 Cor. 4:5, 11 12:10 Eph. 4:32 Phil. 1:29 1 Jn. 2:12 3 Jn. 7 Rev. 2:3

m see note 4 at Jn. 13:35, p. 424 see note 3 at Rom. 12:10, p. 734 Phil. 2:1
n Gk.-"sunagonizomai"- to struggle in company with; i.e. (fig.) to be a partner (assistant)
o see note 1 at Mk. 1:35, p. 68 see note 1 at Lk. 11:1, p. 256 see note 3 at Lk. 22:44, p. 449 see note 28 at Mt. 6:9, p. 79 see note 50 at Mt. 7:8, p. 83 see note 1 at Mt. 9:38, p. 163 see note 4 at Mt. 17:21, p. 213 see note 3 at Lk. 11:5, p. 256 see note 1 at Lk. 18:1, p. 319 see note 2 at Lk. 18:2, p. 320 see note 1 at Acts 4:24, p. 525 see note 2 at Rom. 8:26, p. 707 see note 4 at Rom. 8:26, p. 707
p see note 1 at Jn. 1:1, p. 2
q see note 7 at Mt. 5:10, p. 73 Acts 21:27-31 22:24 23:12-24 24:1-9 25:2, 24 1 Th. 2:15 2 Th. 3:2
r see note 1 at Jn. 4:3, p. 54
s Rom. 15:25
t see note 5 at Acts 9:13, p. 555 Rom. 1:7 1 Cor. 1:2 Eph. 1:1 Phil. 1:1 Col. 1:2 Heb. 6:10

continued on center column

References continued from column 4

u see notes 57-58 at Jn. 15:11, p. 436 see note 91 at Jn. 16:33, p. 442 see note 1 at Lk. 24:4, p. 485
v see notes 10-12 at Rom. 12:2, p. 730 see note 1 at Rom. 12:1, p. 729 Rom. 12:1-2 Acts 18:21 1 Cor. 4:19 Jas. 4:15
w Prov. 25:13 1 Cor. 16:18 2 Cor. 7:13 1 Th. 3:6-10 2 Tim. 1:16 Phile. 7, 20
x Rom. 16:20 1 Cor. 14:33 2 Cor. 13:11 Phil. 4:9 1 Th. 5:23 2 Th. 3:16 Heb. 13:20 see notes 38-39 at Jn. 14:27, p. 434 see note 90 at Jn. 16:33, p. 442 see note 2 at Lk. 24:38, p. 475 see note 2 at Rom. 5:1, p. 681
y Rom. 16:24 Ruth 2:4 Mt. 1:23 28:20 2 Cor. 13:14 2 Tim. 4:22
z Num. 5:22 Dt. 27:15-26 1 Chr. 16:36 Neh. 5:13 1 Cor. 14:16

Footnotes for Romans 15:26-33

5 (Rom. 15:26) The account of Paul's travels in Acts does not give us any details about this collection for the poor saints at Jerusalem. However, Paul does mention it as being the reason he made his last trip to Jerusalem (Acts 24:17), and he wrote about it in his letters to the Corinthians.

In 1 Corinthians 16:1-4, Paul gives instructions for the collection for the saints in Jerusalem. In verse 1, he says he gave the same instructions to the churches of Galatia. It is unclear whether he is saying he had also instructed the churches of Galatia to receive an offering for the Jerusalem saints or whether he was simply instructing the Corinthians to receive the collection in the same manner as the Galatians received their offerings. At any rate, Paul was only delivering the offerings from the churches of Macedonia and Achaia (this verse) during this trip to Jerusalem.

In 2 Corinthians 8:1-5, Paul spoke favorably about the attitude the churches of Macedonia (the churches of Thessalonica and Berea) had towards this offering. He acknowledged that the churches of Achaia (the Corinthian church) had purposed to send an offering a year before the Macedonian churches had(2 Cor. 8:10; 9:2). Paul gave the impression that the offering from the Macedonian churches was unsolicited (2 Cor. 8:4).

Paul encouraged the Corinthians to participate generously in this offering, reminding them that they would reap proportionally to how they sowed (2 Cor. 9:6). He stated clearly that they should not give under compulsion (2 Cor. 9:7) or try to give what they didn't have (2 Cor. 8:11-15). And he gave them a tremendous promise of God's physical blessing on them if they participated (2 Cor. 9:8-11).

This must have been a relatively large sum of money for Paul to be carrying to Jerusalem. Even though Paul could have demanded these people's trust since he was the apostle that brought them the gospel, he made provision for whoever they chose to accompany him to Jerusalem to make sure the money went for what it was intended (2 Cor. 8:20-21 with 1 Cor. 16:3).

This was a benevolence offering for the poor saints in Jerusalem.

6 (Rom. 15:27) Specifically, the carnal things Paul is referring to here is money.

7 (Rom. 15:29) What a statement! Paul had no doubt that he would be walking in the fullness of God. This reveals that walking in the power of the Holy Spirit is our choice.

Some people disagree with this and say you can't make the blessings of God occur. Their argument is that sometimes blessings happen and other times they don't, based on God's choosing; otherwise, it would be like us being able to turn God on and off.

The answer to this is that God is always on. We are the ones who are on and off. Anytime we choose life (Dt. 30:19), we can be assured that the life of God that was given us through Christ Jesus will flow. The responsibility rests on us to stir up the gift that is in us (2 Tim. 1:6).

8 (Rom. 15:30) This shows how important Paul thought prayer was. Paul begs these believers to intercede on his behalf.

9 (Rom. 15:31) Paul's prayer request was that he would be delivered from the religious unbelievers in Jerusalem. The answer to this prayer came in a way that many of us would not have liked. Instead of not having any problems, he was assaulted and wound up spending many years in prison. Yet, he was delivered from the unbelieving Jews. They tried to kill him three times (Acts 21:31; 23:20-21; 25:2-3), but the Lord delivered him through the Roman government.

10 (Rom. 15:31) Paul knew that trouble was waiting for him in Jerusalem. In Acts 20:22-23, Paul said he didn't know exactly what would happen to him in Jerusalem, but he knew it would be bonds and afflictions (see note 4 at Acts 21:4, p. 621).

ROMANS

PAUL SENDS GREETINGS

CHAPTER 16

I COMMEND[a] unto you Phebe[1] our sister,[b]
which is a servant[2c] of the church[2d] which is
at Cen´chre-a:[e]
2 That ye receive[f] her in the Lord, as
becometh saints,[g] and that ye assist[h] her in
whatsoever business she hath need of you:
for[3] she hath been a succourer[i] of many,
and of myself also.

3 Greet Priscilla[j] and Aq´ui-la[j] my
helpers[k] in Christ Jesus:[l]
4 *Who have for my life[4] laid down
their own necks:[m] unto whom not only I
give thanks,[n] but also all the churches[d] of
the Gentiles.[o]
5 Likewise *greet* the church[d] that is in
their house.[p] Salute[q] my wellbeloved E-
pæn´-e-tus,[5] who is the firstfruits[r] of A-
chai´a[s] unto Christ.
6 Greet Mary,[6] who bestowed much
labour on us.

PARALLEL SCRIPTURES FOR ROMANS 16:4

ROMANS 5:7

7 For scarcely for a righteous man will one die: yet peradventure for a good man some would even dare to die.

JOHN 15:13

13 Greater love hath no man than this, that a man lay down his life for his friends.

a 2 Cor. 3:1; 10:12
b Mt. 12:50; 1 Tim. 5:2
c see note 1 at Rom. 1:1, p. 655; see note 9 at Rom. 6:16, p. 692; see note 10 at Rom. 6:18, p. 692
d see note 1 at Acts 12:1, p. 570
e see note 1 at Acts 18:18, p. 606
f Rom. 15:7; Mt. 10:40-42; 25:40; Phil. 2:29; Col. 4:10; Phile. 12, 17; 2 Jn. 10; 3 Jn. 5-10
g see note 5 at Acts 9:13, p. 555; Rom. 1:7; 1 Cor. 1:2; Eph. 1:1; Phil. 1:1; Col. 1:2; Heb. 6:10
h Gk.-"paristemi"- to stand by to help; to succor; aid (Thayer)
i Dict.- one that affords assistance or relief; to render assistance to in time of distress; syn.- help- Rom. 16:3, 4, 6, 9; Phil. 4:14-19; 2 Tim. 1:18
j see note 2 at Acts 18:2, p. 604
k Gk.-"sunergos"- a companion in work; fellow-worker; adjutor (Thayer)- Rom. 16:9; 1 Cor. 16:16
l Eph. 1:1; Phil. 1:1; Col. 1:2; 1 Th. 2:14
m Gk.-"trachelos"- the throat (neck); i.e. (fig.) life- Phil. 2:30; 1 Jn. 3:16
n Col. 3:15; 1 Th. 5:18; see note 1 at Rom. 1:21, p. 660
o see note 45 at Mt. 6:32, p. 83
p Acts 20:20; 1 Cor. 16:19; Col. 4:15; Phile. 2
q Gk.-"aspazomai"- to enfold in the arms; i.e. (by impl.) to salute (fig.) to welcome; Trans. embrace; greet; salute; take leave
r 1 Cor. 16:15; Jas. 1:18; Rev. 14:4
s see note 11 at Acts 18:12, p. 605; Rom. 15:26; Acts 18:12, 27; 2 Cor. 1:1; 9:2

Footnotes for Romans 16:1-6

1 (Rom. 16:1) The only mention of Phebe in scripture is Romans 16:1-2 and the subscript in some Bibles at verse 27. From these passages we can see that Phebe was the one who delivered this epistle to the Romans. She had ministered to many, including Paul, and therefore Paul instructed the Romans to assist her in whatever way they could in her business.

Because the word "servant" in this verse has also been translated "deacon" in other scriptures (see note 2 at this verse, below), many believe that Phebe was actually a deaconess of the church in Cenchrea.

2 (Rom. 16:1) The Greek word that was translated "servant" here is the word "diakonos." This came from the root word "diako" meaning "to run errands." It specified an attendant, i.e. a waiter (at table or in other menial duties). "Diakonos" was specifically a Christian teacher and pastor (technically a deacon or deaconess) [W.E. Vine].

This word was used a total of 28 times in the New Testament. It was translated "deacons" three times (Phil. 1:1; 1 Tim. 3:8,12), "ministers" six times (1 Cor. 3:5; 2 Cor. 3:6; 6:4; 11:15, 23), "minister" fourteen times (Mt. 20:26; Mk. 10:43; Rom. 13:4; 15:8; Gal. 2:17; Eph. 3:7; 6:21; Col. 1:7, 23, 25; 4:7; 1 Th. 3:2; 1 Tim. 4:6), "servant" four times (Mt. 23:11; Mk. 9:35; Jn. 12:26; Rom. 16:1), and "servants" three times (Mt. 22:13; Jn. 2:5, 9).

So, it can be said that the dominant use of this word in the New Testament is to specify a minister or deacon. However, out of the six other times this word was translated "servant" or "servants," it was definitely designating a person who performs menial tasks as a slave. Therefore, it can not be stated emphatically from this verse that Phebe was or was not a deaconess or female minister.

History does supply us with information that there were female ministers in the churches of Bithynia (see note 5 at Acts 16:7, p. 592) as early as A.D. 100. Pliny wrote the emperor Trajan concerning the Christians and reported that he had examined "two old women who were called ministers" (Davis Dictionary of the Bible).

3 (Rom. 16:2) The archaic meaning of the word "for" was "because; since" (American Heritage Dictionary). Paul is saying that the reason they should assist Phebe is because she had assisted others, including Paul. This illustrates the law of reaping what you sow (Gal. 6:7; Lk. 6:38).

Some people become offended when they do not receive assistance from others, yet they have never helped anyone. That is not what Paul is advocating here. Phebe had earned their help. Salvation is by grace, but respect and help from others has to be earned.

4 (Rom. 16:4) Paul does not elaborate and the scriptures do not reveal a specific instance where Priscilla and Aquila *"laid down their own necks"* for Paul's sake. It is possible they were some of the disciples who restrained Paul from entering into the theatre in Ephesus during the uproar caused by Demetrius (Acts 19:28-41).

5 (Rom. 16:5) This is the only mention of Epaenetus in scripture. From this reference we can see that Epaenetus was loved very much by Paul. He was Paul's first convert in Achaia.

6 (Rom. 16:6) There are a number of Marys mentioned in scripture, implying that this was a common name. There is no reason to believe that this Mary in Rome is the same as some other Mary in scripture. This woman had bestowed much labor on Paul and his companions.

ROMANS

PAUL SENDS GREETINGS (continued)

CHAPTER 16

7 Salute An-dro-ni´cus[7] and Junia,[8] my
kinsmen,[9] and my fellowprisoners,[a] who
are of note[b] among the apostles,[c] who also
were in Christ before me.[d]
8 Greet[e] Am´pli-as[10] my beloved[11] in the
Lord.[f]
9 Salute[e] Ur´bane,[12] our helper[g] in
Christ,[h] and Sta´chys[13] my beloved.[i]
10 Salute[e] A-pel´les[14] approved[j] in
Christ. Salute[e] them which are of Ar-is-to-
bu´lus'[15] *household.*
11 Salute[e] He-ro´di-on[16] my kinsman[k]
Greet[e] them that be of the *household* of
Nar-cis´-sus,[17] which are in the Lord.[18f]
12 Salute[e] Try-phe´na[19] and Try-
pho´sa,[19] who labour[l] in the Lord.[f] Salute[e]
the beloved Per-sis,[20] which laboured[l] much
in the Lord.[f]

a my countrymen and once my fellowprisoners (TCNT)- Rom. 16:11, 21 2 Cor. 11:23 Col. 4:10 Phile. 23 Rev. 1:9
b Gal. 2:2, 6
c see note 2 at Lk. 6:13, p. 109 see note 3 at Acts 14:4, p. 581
d and who became Christians before I did (TCNT)
e same as ref. q at Rom. 16:5, p. 753
f see note 3 at Lk. 1:43, p. 12
g Gk.-"sunergos"- a companion in work; fellow-worker; adjutor (Thayer)- Rom. 16:3 1 Cor. 16:16
h Eph. 1:1 2:10 Phil. 1:1 4:21 Col. 1:2 1 Th. 2:14

i see note 11 at Rom. 16:8, this page
j Dict.- to express a favorable opinion of a person, thing, or action; or to signify satisfaction or acceptance
k see note 9 at Rom. 16:7, this page
l Gk.-"kopiao"- to feel fatigue; by impl. to work hard Trans. (bestow) labour; toil; be wearied- Mt. 9:38 1 Cor. 15:10, 58 16:16 Col. 1:29 4:12 1 Th. 1:3 5:12-13 1 Tim. 4:10 5:17-18 Heb. 6:10-11

Footnotes for Romans 16:7-12

7 (Rom. 16:7) The name Andronicus meant "conquering men." This is the only mention of Andronicus in scripture. He and Junia were two of six relatives (see note 9 at this verse, below) Paul mentions in this chapter. He had been imprisoned, presumably for his faith in Christ. Paul said he was "of note" among the apostles. That probably meant Andronicus and Junia were well known, even to the apostles.

Andronicus and Junia were Christians before Paul's conversion. It is very possible that they witnessed to Paul and this may have been part of the "pricks" Paul was fighting against at his conversion (see note 6 at Acts 9:5, p. 553). Since Junia (see note 8 at this verse, below) was a feminine name, it is possible that Andronicus and Junia were married.

8 (Rom. 16:7) This is the only mention of Junia in scripture. The fact that Andronicus and Junia were both imprisoned, both in Christ before Paul, and both Paul's relatives suggests that they were close, possibly man and wife.

They were both "of note" among the apostles, probably meaning that they were well known, even to the apostles. Junia and Andronicus were apparently living in Rome.

9 (Rom. 16:7) The Greek word used for "kinsmen" here is "suggenes" and means "a relative (by blood); by extension, a fellow countryman" (W.E. Vine). In Romans 9:3, Paul used this word to refer to all of the Jews as his countrymen. Therefore, it is not certain whether Paul is using this word to denote blood relatives or fellow Jews. The fact that more of these people were Jews than what Paul designated by the term "kinsmen" would suggest that he was speaking of blood relatives.

There are six (depending on how you interpret v. 21) kinsmen of Paul's referred to in this chapter. These are Andronicus, Junia (this verse), Herodion (v. 11), Lucius, Jason, and Sosipater (v. 21).

It is possible that Tertius is the one speaking in verse 21, and therefore Lucius, Jason, and Sosipater would be his kinsmen (see note 4 at Rom. 16:21, p. 758).

10 (Rom. 16:8) This is the only time Amplias is mentioned in scripture. He was a Christian in Rome to whom Paul sent greetings. His name meant "enlarged."

11 (Rom. 16:8) The Greek word that was translated "beloved" here is "agapetos," the adjective form of "agape" (see note 3 at Rom. 12:10, p. 734). It is signifying the type of love that God has. Paul said Amplias was *"beloved in the Lord"* meaning this was God's love being expressed through Paul.

12 (Rom. 16:9) The name "Urbane" meant "polite." This is the only mention of Urbane in scripture. He had been a companion in work (see ref. g at this verse) with Paul.

13 (Rom. 16:9) The name "Stachys" meant "an ear of grain." This is the only mention of Stachys in scripture.

14 (Rom. 16:10) This is the only mention of Apelles in scripture.

15 (Rom. 16:10) The name "Aristobulus" meant "best counselor." This is the only mention of Aristobulus in scripture.

16 (Rom. 16:11) The name "Herodion" came from the Greek word "Herodes" meaning "hero." This was the name of a number of kings of Palestine (see note 3 at Lk. 3:1, p. 31) and it is possible that Herodion was named after one of the kings named Herod. If so, that would most likely make Herodion a Gentile since it would be very unusual for a Jew to name a child in honor of Herod.

Herodion is the third person Paul mentions in this chapter as being his kinsman (see note 9 at v. 7, above). If Herodion was a Gentile, as his name could imply, then Paul would have to be referring to him as a brother in the Lord and not a natural blood relative.

17 (Rom. 16:11) The name "Narcissus" came from the flower narcissus or the daffodil. This is the only mention of Narcissus in scripture.

18 (Rom. 16:11) This term *"in the Lord"* is referring to the members of Narcissus' household who had been born again through faith in Christ. This is a very appropriate and descriptive term since all believers are in Christ Jesus (2 Cor. 5:17; Col. 2:10).

19 (Rom. 16:12) Tryphena (delicate, dainty) and Tryphosa (delicate) were women at Rome that Paul saluted and commended for their labor in the Lord.

20 (Rom. 16:12) The name "Persis" meant "Persian." He was a Christian at Rome whom Paul greeted. Paul mentioned he laboured much in the Lord. This is the only mention of Persis in scripture.

ROMANS

PAUL SENDS GREETINGS (continued)

m Mk. 15:21
n see note 3 at Mt. 20:16, p. 335
see note 1 at Lk. 22:22, p. 421
see note 2 at Rom. 8:29, p. 709
see note 3 at Rom. 9:11, p. 712
o Mt. 12:49-50
Mk. 3:35
Jn. 19:27
1 Tim. 5:2
p Rom. 8:29
Col. 1:2
Heb. 3:1
1 Pet. 1:22
see note 1 at Rom. 7:1, p. 694

CHAPTER 16

13 Salute Rufus[21m] chosen[n] in the Lord,
and his mother[22o] and mine.
14 Salute A-syn´cri-tus,[23] Phle´gon,[23]
Her´mas,[23] Pat´ro-bas,[23] Her´mas,[23] and the
brethren[p] which are with them.
15 Salute Phi-lol´o-gus,[24] and Julia,[25]
Ne´re-us,[26] and his sister, and O-lym´pas,[27]
and all the saints[q] which are with them.[28]
16 *Salute one another with an holy[29]
kiss.[r] The churches[s] of Christ salute you.

q see note 5 at Acts 9:13, p. 555
see note 35 at Jn. 14:26, p. 434
Rom. 1:7
1 Cor. 1:2
Eph. 1:1
Phil. 1:1
Col. 1:2
Heb. 6:10
r 1 Cor. 16:20
2 Cor. 13:12
1 Th. 5:26
s Gk.-"ekklesia"- a calling out; i.e. a popular meeting; esp. a religious congregation (Jewish synagogue, or Christian community of members on earth or saints in heaven or both)
see note 1 at Acts 12:1, p. 570
Rom. 16:4

PARALLEL SCRIPTURES FOR ROMANS 16:16

ACTS 20:37

37 And they all wept sore, and fell on Paul's neck, and kissed him,

1 PETER 5:14

14 Greet ye one another with a kiss of charity. Peace be *with you all that are in Christ Jesus. Amen.*

Footnotes for Romans 16:13-16

21 (Rom. 16:13) The name "Rufus" meant "red." The name Rufus is mentioned twice in scripture (Mk. 15:21; Rom. 16:13). It is unclear whether this is the same Rufus in both instances. If so, then this Rufus whom Paul sent greetings to in Rome would have been the son of Simon of Cyrene, who was compelled to bear the cross of Jesus. Paul also sent greetings to the mother of Rufus (see note 22 at this verse, below).

22 (Rom. 16:13) Paul greeted the mother of Rufus and called her his own mother. It is unclear whether this is figurative or literal. Most commentators suspect this was a figurative statement, as is the case elsewhere in scripture (see ref. o at this verse).

23 (Rom. 16:14) Asyncritus (incomparable or unlike), Phlegon (burning, scorching), Hermas (variation of Hermes, a Greek deity), Patrobas (father's life), and Hermes (this was the same name as the Greek god that corresponded to the Roman Mercury) were Christians in Rome to whom Paul sent greetings. This is the only mention of these individuals in scripture.

24 (Rom. 16:15) The name "Philologus" meant "fond of words." The wording of this verse suggest that Philologus was the husband of Julia (see note 25 at this verse, below). This is the only mention of Philologus in scripture.

25 (Rom. 16:15) The name "Julia" was the feminine form of the Latin "Julius" as in Julius Caesar. Because of the wording of this verse, many people believe Julia was the wife of Philologus (see note 24 at this verse, above). This is the only mention of Julia in scripture.

26 (Rom. 16:15) The name "Nereus" came from the sea god who, under Poseidon or Neptune, ruled the Mediterranean Sea. This was the name of a Christian in Rome to whom Paul sent greetings. Paul also greets Nereus' sister in this verse who is not named. This is the only mention of Nereus in scripture.

27 (Rom. 16:15) The name "Olympas" meant "excess of wine." This was the name of a Christian in Rome whom Paul greeted. This is the only mention of Olympas in scripture.

28 (Rom. 16:15) This is the second consecutive scripture in which Paul greeted a group of people and the brethren or saints which were with them. This is probably referring to a local group of believers who regularly met in the households of these people. This would have made those who were mentioned in these verses leaders of those local bodies of believers.

29 (Rom. 16:16) This is one of five times in scripture where we are exhorted to greet other believers with a holy kiss or a kiss of charity (see ref. r at this verse).

The culture of Paul's day used a kiss as a greeting, just as we still see in the Arab cultures of today. However, Paul's repeated use of this custom in his instructions to the believers would suggest that he advocated it as a Christian custom. It is certain that Christians have more reason to greet one another with a kiss than anyone else.

It needs to be noted that in each reference to this, there is a specific mention of this being a holy kiss or kiss of charity. That qualifies the manner in which this is to be done. This certainly is not an opportunity for someone to exercise his lusts. This should be motivated only by the holiest Christian love for a fellow believer.

If this kiss of charity is misunderstood or not wanted by the person receiving it, then it would certainly be inappropriate to give it.

ROMANS

WARNING CONCERNING DIVISIONS AND OFFENSES

CHAPTER 16

17 *Now I beseech[a] you, brethren, mark[1]
them which cause divisions[b] and offences[c]
contrary to the doctrine[d] which ye have
learned; and avoid[e] them.
18 *For they that are such[2] serve[f] not our
Lord[g] Jesus Christ, but their own belly;[h]
and by good words and fair speeches
deceive[i] the hearts[j] of the simple.[3]

PARALLEL SCRIPTURES FOR ROMANS 16:17-18

PHILIPPIANS 3:17-19

17 Brethren, be followers together of me, and mark them which walk so as ye have us for an ensample.

18 (For many walk, of whom I have told you often, and now tell you even weeping, that they are *the enemies of the cross of Christ:*

19 Whose end is *destruction, whose God* is their *belly, and* whose *glory* is *in their shame, who mind earthly things.)*

a Dict.- to address an earnest or urgent request; to implore
b Acts 15:1-5, 24; 1 Cor. 1:10-13; 3:3; 11:18; Gal. 1:7-9; 2:4; Phil. 3:2-3; Col. 2:8; 2 Pet. 2:1-2; 1 Jn. 2:19; 2 Jn. 7-10; Jude 19
c Gk.-"skandalon"- a trapstick; i.e. snare (fig. cause of displeasure or sin)- Mt. 18:7; Lk. 17:1
d Gk.-"didache"- instruction (the act or the matter)- Jn. 7:16-17; Acts 2:42; 13:12; Rom. 6:17; Eph. 4:14; 1 Tim. 1:3, 10; 6:1; 2 Tim. 3:10, 16; Ti. 2:1, 7, 10
e Gk.-"ekklino"- to turn aside; deviate; to turn (one's self) away; keep aloof from; to shun one (Thayer)
f Gk.-"douleuo"- to be a slave; serve; do service; to obey; submit to; to yield to; give one's self up to (Thayer); see notes 1-2 at Rom. 1:1, p. 655; see note 21 at Jn. 5:43, p. 100; see note 3 at Lk. 22:27, p. 426; Mt. 6:24; Jn. 12:26; Gal. 1:10; Phil. 2:21; Jas. 1:1; Jude 1; Rev. 1:1
g see note 3 at Lk. 1:43, p. 12
h 1 Sam. 2:12-17, & 29; Mt. 24:48-51; Jude 12
i Mt. 7:15; 24:11, 24; 2 Cor. 2:17; 4:2; 11:13-15; Col. 2:4; 2 Th. 2:10; 1 Tim. 6:5; 2 Tim. 2:16-18; 3:2-6; Ti. 1:10-12; 2 Pet. 2:3, 18-20; 1 Jn. 4:1; Jude 16
j see note 3 at Mt. 12:34, p. 131; see note 14 at Rom. 4:21, p. 680

Footnotes for Romans 16:17-18

1 (Rom. 16:17) This is one of many times that Paul makes a very clear statement about withdrawing from individuals who are causing problems in the church (1 Cor. 5:9-11; Phil. 3:17; 2 Th. 3:6, 14-15; 1 Tim. 6:3-5; 2 Tim. 2:16-17; 3:5; 1 Jn. 2:19; Ti. 3:9-10). We also have an example of Paul separating the true believers from the false and meeting in a separate place in Acts 19:9. These are scriptural precedents for separation based on doctrine.

However, Paul did not say to avoid contact with people who simply had different doctrine. He said to avoid those who caused division and offenses over doctrine. Some people have doctrines that disagree with the Word, but they aren't disagreeable. These people can be loved and restored. But the person who is causing dissension over doctrine is to be treated as contaminated and infectious.

One example of this that Paul used in this epistle would be the matter of observing dietary laws. Paul made it clear that there was nothing wrong with any food (see note 12 at Rom. 14:14, p. 746), but it would be sin for an individual to eat certain foods if he wasn't eating in faith (Rom. 14:23). Therefore, there can be differences of doctrines, but Paul told those that were strong in grace to bear with those who were not. However, if the weak brother became contentious over his doctrine of abstinence from certain meats and began to condemn others (see note 3 at Rom. 14:1, p. 743), Paul would say to mark that man and avoid him.

The first thing Paul said to do was to mark these people. The Greek word that was translated "mark," is the word "skopeo," meaning "to take aim at (spy)" or figuratively, "regard." In modern-day terms, we should "keep an eye" on these people. They are not to be trusted and should not be given the freedom to move about freely among the believers and spread the infection.

The way we choose who is to be marked is based on the doctrine of God's Word. There are those who are indifferent to or don't believe the Word of God, but they aren't out to oppose it. Those we simply love and continue to share the Word with, praying for their eyes to be opened. However, those who actively seek to subvert others from following the doctrine of God's Word are the ones to mark. Paul gives some characteristics of these people in verse 18.

Marking these individuals falls into the category of church discipline and should be done consistently with all those instructions (see note 5 at Mt. 18:17, p. 218).

2 (Rom. 16:18) In this verse, Paul gives us some characteristics of the people he said to mark in the previous verse. These people are not truly serving the Lord Jesus Christ; they are serving themselves. That's what this terminology *"their own belly"* means.

This same description is used in the parallel account of Paul on this same subject in Philippians 3:19 (see Parallel Scriptures, this page). There Paul says that their god is their belly. This is saying that their motive is not the selfless motive of love for God and others, but rather they are motivated by a love for themselves. This is always at the root of all division (see note note 6 at Mk. 15:10, p. 465; see note 4 at Lk. 10:20, p. 251). Philippians 3:19 gives the further explanation that these people glory in their shame and mind earthly things.

Paul says in this verse that these individuals use good words and fair speeches and deceive the hearts of the simple. This means that they flatter people (2 Tim. 4:3) and appeal to the same selfish desires that they themselves have, to draw people after themselves (Acts 20:30).

3 (Rom. 16:18) Paul says that the simple are the ones who are deceived by these sowers of strife. If we will quit being simple, we won't be deceived.

What did Paul mean by "simple"? The Greek word that was translated "simple" in this verse is "akakos." It was only used twice in the New Testament (here; Heb. 7:26). In Hebrew 7:26 it was translated "harmless," meaning "without guile or fraud; harmless; free from guilt" (Thayer).

In this verse, the meaning of this word is "fearing no evil from others, distrusting no one" (Thayer). This is describing those who we today would call "gullible" (Prov. 14:15). Only those who lack discernment between good and evil will fall prey to this deceit.

How do we quit being simple or gullible? It's through God's Word. Many scriptures promise that God's Word will cause the simple to start being wise (Ps. 19:7; 119:130; Prov. 1:4). A good understanding of God's Word is the greatest defense against deception (Jn. 8:32; 17:17).

The English word "simple" is only used twice in the New Testament (here and Rom. 16:19; see note 4 at v. 19, p. 757).

ROMANS

WARNING CONCERNING DIVISIONS AND OFFENSES (cont'd)

k Rom. 1:8
1 Th. 1:8-9
l Eph. 1:15-17
Col. 1:3-9
1 Th. 1:2-3
3:6-10
m 1 Cor. 14:20
Eph. 5:17
Phil. 1:9
Col. 1:9
2 Tim. 3:15-17
Jas. 3:13-18
n Rom. 15:33
1 Cor. 14:33
2 Cor. 13:11
Phil. 4:9
1 Th. 5:23
2 Th. 3:16
Heb. 13:20
see note 38 at
Jn. 14:27, p. 434
see note 39 at
Jn. 14:27, p. 434
see note 90 at
Jn. 16:33, p. 442
see note 2 at
Lk. 24:38, p. 496
see note 2 at
Rom. 5:1, p. 681

CHAPTER 16

19 *For your obedience is come abroad unto all *men.*[k] I am glad therefore on your behalf:[l] but yet I would have you wise unto that which is good, and simple[4] concerning evil.[5m]

20 And the God of peace[n] shall bruise[o] Satan[p] under your feet shortly. The grace[q] of our Lord[g] Jesus Christ *be* with you. Amen.[6r]

o i.e. bruise or tread-
Job 40:12
Isa. 63:3
Lk. 10:19
p Gk.-"Satanas"- the accuser; i.e. the devil-
Rev. 12:10
q see note 5 at
Rom. 1:5, p. 655
see note 8 at
Rom. 3:24, p. 673
see note 15 at
Rom. 5:8, p. 683
Rom. 1:5
12:3, 6
1 Cor. 3:10
15:10
Gal. 1:15-16
2:9
Eph. 3:7-8
1 Tim. 1:11-14
1 Pet. 4:10
r Rom. 16:24
2 Cor. 13:14
Gal. 6:18
Phil. 4:23
1 Th. 5:28
2 Th. 3:18
2 Tim. 4:22
Phile. 25
Rev. 22:21

PARALLEL SCRIPTURE FOR ROMANS 16:19

1 KINGS 3:9-12

9 Give therefore thy servant an understanding heart to judge thy people, that I may discern between good and bad: for who is able to judge this thy so great a people?

10 And the speech pleased the Lord, that Solomon had asked this thing.

11 And God said unto him, Because thou hast asked this thing, and hast not asked for thyself long life; neither hast asked riches for thyself, nor hast asked the life of thine enemies; but hast asked for thyself understanding to discern judgment;

12 Behold, I have done according to thy words: lo, I have given thee a wise and an understanding heart; so that there was none like thee before thee, neither after thee shall any arise like unto thee.

Footnotes for Romans 16:19-20

4 (Rom. 16:19) This is the second and last time that the English word "simple" was used in the New Testament. The first time was in the previous verse. However, this one English word came from two different Greek words. The Greek word that was used in verse 18 was "akakos" (see note 3 at v. 18, p. 756), while the Greek word that was used in this verse is "akeraios" meaning "(1) unmixed; pure as in wines or metals; (2) without a mixture of evil; free from guile; innocent; simple" (Thayer).

Therefore, when Paul presented being simple in verse 18 as something that is not good, and simple in verse 19 as something that is good, he was speaking of two different things. Verse 18 is speaking against being gullible, while verse 19 is speaking in favor of being pure, focused only on things that are good (see note 5 at this verse, below).

5 (Rom. 16:19) This is a wonderful key that the Lord is giving us for living the Christian life and yet very few people use it. It goes contrary to the modern thought that all knowledge is good, even the knowledge of evil.

Satan used Eve's desire to know about evil to entice her to sin (Gen. 3:5-6). All she knew was good, but Satan convinced her she would be better off if she knew about evil. That definitely was not the case.

God never intended for us to know about evil. That's the reason He forbade Adam and Eve to eat of the tree of the knowledge of good and evil. **You cannot be tempted with things that you don't think about** (see note 7 at Rom. 12:2, p. 730; see notes 10-12 at Rom. 8:4-5, p. 701; see note 9 at Rom. 12:2, p. 730). **Therefore, don't think about evil things and you will not be tempted with them.**

Of course, since the fall of man, evil is in the world and there needs to be some knowledge about evil so we can avoid its pitfalls. Paul said, *"we are not ignorant of his devices"* (2 Cor. 2:11). Notice that Paul said we should be "simple," not "ignorant." But most people are indulging in a knowledge of evil that is far beyond what Paul was advocating.

Paul also said, *"For it is a shame even to speak of those things which are done of them in secret"* (Eph. 5:12). Yet many Christians feel it is necessary and beneficial to plumb the depths of the moral debauchery in our world today. That is not so.

We don't have to know **all** about Satanism and what his followers are doing to avoid that pitfall and help those who have already fallen in it. A person who is seeking God with his whole heart and thinking on all the good He has to offer, will never fall prey to Satanism. That individual will also have the wisdom of God to deliver anyone who has become possessed by that spirit. The best defense is a good offense.

Bank tellers don't become astute at recognizing counterfeit money by studying counterfeit bills. It would be impossible to school them on all the possible variations they could encounter. Instead, they become so familiar with the genuine that they recognize a fake.

Likewise, Christians should be wise concerning that which is good and simple (or unmixed, separated from—see note 4 at this verse, above) concerning evil. **Undue attention to what Satan is doing will actually give the enemy inroads into our lives.**

6 (Rom. 16:20) The word "amen" does not mean "the end," as so many people use it in prayer. It means "trustworthy, surely, or so be it." It was used 78 times in the Bible; 56 of those times were in the New Testament.

ROMANS

FINAL GREETING AND BENEDICTION

a see note 1 at Acts 16:1, p. 591

CHAPTER 16

21 *Ti-mo´the-us[a] my workfellow,[b] and
Lucius,[1] and Jason,[2] and So-sip´a-ter,[3] my
kinsmen,[4] salute you.[5]
22 I Ter´tius,[6] who wrote *this* epistle,
salute you in the Lord.[c]

b i.e. fellow worker
c Col. 3:17

PARALLEL SCRIPTURE FOR ROMANS 16:21

ACTS 16:1

THEN *came he to Derbe and Lystra: and, behold, a certain disciple was there, named Timotheus, the son of a certain woman, which was a Jewess, and believed; but his father* was *a Greek:*

Footnotes for Romans 16:21-22

1 (Rom. 16:21) The name "Lucius" meant "illuminative." This name is used twice in scripture (here and Acts 13:1). He is referred to as a kinsman of the apostle Paul (see note 9 at Rom. 16:7, p. 754), or possibly Tertius (see note 4 at this verse, below).

It is unclear whether this is the same Lucius that was mentioned in Acts 13:1. If so, Lucius would have been a long-time associate of Paul and would either be a prophet or a teacher.

Some people suspect that this Lucius is the Luke who traveled with the apostle Paul (see note 2 at Acts 16:10, p. 593) and wrote the books of Luke and Acts (see About the Author in Introduction to the Acts of the Apostles, p. x).

2 (Rom. 16:21) The name "Jason" meant "healing." Jason was a kinsman (see note 9 at Rom. 16:7, p. 754) of the apostle Paul or possibly Tertius (see note 4 at this verse, below).

The name Jason is used five times in scripture. Four of these times are from an account in Acts 17 (Acts 17:5, 6, 7, 9). It is not certain that the Jason mentioned here is the same as the Jason mentioned in Acts 17, but it probably is.

If this is the same Jason as the Jason of Acts 17, then this Jason had been an acquaintance of Paul since Paul first went to Thessalonica (Acts 17:1). This would make it hard to understand Jason as being a kinsman of Paul in the sense of a blood relative. This must be referring to these men as being brothers in the Lord, or possibly, these men were Tertius' relatives (see note 4 at this verse, below).

Jason apparently took Paul and his companions into his household. Because of this, the unbelieving Jews assaulted the house of Jason, and when they didn't find Paul they took Jason into custody.

3 (Rom. 16:21) The name "Sosipater" meant "savior of his father." He is called a kinsman of Paul, or possibly it was Tertius who referred to him as a kinsman (see note 4 at this verse, below).

Most scholars believe that Sosipater is the same man as Sopater of Acts 20:4. If so, this would mean that he was from Berea and was probably a convert of Paul's missionary work there (see note 3 at Acts 20:4, p. 614).

4 (Rom. 16:21) In note 9 at Romans 16:7, page 754, the word "kinsman" has been defined and its normal usage discussed. However, this verse seems to present a problem with the word "kinsman" denoting either a blood relative or a fellow countryman.

There are quite a few scriptures where Paul writes of Timotheus, and nowhere else is it implied that Timothy is related to Paul (see note 1 at Acts 16:1, p. 591). Therefore, most scholars exclude Timothy and believe that Lucius, Jason, and Sosipater are the ones being referred to as kinsmen.

However, if these men were the same men as mentioned in Acts (see notes 1-3 at this verse, above), then it would appear that they were converts of the apostle Paul during his second missionary journey. This would make it doubtful that they were blood relatives as the primary usage of the word "kinsman" would imply.

This could mean that these men were kinsmen in the sense of fellow countrymen. This would mean that these men were of Jewish descent, living in these Gentile cities. There is also the possibility that Paul was referring to them as kinsmen in the sense that they were brothers in Christ.

There is also the possibility that Paul had ceased his comments in the previous verse and that Tertius, the writer of Romans was speaking of these men as his kinsmen.

5 (Rom. 16:21) Whether these men were Paul's kinsmen or Tertius' kinsmen, they were definitely Paul's converts and companions in the ministry. This gives us some insight into Paul's methods.

If these men were the same men as listed in the book of Acts, then they were born again during Paul's second missionary journey (see note 1 at Acts 18:22, p. 607). This means that these men were converted around A.D. 52 and Paul is writing this letter to the Romans around A.D. 57-58 (see Date and Place of Writing in Introduction to the Book of Romans, p. iv).

That means Paul had been discipling these men for approximately five years. Therefore, we have an example of how long it took for Timothy to progress into a position of leadership. Paul is the one who wrote that a novice should not be given a position of authority (1 Tim. 3:6). Timothy was to be left in charge of the church at Ephesus (1 Tim. 1:3) in just a very short time from the writing of this letter, as Paul traveled towards Jerusalem. Some scholars speculate that the church at Ephesus could have had as many as 100,000 members.

6 (Rom. 16:22) The name "Tertius" was of Latin origin and meant "third." This is the only mention of Tertius in scripture. He actually wrote the book of Romans from the apostle Paul's dictation.

ROMANS

FINAL GREETING AND BENEDICTION (continued)

CHAPTER 16

23 Gaius[7] mine host, and of the whole
church,[d] saluteth you. E-ras´tus[8] the
chamberlain[9] of the city saluteth you, and
Quartus[10] a brother.
24 The grace[e] of our Lord[f] Jesus Christ
be with you all. Amen.[g]
25 *Now to him that is of power to
stablish[h] you according to my gospel,[i] and
the preaching[j] of Jesus Christ, according to
the revelation of the mystery,[k] which was
kept secret since the world began,[l]
26 But now is made manifest,[m] and by
the scriptures of the prophets,[n] according
to the commandment of the everlasting
God,[o] made known to all nations for the
obedience of faith:[p]
27 To God only wise,[q] *be* glory through
Jesus Christ for ever. Amen.¶

¶ *Written to the Romans from Corinthus, and sent by Phebe, servant of the church at Cenchrea.*[11]

PARALLEL SCRIPTURES FOR ROMANS 16:25

EPHESIANS 1:9

9 Having made known unto us the mystery of his will, according to his good pleasure which he hath purposed in himself:

COLOSSIANS 1:26-27

26 Even *the mystery which hath been hid from ages and from generations, but now is made manifest to his saints:*
27 To whom God would make known what is the riches of the glory of this mystery among the Gentiles; which is Christ in you, the hope of glory:

Footnotes for Romans 16:23-27

7 (Rom. 16:23) The name Gaius was a common Roman name. This name is used five times in scripture (Acts 19:29; 20:4; here; 1 Cor. 1:14; 3 Jn. 1) and refers to at least three different men.

Acts 19:29 refers to Gaius as being a man of Macedonia (see note 1 at Acts 16:9, p. 593) while Acts 20:4 refers to a Gaius who was of Derbe (see note 5 at Acts 14:6, p. 581), a city of Asia (see note 3 at Acts 16:6, p. 592).

It is probable that the Gaius referred to here is the same man that Paul mentioned in 1 Corinthians 1:14, since the book of Romans was written from Corinth (see Date and Place of Writing in Introduction to the Book of Romans, p. iv). This would make Gaius one of the few people in Corinth that Paul actually baptized. This verse says that Gaius was not only Paul's host, but host of the whole church, implying that he had a house church meeting in his residence.

The apostle John addressed the epistle of 3 John to Gaius. Some speculate that this is the same Gaius that Paul is referring to here.

8 (Rom. 16:23) The name "Erastus" is mentioned three times in scripture (Acts 19:22; here; 2 Tim. 4:20). "Erastus" meant "beloved."

Most scholars agree that this is the same Erastus that Paul sent with Timothy into Macedonia (see note 1 at Acts 16:9, p. 593) while Paul remained in Ephesus (see note 3 at Acts 18:19, p. 606). Paul later wrote to Timothy that Erastus abode in Corinth (2 Tim. 4:20), while this verse reveals that he was the chamberlain of that city (see note 9 at this verse, below).

9 (Rom. 16:23) The word "chamberlain" is only used six times in the Bible (2 Ki. 23:11; Est. 2:3, 14, 15; Acts 12:20; and here). Of the two times this word is used in the New Testament, Acts 12:20 uses "chamberlain" in the sense of an eunuch who keeps the king's bedchamber. In this verse, "chamberlain" was referring to Erastus being the treasurer of the city of Corinth.

10 (Rom. 16:23) The name "Quartus" meant "fourth." This is the only mention of Quartus in scripture. He was a Christian brother in Corinth who sent greetings to the saints in Rome.

11 (Rom. 16:27) This subscript was probably not a part of Paul's original letter to the Romans. It was added at a later date by some scribe. However, it does seem to be accurate and is therefore retained.

d see note 1 at Acts 12:1, p. 570; see note 4 at Mt. 16:18, p. 203
e see note 5 at Rom. 1:5, p. 655; see note 8 at Rom. 3:24, p. 673; see note 15 at Rom. 5:8, p. 683; Rom. 1:5; 12:3, 6; 1 Cor. 3:10; 15:10; Gal. 1:15-16; 2:9; Eph. 3:7-8; 1 Tim. 1:11-14; 1 Pet. 4:10
f see note 3 at Lk. 1:43, p. 12
g see note 6 at Rom. 16:20, p. 757
h variant of establish
i see note 7 at Mt. 24:14, p. 396; see note 3 at Acts 8:4, p. 544; see note 2 at Acts 8:12, p. 546; see note 5 at Acts 20:24, p. 618; see note 3 at Acts 28:28, p. 653; see note 3 at Rom. 1:2, p. 655; see note 1 at Rom. 1:16, p. 658; see note 10 at Rom. 2:16, p. 665; see note 1 at Rom. 10:14, p. 722; see note 3 at Rom. 10:15, p. 723; Rom. 2:16; 2 Cor. 4:3; Gal. 2:2; 2 Th. 2:14; 2 Tim. 2:8

j see note 3 at Mt. 5:2, p. 73; see note 2 at Acts 8:5, p. 545; see note 3 at Acts 8:6, p. 545; see note 2 at Acts 14:4, p. 581; see note 2 at Acts 20:7, p. 615; Acts 9:20; 1 Cor. 1:23; 2 Cor. 4:5
k 1 Cor. 2:7
l Dan. 2:22; Amos 3:7; Mt. 13:17, 35; Lk. 10:23-24; Eph. 3:3-5, 9, 11; 1 Pet. 1:10-12, 20
m Gk.-"phaneroo"-to render apparent-; Col. 1:26; 2 Tim. 1:10; Ti. 1:2-3
n see note 2 at Lk. 7:26, p. 121; see note 1 at Acts 11:27, p. 569; Rom. 1:2; 3:21; 15:4; Acts 8:32-35; 10:43; 26:22-23; Gal. 3:8; Eph. 2:20; Rev. 19:10
o Mt. 28:19-20; Mk. 16:15; Lk. 24:44-47; Acts 13:46-47; 26:17-18
p Rom. 1:5; 15:18; Acts 6:7
q Rom. 11:33-34; Ps. 147:5; Col. 2:2-3; Jude 25

LIFE FOR TODAY

Study Bible and Commentary

ROMANS EDITION

SUPPLEMENTAL
STUDY AIDS

Conversion Chart S1

Footnote Index F1

Page Conversion Chart

The *Life For Today* Program was originally in three-ring binders with looseleaf pages. This chart will help you convert the old looseleaf pages to the new hardbound Romans pages. Use this chart to find corresponding page numbers referred to on tapes and looseleaf pages. To use: (1) locate the page number referred to on tape or pages; (2) locate this page number under the "Old Page Number" column; and (3) the number(s) directly across from the old page number is/are the corresponding page number(s) in the *Life for Today* Study Bible and Commentary - Romans Edition.

OLD PAGE #	NEW PAGE #	OLD PAGE #	NEW PAGE #	OLD PAGE #	NEW PAGE #	OLD PAGE #	NEW PAGE #
740	655	771	683,684,685	802	708,709	833	738,739
741	656,657	772	683,684,685	803	709,710	834	738,739
742	656,657	773	685,686	804	710	835	740,741
743	658,659	774	685,686,687	805	711,712	836	740,741
744	658,659	775	687,688	806	711,712	837	742,743
745	660,661	776	687,688	807	713,714	838	742,743
746	660,661	777	688,689	808	713,714	839	744,745
747	662	778	689	809	715,716	840	744,745
748	662,663	779	690,691	810	715,716	841	746,747
749	663,664,665	780	690,691	811	717,718,719	842	746,747
750	663,664,665	781	691,692	812	717,718,719	843	748
751	665,666,667	782	691,692	813	719,720,721	844	749
752	666,667	783	693,694	814	720,721	845	750,751
753	667,668	784	693,694	815	721,722,723	846	750,751,752
754	667,668	785	694,695	816	721,722,723	847	752
755	669,670	786	694,695	817	723,724,725	848	753
756	669,670	787	696,697	818	723,724	849	754
757	670,671,672	788	696,697	819	725,726	850	755
758	670,671,672	789	698,699	820	725,726	851	756
759	672,673	790	698,699	821	726,727	852	757
760	673,674	791	699,700	822	726,727	853	758
761	674,675,676	792	699,700	823	728,729	854	759
762	675,676	793	701,702	824	728,729		
763	676,677,678	794	701,702	825	729,730,731		
764	677,678	795	702,703,704	826	730,731		
765	678,679,680	796	703,704	827	732,733		
766	679,680	797	704,705	828	732,733		
767	680,681	798	704,705	829	734,735		
768	680,681	799	706,707	830	734,735		
769	682,683	800	706,707	831	735,736,737		
770	682,683	801	707,708,709	832	735,736,737		

Footnote Index

(Footnotes indexed by subject to aid in topical studies)

Footnote Index

ABRAHAM
God counted his faith for righteousness 13 years before his circumcision;
see note 3 at Rom. 4:3, p. 675;
see note 2 at Rom. 4:10, p. 677
had faith before action of circumcision;
see note 5 at Rom. 4:12, p. 677
heir of the world; true seed those who put faith in Christ; see note 1 at Rom. 4:13, p. 678
his faith pleased God, not his actions;
see note 5 at Rom. 4:3, p. 675
justified by faith; God will do the same for us;
see note 15 at Rom. 4:23, p. 680
spiritual offspring of; blessing of Abraham based solely on grace; see note 2 at Rom. 9:8, p. 712

ABRAHAM'S SEED
includes more than his physical descendants;
see note 1 at Rom 4:13, p. 678;
see note 5 at Rom. 4:16, p. 678
spiritual offspring; blessing of Abraham based solely on grace; see note 2 at Rom. 9:8, p. 712

ABSTINENCE FROM MEATS
doing as unto the Lord isn't legalistic;
see note 9 at Rom. 14:6, p. 744
offered to idols is not optional; abstain because of effect on weaker brother's conscience;
see note 16 at Rom. 14:21, p. 747

ACCESS
defined as admission; faith is our admission into the grace of God; see note 3 at Rom. 5:2, p. 681

ACCOUNTABILITY
everyone is accountable to God; don't judge brothers; see note 10 at Rom. 14:11, p. 746

ACCUSATIONS
of others, should not bother us;
see note 6 at Rom. 8:33, p. 709

ACTIONS
an indication of our inner faith; judgments based on actions are for discernment, not condemnation;
see note 9 at Rom. 4:5, p. 675
indicate the condition of our hearts;
see note 14 at Rom. 14:17, p. 747

ADOPTION
sons by; Jesus is son by nature;
see note 32 at Rom. 8:15, p. 704

AFTER
the flesh or Spirit, as opposed to being "in" either one; see note 20 at Rom. 8:9, p. 703

AMEN
see note 6 at Rom. 16:20, p. 757

AMPLIAS
a Christian in Rome to whom Paul sent greetings;
see note 10 at Rom. 16:8, p. 754

ANDRONICUS & JUNIA
relatives of Paul; see note 7 & 8 at Rom. 16:7, p. 754

APELLES
see note 14 at Rom. 16:10, p. 754

AQUILA & PRISCILLA
laid down their own necks for Paul;
see note 4 at Rom. 16:4, p. 753

ARISTOBULUS
see note 15 at Rom. 16:10, p. 754

ASYNCRITUS
Asyncritus, Phlegon, Herman, Patrobas, Hermes, were Christians in Rome to whom Paul sent greetings;
see note 23 at Rom. 16:14, p. 755

BAPTIZED INTO JESUS
not water baptism, but 1 Cor. 12:13 baptism;
see note 5 at Rom. 6:3, p. 688
our spirit; see note 4 at Rom. 6:3, p. 688

BARBARIAN
anyone who did not speak Greek;
see note 13 at Rom. 1:14, p. 657

BE NOT CONFORMED
to the world; the key is our minds;
see note 7 at Rom. 12:2, p. 730

BEAR
Gk. -"bastazo"- "to lift"; lift load of weaker Christian by not offending his weak conscience;
see note 2 at Rom. 15:1, p. 748
infirmities of weak brother; Jesus' example of this kind of love; see note 5 at Rom. 15:3, p. 748
Paul prays God would work this same grace in us;
see note 8 at Rom. 15:5, p. 748

BELIEVE SOMETHING
you'll be alright—wrong!; we must believe the right thing; see note 1 at Rom. 10:2, p. 719

BELIEVETH
present participle—continuous action, faith that results in salvation cannot be abandoned;
see note 2 at Rom. 1:16, p. 658

BELIEVING
glorifies God, unbelief dishonors God;
see note 12 at Rom. 4:20, p. 680

BELOVED
signifying the type of love that God has;
see note 11 at Rom. 16:8, p. 754

BLESSING OF ABRAHAM
based solely on grace, not performance or inheritance by birth; see note 2 at Rom. 9:8, p. 712

BOASTING
bragging, a sign of not understanding justification by grace; see note 11 at Rom. 3:27, p. 673
through Christ Jesus; not done in arrogance or pride;
see note 2 at Rom. 15:17, p. 750

BODIES
a presentation of our bodies to the Lord;
see note 3 at Rom. 12:1, p. 729

BODY
not all believers have been given the same job; we all have different functions;
see note 1 at Rom. 12:4, p. 732

BODY IS DEAD
because of sin; see note 23 at Rom. 8:10, p. 703
flesh has been corrupted; spirit is releasing life;
see note 24 at Rom. 8:10, p. 703

BODY OF DEATH
i.e. body of sin; the lingering influence of the sin nature; see note 2 at Rom. 7:24, p. 699
Paul thanking God for deliverance from;
see note 3 at Rom. 7:25, p. 699

BRETHREN
fellow countrymen or fellow believers;
see note 1 at Rom. 7:1, p. 694

CALLED
of Jesus Christ, to be saints; many are called, few are chosen; see note 7 at Rom. 1:6, p. 656

CAPITAL PUNISHMENT
God has delegated power to restrain or kill to governments; see note 7 at Rom. 13:4, p. 739

CARNAL
many ways "carnal" is used;
see note 16 at Rom. 8:7, p. 702
used interchangeably with "flesh";
see note 13 at Rom. 8:6, p. 702

CARNAL MIND
is hostile to God; see note 17 at Rom. 8:7, p. 702
see also **MINDED, CARNALLY**

CHAMBERLAIN
definition of; see note 9 at Rom. 16:23, p. 759

CHARACTER
produced as a result of having fought battles and won;
see note 11 at Rom. 5:4, p. 683

CHILD OF GOD / SON OF GOD
terms used interchangeably;
see note 30 at Rom. 8:14, p. 704

CHRIST
is in every born-again believer;
see note 23 at Rom. 8:10, p. 703

CHRIST IN YOU
partaker of His glory; Christian's spirit is complete;
see note 1 at Rom. 8:18, p. 705

CHRIST'S DEATH
beliefs that deny its sufficiency;
see note 7 at Rom. 10:6, p. 720

CHRISTIAN FREEDOM
not to do your own thing, but serve Christ in newness of spirit; see note 6 at Rom. 7:4, p. 695

CHRISTIAN LIFE
impossible to live in our own ability;
see note 19 at Rom. 8:8, p. 702
out of our own resources;
see note 1 at Rom. 7:15, p. 698

CHRISTIANS
why they can serve as police officers or soldiers, enforcing what's right;
see note 7 at Rom. 13:4, p. 739

CIRCUMCISION
an outward sign of inward reality; condition of the heart makes a child of God;
see note 1 at Rom. 2:28, p. 667
and religious rites not necessary for justification;
see note 3 at Rom. 4:10, p. 677
justification of Abraham was 13 years before;
see note 2 at Rom. 4:10, p. 677;
see note 3 at Rom. 4:3, p. 675
salvation by grace; see note 1 at Rom. 4:9, p. 676
true; is a born-again nature, not a mark in the flesh;
see note 4 at Rom. 2:29, p. 667
was a confirmation of the righteousness Abraham already had; was not intended to be used as a judge of anyone's righteousness;
see note 4 at Rom. 4:11, p. 677

CIVIL DISOBEDIENCE
as relates to submission;
see note 1 at Rom. 13:1, p. 738
relating to not resisting the authority of our government; see note 3 at Rom. 13:2, p. 739

COALS
of fire heaped on his head; not torment, but conviction; see note 15 at Rom. 12:20, p. 737

CONCLUSION
to Romans 7; see note 4 at Rom. 7:25, p. 699
to Romans 9; see note 1 at Rom. 9:30, p. 717

CONDEMNATION
Jesus is making intercession for us, therefore He couldn't be ministering condemnation;
see note 7 at Rom. 8:34, p. 709
how to escape it; see note 5 at Rom. 8:1, p. 700
sin ruled like a king through; loss of knowledge of righteousness by faith causes grace to lose its power;
see note 10 at Rom. 5:21, p. 687

CONDEMNING
judging; Gk. -"krino";
see note 3 at Rom. 2:1, 3, p. 662
no justification for; if one condemns he can no longer claim ignorance of his own offenses;
see note 2 at Rom. 2:1, p. 662

CONFESS
1Jn. 1:9; see note 11 at Rom. 4:8, p. 676

CONFESSION
with the mouth, belief from the heart;
see note 10 at Rom. 10:10, p. 721

CONFLICT
arises when individuals refuse to use faith in God's grace as the only means of salvation;
see note 3 at Rom. 1:2, p. 655

CONFORMED
meaning of, in "be not conformed to this world";
see note 7 at Rom. 12:2, p. 730

CONQUEROR
what is being more than?;
see note 9 at Rom. 8:37, p. 710

CONSCIENCE
essential to faith; part of our soul bearing witness to right and wrong; see note 9 at Rom. 2:15, p. 665
intuitive knowledge of God;
see note 8 at Rom. 2:14, p. 665
see also **DEFILED CONSCIENCE**

CONSIDER
definition of, in reference to Abraham considering not his body; see note 9 at Rom. 4:19, p. 680

CONVICTION
heaping coals of fire on someone's head;
see note 15 at Rom. 12:20, p. 737
people don't want to retain God in their knowledge;
see note 5 at Rom. 1:28, p. 661

CONVICTIONS
abstain from meats sacrificed to idols because of effect upon weaker Christian's conscience;
see note 16 at Rom. 14:21, p. 747
clear about eating meat sacrificed to idols; should not be practiced openly, lest weaker brother be offended;
see note 17 at Rom. 14:22, p. 747
concerning eating meat or only herbs;
see note 4 at Rom. 14:2, p. 744
love; how to get along with someone with different convictions; see note 4 at Rom. 15:1, p. 748
receive people who are not judging others by their own personal convictions;
see note 5 at Rom. 14:3, p. 744
will condemn us if we aren't subject to civil government; see note 8 at Rom 13:5, p. 740
see also **PERSONAL CONVICTIONS**

COUNTED
i.e. imputed; see note 6 at Rom 4:3, p. 675

CREATION
i.e. animal creation plunged into degenerate state so it may be redeemed with us;
see note 5 at Rom. 8:20, p. 705
fall and redemption; creation involuntarily subject to same corruption as mankind;
see note 7 at Rom. 8:21, p. 706
not in perfect balance; corrupted; will be relieved at manifestation of children of God;
see note 8 at Rom. 8:22, p. 706
that which is created; creature;
see note 3 at Rom. 8:19, p. 705

CREATURE
same word translated "creation";
see note 3 at Rom. 8:19, p. 705

CURSE
our vicious talk about others; releases death;
see note 8 at Rom. 12:14, p. 735

DAMNATION
meaning of Gk. word for, in reference to resisting power of government;
see note 4 at Rom. 13:2, p. 739

DAMNED
Gk. -"katakrino"- to judge against; different from "krino" used for eternal damnation; defiled conscience will not eternally damn a Christian;
see note 18 at Rom. 14:23, p. 747

DAVID
example from his life that God's holiness was clearer in David's sinfulness; see note 8 at Rom. 3:4, p. 668
(King) his revelation of salvation by grace;
see note 10 at Rom. 4:6, p. 676

DEAD TO SIN
see **SIN, DEAD TO**

DEATH
experiencing defeat; see note 27 at Rom. 8:13, p. 703
(ours) and resurrection with Christ; an accomplished fact; our new identity in our spirit;
see note 6 at Rom. 6:4, p. 688
the only way to get out from under the law and the old man; see note 2 at Rom. 7:1, p. 694
why were men dying if their sins weren't being counted against them?; see note 3 at Rom. 5:14, p. 685
see also **LAW OF SIN AND DEATH**

DEBT
being in debt isn't a sin;
see note 1 at Rom. 13:8, p. 740
love for our fellow man is a debt;
see note 2 at Rom. 13:8, p. 740

DEBTOR
in a spiritual sense, to share the gospel;
see note 12 at Rom. 1:14, p. 657

DEFILED CONSCIENCE
damaging results to our weaker brother if he follows our actions; it will offend, weaken and damn him; it is sin for him; see note 15 at Rom. 14:20, p. 747
will not eternally damn a Christian;
see note 18 at Rom. 14:23, p. 747

DELIVERANCE
from Rom. 7; see note 4 at Rom. 7:25, p. 699

DIETARY LAWS
see **O.T. DIETARY LAWS**

DISBELIEF
dishonors God; believing brings glory to God;
see note 12 at Rom. 4:20, p. 680

DISCIPLED
not just evangelized; attitude of Paul's that we should also have ; see note 6 at Rom. 15:20, p. 751

DISCIPLING
to a position of leadership; one of Paul's methods;
see note 5 at Rom. 16:21, p. 758

DISOBEDIENCE
see **CIVIL DISOBEDIENCE**

DIVISION
in the Church is due to lack of foundational truth of justification by grace through faith;
see note 11 at Rom. 3:27, p. 673

DOCTRINAL TRUTH
and personal convictions are two different things; observation of special days;
see note 8 at Rom. 14:5, p. 744

DOCTRINE OF DEVILS
vs. personal convictions concerning the eating of certain meats; see note 5 at Rom. 14:3, p. 744

DOCTRINES
which are negotiable and which aren't? If Christ received someone regardless of doctrinal errors, we should also; see note 9 at Rom. 15:7, p. 748

DOUBT
that God can perform His promises;
see note 14 at Rom. 4:21, p. 680

DUTY TO MANKIND
walking in law of love; loving neighbor as self;
see note 13 at Rom. 14:15, p. 746

EARNEST EXPECTATION
creation waiting with, for the day when the glory of God in us is revealed;
see note 2 at Rom. 8:19, p. 705

EATING MEAT
Gentile Christians who didn't have any convictions about, vs. Jewish Christians who did;
see note 4 at Rom. 14:2, p. 744

EATING MEAT SACRIFICED TO IDOLS
lawful, but not correct for strong believer who must bear infirmities of weaker brother;
see note 1 at Rom. 15:1, p. 748

EFFECT
is God's Word made of no effect through unbelief?;
see note 5 at Rom. 3:3, p. 668

ELDER
shall serve the younger;
see note 5 at Rom. 9:12, p. 712

ELECTION
based on God's foreknowledge;
see note 4 at Rom. 9:11 p. 712
God's election not based on birth or performance; predestination; see note 3 at Rom. 9:11, p. 712
not based on performance, but one's choices;
see note 6 at Rom. 9:13, p. 713

EMOTIONS
our knowledge or perception of truths control our emotions; see note 7 at Rom. 6:6, p. 689

EPAENETUS
Paul's first convert in Achaia;
see note 5 at Rom. 16:5, p. 753

ERASTUS
see note 8 at Rom. 16:23, p. 759

ESAU
referred to the nation of Edom in "Jacob I loved and Esau I hated"; see note 6 at Rom. 9:13, p. 713

EVIL
must be overcome with good;
see note 16 at Rom. 12:21, p. 737

EXHORTATION
encouraging people; see note 6 at Rom. 12:8, p. 733

EXPERIENCE
approved character; see note 11 at Rom. 5:4, p. 683

FAITH
Abraham's counted for righteousness 13 years before circumcision;
see note 2 at Rom. 4:10, p. 677;
see note 3 at Rom. 4:3, p. 675
and confession; how truths of will work;
see note 10 at Rom. 10:10, p. 721
and obedience closely related;
see note 6 at Rom. 1:5, p. 655
any action not of is sin;
see note 19 at Rom. 14:23, p. 747
calling things which be not as though they were;
see note 6 at Rom. 4:17, p. 679
comes by "hearing" not by "having heard";
see note 6 at Rom. 10:17, p. 723
God has dropped all charges against us because of;
see note 6 at Rom. 8:33, p. 709
governed by law; see note 12 at Rom. 3:27, p. 673
has actions; final judgment;
see note 7 at Rom. 2:6, p. 663
hope is an important part of;
see note 12 at Rom. 8:24, p. 706
in Jesus' atonement, not our actions, grants us righteousness; see note 9 at Rom. 4:5, p. 675
in what Christ did for us is only requirement for salvation; see note 1 at Rom. 14:1, p. 743
is based on God's Word; considers only God's Word; will believe only God's Word;
see note 8 at Rom. 4:18, p. 679
is the direct result of what we think and focus on;
see note 9 at Rom. 4:19, p. 680
justification by; Abraham and us;
see note 15 at Rom. 4:23, p. 680
justification by; purpose of the law;
see note 8 at Rom. 5:20, p. 687
must be mixed with God's Word for the Word to profit us; see note 5 at Rom. 3:3, p. 668
not produced by actions but faith produces actions;
see note 5 at Rom. 4:12, p. 677
pleased God, not Abraham's actions; was accounted as righteousness, not Abraham's holy life;
see note 5 at Rom. 4:3, p. 675
spoken of throughout the whole world;
see note 9 at Rom. 1:8, p. 656
the just shall live by; see note 4 at Rom. 1:17, p. 658
the only way by which God's grace can be accessed;
see note 3 at Rom. 5:2, p. 681
the way for both Jew and Gentile to achieve justification; see note 13 at Rom. 3:30, p. 674
those in the flesh cannot have faith;
see note 18 at Rom. 8:8, p. 702
to eat meat sacrificed to idols; keep it to yourself and don't offend the weaker brother;
see note 17 at Rom. 14:22, p. 747
won't work without hope;
see note 12 at Rom. 5:4, p. 683
see also **SALVATION BY FAITH**

FAITH OF GOD
is the Word of God; see note 4 at Rom. 3:3, p. 668

FAITH, STRONG
the result of being fully persuaded;
see note 13 at Rom. 4:21, p. 680

FAITH, THE MEASURE OF
a gift from God; see note 15 at Rom. 12:3, p. 731
we all have; see note 16 at Rom. 12:3, p. 731

FAITH TO FAITH
the means whereby righteousness is given;
see note 3 at Rom. 1:17, p. 658

FAITHFUL
God has never had anyone qualified working for Him yet; it's not because of our great faithfulness that God uses us; see note 8 at Rom. 9:16, p. 713

FALL
of Jews, not irrevocable;
see note 3 at Rom. 11:11, p. 726

FEAR
not as good a motivator as the goodness of God;
see note 5 at Rom. 2:4, p. 663

FIRSTBORN
first in order or importance;
see note 3 at Rom. 8:29, p. 709

FIRSTFRUITS OF THE SPIRIT
see note 9 at Rom. 8:23, p. 706

FLESH
and carnal, terms used interchangeably; Gk. -"sarx";
see note 13 at Rom. 8:6, p. 702
explanation of term; how used in scripture;
see note 3 at Rom. 7:18, p. 698
has been rendered powerless through sin;
see note 26 at Rom. 8:12, p. 703
how to escape it; see note 4 at Rom. 7:25, p. 699
in the flesh and after the flesh;
see note 8 at Rom. 7:5, p. 695
"O wretched man that I am!"; describing the absolute wretchedness of his flesh;
see note 1 at Rom. 7:24, p. 699
of Jesus taking our place;
see note 8 at Rom. 8:3, p. 701
part of man not changed by Christ;
see note 3 at Rom. 13:14, p. 742
serving God in our own power;
see note 1 at Rom. 7:15, p. 698
those that are in the flesh cannot have faith;
see note 18 at Rom. 8:8, p. 702

FOCUS
man's focus is on external; God's is on condition of man's heart; we need to focus on inner condition of our brothers to tolerate minor differences;
see note 14 at Rom. 14:17, p. 747

FOREKNOWLEDGE
doctrine of election is based on;
see note 4 at Rom. 9:11, p. 712
God knowing who would accept His offer of salvation; see note 1 at Rom. 8:29, p. 708
God's predestination based on;
see note 3 at Rom. 9:11, p. 712

FORGIVENESS
Jesus dealt with all sin;
see note 4 at Rom. 5:16, p. 686

FORGIVENESS OF SIN
past, present, and future;
see note 11 at Rom. 4:8, p. 676

"FREED"
from sin, as opposed to being "free";
see note 9 at Rom. 6:7, p. 690

FREEDOM
a Christian's ; see note 6 at Rom. 7:4, p. 695
in Christ; don't offend weaker brother;
see note 1 at Rom. 14:1, p. 743

FREEDOM IN CHRIST
don't despise those who don't have the revelation of; temper it with love for our fellow Christians;
see note 6 at Rom. 14:3, p. 744

FREEDOM OF CHOICE
not taken away by God;
see note 2 at Rom. 11:9, p. 725

FREEWILL
vs. predestination; example of Pharaoh;
see note 9 at Rom. 9:17, p. 714

FRUIT, ACTIONS
judgment of actions for discernment, not condemnation; see note 9 at Rom. 4:5, p. 675

FULL GOSPEL
Paul "fully" preaching the gospel; miracles;
see note 5 at Rom. 15:19, p. 750

FULLNESS OF GOD
walking in the power of the Holy Spirit, our choice;
see note 7 at Rom. 15:29, p. 752

"FULLNESS OF THE GENTILES"
expression explained;
see note 2 at Rom. 11:25, p. 727

GAIUS
see note 7 at Rom. 16:23, p. 759

GENTILES
Christ opened door of salvation to; do not have to become Jews; see note 2 at Rom. 15:9, p. 749
salvation wasn't earned, it was God's grace; they must stand by faith; see note 2 at Rom. 11:18, p. 726

GIFT
eternal life; see note 4 at Rom. 6:23, p. 693

GIFT OF RIGHTEOUSNESS
see note 3 at Rom. 5:15, p. 686

GIFTS
different, not better; see note 13 at Rom. 12:3, p. 731
differing one from another;
see note 2 at Rom. 12:6, p. 733
some live up to more of their potential than others, but it's God's mercy that makes it possible;
see note 15 at Rom. 12:3, p. 731
spiritual; can be imparted; help strengthen;
see note 10 at Rom. 1:11, p. 657

GIFTS AND CALLINGS
of God without repentance; some people in sin see supernatural gifts in their ministries;
see note 4 at Rom. 11:29, p. 728

GIVING
ministry of; should be generous;
see note 7 at Rom. 12:8, p. 733

GLORY
Gk. -"doxa"; falling short of Jesus; we need a savior;
see note 6 at Rom. 3:23, p. 672

GLORY OF GOD
complete in us; see note 1 at Rom. 8:18, p. 705
deposited within God's saints; creation anticipates day when it will be revealed;
see note 2 at Rom. 8:19, p. 705

GOD
calls things which be not as though they were; this illustrates faith; see note 6 at Rom. 4:17, p. 679
freely giving us all things;
see note 5 at Rom. 8:32, p. 709
used Pharaoh's choice;
see note 9 at Rom. 9:17, p. 714
"who hath resisted His will?"; an abusive interpretation which Paul counters;
see note 10 at Rom. 9:19, p. 714

GOD BE TRUE
but every man a liar; applications of this truth;
see note 7 at Rom. 3:4, p. 668

GOD FORBID!
see note 6 at Rom. 3:4, p. 668

GOD GAVE THEM UP
or God gave them over; reprobate mind;
see note 2 at Rom. 1:24, p. 660

GOD'S LOVE
we are the objects of; see note 8 at Rom. 1:7, p. 656

GOD'S PERFECT WILL
manifest when we make total sacrifice of our lives; see note 1 at Rom. 12:1, p. 729

GOD'S WILL
i.e. finding God's will for our lives; see note 10 at Rom. 12:2, p. 730
good and acceptable and perfect; see note 11 at Rom. 12:2, p. 730
to present ourselves to Him; vocation is secondary; see note 12 at Rom. 12:2, p. 730

GODHEAD
a revelation of His divine nature; see note 3 at Rom. 1:20, p. 659

GOODNESS OF GOD
leads to repentance; is a better motivator than fear; see note 5 at Rom. 2:4, p. 663

GOSPEL
has to be heard; see note 1 at Rom. 10:14, p. 722
my; Paul received his revelation of the gospel from God; see note 10 at Rom. 2:16, p. 665
not new; woven throughout O.T. ; law and grace do not mix; see note 3 at Rom. 1:2, p. 655
sharing of—its importance; see note 3 at Rom. 10:15, p. 723
the power of God that releases the effects of salvation; see note 1 at Rom. 1:16, p. 658

GOVERNMENTS
be subject to for wrath and conscience sake; see note 8 at Rom. 13:5, p. 740
being "subject to" includes paying taxes; see note 9 at Rom. 13:6, p. 740
given God's power to restrain or kill; "sword"; see note 7 at Rom. 13:4, p. 739
"not a terror to good works"—meaning of; see note 5 at Rom. 13:3, p. 739
officials of are to be ministers to us; see note 6 at Rom. 13:4, p. 739
results of resisting the power of government; see note 4 at Rom. 13:2, p. 739
to what extent they are ordained by God; see note 2 at Rom. 13:1, p. 738
we are not to fight against (resist) the authority of the government we live under; see note 3 at Rom. 13:2, p. 739

GRACE
Gk. -"charis"; Gk. -"charisma"- "gift"; definition of; see note 5 at Rom. 1:5, p. 655
God's; faith is our admission into; see note 3 at Rom. 5:2, p. 681
God's ability given to us; unearned; no grace apart from faith in Jesus; see note 8 at Rom. 3:24, p. 673
gospel of; misinterpreted as encouraging sin; see note 1 at Rom. 6:1, p. 688
how great God's grace is, just as sin nature came independently of our actions, so does righteous nature—through one man; see note 1 at Rom. 5:12, p. 684
justification by, not works; grace and works won't mix; see note 2 at Rom. 11:6, p. 725
loses its power; see note 10 at Rom. 5:21, p. 687
preaching of by Paul; accused falsely of encouraging people to sin; see note 12 at Rom. 3:8, p. 669
revelation of; danger is to become insensitive and impatient with brothers who haven't yet come to that knowledge; temper freedom in Christ with love; see note 6 at Rom. 14:3, p. 744
salvation by grace, David and Abraham examples of; see note 4 at Rom. 4:3, p. 675
we begin and continue our Christian walk by faith in God's grace; see note 15 at Rom. 5:8, p. 683
why resist sin? why live holy?; see note 2 at Rom. 6:2, p. 688
see also **LAW AND GRACE; SALVATION BY GRACE**

GRACE AND WORKS
Jewish and Gentile Christians had controversy over; see note 1 at Rom. 14:1, p. 743

GROANING IN THE SPIRIT
see note 5 at Rom. 8:26, p. 707

GUILTY
both Jew and Gentile; all saved by one method, through faith; see note 1 at Rom. 2:1, p. 662

HEARING
faith comes by "hearing," not "having heard"; must open your spiritual ears; see note 6 at Rom. 10:17, p. 723

HEART
God is concerned with the heart while man focuses on externals; we need to focus on inner condition of our brothers; see note 14 at Rom. 14:17, p. 747
pure; change of to serve God; see note 12 at Rom. 7:6, p. 695
will believe what we focus our attention on and disbelieve whatever we neglect; see note 14 at Rom. 4:21, p. 680

HEART AND SPIRIT
not the same; see note 3 at Rom. 2:29, p. 667

HEIRS
i.e. joint-heirs with Christ; we share equally with the one who has inherited everything; it cannot be taken advantage of without our cooperation; see note 34 at Rom. 8:17, p. 704

"HELPETH"
the Holy Spirit helps us as we are interceding; see note 2 at Rom. 8:26, p. 707

HERMAS
see note 23 at Rom. 16:14, p. 755

HERMES
see note 23 at Rom. 16:14, p. 755

HERODION
Paul mentions as being his kinsman; see note 16 at Rom. 16:11, p. 754

HINDERED
"let"; Paul from coming to Rome; see note 11 at Rom. 1:13, p. 657

HOLINESS
reasons for living a holy life; see note 8 at Rom. 6:16, p. 692

HOLINESS OF GOD
God retains His holiness even when people are unholy; example from David's life; see note 8 at Rom. 3:4, p. 668

HOLY
why live holy?; see note 2 at Rom. 6:2, p. 688

HOLY KISS
see note 29 at Rom. 16:16, p. 755

HOLY SPIRIT
indwelling; the hope of living in victory; see note 26 at Rom. 8:12, p. 703
knows how to convey our needs to the Father; intercession; see note 6 at Rom. 8:27, p. 707
one cannot believe God and receive salvation without quickening power of; see note 19 at Rom. 8:8, p. 702

HOMOSEXUALITY
and lesbianism; an abomination to God; see note 3 at Rom. 1:26, p. 661
emotional and physical consequences of; see note 4 at Rom. 1:27, p. 661

HOPE
and patience; see note 13 at Rom. 8:25, p. 706
and rejoicing closely related; see note 5 at Rom. 5:2, p. 681
helps us endure; Holy Spirit helps our frailties; see note 1 at Rom. 8:26, p. 707
i.e. the blessed hope of Jesus' return; see note 6 at Rom. 5:2, p. 681
natural and supernatural; see note 7 at Rom. 4:18, p. 679
saved by hope; it's an important part of faith; see note 12 at Rom. 8:24, p. 706
the first step towards faith; see note 12 at Rom. 5:4, p. 683

HUMILITY
key factor in success; servitude to Christ: see note 2 at Rom. 1:1, p. 655

"I SPEAK AS A MAN"
this was not God's wisdom, but man's; see note 10 at Rom. 3:5, p. 669

ILLYRICUM
see note 4 at Rom. 15:19, p. 750

IMPUTED
counted; to take an inventory; see note 6 at Rom. 4:3, p. 675
God was not imputing men's sins (from time of Adam to Moses); see note 2 at Rom. 5:13, p. 685
righteousness through Christ being like imputed sin through Adam; see note 1 at Rom. 5:15, p. 686
why were men still dying if sins not imputed? Satan's inroad; see note 3 at Rom. 5:14, p. 685

"IN"
the flesh or "in" the Spirit; as opposed to being "after" either one; see note 20 at Rom. 8:9, p. 703

IN THE LORD
born-again believers; see note 18 at Rom. 16:11, p. 754

INFIRMITIES
Gk. -"astheneia"- feebleness (of body or mind); not knowing how to pray; see note 3 at Rom. 8:26, p. 707

INFIRMITY
Gk. -"asthenema"- ; "a scruple of the conscience"; strong brother bears infirmities of the weaker brother; see note 3 at Rom. 15:1, p. 748

INTEGRITY
in the sight of man; see note 12 at Rom. 12:17, p. 736

INTERCESSION
opposite of condemnation; Jesus is making intercession for, not condemning us; see note 7 at Rom. 8:34, p. 709
the Holy Spirit conveying our needs; see note 6 at Rom. 8:27, p. 707

INTUITIVE KNOWLEDGE
of God; see note 8 at Rom. 2:14, p. 665; see note 2 at Rom. 1:18, p. 659
or revelation; see note 3 at Rom. 1:20, p. 659
preventing man from committing depraved acts; see note 2 at Rom. 1:24, p. 660

ISRAEL
knew the gospel of salvation by faith; see note 7 at Rom. 10:19, p. 723
will be saved; restoration of; see note 1 at Rom. 11:23, p. 727; see note 3 at Rom. 11:26, p. 727; see note 1 at Rom. 11:15, p. 726

JACOB
have I loved, Esau have I hated; see note 6 at Rom. 9:13, p. 713

JASON
see note 2 at Rom. 16:21, p. 758

JESUS
example of God's love in relation to bearing infirmities of our weaker brother;
see note 5 at Rom. 15:3, p. 748
Paul prays God would work this same grace in us;
see note 8 at Rom. 15:5, p. 748
was Son of God by nature, we are sons of God by adoption; see note 32 at Rom. 8:15, p. 704

JEWS
did not have monopoly on God; Gentiles could come directly to God; future restoration of Israel;
see note 1 at Rom. 11:15, p. 726
had rejected God but He is still going to bring His promises to the Jews to pass; a total act of grace;
see note 4 at Rom. 11:29, p. 728
had superior knowledge of God which made them more accountable; see note 1 at Rom. 2:17, p. 665
have no advantage over others; haven't kept the law perfectly so they are the same as the uncircumcised;
see note 3 at Rom. 2:25, p. 666
main advantage; God committed His Word unto them;
see note 2 at Rom. 3:2, p. 668
Paul's great love for; see note 3 at Rom. 9:3, p. 711
true Jew; those born again are God's people;
see note 2 at Rom. 2:29, p. 667;
see note 1 at Rom. 2:1, p. 662
what advantage in being one?;
see note 1 at Rom. 3:1, p. 668

JOB
and Paul's question, "Why hast thou made me thus?";
see note 11 at Rom. 9:20, p. 714

JUDGE
don't judge brethren, God will; everyone is accountable to God; see note 10 at Rom. 14:11, p. 746
ourselves so as not to cause another to stumble in his faith; see note 11 at Rom. 14:13, p. 746
we are servants, God is judge; only judge ourselves, that we aren't a stumbling block;
see note 7 at Rom. 14:4, p. 744

JUDGE THE WORLD
God will, arguments against must be rejected;
see note 11 at Rom. 3:6, p. 669

JUDGEST
Gk. -"anakrino" signifies discernment;
Gk. -"krino" condemning type of judging;
see note 3 at Rom 2:1, 3, p. 662

JUDGING
and condemnation of others not allowed;
see note 2 at Rom. 2:1, p. 662

JUDGMENT
result of resisting the power of government;
see note 4 at Rom. 13:2, p. 739

JUDGMENT, FINAL
and salvation by faith; faith has actions;
see note 7 at Rom. 2:6, p. 663

JUDGMENT (GOD'S)
contains mercy; see note 3 at Rom. 11:22, p. 727

JUDGMENTAL
those who recognize their freedom in Christ should not judge brothers who don't; likewise, those still emphasizing works should not judge those who aren't; see note 6 at Rom. 14:3, p. 744

JUDGMENTS
based on actions are for discernment, not condemnation; see note 9 at Rom. 4:5, p. 675

JULIA
see note 25 at Rom. 16:15, p. 755

JUNIA
Paul's relative; well known to the apostles;
see notes 7-8 at Rom. 16:7, p. 754

JUSTIFICATION
Abraham believed God; justified 13 years before his circumcision; by faith, not law;
see note 3 at Rom. 4:3, p. 675;
see note 2 at Rom. 4:10, p. 677
by faith, Abraham and us also;
see note 15 at Rom. 4:23, p. 680
by faith, apart from the law;
see note 8 at Rom. 5:20, p. 687
by faith, not by holy life;
see note 5 at Rom. 4:3, p. 675
by grace; failure to understand denies the sufficiency of Christ's death; see note 7 at Rom. 10:6, p. 720
by grace, through faith, not works;
see note 2 at Rom. 11:6, p. 725
faith is the way, for Jews and Gentiles;
see note 13 at Rom. 3:30, p. 674
is apart from religious ordinances;
see note 3 at Rom. 4:10, p. 677
not to be earned, it's a gift;
see note 7 at Rom. 3:24, p. 673
of the ungodly; see note 8 at Rom. 4:5, p. 675

JUSTIFIED
by faith; can be and still have personal conviction about keeping the Jewish ceremonial law;
see note 5 at Rom. 14:3, p. 744
"in thy sayings and mightest overcome when thou art judged"; quoted from David in Ps. 51:4;
see note 8 at Rom. 3:4, p. 668

KINSMEN
i.e. fellow countrymen of Paul;
see note 4 at Rom. 16:21, p. 758
Paul's kin or Tertius'?;
see note 5 at Rom. 16:21, p. 758
six blood relatives of Paul;
see note 9 at Rom. 16:7, p. 754

KISS
i.e. a holy kiss of charity;
see note 29 at Rom. 16:16, p. 755

KNOWLEDGE
"My people are destroyed for lack of"; our perception of truths control our emotions and experiences;
see note 7 at Rom. 6:6, p. 689
see also **INTUITIVE KNOWLEDGE**

LAW
and our flesh linked together; law couldn't accomplish righteousness; see note 7 at Rom. 8:3, p. 701
brings sin into focus, all blindness is removed;
see note 2 at Rom. 7:7, p. 696
Christ the end of, to everyone that believeth; law still in effect for unbeliever;
see note 4 at Rom. 10:4, p. 719
comes; sin is imputed; can only be remedied by new birth; see note 4 at Rom. 7:9, p. 697
controversy over keeping the O.T. law between the Jewish and Gentile Christians;
see note 1 at Rom. 14:1, p. 743
could not produce life; it is spiritual, we are carnal; we benefit from Jesus' keeping the law;
see note 7 at Rom. 7:14, p. 697
dead to the law; law was only for the old man;
see note 5 at Rom. 7:4, p. 695
end of the law for righteousness; still useful purposes of law for N.T. believers;
see note 3 at Rom. 10:4, p. 719
for justification was never God's intent;
see note 1 at Rom. 3:21, p. 672
fulfilling the righteousness of the law by the Holy Spirit;
see note 9 at Rom. 8:4, p. 701
gave sin an occasion against us; revives sin; brings knowledge of sin; see note 5 at Rom. 7:11, p. 697
God's kind of love automatically meets requirements of; see note 4 at Rom. 13:10, p. 741
imputes sin; age of accountability;
see note 3 at Rom. 7:9, p. 696
keeping the "righteousness" of; no one can keep the law; see note 4 at Rom. 2:26, p. 666
made clear our depraved nature;
see note 1 at Rom. 7:7, p. 696
ministration of death; drew out what was already there;
see note 6 at Rom. 7:13, p. 697
not given for justification or salvation; but to kill, condemn, strengthen sin; God doesn't grade on a curve; only hope is faith in a Savior;
see note 4 at Rom. 3:19, p. 671
not intended for believer; law produces guilt; return to bondage; see note 3 at Rom. 3:19, p. 671
not kept by Jews; same as uncircumcised;
see note 3 at Rom. 2:25, p. 666
not made for born-again Christian;
see note 11 at Rom. 7:6, p. 695
only way to get out from under is through death;
see note 2 at Rom. 7:1, p. 694
purpose of the law; N.T. man fulfilling the law;
see note 3 at Rom. 13:8, p. 740
true purpose of; to drive us to God;
see note 14 at Rom. 3:31, p. 674
what is the purpose of?;
see note 8 at Rom. 5:20, p. 687
worketh wrath; no law, sin is not imputed;
see note 3 at Rom. 4:15, p. 678

LAW AND GRACE
don't mix; no self-salvation or justification;
see note 3 at Rom. 1:2, p. 655

LAW AND GRACE MENTALITY
see note 5 at Rom. 10:5, p. 720

LAW MENTALITY
denies Christ's substitutionary work;
see note 7 at Rom. 10:6, p. 720

LAW OF FAITH
see note 12 at Rom. 3:27, p. 673

LAW OF LOVE
love neighbor as self; our actions have influence on others; see note 13 at Rom. 14:15, p. 746

LAW OF SIN
a force or influence impelling action; not the sin nature; the body of the "old man";
see note 5 at Rom. 7:23, p. 699
in our members; "old man" is dead;
see note 2 at Rom. 7:17, p. 698
Paul not living under its dominance;
see note 4 at Rom. 7:21, p. 699

LAW OF SIN AND DEATH
influences of sin and its resulting wages;
see note 6 at Rom. 8:2, p. 700

LAWS
why the government's should be kept;
see note 8 at Rom. 13:5, p. 740

LEARNING
from O.T. scriptures rather than from "hard knocks";
see note 6 at Rom. 15:4, p. 748

LED BY THE SPIRIT
of God; see note 29 at Rom. 8:14, p. 704

LEGALISTIC MENTALITY
passes judgment on others;
see note 6 at Rom. 14:3, p. 744

LESBIANISM
and homosexuality; an abomination to God;
see note 3 at Rom. 1:26, p. 661
emotional and physical consequences of;
see note 4 at Rom. 1:27, p. 661

LET
i.e. hindered; Paul hindered from coming to Rome; see note 11 at Rom. 1:13, p. 657

LET GOD BE TRUE
see **GOD BE TRUE**

LIKEWISE
the Holy Spirit helps us; see note 1 at Rom. 8:26, p. 707

LIVE BY THE LAW
i.e. to continue to remain alive by keeping the law; see note 6 at Rom. 10:5, p. 720

LIVING SACRIFICE
God's will for every individual; see note 12 at Rom. 12:2, p. 730
the way to true success; see note 13 at Rom, 12:3, p. 731
we need to reaffirm this decision daily; see note 4 at Rom. 12:1, p. 729

LORD
Jesus is; confession of—heartfelt enough to involve actions; see note 9 at Rom. 10:9, p. 721

LOVE
a handout doesn't help a lazy person; see note 5 at Rom. 12:11, p. 735
by hating and abhorring evil; see note 2 at Rom. 12:9, p. 734
for our fellow man is a debt; see note 2 at Rom. 13:8, p. 740
God's kind of fulfills the law; see note 3 at Rom. 13:8, p. 740
see note 4 at Rom. 13:10, p. 741
how to get along with brother who has different convictions than you; see note 4 at Rom. 15:1, p. 748
preferring one another; see note 4 at Rom. 12:10, p. 734
responding in causes "heaps" of conviction; see note 15 at Rom. 12:20, p. 737
the three major Gk. words for; see note 3 at Rom. 12:10, p. 734
walking in love is important as the Lord's return nears; see note 1 at Rom. 13:11, p. 742
without dissimulation; see note 1 at Rom. 12:9, p. 734
see also **LAW OF LOVE**

LOVE FOR SELF
serving their own belly; see note 2 at Rom. 16:18, p. 756

LOVE, GOD'S
we are the object of His love; see note 8 at Rom. 1:7, p. 656

LOVE, GOD'S KIND OF
Jesus is the supreme example of; submitted Himself lest He offend people, we should too; see note 5 at Rom. 15:3, p. 748

LOVE, LAW OF
see **LAW OF LOVE**

LOVE OF CHRIST
nothing can separate us, except denying the faith; see note 8 at Rom. 8:35, p. 710

LOVE OF GOD
is much more toward us now that we are justified; see note 16 at Rom. 5:9-10, p. 684
shown to us through grace; see note 14 at Rom. 5:7, p. 683

"MAKE HASTE"
Isa. 28:16 cp. Rom. 9:33; shamed in battle; see note 7 at Rom. 9:33, p. 718

MANIFESTATION
of the sons of God; see note 4 at Rom. 8:19, p. 705

MANY YEARS
of Rom. 15:23; see note 2 at Rom. 15:23, p. 751

MARK
them that cause divisions; see note 1 at Rom. 16:17, p. 756

MARRIAGE
physical, to produce children; to Christ to bring forth fruit; see note 7 at Rom. 7:4, p. 695
to the old man and deliverance; see note 3 at Rom. 7:2, p. 694

MARY
bestowed much labor on Paul and his companions; see note 6 at Rom. 16:6, p. 753

MENTALITY
see **LAW MENTALITY**

MESSENGER
anointed messenger and anointed message not always well received; see note 4 at Rom. 10:16, p. 723

MESSIAH
(Jesus) to the Jews, Savior to the Gentiles; see note 1 at Rom. 15:8, p. 749
the Jewish Messiah; tragic rejection of Jesus; the true Israel of God; see note 1 at Rom. 9:6, p. 711

MERCIES OF GOD
not wrath; encourage people to give themselves to God; see note 2 at Rom. 12:1, p. 729

MERCY
show mercy to be shown mercy; see note 6 at Rom. 2:5, p. 663
of God; extra to certain individuals; God is not unfair; see note 7 at Rom. 9:14, p. 713
gift of; should be hilarious with; see note 9 at Rom. 12:8, p. 733
we cannot give people what they deserve; see note 11 at Rom. 12:17, p. 736

MIND
can't be tempted with things you don't think about; see note 5 at Rom. 16:19, p. 757
conform not to the world; see note 7 at Rom. 12:2, p. 730
important in walking after the Spirit; see notes 10-12 at Rom. 8:4-5, p. 701
make our thinking line up with God's Word; see note 8 at Rom. 12:2, p. 730
meditating of God's Word until fully persuaded; see note 13 at Rom. 4:21; p. 680
praise keeps our minds stayed on God; see note 11 at Rom. 4:20, p. 680
renewing of; see note 9 at Rom. 12:2, p. 730
stayed on God's promises; nothing too difficult for God; see note 14 at Rom. 4:21, p. 680
strong faith, the result of what we focus on; see note 9 at Rom. 4:19, p. 680
unbelief, the result of thinking on natural facts; see note 10 at Rom. 4:20, p. 680
unrenewed; the reason a Christian tends to sin; see note 8 at Rom. 6:6, p. 689
see also **RENEWING OUR MINDS; REPROBATE MIND**

MINDED, CARNALLY
results in death; all the miseries arising from sin; see note 14 at Rom. 8:6, p. 702
is death; spiritually minded is life; see note 15 at Rom. 8:6, p. 702

MINISTERS
government officials are to be; see note 6 at Rom. 13:4, p. 739

MINISTRY
practical service; see note 4 at Rom. 12:7, p. 733

MIRACLES
working through Paul; see note 3 at Rom. 15:19, p. 750

MORE THAN A CONQUEROR
see note 9 at Rom. 8:37, p. 710

MORTIFY
deaden ourselves to the flesh; see note 28 at Rom. 8:13, p. 703

MOSES
prophesying the day of justification; word of faith, which we preach; see note 8 at Rom. 10:8, p. 721

MOTIVATION FOR SALVATION
goodness of God superior to fear; see note 5 at Rom. 2:4, p. 663

NARCISSUS
see note 17 at Rom. 16:11, p. 754

NATURAL HOPE
vs. supernatural hope; example of Abraham; see note 7 at Rom. 4:18, p. 679

NATURAL MIND
carnal mind; see note 17 at Rom. 8:7, p. 702

NATURE
ours; good acts could not change our sinful nature; sinful acts cannot change our righteous nature; see note 1 at Rom. 6:20, p. 693
two natures; Christian with 2 natures would be living in adultery; old man (our first husband) is dead; see note 4 at Rom. 7:3, p. 695

NEGOTIABLE & NON-NEGOTIABLE DOCTRINES
how are they determined? If Christ has received an individual, overlooking errors, we should also; see note 9 at Rom. 15:7, p. 748

NEREUS
a Christian in Rome; see note 26 at Rom. 16:15, p. 755

NEWNESS OF SPIRIT
see note 12 at Rom. 7:6, p. 695

OBEDIENCE
faith and obedience closely related; see note 6 at Rom. 1:5, p. 655
difference between obedience and submission; see note 1 at Rom. 13:1, p. 738

OBSERVING SPECIAL DAYS
personal convictions vs. bondage to a "command"; see note 8 at Rom. 14:5, p. 744

OFFENDED
persecutors of Christians; trusting in themselves; see note 6 at Rom. 9:33, p. 718

OFFERING
for saints in Jerusalem; instruction on; see note 5 at Rom. 15:26, p. 752

OLD MAN
and law; freed from by death; see note 2 at Rom. 7:1, p. 694
deliverance from; see note 3 at Rom. 6:11, p. 690
died with Christ; see note 4 at Rom. 6:3, p. 688
died with Christ but didn't rise; see note 3 at Rom. 7:2, p. 694
is dead; Christian tends to sin because of an unrenewed mind; see note 8 at Rom. 6:6, p. 689
is dead; law of sin is in our members; see note 2 at Rom. 7:17, p. 698

is dead and gone; renew our minds and end sin's dictatorship; see note 5 at Rom. 6:12, p. 691
is not being resurrected;
see note 1 at Rom. 6:11, p. 690
law was made for; when he's dead we are no longer under the law; see note 5 at Rom. 7:4, p. 695
residual old man; lingering effects; God's grace and freedom from law are the keys to breaking dominance of sin; see note 6 at Rom. 6:14, p. 691

OLD TESTAMENT
written for us to learn from rather than "hard knocks"; heeding not is like reinventing the wheel;
see note 6 at Rom. 15:4, p. 748

OLD TESTAMENT DIETARY LAWS
shadows of things to come; nothing is unclean;
see note 12 at Rom. 14:14, p. 746
weak Jewish Christian eating herbs for fear of breaking one; see note 4 at Rom. 14:2, p. 744

OLD TESTAMENT QUOTE
possible scriptures Romans 11:8 refers to;
see note 1 at Rom. 11:8, p. 725

OLYMPAS
see note 27 at Rom. 16:15, p. 755

ORACLES
of God; God's Word committed to the Jews;
see note 3 at Rom. 3:2, p. 668

OURSELVES
correct view of ; see note 14 at Rom. 12:3, p. 731

OWE NO MAN
what this really means;
see note 1 at Rom. 13:8, p. 740

PATIENCE
faith sustained over a long period of time;
by-product; see note 9 at Rom. 5:3, p. 682
is linked together with hope;
see note 13 at Rom. 8:25, p. 706

PATIENCE, COMFORT, AND HOPE
come through scriptures, not tribulation;
see note 7 at Rom. 15:4, 748

PATROBAS
see note 23 at Rom. 16:14, p. 755

PAUL
called it "my gospel"; received his revelation from God;
see note 10 at Rom. 2:16, p. 665
his great love for the Jews;
see note 3 at Rom. 9:3, p. 711
knew that trouble was waiting for him in Jerusalem;
see note 10 at Rom. 15:31, p. 752
reaping carnal things, i.e. money;
see note 6 at Rom. 15:27, p. 752
Romans helping with his expenses to Spain;
see note 4 at Rom. 15:24, p. 751
spoke "as a man" to expose error in a thought belonging to opponents of the gospel;
see note 10 at Rom. 3:5, p. 669
verifying the truth; clarifying his statements in Rom. 9:3; see note 1 at Rom. 9:1, p. 710

PAUL'S
greetings to leaders of local bodies;
see note 28 at Rom. 16:15, p. 755
sorrow in heart, longing for salvation of the Jew;
see note 2 at Rom. 9:2, p. 710

PEACE
performance-based acceptance;
see note 2 at Rom. 5:1, p. 681

PEACE WITH ALL MEN
see note 13 at Rom. 12:18, p. 736

PEOPLE
no difference between moral, immoral, religious, nonreligious, all need salvation;
see note 12 at Rom. 10:12, p. 722

PEOPLE OF GOD
not based on nationality, but on faith in God; quotes from O.T.; see note 13 at Rom. 9:24, p. 715

PERSIS
see note 20 at Rom. 16:12, p. 754

PERSONAL CONVICTIONS
and doctrinal truth are two different things; observing certain days; see note 8 at Rom. 14:5, p. 744
see also **CONVICTIONS**

PHARAOH
was his hardened heart caused by predestination or free will?; see note 9 at Rom. 9:17, p. 714

PHEBE
assisted others; put to work the law of sowing and reaping; see note 3 at Rom. 16:2, p. 753
deaconess of the church in Cenchrea;
see note 1 at Rom. 16:1, p. 753
may or may not have been a deaconess, or female minister; see note 2 at Rom. 16:1, p. 753

PHILOLOGUS
see note 24 at Rom. 16:15, p. 755

PHLEGON
see note 23 at Rom. 16:14, p. 755

POTENTIAL
everyone has been given the same; "the" measure of faith; see note 15 at Rom. 12:3, p. 731

PRAISE
keeps mind stayed on God; makes us strong in faith;
see note 11 at Rom. 4:20, p. 680

PRAYER
for deliverance from unbelieving Jews;
see note 9 at Rom. 15:31, p. 752
Holy Spirit helps our infirmities; helps us when interceding; does not automatically do it for us;
see note 2 at Rom. 8:26, p. 707
Holy Spirit helps us as He helped Jesus;
see note 4 at Rom. 8:26, p. 707
importance of; see note 8 at Rom. 15:30, p. 752
infirmities in Rom. 8:26 are weaknesses from not knowing how one should pray;
see note 3 at Rom. 8:26, p. 707

PREACHING THE GOSPEL TO EVERYONE
see note 1 at Rom. 15:22, p. 751

PREDESTINATION
election; see note 3 at Rom. 9:11, p. 712
is dependent on foreknowledge;
see note 2 at Rom. 8:29, p. 709
we are predestined to be just like Jesus the firstborn;
see note 3 at Rom. 8:29, p. 709

PRELIMINARIES
being dispensed; presenting defense of the gospel;
see note 14 at Rom. 1:15, p. 657

PRIDE
the root of all divisions in the Church today;
see note 11 at Rom. 3:27, p. 673

PRISCILLA AND AQUILA
laid down their own necks for Paul;
see note 4 at Rom. 16:4, p. 753

PROMINENT PEOPLE
great in kingdom are greatest servants;
see note 10 at Rom. 12:16, p. 736

PROPHECY
speaking forth of the mind and counsel of God;
see note 3 at Rom. 12:6, p. 733

PROVE
God's will in our lives;
see note 10 at Rom. 12:2, p. 730;
see note 13 at Rom. 12:3, p. 730

PSALMS 69
a prophetic psalm; see note 2 at Rom. 11:9, p. 725

QUARTUS
a Christian brother in Corinth;
see note 10 at Rom. 16:23, p. 759

QUICKENING
of our mortal bodies; quickening power for this life; the resurrection; see note 25 at Rom. 8:11, p. 703

REAPING
what you sow; see note 3 at Rom. 16:2, p. 753

REASONABLE SERVICE
a totally consecrated life;
see note 5 at Rom. 12:1, p. 729

REDEMPTION OF OUR BODY
ransom in full; see note 11 at Rom. 8:23, p. 706

REJOICE
Gk. -"kauchaomai"- rejoicing in the midst of tribulation; see note 4 at Rom. 5:2, p. 681

REJOICING
and hope closely related;
see note 5 at Rom. 5:2, p. 681
in tribulations; God works for good whatever comes against us; see note 7 at Rom. 5:3, p. 682

REMNANT SHALL BE SAVED
very few Jews are truly God's people;
see note 14 at Rom. 9:27, p. 716

RENEWING OUR MINDS
see note 9 at Rom. 12:2, p. 730
and total commitment;
see note 6 at Rom. 12:2, p. 730

REPROBATE MIND
God gave them over to;
see note 2 at Rom. 1:24, p. 660
lose God's conviction about sin;
see note 9 at Rom. 1:32, p. 662

REPROBATE PERSON
past feeling remorse or conviction;
see note 6 at Rom. 1:28, p. 661

RESIST
results of resisting the power of government;
see note 4 at Rom. 13:2, p. 739
what the word implies relating to fighting against the authority of government;
see note 3 at Rom. 13:2, p. 739

RESURRECTION LIFE
dependent on knowing that our death with Jesus to sin is one time only, no need for a repeat;
see note 10 at Rom. 6:9, p. 690
does not automatically manifest itself in our flesh;
see note 7 at Rom. 6:6, p. 689

RESURRECTION OF JESUS
validity of Jesus' claims;
see note 4 at Rom. 1:4, p. 655

RESURRECTION, SPIRITUAL
not manifested automatically, our knowledge is important; see note 7 at Rom. 6:6, p. 689

ours with Christ; an accomplished fact at salvation, not something yet to be accomplished;
see note 6 at Rom. 6:4, p. 688

REVELATION
of God to mankind; men without excuse;
see note 2 at Rom. 1:18, p. 659
not always received; won't glorify God or be thankful;
see note 1 at Rom. 1:21, p. 660

RIGHT AND WRONG
infallible system for determining; having faith (or doubt) in the correctness of an action for us;
see note 19 at Rom. 14:23, p. 747

RIGHTEOUS ACTS
used for discernment, not condemnation;
see note 9 at Rom. 4:5, p. 675

RIGHTEOUSNESS
a gift; the general of grace defending us against the devil's wiles; see note 10 at Rom. 5:21, p. 687
Abraham counted as righteous 13 yrs. before his circumcision; see note 2 at Rom. 4:10, p. 677;
see note 3 at Rom. 4:3, p. 675
apart form the Law was unthinkable to the Jews;
see note 1 at Rom. 3:21, p. 672
granted by faith in Jesus' atonement, not our actions;
see note 9 at Rom. 4:5, p. 675
received by faith; see note 3 at Rom. 1:17, p. 658
through the faith of Christ;
see note 3 at Rom. 3:22, p. 672
two kinds of; our own righteousness and God's righteousness; see note 2 at Rom. 10:3, p. 719

RIGHTEOUSNESS BY FAITH
independent of actions;
see note 7 at Rom. 5:19, p. 687

RIGHTEOUSNESS BY GRACE
see note 2 at Rom. 9:30, p. 717

RIGHTEOUSNESS OF GOD
a gift; though faith of Christ;
see note 2 at Rom. 3:22, p. 672

RIGHTEOUSNESS OF JESUS
given to us; see note 10 at Rom. 3:26, p. 673

RIGHTEOUSNESS OF THE LAW
can be kept; but no one can keep the law;
see note 4 at Rom. 2:26, p. 666

RIGHTEOUSNESS, THE GIFT OF
see note 3 at Rom. 5:15, p. 686

RIGHTEOUSNESS THROUGH CHRIST
sin through Adam; see note 2 at Rom. 5:15, p. 686

ROMANS
letter of; subscript to Paul's original letter;
see note 11 at Rom. 16:27, p. 759

ROYAL LAW
loving one another is a debt;
see note 2 at Rom. 13:8, p. 740

RUFUS
see note 21 at Rom. 16:13, p. 755
mother of; see note 22 at Rom. 16:13, p. 755

RULING
a gift, commonly called administration;
see note 8 at Rom. 12:8, p. 733

SACRIFICES OF OLD TESTAMENTS
the credit card waiting for the real sacrifice—Jesus;
see note 9 at Rom. 3:25, p. 673

"SAVED"
used interchangeably with "delivered";
see note 13 at Rom. 10:13, p. 722

SAVED BY FAITH
not actions; see note 7 at Rom. 2:6, p. 663

SAVIOR
all are guilty and need salvation; any deviation from trust in Jesus is error; see note 1 at Rom. 3:9, p. 669

SALVATION
cannot be received without quickening power of Holy Spirit; see note 19 at Rom. 8:8, p. 702
Jews are not excluded, they just aren't favored over Gentiles; see note 1 at Rom. 11:1, p. 724
keeping O.T. laws unnecessary for; only 1 requirement for; see note 1 at Rom. 14:1, p. 743
legalism vs. personal convictions; Paul and the "weaker brother"; see note 3 at Rom. 14:1, p. 743
seeking to earn it prevents one from being saved;
see note 7 at Rom. 3:24, p. 673
three areas of responsibility for; individual believes, someone preaches, others send;
see note 2 at Rom. 10:14, p. 722
through faith in Jesus, not moral goodness;
see note 2 at Rom. 3:19, p. 671
true; must have confession with mouth and belief from heart; see note 10 at Rom. 10:10, p. 721

SALVATION BY FAITH
not by circumcision, water baptism, or any other act of obedience; see note 3 at Rom. 4:10, p. 677
not our holiness; see note 4 at Rom. 4:16, p. 678

SALVATION BY GRACE
Abraham and David examples of;
see note 4 at Rom. 4:3, p. 675
Abraham in uncircumcision;
see note 1 at Rom. 4:9, p. 676
through faith; King David had a revelation of;
see note 10 at Rom. 4:6, p. 676

SCRIPTURES
produce patience, rather than tribulations;
see note 7 at Rom. 15:4, p. 748

SECOND RETURN OF CHRIST
as time is growing short we must be more sensitive to God; see note 1 at Rom. 13:11, p. 742

SEED, ABRAHAM'S
includes more than physical descendants;
see note 5 at Rom. 4:16, p. 678;
see note 1 at Rom. 4:13, p. 678;
see note 2 at Rom. 9:8, p. 712
see also **ABRAHAM'S SEED**

SELF-CENTERED PERSON
see note 9 at Rom. 12:15, p. 735

SERVANT
love-slave, Jesus as absolute Master;
see note 1 at Rom. 1:1, p. 655
a minister or deacon; a person performing menial tasks as a slave; see note 2 at Rom. 16:1, p. 753

SERVANTS
to Satan or God; see note 9 at Rom. 6:16, p. 692;
see note 10 at Rom. 6:18, p. 692

SERVING GOD
in our own power (flesh); "spirit" used once in Rom. 7; 21 times in Rom. 8;
see note 1 at Rom. 7:15, p. 698

SERVING THE LORD
even in our business endeavors;
see note 7 at Rom. 12:11, p. 735

SERVITUDE
to Christ; humility key factor in success;
see note 2 at Rom. 1:1, p. 655

SHADOWS
rituals (dietary laws) are shadows of things to come; after Christ they are meaningless if used as requirements for acceptance with God; illustration of shadow of person around corner;
see note 12 at Rom. 14:14, p. 746

SIGN
circumcision an outward sign; condition of heart makes a child of God;
see note 1 at Rom. 2:28, p. 667

SIGN OF THE COVENANT
circumcision; see note 4 at Rom. 4:11, p. 677

SIMPLE
concerning evil; can't be tempted with things you don't think about; see note 5 at Rom. 16:19, p. 757
gullible, easy to deceive;
see note 3 at Rom. 16:18, p. 756
two different things; gullible and speaking in favor of being pure; see note 4 at Rom. 16:19, p. 757

SIN
Adam's produced a sin nature; Jesus dealt with original sin and acts of sin;
see note 4 at Rom. 5:16, p. 686
definition of; any action we don't have faith in the correctness of; see note 19 at Rom. 14:23, p. 747
grace teaching encouraging people to sin; sin gives Satan an inroad; see note 7 at Rom. 6:15, p. 692
i.e. sin nature (a noun);
see note 9 at Rom. 5:21, p. 687
inroad of Satan; see note 3 at Rom. 5:14, p. 685
Jews argued not committing the same sins as heathens in Rom. 1— adultery, idolatry, etc.;
see note 4 at Rom. 2:3, p. 663
law of in our members; old man dead;
see note 2 at Rom. 7:17, p. 698
ruled like a king; loses its strength to rule;
see note 10 at Rom. 5:21, p. 687
when we sin we yield ourselves to Satan;
see note 8 at Rom. 6:16, p. 692
you don't have to sin; see note 4 at Rom. 6:12, p. 691
wages of; see note 3 at Rom. 6:23, p. 693
see also **LAW OF SIN**

SIN, DEAD TO
an accomplished work of Christ we appropriate; reckon; see note 2 at Rom. 6:11, p. 690
died to sin once; see note 1 at Rom. 6:11, p. 690
focus on our resurrected union with Christ;
see note 3 at Rom. 6:11, p. 690
if struggling with sin, have not recognized their death with Christ; see note 12 at Rom. 6:9, p. 690
meaning of; see note 3 at Rom. 6:2, p. 688
not dying over and over but renewing the mind;
see note 11 at Rom. 6:9, p. 690

SIN NATURE
came by Adam; trying to obtain righteousness by actions cannot change sin nature;
see note 6 at Rom. 5:19, p. 687

SINFUL CONDITION OF JEWS
and Gentiles; see note 2 at Rom. 2:21, p. 666

SINNED
all have; no difference in God's sight;
see note 4 at Rom. 3:22, p. 672

SINNER
God saves the sinner; salvation provided by grace, received through faith;
see note 5 at Rom. 3:23, p. 672

SINS
defined; see note 7 at Rom. 1:29, p. 662
not imputed from time of Adam to Moses;
see note 2 at Rom. 5:13, p. 685

not imputed to those who receive forgiveness; will not, not ever; even future sins have been dealt with; see note 11 at Rom. 4:8, p. 676

SLOTHFULNESS OR LAZINESS
see note 5 at Rom. 12:11, p. 735

SON OF GOD/CHILD OF GOD
terms used interchangeably;
see note 30 at Rom. 8:14, p. 704

SONS OF GOD BY ADOPTION
we are; Jesus is Son of God by nature;
see note 32 at Rom. 8:15, p. 704

SORROW OF HEART
longing for salvation of the Jews;
see note 2 at Rom. 9:2, p. 710

SOSIPATER
see note 3 at Rom. 16:21, p. 758

SPAIN
Paul's intentions to travel to;
see note 3 at Rom. 15:24, p. 751

SPIRIT
Gk. -"pneuma"-; Holy Spirit, mental disposition, a prevailing mood or attitude;
see note 6 at Rom. 12:11, p. 735
how to walk in the Spirit and escape the flesh;
see note 4 at Rom. 7:25, p. 699
newness of; see note 12 at Rom. 7:6, p. 695
the Christian's spirit is already complete;
see note 1 at Rom. 8:18, p. 705

SPIRIT BEARING WITNESS WITH OUR SPIRIT
assuring us we are children of God;
see note 33 at Rom. 8:16, p. 704

SPIRIT-CONTROLLED LIFE
Rom. 8; an exclamation of victory; God for us;
see note 4 at Rom. 8:31, p. 709

SPIRIT OF BONDAGE
a reference to old sin nature;
see note 31 at Rom. 8:15, p. 704

SPIRIT OF CHRIST/SPIRIT OF GOD
see note 22 at Rom. 8:9, p. 703

SPIRIT OF GOD INDWELLING
anyone who is born again has;
see note 21 at Rom. 8:9, p. 703

STACHYS
see note 13 at Rom. 16:9, p. 754

STUMBLING STONE
Jesus is; see note 5 at Rom. 9:32, p. 717

SUBJECT
meaning of Gk. word for;
see note 1 at Rom. 13:1, p. 738
two reasons for being subject to civil government;
see note 8 at Rom. 13:5, p. 740

SUBMISSION
an attitude, not an action; eight major areas of; meaning of; contrasted with obedience; examples from life of Apostles and Peter; is voluntary; submission and civil disobedience; see note 1 at Rom. 13:1, p. 738
to God and to government are intertwined;
see note 8 at Rom. 13:5, p. 740
to government includes paying taxes;
see note 9 at Rom. 13:6, p. 740

SUBSTITUTE DEATH OF JESUS
see note 8 at Rom. 8:3, p. 701

SUPERNATURAL HOPE
vs. natural hope; example from Abraham's life;
see note 7 at Rom. 4:18, p. 679

SWORD
symbolic of power to restrain or kill given to governments; see note 7 at Rom. 13:4, p. 739

TAXES
Jesus paid taxes and commands us to also;
see note 9 at Rom. 13:6, p. 740
one of the laws we should comply with;
see note 8 at Rom. 13:5, p. 740

TEACHING
gift of; see note 5 at Rom. 12:7, p. 733

TEMPTATION
is linked to what we think on; flesh seems strong when fed; see note 3 at Rom. 13:14, p. 742

TERTIUS
wrote Romans from Paul's dictation;
see note 6 at Rom. 16:22, p. 758

THEREFORE
benefits of being justified by faith;
see note 1 at Rom. 5:1, p. 681

TOLERANCE
of believers with differing views;
see note 5 at Rom. 14:3, p. 744

TRANSFORMED
making our thinking line up with God's Word;
see note 8 at Rom. 12:2, p. 730

TRIBULATION
doesn't produce patience, scripture does;
see note 7 at Rom. 15:4, p. 748

TRIBULATIONS
are not blessings from God; spoils to be gained;
see note 8 at Rom. 5:3, p. 682
do not produce patience, the scriptures do; tribulations cause us to use what God has already given us through His Word; see note 9 at Rom. 5:3, p. 682

TRUSTING IN ONESELF
see note 6 at Rom. 9:33, p. 718

TRYPHENA AND TRYPHOSA
Paul saluted and commended them for their labor in the Lord; see note 19 at Rom. 16:12, p. 754

UNBELIEF
comes through thinking on natural facts;
see note 10 at Rom. 4:20, p. 680
doubts that God can perform His promises;
see note 14 at Rom. 4:21, p. 680

UNCLEAN
nothing is!; dietary laws were shadows of things to come; see note 12 at Rom. 14:14, p. 746

UNGODLY
God saves only; see note 5 at Rom. 3:23, p. 672
justification of; see note 8 at Rom. 4:5, p. 675

UNRIGHTEOUSNESS
ours; brings out God's righteousness even more;
see note 9 at Rom. 3:5, p. 669

UNTHANKFUL
not glorifying God; see note 1 at Rom. 1:21, p. 660

URBANE
a companion in work with Paul;
see note 12 at Rom. 16:9, p. 754

VANITY
nonhuman creation being subjected to corruption;
see note 6 at Rom. 8:20, p. 705

VENGEANCE
see note 11 at Rom. 12:17, p. 736
is God's; turning the other cheek; takes the faith of God; see note 14 at Rom. 12:19, p. 737

VESSEL
of honor and dishonor; God can use someone who has rejected Him; see note 12 at Rom. 9:21, p. 715

WALK AFTER THE SPIRIT
the mind stayed on spiritual things; walk after the flesh—the mind is focused on carnal things;
see note 10 at Rom. 8:4, p. 701
whatever a person thinks on is what he is going to become or do; see note 11 at 8:5, p. 701

WANTON
definition of; see note 2 at Rom. 13:13, p. 742

WATER BAPTISM
or religious rites; not necessary for justification;
see note 3 at Rom. 4:10, p. 677

WEAK, UNGODLY, SINNERS AND ENEMIES
God is willing to save us in spite of our actions;
see note 13 at Rom. 5:6, p. 683

WEAKER BROTHER
abstain from meat offered to idols because of effect upon; see note 16 at Rom. 14:21, p. 747
damage to him if he follows our actions with a defiled conscience: it's evil, will offend, weaken, and damn him, it's sin for him;
see note 15 at Rom. 14:20, p. 747
don't be critical of his convictions; Paul wasn't inconsistent in his actions; difference between legalism and salvation by grace;
see note 3 at Rom. 14:1, p. 743
don't display freedom in Christ in a way that offends him; see note 1 at Rom. 14:1, p. 743
don't offend him by practicing openly your clear conscience about eating meat sacrificed to idols;
see note 17 at Rom. 14:22, p. 747
lift his load ("bear") by not offending his weak conscience; see notes 2-3 at Rom. 15:1, p. 748
strong believer is to bear infirmities of; "lawful" doesn't mean "correct"; see note 1 at Rom. 15:1, p. 748
who is he?; see note 2 at Rom. 14:1, p. 743
why we should bear infirmities of; example of Jesus;
see note 5 at Rom. 15:3, p. 748

WHOSOEVER
Gentiles did not have to become Jews to be saved;
see note 11 at Rom. 10:11, p. 722

WITHOUT NATURAL AFFECTION
Gk. -"astorgos"- hard-hearted towards kindred;
see note 8 at Rom. 1:31, p. 662

WORD OF GOD
God's Word produces God's faith;
see note 5 at Rom. 10:17, p. 723
is the faith of God; see note 4 at Rom 3:3, p. 668
Jews' unbelief did not make it of no effect;
see note 5 at Rom. 3:3, p. 668

WORKS
Abraham's were not good for justification, was justified by faith for 13 years. before circumcision;
see note 1 at Rom. 4:1, p. 674
allow us boasting only if compared to others; all come short in God's sight; see note 2 at Rom. 4:2, p. 674
justified by works or justified by faith;
see note 2 at Rom. 4:14, p. 678
salvation not by; see note 7 at Rom. 4:4, p. 675
the object of faith; faith in oneself;
see note 3 at Rom. 9:32, p. 717
won't mix with grace; see note 2 at Rom. 11:6, p. 725
see also **GRACE AND WORKS**

WORKS OF FAITH/WORKS OF THE LAW
see note 4 at Rom. 9:32, p. 717

WORSHIP
sanctified by the Holy Ghost;
see note 1 at Rom. 15:16, p. 750

WRATH
God's; people need to know the good news of the Gospel more; see note 1 at Rom. 1:18, p. 659

ANDREW WOMMACK

Andrew Wommack's ministry is centered in a strong emphasis on God's grace and unconditional love. He believes in and teaches the victorious Christian life.

Andrew was raised in a Baptist home, having committed his life to the Lord as a young child. However, on March 23, 1968, he had a decisive experience with God's love and grace that changed his life forever.

Since then, he has spread the message of God's love far and wide—first, as a pastor of three churches, and now as an independent Bible teacher and speaker. He fulfills his ministry by traveling throughout the United States and the world, speaking in churches, seminars, retreats, and special events. He is heard on numerous radio stations across the country, and to date has distributed millions of cassette teaching tapes free of charge. With the main office in Colorado Springs, Colorado, Andrew Wommack Ministries also has an office in Great Britain and has made outreach into formerly communist Romania, Hungary, and Poland. Andrew has written two books—*Grace & Faith* and *Hardness of Heart*. In addition to the *Life For Today* study series, he has a six-hour marriage seminar on video cassette.

In September, 1994, Andrew opened the doors of Colorado Bible College to a first class of 50 students. This is a totally unique concept of preparing for ministry with a strong emphasis on the practical and personal discipleship. This two year program actually includes internship and overseas ministry trips as part of the curriculum.

Today, Andrew Wommack Ministries continues to expand both at home and abroad. Wherever he travels, his powerful emphasis on God's Word continues to set people free from sin, self-righteousness, and religiosity—often with signs and wonders following. As it began, Andrew's ministry continues to embody the scripture, *"And ye shall know the truth, and the truth shall make you free"* (Jn. 8:32).